THE INTERACTIVE DOCUMENTARY IN CANADA

Edited by

Michael Brendan Baker

and Jessica Mulvogue

McGill-Queen's University Press
Montreal & Kingston • London • Chicago

ISBN 978-0-2280-2107-0 (cloth)
ISBN 978-0-2280-2108-7 (paper)
ISBN 978-0-2280-2161-2 (ePDF)
ISBN 978-0-2280-2162-9 (ePUB)

Legal deposit second quarter 2024
Bibliothèque nationale du Québec

Printed in Canada on acid-free paper that is 100% ancient forest free (100% post-consumer recycled), processed chlorine free

This book has been published with the help of a grant from the Canadian Federation for the Humanities and Social Sciences, through the Awards to Scholarly Publications Program, using funds provided by the Social Sciences and Humanities Research Council of Canada.

Funded by the Government of Canada | Financé par le gouvernement du Canada | Canada | Canada Council for the Arts | Conseil des arts du Canada

We acknowledge the support of the Canada Council for the Arts.
Nous remercions le Conseil des arts du Canada de son soutien.

McGill-Queen's University Press in Montreal is on land which long served as a site of meeting and exchange amongst Indigenous Peoples, including the Haudenosaunee and Anishinabeg nations. In Kingston it is situated on the territory of the Haudenosaunee and Anishinaabek. We acknowledge and thank the diverse Indigenous Peoples whose footsteps have marked these territories on which peoples of the world now gather.

Library and Archives Canada Cataloguing in Publication
Title: The interactive documentary in Canada / edited by Michael Brendan Baker and Jessica Mulvogue.
Names: Baker, Michael Brendan, editor. | Mulvogue, Jessica, editor.
Description: Includes bibliographical references and index.
Identifiers: Canadiana (print) 20240293177 | Canadiana (ebook) 20240293207 | ISBN 9780228021087 (paper) | ISBN 9780228021070 (cloth) | ISBN 9780228021629 (ePUB) | ISBN 9780228021612 (ePDF)
Subjects: LCSH: Documentary films—Canada—History and criticism. | LCSH: Interactive multimedia—Canada.
Classification: LCC PN1995.9.D6 I58 2024 | DDC 070.1/8—dc23

For Patty

CONTENTS

PART 2

Encounters with Others: Activism, Agency, and Ethics

PART 3

Image and Sound beyond "the Real": Media Pasts, Presents, and Futures

FIGURES

ACKNOWLEDGMENTS

This collection was first imagined in 2014 over the course of a series of conference presentations in Canada and the United States that revealed the breadth and depth of work undertaken to address the still-emerging interactive documentary form. It was further developed within the collegial space of the Film and Media Studies Association of Canada's annual conference, and many of the contributors count themselves as members of that lively, engaged, and dedicated community of media scholars. The collection would not have come into existence were it not for this supportive network of graduate students, faculty, and filmmakers that commits itself to the study of the moving image within the often messy context of "Canada." A sincere thank you to oh, so many unnamed collaborators, mentors, and friends for their intellectual and emotional guidance and support, and our profound gratitude to all our contributors for dedicating their time, energy, and intellect to this project.

The editors would like to extend a heartfelt thank you to McGill-Queen's University Press, especially our editor, Jonathan Crago, who supported this project from its earliest inception and demonstrated endless patience when pandemic lockdowns and epoch-defining anxieties necessitated that we slow our work to a snail's pace. Additional thanks to the production, design, and editorial staff at MQUP who tirelessly set the highest bar for the publication and presentation of scholarly work in Canada and abroad. Importantly, this book would not have been possible without the generous funding of the Social Sciences and Humanities Research Council of Canada Awards to Scholarly Publications Programme.

Sadly, as work concluded on the collection, word was received of the unexpected passing of Patricia Zimmermann, a contributor here and a titan within the global documentary studies community. Patty's boundless enthusiasm, encouragement, and generosity will not soon be forgotten, and this collection is dedicated to her memory.

Last, on a personal note, Michael and Jessica would like to thank our partners, Laurel and Pehr, and our children, Charlotte and Cleo, who provide that most essential motivation when one is pursuing a project of considerable depth and scope: a reason to step away from our desks.

THE INTERACTIVE DOCUMENTARY IN CANADA

INTRODUCTION

THE INTERACTIVE DOCUMENTARY IN CANADA

Michael Brendan Baker and Jessica Mulvogue

When the idea for this collection first emerged, we were motivated both by the status of Canadian interactive documentary creators as global leaders in the field and by the sense that the interactive documentary in Canada and elsewhere was flirting with obsolescence. We hypothesized that the interactive documentary would be reduced to a mere blip in Canadian film history – a decade or two of intense innovation in the area of digital storytelling with its origins in the mid-2000s – if it were not properly observed, historicized, and critiqued. It is an extended moment in which fast technological change, along with digital fatigue (and the overuse of the descriptor "interactivity"), is rendering many of the interactive documentaries we study, teach, and admire inaccessible or unviewed. We thus felt it urgent to try to document, analyze, and think alongside the interactive documentary in Canada while it was still thriving.

In the course of producing this collection we have seen developments that both confirm and challenge our hypothesis. Technological change has been swift. Early, database-driven forms of interactive documentary – or "i-docs" – now seem ancient in the face of new technological forms of immersion and interactivity. We have witnessed how certain web-based i-docs have become increasingly difficult to access due to technological obsolescence, while artistic strategies to embrace and work alongside accelerating technological change have flourished. For instance, interactive documentaries originally made for the web with now dated software have been given new life in the form of apps, and the surge in development of virtual reality storytelling over the last five years has been a site of exploration for a new form of i-doc by storytellers and institutions alike. While the web-based, often database-driven form of interactive documentary aptly described the pool of i-docs in Canada at the outset, the term "i-doc" here and elsewhere now designates a wide variety of new media works that tell stories and engage spectators in many different ways. We might best describe this period of Canadian media history as a transitional moment in non-fiction digital storytelling, a moment that saw numerous Canadian artists and filmmakers experimenting with and expanding the documentary film form through the use of varied platforms, novel modes of interactivity, and networked media.

What we understand as an interactive documentary has never been a singular or stable form. As Judith Aston and Stefano Odorico (2018, 65) write, i-docs are "a constantly evolving set of forms and practices." The term thus encompasses a variety of projects that are alternatively referred to as web-docs, transmedia documentaries, locative docs, docu-games, computational non-fiction (Miles 2017), and open space new media documentary (Zimmermann and de Michiel 2018). The projects employ different image-making technologies (from photography and film to virtual reality and volumetric imaging) as well as different platforms (from websites and smartphone apps to VR headsets and hybrid screen/live performance events). We have chosen in this collection to stick with the term "interactive documentary" and its short form, "i-doc," for the simple reason that this is the most widely used term to describe – in both industry and scholarly parlance – this ever-changing group of practices. That said, some of our contributors take issue with this term, pointing out its descriptive limitations. We welcome these challenges to the designation and support the need to keep the debate on the matter open and alive.

The malleability of the form and term itself has resulted in attempts to define it that are "deliberately open" (Aston, Gaudenzi, and Rose 2017, 1). For instance, Galloway, McAlpine, and Harris (2007, 330) define it as "any documentary that uses interactivity as a core part of its delivery mechanism," while Aston, Gaudenzi, and Rose (2017, 1) maintain that the i-doc is "any project that starts with an intention to document the 'real' and that uses digital interactive technology to realize this intention."

The obstacle in trying to define the interactive documentary is that the terms used to designate and specify it are as ambiguous and unstable as the form itself: "documentary," "interactivity," "reality," or "the real" are all contested and fluctuating concepts. If, as Kate Nash (2022, 2) reminds us, "traditional" documentary film has never been a static form as it describes a tradition of work and corpus that conveys a very broad spectrum with regard to any perceived link to "reality" or "truth," then the attempt to secure a definition of an arguably even more fluid category of documentary media, one that is quickly morphing and adapting to new technologies, is a difficult if not futile task. For some scholars, such as Arnau Gifreu-Castells (2011), that there even exists an evolutionary link between documentary film and interactive documentary, as such "a complex and varied genre," is called into question. Interactive documentary, for Castells, may have more in common with other forms of digital media storytelling than with documentary film. However, we believe, as is presented later in this introduction, that there is an important and meaningful link between the history of documentary filmmaking practice in Canada and the emergence of interactive documentary. We thus regard the interactive documentary as an evolution of documentary film, one made possible by Web 2.0 technologies and the innovation of a more open, participatory, and social internet.

The concept of "interactivity" is central to Web 2.0, but, given that this term has been used inconsistently and indeterminately, it adds further complications to the attempt to define the i-doc. Interactivity can designate something as broad as participation to something as specific as human-computer interaction. As Inke Arns (n.d.) asserts, the term "encompasses both the theory of interrelated social action as well as the primarily technological category of human-computer communication." In other words, digital interactive technology may provide the foundation for the interactive documentary, but how it generates "interactivity" may take many shapes. We agree with Nash (2012, 199) that interactivity in i-docs is "most often understood in terms of the user's ability to exert control over content" and thus often involves human-computer interaction and both an active physical and mental role on the part of the users. But the levels of choice and control over the contents of the work vary greatly. At minimum, this may be simply the choice over chronology and, at maximum, this may be the ability to add or generate content. But the complexity of the term is not simply found in the varying degrees of interaction; interactivity, and, more important, its effects and affects, emerges at the intersection of spectator/user, technological platform, and documentary subject matter. What interactivity *does*, how it changes the documentary media content and, likewise, the spectator, is revealed in the experience of the i-doc. It is for this reason that we refrain from locating interactivity as a particular mode of engagement and, instead, leave its theorizing to the close analyses of i-docs provided by the individual chapters.

While interactivity is a tricky descriptor, there are nonetheless important transformations from the norms of traditional non-fiction film that result from the use of interactive devices in documentary storytelling.

Broadly speaking, interactivity loosens the "absolute control of the classical authorship and [of an] unmodified narrative" (Alkarimeh and Boutin 2017, 5). Through interactive modalities, for instance, non-linearity, polyvocality, participation, even co-creation become formative of the story being told. As such, the so-called passive spectator is ostensibly turned into a more active user, player, or navigator insofar as the i-doc allows its user/player/navigator to generate their own narrative paths within a given set of content and, thus, to determine how (and whether or not) the story unfolds. In this way, interactivity has altered the "traditional" structures of author, narrative, and viewer of the classical documentary (ibid.). Interactivity guides a movement away from a pre-constituted causality towards "new architectures for knowledge and experience," in which "explanatory structures of continuity" are replaced with "architectures of contiguities" (Zimmermann 2018, 10). Indeed, for many of this volume's contributors, especially the chapters collected in Part 2, the fragmentation and plurality of narrative plays a crucial role in the political, ethical, and pedagogical import of the interactive documentary. Rather than a *voice*, i-docs present a variety of *voices*: snippets of different, and sometimes divergent, worlds. In this way, interactive documentary offers a means by which to radically reshape storytelling and spectator experience.

At their best, i-docs have the potential to offer new forms of agency and critical thinking, novel sites of collectivity, and innovative modes of learning. They do so through the implementation of media tools and design philosophies that leverage the accumulated knowledge of the documentary tradition. At their worst, however, i-docs can appear as experiments in non-fictional new media that fail to innovate a tradition with well-established representational strategies and other conventions that ably serve to orient and engage audiences. This volume acknowledges that many interactive documentaries are imperfect media: many are works that do not necessarily live up to some of the hype that accompanied them when they first emerged. Nonetheless, these media objects are still worthy of analysis, not only because they are indicative of a transitional moment in digital media and documentary history whose full effects are yet to be seen but also because they speak to wider ideas of the social function of media technologies in a period defined by a deepening influence of screen media upon everyday life.

While this collection largely upholds the evolutionary link between documentary film and interactive documentary, and while most of our contributors understand interactivity as a mode that allows the spectator to have some amount of control over the content, we also include contributions that discuss digital media projects that challenge these understandings of the interactive documentary altogether. Both Brenda Longfellow's and Randolph Jordan's chapters consider VR and AR projects, respectively, that may not be conventionally understood within the category of documentary but that nonetheless allow the user to take part in futures and pasts connected to "the real" of the spectator. Cindy Poremba and Amy Siegel's exploration of hybrid image capture takes up the issue of filmic indexicality, a perceived link to the "real" central to foundational ideas of a documentary "truth." Chelsea Birks's contribution considers an unconventional form of interactive documentary – a public art installation – that invites *passivity* on the part of the viewer rather than any form of control over content. And Monika Kin Gagnon and Matt Soar contest the term "interactive documentary" altogether, taking the position that the term "interactive" limits what is in fact a much broader range of novelties and possibilities that different technologies and software offer the documentary form.

We believe that it is important to include these perspectives and case studies because they point to new directions in i-doc practice and to novel ways of conceiving of their significance. Indeed, no longer only web-based, human-computer engagements dominated by a point-and-click function, artists and media practitioners as well as scholars are exploring the affordances of new technologies in the production of documentary content and new modes of exhibition, and in ways that shift both what we understand as the "reality" of documentary content and of "interactivity." Given the overall variability of interactive documentary and the difficulty of pinning it down, this volume avoids circumscribing it within specific terms or technologies. Rather, *The Interactive Documentary in Canada* embraces what Patricia Zimmermann (2018, 9) calls the "polyphonic" nature of the interactive documentary: "A polyphonic model for new media documentary moves from the one to the many on all levels: concept, distribution, exhibition, iterations, interfaces, issues, people, platforms, skills, technologies." The present volume makes evident that such a conception allows for a field of heterogenous non-fiction forms and modes of engagement, but it also complicates the practice of archiving these cultural texts. While the i-doc is less than two decades old, technological obsolescence has already greatly affected the field, making more than a few web-based i-docs inaccessible. Multiple contributors to this book touch upon this challenge, and it is the central focus of Daniel Keyes and Mike Robbin's chapter.

Trying to capture something of the malleable, diversified nature of new media documentary in book form – a rather fixed, conventional form of "old media" – harbours some incongruity. At its base, however, the collection aims to draw attention precisely to the heterogeneity of this form, its technologies, and its uses within a historical period that has seen an explosion of interest in new forms of digital storytelling, reflecting wider shifts in popular digital visual culture towards forms of interactive, immersive, and embodied experiences. To do so, a spectrum of methodologies – ranging from oral history, close textual analysis, and reception study to media theory, pedagogy, and posthumanism – are brought to bear upon a diverse corpus of work, exemplifying the critical tools and theoretical frameworks that can open up and reveal the intentions of creators, the experiences of audiences, the promise of interactive design, and the connections between this work and the broader fields of moving images and new media. But *The Interactive Documentary in Canada* isn't simply concerned with a relatively new way of non-fiction storytelling; as the title suggests, the heterogeneity of works and chapters are brought together here by the specific national context of Canada.

In this way, this book extends and deepens the study of interactive documentary by situating it historically within a particular national context. The few extant books on the interactive documentary explore, in general terms, the nature of the interactive documentary from an ontological lens and consider explicitly how the i-doc shifts and expands the traditional documentary film form. Notable here are *Interactive Documentary: Theory and Debate* (Nash 2022); *I-Docs: The Evolving Practices of Interactive Documentary* (Aston, Gaudenzi, and Rose 2017), and *The Interactive Documentary Form: Aesthetics, Practice, and Research* (Odorico 2019). These works thoroughly consider the i-doc from key angles of documentary culture: the nature of image and "reality," the ethical potentials and pitfalls of the form, the role of the "documentary voice" or lack thereof, and the role of the viewer or user in shaping documentary discourse. This scholarship is accompanied by numerous articles that engage with similar questions surrounding the documentary form through analyses of particular case studies.

By focusing on the specificities of Canada, the volume shifts the inquiry of i-docs away from ontological questions about the nature of the form and instead emphasizes contexts related to the social, political, institutional, and technological histories and networks that enabled the i-doc to flourish within Canada and that inform the content, form, and experience of the case studies discussed. This is not to say that the abiding questions surrounding the nature of the i-doc aren't taken up in the volume's chapters but that, read as a whole, the collection takes up these questions within the specificities of histories, institutions, communities, and cultures of the many regions of Canada.

The nation provides a special case for the study of interactive documentary: for such a small country (in terms of population), there have been an extraordinary number of works produced here, with numbers comparable only to France (Mulvogue 2019). In part this is due to institutional structures and funding models that have historically supported the production of documentary film (over other forms of cinema in Canada) and, in the last decade or so, have had a particular focus on digital innovation in storytelling. The National Film Board of Canada (NFB) looms large in this collection, both in its recent past – as a producer of i-docs – and its longer history of innovation in film form. The NFB has been central to developments in Canadian cinema, playing a major or supporting role, for instance, in the creation of direct cinema, IMAX cinema, and advancements in computer animation built upon the innovative works of traditional animation that introduced the Board to global audiences in its earliest decades. It is the primary institutional space supporting, championing, and innovating the documentary form in Canada. While many of the i-docs discussed in this collection were made in participation with a range of other institutions and organizations, both private and public, the legacy of NFB innovation can arguably be seen in the formal and conceptual strategies, the visions, and the goals of many interactive documentaries produced across Canada no matter their home. Indeed, the impetus for interactive documentary in Canada is often attributed to the 2004 NFB Filmmaker-in-Residence initiative, which itself was an attempt to renew the participatory and socially engaged impulses behind the Challenge for Change and Société nouvelle programs (1967–80) and ran parallel to the institution's early efforts at creating an online space for social and political engagement, epitomized by the CitizenShift website and its French-language partner site, Parole Citoyenne. Conceived as an experiment in interventionist filmmaking and marketed as "the world's first documentary experience that's totally online," the

Filmmaker-in-Residence program involved filmmaker Katerina Cizek working alongside doctors, nurses, patients, and researchers at St Michael's Hospital in Toronto to document stories emerging from the frontlines of inner-city healthcare. The program resulted in multiple short web-based "interventions" that each focus on different stories of urban health and that reached wider audiences as a DVD compendium, *The 7 Interventions of Filmmaker-in-Residence* (Frise and Cizek 2009). These projects began the NFB's experimentation with documentary on the web and Cizek's subsequent project, the *Highrise* series, would establish the NFB as a key player in digital interactive storytelling and place it at the vanguard of the international i-doc boom.

In many ways, i-docs uphold and continue the legacy of the NFB and its experiments in documentary film. But, from another perspective, the i-doc is a product of specific mandates that change substantially with each new government and each new strategic plan. The boom in interactive documentary at the NFB throughout the early 2010s is clearly a manifestation of the mandate language contained in the 2008 Strategic Plan, with its goal of "supporting creators, privileging imagination and socially engaged creation in all technological forms, and making the results accessible to all Canadians" (National Film Board of Canada 2009). However, it comes at a time of diminishing resources imposed upon the institution by the Stephen Harper government. One might speculate that the Digital Studio initiative was not only a response to emerging technology but also cover to fund the sort of innovative, socially engaged, and thought-provoking work that is more difficult to rationalize under orders to exercise fiscal restraint. Nonetheless, a consequence of this commitment – referenced elsewhere as "the digital opportunity" – is the mobilization of interactive media creators across both the public- and private-sector production industries and a great deal of important cross-collaboration between those two groups. Indeed, this cross-collaboration is one aspect of the "story" this collection seeks to tell. Discussions of public/private partnerships appear in several chapters, and the labour conditions of several projects are also addressed in a small number of contributions. However, the production workflow of these projects is too fluid to generalize and is often actuated in personal (which is to say, not institutional) workspaces that fall beyond the reach of most research methodologies.

The longer history of documentary filmmaking in Canada, both in and beyond the NFB, is a valuable means of understanding interactive documentary initiatives in Canada today because it provides a broad interpretative framework that brings together institutional, socio-political, and cultural histories. Positioning the interactive documentary within the context of Canada does not mean asserting a uniform national lens on the i-doc. Like the i-doc, Canada is heterogenous: it comprises many nations, bound by regional, linguistic, and ethnic differences. The condition of being many-nations-in-one-land is evident and at times directly taken up by the chapters in this collection.

Janine Marchessault and Will Straw (2019, xvii) state in their introduction to the *Oxford Handbook of Canadian Cinema* that it could "be argued that Canadian *places* have displaced the nation-state as the context in which cultural initiatives are conceived and in relation to which they become meaningful" (emphasis in original). The specificity of place is important for understanding the particularities of the national context of this collection. In a country so vast and relatively sparsely populated as Canada, the formation of "imagined communities" is region-based rather than nation-based. The situatedness and specificities of *place* are key to many i-docs discussed in this book: from Hogan's Alley in Vancouver, British Columbia, to Marshville Middle School in Sackville, New Brunswick, this collection illustrates the ways in which local or regional contexts and stories ground many interactive documentaries. For a form that for the most part is itself situated in cyberspace, place in interactive documentary is, as Zimmermann (2018, 10) notes, "a location in the material world that serves as a nodal point for people, relations, nature, and the built environment to mark space as specific and complex."

Within Canada, place as land and territory is highly political. As a colonial power, the nation of Canada is built upon the displacement and dispossession of Indigenous bodies from Indigenous land (Coulthard and Simpson 2016). The link between culture and land is critical; as Coulthard and Simpson write, it is the relationship to the land that "itself generates the processes, practices, and knowledges that inform [Indigenous] political systems, and through which we practice solidarity" (254). Land, in the context of Canada, can also not be divorced from the present realities of environmental catastrophe and climate change, nor from struggles for environmental justice, often being fought by Indigenous Peoples across different regions of Canada. This is a major thematic in i-doc practice in Canada. Multiple contributions in this volume address historical and ongoing settler-colonial extractivist practices that have negatively affected communities of humans and non-humans alike. While we cannot forget that the technological substrata that support the production and exhibition of i-docs are themselves comprised by materials of the Earth, many of the contributions show how technologies can be put to use as creative modes of addressing these issues, either by augmenting pedagogical practices (Miller and Jekanowski); offering the potential for non-human perspectives (Birks); or disrupting easy solutions or neat narrative endings (Mulvogue). Innovation and thinking beyond traditional documentary storytelling also provides a means for projecting possible, and more just, Indigenous futures (Longfellow).

Given their mostly web-based platforms and interactive modalities, even the most locally focused i-docs discussed in this volume invite viewership and participation that extend beyond borders, forging connections across Canada and with the rest of the world. For example, in *A Journal of Insomnia* (Hugues Sweeney, 2013), discussed in this book by Zoë Druick, and *The Space We Hold* (Tiffany Hsiung, 2017), examined by Freya Wright-Brough, the goal to connect people across regional and national borders is central to the subject matters and integrated into the works' participatory design. The input of viewers is crucial to the meaning and structure of the works themselves, and their interactive modalities encourage connections, and the acknowledgment of difference, to be made across geographic boundaries. Specificities of place thus come to speak to larger, global issues: from environmental sustainability and justice to histories of racial and gender-based violence; from negotiations of changing technologies to the economization of consciousness; and from the ways in which we recall the past to the possibilities for imagining different futures.

The historical context offered in the early chapters as well as in the introductory sections of most contributions is essential to a proper understanding of the i-doc on a global level; equally important is the diversity of creators, projects, and critical methods that are examined. The role played by Canadian institutions and Canadian creators is too often reduced to a small number of directors (e.g., Katerina Cizek) and projects (e.g., *Highrise*) that are not truly representative of the scale, breadth and diversity of projects made by the NFB, their private-sector partners, and smaller-scale producers over the last decade-plus. Our collection serves as something like a corrective to accepted narrative of Canada's contribution to the i-doc boom of the 2010s. If there is a critical dialogue between the local and the global in many interactive documentaries, and from the specific context of film in Canada, there is also an important interplay, if not a tension, between the national and the local: the histories, policies, and funding strategies of federal institutions that historically supported documentary filmmaking in Canada and that today support i-docs versus the specificities of place, language, and culture that constitute the unique stories featured within these works. This same tension appears within, at times drove, and ultimately contributed to the fate of the Challenge for Change and Société nouvelle programs, identified above as an influential force within the NFB upon the Digital Studio initiative responsible for so much Canadian i-doc production over the last decade-plus. The value proposition of projects that are at times technologically bound, limited by devices-in-use, and regionally specific in their subject matter or appeal to discrete audiences can be difficult to assess, evaluate, and therefore legitimize within such a monolithic institutional space that nonetheless claims that its mandate is to "create, produce, and distribute distinctive and original audiovisual works that reflect the diverse realities and perspectives of Canadians, and to share these works with the people of Canada and the rest of the world" (Government of Canada 2023). It is the risk that such tensions might have a negative impact upon the continued visibility and legacy of interactive works that this collection seeks to mitigate.

Part 1, "Technologies, Innovation, Experimentation: Histories and Case Studies of I-Doc Production and Exhibition in Canada," brings together six chapters that situate the i-doc within specific historical-technological junctures from the intersecting perspectives of production, innovation, and exhibition. These chapters engage with the still-emerging history of the interactive documentary in Canada at both the macro and micro levels, balancing inquiries of broad institutional spaces with those of individual projects and technologies. While it is possible to offer a fulsome study of an individual i-doc without either detailing its production and reception or fully engaging with the technologies upon which it is designed and distributed, the chapters presented in Part 1 offer such detailed histories and serve to contextualize much of the work that follows in subsequent parts.

In "The National Film Board of Canada's Digital Studio: An Oral History," Michael Brendan Baker adopts the oral history form as a means to track the development of storytelling technologies, production practices, and preservation protocols within the institutional framework of the National Film Board of Canada's Digital Studio, once the largest i-doc producer in the world. Hours of interviews with leading figures involved at the founding of the Digital Studio, in combination with supporting documents (including internal memos and government white papers) detail the philosophies, evolving prospects, and legacy of the first decade of i-doc production at the NFB.

With "Notes on Impact: The Case of the Interactive Documentary *GDP*," maker and scholar Frédéric Dubois revisits the National Film Board's 2010 i-doc *GDP* for the purpose of better conceptualizing the notion of impact with regard to interactive media. Drawing on impact scholarship in journalism and documentary, field experience and impact guides, this chapter calls into question current discourse on media impact while providing a first-person glimpse into the development and launch of an i-doc. Dubois seeks to make a practical contribution to production studies by stressing some of the shortcomings resulting from the current focus on short-term impact assessment in the field and points to the limitations of impact evaluation solely based on the reception of an interactive documentary, insisting on the importance of accounting for the effects of innovative production processes on subsequent work.

With "*Fort McMoney*: The Challenge of Maintaining Interactive Documentary," Daniel Keyes and Mike Robbins shift the focus upon a singular NFB work from production processes and impact assessment to the complicated issues of technological obsolescence and the archiving of interactive media projects. Synthesizing textual analysis, media theory, and interviews, Keyes and Robbins explore the diminished state of one of the Digital Studio's first "big hits" and consider whether the NFB's strategy to archive a project as complex and multifaceted as *Fort McMoney* is necessary and noble or misdirected and ill-conceived.

Moving away from the institutional space of the NFB, the study of a mobile device-focused "international collaborative creative arts research project" preoccupies Gerda Cammaer and Max Schleser in "*Viewfinders*: Exploring Travelling and Landscapes via Augmented Reality." The *Viewfinders* project crosses the boundaries of augmented reality, expanded cinema, photojournalism, and documentary media, and the authors here explore a form of interactive documentary that allows user-audiences to engage critically with the world through mobile technology. Cammaer and Schleser contemplate the smartphone as a widely available technology that might possibly democratize the i-doc form and consider the specific mechanism of Canadian research-creation funding as an institutional tool supporting innovation in the field.

Matt Soar and Monika Kin Gagnon, meanwhile, present a comprehensive history of Korsakow, a critical tool in the first wave of database documentaries. The software, designed for the creation of interactive storytelling and adopted in large numbers by creators with a preoccupation with non-fiction, is examined from the perspective of its niche institutional development, its creative possibilities, and its debts to extant modes of cinematic expression. "Always Already Old: Looking Back with the Korsakow System" details how the authors themselves adopted and shepherded the software and leveraged institutional resources within Canada to guarantee the accessibility of Korsakow for both their own projects and those of their peers. Their work includes numerous case studies as well as a critical evaluation of Korsakow's affordances as an interactive media-making tool and its shortcomings as a piece of software facing obsolescence.

Finally, Caroline Klimek offers a close reading of a singular interactive documentary and its exhibition history as a unique instance of the "live performance" of an interactive object. With "I-Docs and Live Performance: *Highrise: Universe Within* at Hot Docs," Klimek deftly situates Katerina Cizek's *Highrise* project within the larger context of film festivals and considers the challenges posed by i-docs within this exhibition and marketing space. The chapter serves as an interesting bookend to the oral history of the Digital Studio presented at the outset of Part 1 as Klimek considers the life of an i-doc generally regarded as symbolizing the end of the (first) Golden Age of work produced within that institutional space.

Part 2, *Encounters with Others: Activism, Agency, and Ethics*, offers five chapters that specifically discuss both the political and pedagogical potential of the interactive documentary and the ethics of the i-doc experience as shaped by its creators. Contributors here take up important questions regarding the relationship between interactivity and agency, in particular, how interactive documentaries may or may not heighten the potential for social change. Central to these chapters are the notions of care and responsibility in turbulent, troubling times: they highlight how i-doc practitioners employ specific digital technologies to achieve various levels of interaction with a user or audience, and how these design decisions generate novel encounters with the other (human and non-human) and shape our political understanding of space, place, and history.

In "Collaborative Encounters: I-Docs and Environmental Pedagogy in and beyond the Classroom," Rachel Webb Jekanowski and Elizabeth Miller argue that, given its polyphony, interactive documentary is ideal for telling the complex, "thick" (Tsing 2015), and diverse stories of climate change and thus is an innovative and effective tool for environmental pedagogy. The chapter draws on scholarship from environmental pedagogy, environmental humanities, and critical Indigenous studies as well as on the authors' experience of creating, teaching, and distributing *The Shore Line* (2017), an i-doc created by Miller and for which Jekanowski was a curriculum designer. In doing so, they show how the i-doc apparatus and its content can transcend boundaries of time, space, and discipline, bringing together divergent voices and forms of communication that foster comparative and collaborative learning. Through concrete examples, Jekanowski and Miller exemplify how an i-doc such as *The Shore Line* can be used by educators to mobilize environmental action and to build a politics of care for the non-human world.

Laura Ann Fox similarly takes up the relationship between activism and pedagogy by examining the theoretical underpinnings and the political potentials of an i-doc she made as part of a grassroots movement for educational reform in Sackville, New Brunswick. "Thinking in Networks: The Interactive Documentary as a Tool for Social Change," brings Latour's actor-network theory into the digital era as it considers the networks and agents involved in the relationship between the real and the virtual. Like Jekanowski and Miller, Fox sees a political urgency to breaking down barriers in knowledge creation, to diversifying forms of socially valued knowledge, and to thinking in networks. Through an analysis of and reflection on her creation of the i-doc *Sackville Schools 2020*, she shows how interactive documentary can be a tool to facilitate such tasks.

While not explicitly focused on pedagogy, Freya Wright-Brough takes up crucial questions about how we learn about others through media representation in "Interactivity as Ethical Encounter in *The Space We Hold*." She examines the encounter with an Other through Levinasian ethics and an analysis of *The Space We Hold*, an i-doc about the history and legacy of forced sexual slavery. Wright-Brough is concerned particularly with the ways in which *The Space We Hold* invites and exemplifies practices of responsibility – from filmmaker, spectator, and subject – for the Other through its participatory mode and interactive functions. Using Levinas's concepts of transcendent face-to-face encounter and infinity, she focuses on the construction of the i-doc and its potential for the formation of ethical relations between filmmaker and documentary subject, and spectator and subject, that resist the totalization of the Other.

Chelsea Birks's "Fish Love: Digital Technology and Passivity in Nettie Wild's *Uninterrupted*" continues the theme of documentary ethics but with a focus on the non-human world. Looking at *Uninterrupted* – a transmedia work about the lifecycle of BC salmon featuring both an online and urban-installation component – Birks approaches questions of agency and action in i-docs from a posthumanist perspective, showing how the work asks the spectator to see the fish as agents. Moreover, and in an important counter-example to the subject of action and i-docs, Birks understands *Uninterrupted* as provoking a form of passivity or a loss of control of the image. Via Anat Pick and Simone Weil, she theorizes this passivity as an experience of vulnerability, one that allows spectators to empathize with the fish on screen and that, ultimately, is a form of love.

To conclude Part 2, Jessica Mulvogue's contribution follows a parallel line of thinking to Birks's focus on passivity in interactive documentary. "Playing with Extreme Oil: Slow Catastrophe and the Melancholic Imaginary in *Offshore* and *Fort McMoney*" considers the possible meanings of inertia and inaction in two docu-games about extreme modes of fossil fuel extraction. Positioning the works as exemplary of twenty-first-century fossil-fuel narratives (Buell) that articulate the slow violence of oil industries, Mulvogue explores how the game function of the works gives way to an open-ended play mode, in which resolution is denied. Coupled with the apocalyptic tones of the projects and their contents, Mulvogue theorizes the ultimate inertia of the works as a "melancholic" imaginary that speaks to a wider affective state of living within climate catastrophe. Contrary to regressive or reactionary understandings of melancholia, Mulvogue sees the elements of stasis found in the work as a means to resist or counter narratives of progress, which are built upon the fossil fuel industries and thus on the destruction of the Earth.

The final part of the collection, "Image and Sound beyond 'the Real': Media Pasts, Presents, and Futures," considers the relationship of the interactive documentary to previous forms of non-fiction storytelling and technology, its lifespan within the contemporary media moment, and its prospects – technologically and otherwise – for the future. Our knowledge of, and comfort with, older media forms is considered in relation to the question of how the interactive documentary engages an audience both intellectually and affectively. Volumetric imaging and highly specialized executions of augmented reality and virtual reality are considered not only for their role in the evolution of the i-doc but also for the ways in which they will almost certainly force a reconsideration of the ontology of the documentary image in the realm of digital media. The chapters in this section include the reflections of two i-doc maker scholars who seek to understand the implications of virtual reality in the areas of social change and restorative justice, while a third author makes a pioneering contribution to our understanding of sound within the i-doc.

Peter Urquhart's "Nostalgia, 'Old' Media and *Welcome to Pine Point*" considers the complex, often competing relationships between new and old technologies and their (mediating) ties to the past. A case study presenting one of the NFB Digital Studio's earliest projects becomes a vehicle for exploring the ways in which i-docs might shape our engagement with subject matter by leveraging our familiarity with older, conventional forms of media and technology. Theories of nostalgia are adopted here as a means of exploring our relationship to an imagined past as well as to "possible futures of progress, stability, and comfort." Urquhart's contribution is given added dimension in light of the fact the project under examination itself disappeared for several years when modern browsers were briefly incompatible with its original programming (the project has since been converted and, for a time, future-proofed for use in many browsers).

In "Acoustic Profiling in Hogan's Alley: Mapping Intersectional Soundways in the Lost Vancouver Neighborhood of Stan Douglas's iOS app *Circa 1948*," Randolph Jordan considers an augmented reality app that brings a largely forgotten history into the present. He argues that the soundworld of Douglas's i-doc serves to re-establish and reassert the place of marginalized communities within a troubling chapter of Vancouver's urban history. Jordan leverages his expertise in the area of sound theory to explore the potential for i-docs to use the soundtrack to more fully engage with space and place. Most important, he sees sound design in Douglas's project as a call to action for housing activists in contemporary Vancouver in their fight against "urban renewal."

Zoë Druick's chapter, "*A Journal of Insomnia*: The Individualization of Sleep in a Wired World," similarly considers sound in interactive documentary, focusing on the affective affordances of "haptic listening" in the NFB Digital Studio project *A Journal of Insomnia*. The chapter interrogates the potential for i-docs to engage in the field of illness and examines, among other things, "the role of voices ... in terms of the creation of authenticity and intimacy in relation to narratives of dis-ease" (00). Druick adopts a complex citational regimen spanning the fields of sound studies, health and illness studies, media studies, and critical theory to explore the rise of digital capitalism and its demand that our consciousness become coterminous with productivity.

With "Going Deep: Hybrid Capture in Documentary," Cindy Poremba and Amy Siegel introduce readers to "hybrid captured images" and highlight the role a constellation of innovative technologies plays within individual interactive documentaries and the challenge they present to conceptions of the documentary image more broadly. Poremba and Siegel adopt a new materialist approach as they argue "volumetric images present a powerful focal object for exploring late postmedia through the intra-action of human and computational agencies, the increasing blur between data and images, and desires and expectations surrounding digital capture" (00). They highlight the ways in which i-docs featuring hybrid capture complicate foundational notions of non-fiction media and present case studies from the leading edge of Canadian technologists and creators.

Last, in "Indigenous Futurism and the Immersive Worlding of *Inherent Rights, Vision Rights*, *2167*, and *Biidaaban: First Light*" Brenda Longfellow considers the world-building potential of i-docs as Indigenous creators adopt the form to contest settler-colonial authority and imagine a future of secured Indigenous sovereignty. Longfellow, herself an i-doc creator, situates five case studies of contemporary works of virtual reality within larger histories of Indigenous cinema, experimental film, video art, and new media production and highlights the ways in which these projects adopt VR in an effort to provide user-audiences with an embodied and participatory form of engagement. The chapter privileges the work of Indigenous media scholars and artists alike, and productively challenges the descriptors of "Canada" and "documentary" used throughout this collection.

The book concludes with an afterword prepared by US media scholars Patricia Zimmermann and Dale Hudson, who offer an appreciative, descriptive assessment of the text that helps underscore some key questions about individual contributions as well as the overarching scope of the collection. The editors sought to include the perspective of leading figures within the field of interactive media studies who might speak not only to the character and content of Canadian i-docs from their informed positions but also to the state of new media scholarship as reflected in the work of the contributors featured herein. It is interesting to observe where Zimmermann and Hudson's sense of the field and the realities of cultural production in Canada depart from those of the editors and contributors, a tension we find productive and ultimately illuminating.

As preliminary work on this collection drew to a close in early 2021, deep within lockdowns on both sides of the Atlantic due to the Covid-19 pandemic and only a few weeks after the storming of the US Capitol by a mob led by domestic terrorists who organized themselves using social media, we observed a renewed need for theorizing the significance of digital interactivity and the ways in which digital technologies can help or hinder our connection to people, places, and stories. Interactive documentary represents just one small mode of online digital engagement. However, the tumult of the last few years brought to the fore the possibilities and pitfalls of communicating, sometimes solely, via our computers and phones. Many of us found solace in establishing and connecting with online communities during the pandemic; given strict restrictions, we created and shared stories of ourselves and others' lives online and we used video, photo, and text to do so. As educators, for better or for worse, we found new strategies for delivering lectures and engaging students remotely, often with the help of software developed to create interactive learning experiences. However, the dangers of algorithmic bias in online social and news media permeate these online spaces: the strong virality of false information and the ways in which online information is easily manipulated has had crippling effects on societies. Solace may be found in online communities, but sometimes the strength of these communities has arguably created deeper divisions in societies as a whole. While the contributions to this collection were for the most part written prior to the Covid-19 pandemic, the inquiries, arguments, and histories presented here will, we believe, play a role in contributing to conversations and studies that will surely emerge about the kinds of digital communication and storytelling that, out of necessity, flourished during these years.

References

Alkarimeh, Baker, and Eric Boutin. 2017. "Interactive Documentary: A Proposed Model and Definition." *French Journal for Media Research*, no. 7: 1–22.

Arns, Inke. n.d. "Interaction, Participation, Networking Art and Telecommunication." *Media Art Net/Medien Kunst Netz.* http://www.mediaartnet.org/themes/overview_of_media_art/communication/print.

Aston, Judith, and Stefano Odorico. 2018. "The Poetics and Politics of Polyphony." *Alphaville: Journal of Film and Screen Media*, no. 15 (Summer): 63–93.

Aston, Judith, Sandra Gaudenzi, and Mandy Rose, eds. 2017. *I-Docs: The Evolving Practices of Interactive Documentary*. London and New York: Wallflower.

Coulthard, Glen, and Leanne Betasamosake Simpson. 2016. "Grounded Normativity/Place-Based Solidarity." *American Quarterly* 68 (2): 249–55. https://doi.org/10.1353/aq.2016.0038.

Galloway, Dayna, Kenneth B. McAlpine, and Paul Harris. 2007. "From Michael Moore to JFK Reloaded: Towards a Working Model of Interactive Documentary." *Journal of Media Practice* 8 (3): 325–39. https://doi.org/10.1386/jmpr.8.3.325_1.

Gifreu-Castells, Arnau. 2011. "The Interactive Documentary: Definition Proposal and Basic Features of the New Emerging Genre." In *McLuhan Galaxy Conference: Understanding Media Today, Barcelona, 25–26 May*, 367–78. Barcelona: Editorial UOC.

Government of Canada. 2023. "The National Film Board: Mandate and Values." Last modified 14 February 2023. https://www.canada.ca/en/national-film-board/corporate/about/mandate-values.html.

Marchessault, Janine, and Will Straw, eds. 2019. *The Oxford Handbook of Canadian Cinema*. New York: Oxford University Press.

Miles, Adrian. 2014. "Interactive Documentary and Affective Ecologies." In *New Documentary Ecologies: Emerging Platforms, Practices and Discourses*, ed. Kate Nash, Craig Hight, and Catherine Summerhayes, 67–82. Basingstoke: Palgrave Macmillan.

Mulvogue, Jessica. 2019. "The World Navigated: Interactive Documentaries in Canada." In *The Oxford Handbook of Canadian Cinema*, ed. Janine Marchessault and Will Straw, 409–22. New York: Oxford University Press.

Nash, Kate. 2012. "Modes of Interactivity: Analysing the Webdoc." *Media, Culture and Society* 34 (2): 195–210. https://doi.org/10.1177/0163443711430758.

– 2022. *Interactive Documentary: Theory and Debate*. London: Routledge.

National Film Board of Canada. 2009. *Report on Plan and Priorities*. Ottawa: Government of Canada. Last modified 13 November 2009. https://www.tbs-sct.canada.ca/rpp/2010-2011/inst/nfb/nfb01-eng.asp.

Odorico, Stefano. 2019. *The Interactive Documentary Form: Aesthetics, Practice, and Research*. New York: Columbia University Press.

Tsing, Anna Lowenhaupt. 2015. *The Mushroom at the End of the World: On the Possibility of Life in Capitalist Ruins*. Princeton, NJ: Princeton University Press.

Zimmermann, Patricia R. 2018. "Thirty Speculations towards a Polyphonic Model for New Media Documentary." *Alphaville: Journal of Film and Screen Media*, no. 15 (Summer): 9–15. https://doi.org/10.33178/alpha.15.01.

Zimmermann, Patricia R., and Helen de Michiel. 2018. *Open Space New Media Documentary: A Toolkit for Theory and Practice*. New York: Routledge.

PART ONE

Technology, Innovation, Experimentation

Histories and Case Studies of I-Doc Production and Exhibition in Canada

1

THE NATIONAL FILM BOARD OF CANADA'S DIGITAL STUDIO

AN ORAL HISTORY

Michael Brendan Baker

The interactive documentary space was, in many important ways, largely established and defined within the context of Canada by the new media works produced by the National Film Board of Canada's Digital Studio. The Digital Studio, founded during Tom Perlmutter's time as commissioner (2007–13) as he sought to modernize the institution, not only centralized and incubated the efforts of the leading interactive designers and non-fiction filmmakers in Canada but also reflected the emergent "digital culture" mandate of the federal government and its various agencies at the time. The mandate of the studio was and remains to "'create' and 'connect' with Canadians in the age of the Internet" through "experimenting with the creative application of digital technologies and interactivity as it relates to story, expression and community" (National Film Board of Canada 2010). The NFB regarded such a shift towards interactive and transmedia storytelling as the "digital opportunity." Meanwhile, the establishment of the Digital Studio within the NFB signalled a larger shift in the funding priorities of the institution as less and less in-house production of conventional film work was supported by ever-diminishing budgets across all categories of production, necessitating an expansion of international partnerships and private financing contributions. However, these new models for production and partnering resulted in a rapid rise in both output and international profile for interactive works and their creators, quickly establishing the Digital Studio as a world leader in interactive storytelling with a particular aptitude for the sort of non-fictional work that has defined the NFB since its founding. Across this body of work, the NFB's Digital Studio established a benchmark for the form, content, and possibilities of the interactive documentary in its earliest years and maintained this pride of place for the first decade of its existence.

Method

It is my intention to track the development of institutional strategy, storytelling technologies, production practices, and preservation protocols within the framework of the National Film Board of Canada's Digital Studio, among the largest i-doc producers in the world. In a previous project examining the pioneering Challenge for Change and Société nouvelle programs (CFC/SN), I undertook interviews with filmmakers and other principals to privilege the voices of those directly involved in the initiative. At the same time, it was necessary to search the NFB archives to collect materials that would present the views of CFC/SN participants with whom I was unable to speak. In a collection of historical newsletters published by these participants and kept on file by the Board, I took note of the pride-of-place interviews, Q&AS, and other printed forms of oral testimony occupied in this narrative and the important role they played in my pursuit of presenting the story of their activities in a rigorous and comprehensive manner. Recognizing the historical value of these materials, I choose to adopt the oral history form to capture and better understand the launch of the Digital Studio and its preliminary activities through to the departures of its founding personnel.

When undertaken in a studious and respectful manner that acknowledges the ethical issues that can arise within such an undertaking, oral history as a narrative research methodology can help reconstruct the past and document aspects of the historical record that have been obscured or are otherwise missing (Perks and Thomson 2015). Moreover, it provides an opportunity to explore, analyze, and interpret the history and culture of an institutional space such as the NFB when such an enterprise was not prioritized contemporaneously with the events under consideration. This method is well established in both documentary filmmaking practice and in the study of documentary cinema history (see Kahana 2016; Rosenthal 1980; Waugh, Baker, and Winton 2010) and strikes me as particularly important in relation to the efforts and achievements of the Digital Studio.

It is of interest to me and vital to the historical record to share perspectives on the founding of the Digital Studio and the immediate impact of the first projects produced under the NFB Interactive brand, the evolution of the Digital Studio over the first several years of the initiative and the development of resources to support its growth, and the response to Digital Studio projects and their institutional home from the perspective of those outside Canada in an effort to confirm and clarify the broader impact of the work.

The primary subjects of this inquiry include Cindy Witten (director general, English Programming, NFB, 2008–12); Monique Simard (director general, French Programming, NFB, 2008–13); Hugues Sweeney (executive producer of the Digital Studio, French, NFB, 2008–19); Loc Dao (executive producer and creative technologist, then chief digital officer, NFB, through 2020); Robert McLaughlin (director of digital content and strategy, then executive producer of the Digital Studio, English, NFB); Jimmy Fournier (director, research and development, NFB); Shari Frillot (chief curator, New Frontier Program, Sundance Film Festival); and Ingrid Kopp (director of interactive, Tribeca Film Institute). All of these individuals were directly involved with the launch of the NFB Digital Studio or directly engaged with the NFB when the first wave of work was produced. Supplementing these long-form interviews are primary sources, including planning documents shared by the interviewees, publicly available government white papers, and public presentations delivered by NFB personnel to creative professionals at industry conferences and events. Secondary sources include journalistic coverage of the NFB's announcement of its digital strategy, NFB press releases, and critical responses to its first slate of interactive projects. Wherever necessary, the interviews were cross-referenced both with each other and with the supplemental resources as a means of fact-checking and verifying claims made by participants.

The Formation of the Digital Studio(s)

It is interesting to note, but generally unremarked upon, that nearly all of the key personnel involved with the NFB Digital Studio at its founding in 2008 under the commission of Perlmutter were previously involved with the Canadian Broadcasting Corporation's (CBC) and Radio-Canada's digital initiatives and were brought to the NFB for precisely their new media experience. Founded in 2000 as the traditional broadcasting institutions sought to attract a younger, more engaged audience, CBC's *Radio 3* and Radio-Canada's *Bande à part* were regarded as among the web's most sophisticated and forward-looking new media projects of the decade. Loc Dao and Robert McLaughlin were among the first to join Cindy Witten, director general, English Programming, at the NFB offices in Vancouver following their time with the CBC – time spent, in part, launching *Radio 3* as an online webcasting initiative with a team that included Susan Englebert and Robert Ouimet. Meanwhile, at Radio-Canada, Hugues Sweeney worked as head of the pioneering *Bande à part* multi-platform project involving webcasting, traditional radio, and broadcast television. Sweeney would be Monique Simard's first hire upon her arrival at the NFB as director general, French Programming, following a successful career as an independent producer of documentaries. Simard's appointment was not insignificant and might be understood as an effort on the part of the NFB to stabilize the institution at a time when it was regularly under fire and facing something like an existential crisis. She recalls, "I've been associated all my life with the NFB. When I was 18 years old, I was in a documentary by Claude Jutra [*Wow*, 1970] – I knew the place by heart. There were pictures of me on the walls of the NFB! I think that everybody knew I loved the NFB as an institution, that I believed in its existence, because over the years there were instances where Heritage wanted to close down the NFB, private producers wanted to close them down and get the money. So I had credibility as a producer which was very, very important. There was trust in me and, of course, I was well known" (Simard 2018).

The new media experience shared by most of this core group (at the CBC and elsewhere) would prove essential to their efforts in establishing a similar creative space within the NFB. Dao (2018) explains:

> Rob and I started working together at CBC in 2000 and we were experimenting with the shift from new media to – well, we didn't know what to call it at the time. That was near the beginning of social media and UGC (user-generated content) and it was the early days of MySpace and before YouTube existed. We started creating these communities to reach musicians and performers and digital artists and we created these niche sites that served those communities. The music community that we built at the time was a site called New Music

Canada. In fact, the database we built for that has today become CBC Music. We had just come off the demise of the original Napster and we were all living in a world of music albums and anticipating album releases. With that project we decided, "Okay, the song – that's how music is going to change. Everything is going to be about the track now." And it was that simple decision that led to this little database that all indie Canadian musicians at the time contributed to and ultimately established the CBC Music database as it is today.

He continues:

> In terms of moving into interactive, we created 120seconds.com which was a website for digital artists, artists that we work with today like Vincent Morrissette. He first got interested in creating digital art back in 2000 with this user-generated site where people could experiment with art and story and upload it online. That was another kind of feed for us into interactive and then it was really in 2002 to 2005 that we created the CBC Radio 3 digital magazine that took from all these sources [including New Music Canada and JustConcerts.com] and created regional storytelling in arts and news and music and put it together in a weekly format. I think because we cut our teeth making [over one hundred] issues over three years that, by the end of it, Rob and I and our team (which included Alicia Smith and Jeremy Mendes) had this idea of what I now like to call our "Interactive 1.0."
>
> Around that time, you might recall the CBC had a big lockout in 2005–06, so we started looking for other things to do and it was then that Kat Cizek – along with Gerry Flahive – reached out to me. Rob and I collaborated with them on the Filmmaker-in-Residence project [in 2004], which was a first foray into interactive at the Board. You'll see that the design style and layer of immersive-ness that we developed before leaving CBC Radio 3 merged with the long-form storytelling of the NFB and resulted in the Filmmaker-in-Residence project. When Tom Perlmutter became commissioner, interactive was clearly one of the things that was in his head, this shift to be engineered within the NFB, and that resulted in the hiring of Cindy and Monique which, in turn, ultimately brought Rob and I back to the NFB and the public service on a more permanent basis.

Sweeney recalls arriving at the Montreal offices to discover "empty workspaces"; while a structure had quickly been established in the Vancouver studios, it would be left to Simard and Sweeney, the latter hired with the interim title "Creative Consultant," to establish policies and procedures as well as to hire additional staff. He was cognizant of the rigid structures previously in place at the NFB but was optimistic that this new venture would afford both the English and French teams a degree of freedom and a wealth of opportunities. He explains:

> On the one hand, it felt like a place where a lot of habits were deadlocked over [the previous] two or three decades. Linear production [was the expectation] and a rigid process was developed to deliver a documentary feature or short animated film. In a positive sense, it was very rigorous, but on the other hand that meant absolutely no flexibility because everything is determined by the process. But at the same time, for me, it was an ocean of potential, an endless sea of possibility.
>
> When you look beyond who [the NFB] caters to, when you look at the longer history of the NFB, major disruptive moments happened there and at multiple points in history it was a very important place for innovation. Direct cinema was born at the NFB, IMAX was born at the NFB, among the first computer animations were born at the NFB. And then you look at the long tradition of animation through the 1950s, 60s, and 70s – it's incredible to consider the work of Norman McLaren and so many other creators. So it was very exciting to kickstart something completely new at a place where, at its roots, there was a very strong appetite for innovation and transformation. (Sweeney 2018)

The broader institutional context for the Digital Studio's emergence is found within several planning documents circa 2009 and a published white paper from 2010 entitled, "The Digital Opportunity," which laid out the NFB's proposed shift towards digital creation, distribution, and transmedia storytelling alongside a mandate to digitize and make available online a larger portion of its audiovisual library. Publicly, this initiative was first understood as the NFB "going online" in 2008 by finally making a large number of its titles – approximately two thousand at launch – free to stream at NFB.ca. Internally, conversations about establishing resources for the creation of new media projects began at the same time. Planning documents drafted by English Programming in early 2009 highlight "digital" as providing "increasing control over direct means of distribution" and stress it has "never been more cost effective to produce new kinds of innovative NFB programming or measure its ultimate impact upon audiences, attitudes, and policy" (NFB English Programming 2009, 2–3). English Programming cites the success of earlier digital initiatives, including the aforementioned Filmmaker-in-Residence project and the (regrettably named) mobile shorts program, *Shorts in Motion: The Art of Seduction*, as the foundation upon which it could build a new digital strategy (4). Interactive documentaries, as well as digital animation, are explicitly referenced as the storytelling forms for which the NFB would seek to establish itself as a leader and innovator. Simard cites her own professionalization as a documentary filmmaker and McLaughlin his background and training in journalism as logical explanations for the Digital Studio's preoccupation with non-fiction as it moved into the field of interactive. And while it was never the mandate of the Digital Studio to focus wholly on works of non-fiction – indeed, it is not accurate to singularly characterize the works available at NFB Interactive as "interactive documentary" – the fact remains that the vast majority of works produced by the institution are suitably categorized as i-docs.

Witten described the impulse behind the formation of the Digital Studio in terms of its link to the first phase of the NFB's digital strategy and its connection to the history of innovation at the institution. "The streaming project was happening, but it was happening in another department at the Film Board," she explains, "so while we were certainly keeping each other in the loop, one didn't build on the other except that we all knew that we wanted to reach Canadians with the work" (Witten 2018). She continues:

> DVDs were sitting in dusty jackets on public library shelves and the odd piece would go up on television, but nobody really knew it was an NFB film because to them it looked like a CBC film. Audiences would hear about an animation that won an Oscar or was nominated for an Oscar but even that was difficult to find and watch, so we were all united in this excitement and urgency around getting the work out to Canadians in a much more direct way. I would say the work English Programming and English Distribution were doing was certainly complementary, but it was a very separate thing.

> Distribution was about archiving and data management and such, and we were trying to figure out how to create in the digital space.

It is important to highlight here the purposeful division and organizational disconnection between the production side and the distribution side at the Board, particularly where matters of archiving are concerned; the tension produced by this siloing of work was evident in my conversations with all of the principals involved. In fact, this gap between the two departments, each with its own budget and responsibilities, would prove perilous to the ongoing access of the NFB's interactive projects. Witten, echoing Sweeney above, explains that the Board was preoccupied with a unique set of questions related to new media production that distracted it at the time from matters relating to preservation and access:

> What does interactive mean? What tools do we need? What is the process? We were in an institution where you went out and shot and then you edited and it was a very linear process and we could describe it very easily to anyone. We had many forms that accompanied every step of that process and different budgets that were tapped throughout that process but now we were in a space where we were defining it as we went along, putting one foot down in front of the other … It seemed to me that it was part of the continuum of innovation at the Film Board, with the Direct Cinema films of the late 1950s and early 60s, the work that they were doing in animation, all springing forth from one dusty corner or another in that building on the highway in Montreal. It just made sense to me that we would tackle interactive and define it and help others figure it out. (Witten 2018)

A year later, the official mandate of the studio was publicly declared. At the time, then NFB commissioner Perlmutter wrote: "We need to support content that is not tied to existing broadcast properties and may never have a broadcast component. This is perhaps the riskiest and most difficult content to develop and, in some ways, the most important. It is here that the language, aesthetics and dynamics of new media programming will be developed" (Canada 2009).

Often obscured by the formality of the white papers and other policy communications, however, is the vision and invaluable impact borne of the close working relationship of the two women, Simard and Witten, hired months apart and tasked with making tangible the abstract goals laid out in internal communications and press releases. Simard (2018) explains: "[Cindy and I] got along very well the first day we met, and that made a huge difference in the years we were there together. Before Cindy and I were the head of our programs, and many people have told us this, it was like a wall. There was no collaboration, no communication, between the English and French programs. And I'm very happy to say we did change that – fabulously." Simard and Witten boldly dedicated 20 per cent of their respective production budgets to interactive works at a time when it was not a popular decision among the rank-and-file despite the Board's public commitment to digital production and distribution. Simard continues: "It's very much a legacy of our time there. Because [we were] getting along and seeing things the same way and sharing our ideas and sharing the same vision, we did things that would have been difficult for [Cindy] alone on her side or me alone on my side. And one of the major things was opening the interactive studios and saying, 'We're putting 20 percent of our money in interactive.' It would have been very difficult if either of us had tried to do it alone." The direct result of that budget commitment was the formal creation of the Vancouver and Montreal interactive studios now referred to as the NFB Digital Studio.

Production Processes, Support, and Resource Management

In conversations with the principal founders of the Digital Studio, stories of establishing workflows, access to technology, and resource management within the NFB are a recurring topic. It is an understatement to say the formula-driven systems of the NFB's long-standing bureaucracy was mismatched to the exploratory, dynamic nature of the web-based multimedia projects the new teams were developing. Moreover, the traditional role of producer within the NFB necessarily evolved as a consequence of new media production. Where once producers effectively managed productions from the top down within a strict bureaucracy, securing and managing budgets from available funding envelopes, overseeing the logistical and administrative aspects of a film's production, and working with the creative team to support and guide a project to its completion, the role of producer within the Digital Studio became more creative, more multifaceted, more technologically adept, and more likely to seek change to existing systems at the Board – but they were forced to do so while still navigating that bureaucracy.

"Generally speaking, the Board was not at all the most technical or the most forward-thinking in terms of systems and tools," McLaughlin (2018) recalls:

> It remains a place that tries to use enterprise-level systems for an organization that is under four hundred people. The other consideration is we are tied to the government, so there's a belief that as a government agency every rule that is set out must apply equally to all agencies. I think we're now much better at understanding how those rules can be interpreted to apply to different organizations rather than just assuming the Canadian Revenue Agency has to have the same rules as the National Film Board. I think the Board has advanced a little bit in terms of understanding there's more flexibility for us, but at the beginning of my time it was the most rigid, bureaucratic place including everything surrounding technology. It was brutal.
>
> I was coming from CBC at a time when production was rooted at everyone's desk, especially in the world of radio. Digital audio production was enabled by laptops and personal computers; it was simple to make audio programming and so the collective agreements allowed for anyone to edit audio. Returning to the NFB in 2008 after my earlier experience preceding the CBC lockout, it felt like I was stepping back twenty-five years. The systems and processes were not in place to support production in the age of the internet or especially around 2008 – we're not talking about the year 2000, we're not talking about the dot-com bubble. This is 2008, so for me it was quite a shock and there was a lot of head-butting and turbulence. It wasn't so much on the production side, it was mostly on the institutional side: What form do you need to fill out in order to do what you want to do? And on the labour side, how do you contract [new roles in the digital arts]?
>
> If you want to contract someone at the Film Board, you must fill out the appropriate form. In order to fill out the appropriate form, you must use the appropriate tool. And within that tool there will be a drop-down menu, and in that drop-down menu there will be six titles that you can choose from in order to fill out the

contract. If your description isn't on that drop-down list, you can't get a contract written. So if I want a contract for a creative director who only works on the internet, and they are not a filmmaker, and they are not represented by the Directors Guild of Canada, it's a problem ... At the time, every title listed in the drop-down menus of those forms was a film term, and every title had already been considered by the collective agreements that might be attached to the work that was happening. If you're a sound design person, is [that] a "composer"? Is [she] a Writer's Guild member? Is he also writing a programming script? [Nothing to support that type of creative professional] was in place. So you need to talk to the legal department and you start explaining to them there's going to be a different kind of work happening, and even if they agree to make the change it would require a meeting. In fact, it would require a series of meetings – it's not one meeting, it's not like I go for a coffee and convince someone that [the change is necessary]. Everyone involved in the decision needs to be in the room in order to make a change like that, and only after three or four meetings with people will they nod their heads [in agreement]. And then you have to go find the person at the Board that made the tool which in those days was custom-made by NFB staff. And *then* you have to convince *them* that they needed to change the tool.

To be honest, I sort of felt like ... while I wasn't being asked to change the institution, that's what I had to do in order to get the work done. I had to change systems and processes and ways of thinking about what art is, change ways of thinking about how work happens, change ways of thinking about all of that stuff and that was the most frustrating and turbulent part.

McLaughlin's commitment to execute on the shared vision for the Digital Studio despite the day-to-day frustrations of working within such a traditional institutional structure is something shared by all of the key personnel who discussed their experiences. Dao describes "bureaucratic gotchas" in the early years that regularly interrupted (though rarely derailed) the production process at all levels as the team sought to establish best practices and find firm footing for the production of non-linear projects within an institutional space otherwise dedicated to traditional linear forms. Disagreements between producers and marketing were not uncommon (indeed, they are a feature, not a bug, of the industry), but Witten (2018) explains, "Every time we decided to produce a project we had a very particular community in mind, we had a very particular audience in mind, and we had ideas right from the development stage about how we would reach those people."

While no single workflow captured the many approaches explored and adopted by the teams at the Digital Studio, over time, producers and creators established a routine that "fit" within the Board's administrative framework yet allowed them to remain open to chance and outside influence. Sweeney (2018) explains:

> There are three ways to start a project. We're not a granter or a funder, so it's less rigid in its methodology [in terms of how] the project begins; it's not like a submission to Telefilm [wherein] you have to submit on a deadline and with very specific materials. Digital Studio projects will often come from outside. It could be an individual, a group of creators, another producer or organization that has an idea or an intuition about something.
>
> We could also, as a studio, have an idea or an intuition or an opportunity that we will offer to those outside [the Board]. For example, for several years, mental health was one of the priority thematics that we wanted to develop, so we did a project on insomnia [*Journal of Insomnia*] in 2013. The idea came from inside the studio, just the broad strokes, saying, "Okay, we know that 30 percent of the population is insomniac, we know that it is a very solitary experience, but at the same time we know we have all of those people experiencing the same thing at the same time, so the internet is probably the best way to tell that story." So, we reached out to a team of creators and gave them the project and they created it from inside-out.
>
> The third way is more about the context that we'll create with a partner in which people can pitch an idea or concept or project. For instance, we do that a lot with Arte France or with Quartiers des Spectacles in Montreal. We will call for ideas with a [specific] editorial and artistic frame; for instance, with Arte we did a project called "60 seconds" and the idea was for people to pitch ideas for an interactive documentary for a mobile phone that is lived inside sixty seconds and is about mobility. And we had dozens of proposals

> coming from all over the globe; we had an international jury gather in Montreal, and we selected ten projects that we produced. So that is an example of the frame defined [by the Board] but the ideas sourced from the outside. These are the three principal ways of how projects are started.

Sweeney and McLaughlin describe the process following a successful proposal as fairly well established and quite typical relative to similar interactive design projects produced elsewhere. Sweeney (2018) continues:

> We always have fifteen projects on the go at some point in their evolution. Let's say one-third is in the conception phase, one-third is in the R&D phase, and one-third is in the production phase, so we have this constant flow of things ready to go and in evolution, etc. The cycle of production averages between twenty-four and thirty-six months, so it's a lot of planning. We keep ourselves at capacity and have a fast track for smaller projects because [many of] our projects are quite large in scale. These large-scale projects are always around $200,000 to $300,000 in terms of budget, but if we keep a fast track of smaller projects that cost something between $10,000 and $25,000 and take between three and six months to be made, they can correspond to the zeitgeist or something going on at that specific moment.
>
> That being said, [we] try to value our allocation not as investment money but instead use our network of collaborators and potential collaborators, both nationally and internationally, to raise the overall capacity of production. On average, depending on the year, for every dollar we receive by allocation we can raise another three or four dollars through collaboration structures so that the project gets more capacity or we increase our overall capacity to do more projects. The majority of things that come out of the Montreal studio are built in collaboration with national or international partners. It's very diverse but we try to find other institutions or organizations that have a similar philosophy and desire to bring those kinds of projects into the public space.

This practice of third-party partnerships, endorsed by the NFB in its traditional film production, provided the Digital Studio with increased financial resources, access to a pool of leading-edge creatives, and an international reach for its projects that quickly helped establish its work as leading edge and in keeping with the legacy of artistic quality generally associated with the Board. It must be acknowledged, however, that these strategies were in part a consequence of funding cuts to the NFB (and other cultural institutions) under the direction of Prime Minister Stephen Harper's government (2006–15), which prioritized fiscal responsibility and efficiency while demanding the Board still meet its obligations to promote Canadian culture despite greatly reduced resources relative to those provided by his predecessors, Paul Martin (2003–06) and Jean Chrétien (1993–2003). The decision to leverage the expertise of contract and freelance employees from the digital arts and technology sectors was crucial to the Digital Studio's innovative work but highlights long-simmering concerns about the diminishing role of union employment at the NFB, an institution that regularly deals with questions about working conditions and job security in the face of such cuts. Indeed, many of the Digital Studio's early collaborators (e.g., ARTE, RTS) were likewise publicly funded cultural institutions responding to new challenges posed by online production and dissemination.

The distinction between the English and French units within the Digital Studio was both organizational and budgetary, but there were not philosophical or aesthetic differences that defined each body of work (as was the case with the competing visions of Challenge for Change and Société nouvelle decades earlier). Sweeney explains (2018): "Rob and I have total independence on the projects we choose, the way we allocate the money, the creators we work with, the partnerships we build. But at the same time, Rob and I are talking almost every day and are very close on strategy, point-of-view, philosophy, and just sharing ideas and decision making, trying to bring audiences together." This partnership between McLaughlin and Sweeney at the production level mirrored the partnership between Witten and Simard at the executive level and created working conditions within the Digital Studio that allowed NFB creators and their outside partners to thrive.

Recognition and Impact

The work produced during the first several years of the Digital Studio set a standard that inspired creators inside and outside of the NFB. While a wide diversity of approaches to new media creation and transmedia storytelling was on display, it was not long before the work of the Digital Studio became synonymous with the emerging field of interactive documentary. This perception was bolstered equally by the tradition of documentary associated with the Board as well as the specific contours of the most acclaimed and highest profile of works made available at the NFB Interactive website (which serves as the public-facing home for the studio) during the first half-decade of the Digital Studio's operations. *GDP* (Hélène Choquette, 2009), *Water Life* (Rob McLaughlin, Loc Dao, Jam3, 2009); *Here at Home* (Manfred Becker, Sarah Fortin, Darryl Nepinak, Louiselle Noël, and Lynne Stopkewich, 2012); *Highrise* (Katerina Cizek, 2009); *Fort McMoney* (David Dufresne, 2013); and *Bear 71* (Jeremy Mendes and Leanne Allison, 2012) were among many early projects received with acclaim and easily squared with the NFB's legacy of non-fiction filmmaking. Perhaps just as important, the success of this work helped to establish networks of third-party collaborators as well as to lay the foundation for further partnerships beyond those leveraged in these early years, which included technology partners like Jam3, Helios Design, and Mozilla; journalistic outfits including the *Globe and Mail*, the *Guardian*, and the *New York Times*; industry partners like IDFA DocLab and the Sundance Film Festival; and other agencies of the Canadian government.

Metrics for assessing the success or perceived failure of a project were fluid and, at the outset, handicapped by the Canadian government's privacy policies for its various branches (including a limitation on the use of trackers on any government-hosted website), the National Film Board of Canada included. It took some time for the Digital Studio to arrive at a place where visitor statistics and user-engagement metrics became a basic feature for all projects. Dao (2018) explains:

> It is one of those jurisdictional challenges with us working as part of the government. Early on, we weren't allowed to use some of the tools that we were used to using [in web design,] and so we had to use what the NFB had in place, which excluded the trackers that we had chosen. There was an old system called NET Insights, a product subsequently bought up by IBM and then and soon thereafter no longer used or supported, but that's what the institution had at the time. We had those [tools] on the first eleven projects, except, for whatever reason, with *Water Life* we decided to track it anyway with Google Analytics and that gave us a lot of early visibility on that

> project. And then somewhere in 2011, we pointed out something ironic: the prime minister's website at the time was using Google Analytics. That basically opened the door to allow us to use it and so we added it in arrears to everything. So from about 2012 on, the analytics got better and then from 2013 they were very accurate.

Dao observed that these analytics were rarely used against producers and creators within the Digital Studio because they were simply not sufficiently understood by anyone outside the studio or the marketing department (who served as key partners within the Board to get the work in front of audiences). "If anything," Dao adds, "we used those numbers to try and do better, and that was something we held ourselves to: a desire to improve based on those metrics."

Another important role analytics played in the ongoing development of Digital Studio projects was the way in which they clarified expectations for projects with a more focused appeal while simultaneously encouraging producers and creators to go "big" with various modes of delivery and outreach that might serve to grow an audience beyond its initial reach. "In our early projects, we thought of audiences as a thing at launch as opposed to partners in a project from early on through to its long tail," Dao (2018) recalls:

> We had this ceiling of a hundred thousand unique visitors [with many of our projects] that we couldn't cross with that approach. And then with *Bear 71* we introduced the notion of the story world, so from that project on we [explored] multifaceted projects. With *Bear 71* there is the live version [which, on at least one occasion, featured a live score performed by Tim Hecker], the installation, the interactive documentary, and the Twitter role-playing game. When we unveiled all of that in partnership with Sundance, we were able to show numbers that quadrupled [the audience of earlier projects] just by taking that different approach.
>
> It's also been sobering at points. We've had projects like Guy Maddin's *Seances* (2016) where we thought his audience was much bigger – and it doesn't take away at all from the project – but it showed us in real stark numbers what the size of the audience for that project was as opposed to what we anticipated.

Water Life achieved 2.5 million views during the time it was actively marketed by the Board, making it the project with the largest audience in the Digital Studio portfolio. *A Short History of the Highrise* (Katerina Cizek, 2014) and *Do Not Track* (Brett Gaylor, 2015) both achieved over a million views during this same period, while *Seven Digital Deadly Sins* (Pablo Vio, 2014) and *Bear 71* reached over 700,000 and 600,000 views, respectively (with the latter almost certainly approaching the million mark after the subsequent launch of a virtual reality version available to home users).

Despite the initial challenges of defining the parameters of an emergent media form and establishing a place for such work within a traditional filmmaking institution like the NFB, these and other obstacles were overcome. The impact of the Digital Studio's work was felt within the digital arts world almost immediately, and the importance of the work it was producing was widely recognized – but in typically Canadian fashion, this acclaim came from abroad. "We got a lot of our validation internationally before we felt like we received validation back home," Dao (2018) explains, "so individuals like Shari Frillot, Ingrid Kopp, and Caspar Sonnen at the IDFA DocLab were key in that regard."

Frillot, of the New Frontier program at the Sundance Film Festival, was not only a champion of the work but of the leadership role played by Digital Studio personnel within the larger field of interactive digital arts. "The NFB folks were very active in the beginning and really got people talking about the newness of 'interactive,' what was the importance of it, the texture of it," Frillot (2018) explains:

> You could really feel a shift away from the proprietary or profit-driven aspects of the medium. They always fostered and made a space for forums [of exchange] and I've always been thankful for that because there's something about what the Board is doing that is very in line with the spirit of what we were trying to do at Sundance, which is always about ideas and not just keeping up with where the media landscape is right now. [The Digital Studio] is not putting the cart in front of the horse in terms of asking what kind of [project] can get us this much currency on the international film festival circuit or this kind of box office in release. They've made a decision to ask the opposite set of questions, "What if we talked to artists who were working within a new medium? With YouTube or with HTML as a

> [creative] platform? Or what this musician is working on or this painter? What if we look at the thing that's being created as we speak – as opposed to the thing that's tested and tried and profitable – and see where that takes us?"

Ingrid Kopp, director of interactive at the Tribeca Film Festival, played a central role in introducing NFB Interactive projects to US and international audiences, supporting the work through the TFI Media Fund, and encouraging networking, discourse, and debate about the work through the TFI Interactive Conference. "I was always very impressed with how they combined experimentation and brave experiments with clear strategy and how thoroughly they executed projects," Kopp (2019) explains. She continues:

> I think what always stood out for me is how the work is allowed to be what it needs to be – the NFB are open to new technologies and platforms but not led by them, they are always led by the needs of the work. I think one of the biggest hurdles is always reaching audiences and also nurturing and developing and educating audiences for this kind of work. It defies categorization in many ways, which is exciting creatively but often frustrating for people who need to put things in certain buckets (press, PR, and yes, audiences who may not have the equipment needed to experience certain interactive work) … I think one of the biggest obstacles is holding one's nerve when access to audiences and markets seems a bit wobbly. The NFB have really invested in this space and that has been invaluable in terms of building the field and creating more opportunities. But the work needs to continue, particularly now as VR and AR are shifting everything around. Carving out a mission-driven space for this work that is slightly protected from the market is vital if we are to continue to support brave and interesting work and take the time to nurture new audiences and experiment with new platforms and technologies.

Witten fondly recalls the great heights of the Digital Studio's achievements during her tenure but balances this pride with thoughtful self-reflection upon what could have been handled better. "In the sphere [of interactive design], we were rock stars," she explains.

> We were considered leading-edge. All of the big interactive studios we're looking at what we were doing. When we went to Sundance and other high-profile events, we realized the position we held, that we were doing something really special, and that we were at the edge of innovation in that space. But I think at times, the Board – and I was very much a part of this, I was right in the middle of it – may have been a little bit too focused on innovation and our international reputation … I felt that we spent a little too much time [focused on brand and reputation] and could have spent a little bit more time on the programming, specifically for Canadians, really trying to push the impact here at home. To create something that people would come to, that they would be nourished by, that they'd be provoked by, and that would cause conversations. I felt like we erred on the side of innovation, and we needed to be more of a consistent presence in people's lives … I was there, so I'll take responsibility for that – we needed to transition to a more deliberate attempt to engage people in a more regular way and I feel like we didn't make that transition [during my time]. (Witten 2018)

Nonetheless, the Digital Studio would go on to win "over 150 international awards and honours including a Gold Medal at Cannes Cyber Lions, over a dozen Webby Awards," an International Emmy Award and numerous Canadian Screen Awards in the first decade-plus of its existence (National Film Board of Canada 2020). These successes both established the Digital Studio as a global leader in the area of interactive design and helped elevate the art form beyond a niche of tech-savvy multimedia designers. While still limited to audiences with the time, interest, and technology required to explore these experiences, that audience was expanding both in terms of its size and its scope, and the impact of these projects was felt from classrooms and public spaces to gallery installations and mobile devices the world over.

New Directions and the Challenge of Technological Obsolescence

A major turning point in the history of the Digital Studios was the resignation of NFB commissioner Perlmutter in December 2013 and his complete departure from the Board in February 2014 alongside then-director general of English Programming Ravinda Din amidst allegations of conflict of interest and a failure to disclose a romantic relationship at the workplace between an executive and a deputy officer (Houpt 2014; Taylor 2014). Given the private and deeply personal nature of these circumstances, none of the individuals interviewed would speak on the record about the impact of these events on the activities of the Digital Studio in the months that followed. It should suffice to say, however, that the period of activity generally regarded as the first peak of the Digital Studio's strategy and output – regarded by some as its "golden age" – concludes with the departures of Witten, Simard, and the resignation of Commissioner Perlmutter all in close succession. At the time of their respective interviews for this project in the autumn of 2018, Loc Dao, Rob McLaughlin (after a brief return to the private sector), and Hugues Sweeney remained in leadership positions at the Digital Studio, navigating a new era of creative possibility and technological innovation while at the same time reconciling with the difficult truth that the long-term availability of this vital body of work may be compromised by the very platforms and technologies upon which it was innovated.

Over the first decade of the Digital Studio's existence, nearly seventy works of one kind or another were produced. These works ranged from big-budget immersive projects well suited for a roadshow experience to small-scale, low-overhead social media experiments with a quick development period. Across these projects, a broad range of creative tools and platforms were leveraged by the Digital Studio within the larger context of dynamic changes in the world of multimedia design and the evolution of personal internet-enabled devices. As a result, it was not uncommon, and this remains the case, to discover that an interactive project launched on a particular device or platform – be it web-based experience using Adobe Flash or a self-contained app requiring a particular mobile operating system – no longer works without difficulty on that same device or platform a year later. Witten (2018) explains:

> We talked about the ephemeral nature of the work. "Maybe not everything's meant to be there in perpetuity? Maybe some of it can be let go? Maybe some of it can be put on a particular server and stored in a particular way so there could still be access to it even long after the technology has been eclipsed?" It's completely different in its nature [from conventional film work] so there were very early

> conversations around that ... It is interesting in that, in this space where it is resource heavy and you are on the edge of innovation, what are the requirements around making it accessible to all and making it accessible to everyone in perpetuity?

Ultimately, however, responding to the challenge of technological obsolescence was not the responsibility of the creators in the Digital Studio but, rather, the team of archivists and technologists working in research and development at an arm's length from both the English and French production branches.

As director of research and development at the NFB, it fell to Jimmy Fournier and his team to identify best practices and to establish policies that would best serve the maintenance of the digital media works produced by the Digital Studio. It was a process that ran in parallel with the early activities of the Digital Studio and one that was not formalized until 2015. It was at this time that the NFB published its "golden rules of archiving" for the institution at-large alongside an announcement that it would partner with ASG Software Solution for the purpose of ensuring that "Canada's audiovisual legacy will be better preserved and safeguarded for generations to come" (National Film Board of Canada 2015). Inherent to this strategy was a recognition that the well-established archival workflow best suited for linear production had been transformed by video production and digital storage. Fournier explains: "First, we have put a process in place that continuously checks the integrity of the stored data. Second, we choose open-file formats, which will last for well over a decade, to avoid frequent data migrations. Third, we proactively anticipate the obsolescence of the storage hardware. Fourth, and finally, we will keep two copies of every media asset on two very different storage technologies, in two completely different locations" (ibid.). The document was not specific to interactive work and, as a result, did not attend to the fact that interactive works disrupted this archiving continuum; the announcement made no mention of the consequences of using proprietary tools to create work routinely published on platforms regularly facing obsolescence. Practically and philosophically, the best practices for preserving the assets of a linear work were somewhat at odds with the need to preserve the experience of an interactive media object.

Seeking to expand both its pool of resources and technological expertise in the specific area of archiving interactive media, the National Film Board of Canada, in December 2018, made public its partnership with Rhizome, a not-for-profit digital arts collective affiliated with the New Museum in New York City and the creator of Webrecorder, an open-source web archiving platform. The purpose of the partnership was to leverage the resources and institutional support of the NFB to facilitate Rhizome's enhancement and continued support of Webrecorder in order to meet and serve the needs of the NFB as it set out to "preserve more than 100 interactive web-based productions in its collection" and to ensure that "Canada's audiovisual legacy will be better preserved and safeguarded for generations to come, even in the midst of major changes in web technology such as the discontinuation of support for Adobe Flash Player" (National Film Board of Canada 2018). The partnership and its purpose date back to the goals the NFB set for itself in the 2015 white paper, but it remains difficult to declare the initiative a success. Browsing NFB Interactive in 2022, several of the earliest projects are simply missing from the directory, while others feature a disclaimer that reads: "Technology is moving fast, and we were no longer able to support this format. Because conservation is part of our DNA, we carefully archived this web experience." However, that archived experience is not available to the public; instead, visitors are asked to "check out [the Digital Studio's] most recent works."

It must be said that the impact of the global pandemic beginning March 2020 upon the NFB's archiving and preservation of decommissioned Flash-based i-docs was profound; much of the budget previously earmarked and available to these teams was redirected to support remote production during the closures of the NFB's offices. Work on this initiative resumed in 2022, but, at the time of writing, the NFB's archive (or "vault," if I might offer a more accurate descriptor) remains available by request only, and access is limited both in terms of the time one is allowed to explore a project and which projects have been prepared for non-institutional users. Speaking to the International Internet Preservation Consortium (IIPC) in 2021, Fournier explained that it was quite possible programmed or curated access to a limited number of archived projects was just as likely as was a complete public-facing free-to-use library of preserved works. If this is the case, the creative legacy of the Digital Studio remains imperiled.

In February 2022, under Commissioner Claude Joli-Couer, the National Film Board announced that the English-language Digital Studio would be subsumed by the Animation Studio to form a new organizational unit within the English branch, the Animation and Interactive Studio. McLaughlin was named the first head of this unit following time as the executive producer of English Programming on an interim basis; the organizational structure of the French-language unit remained in place (Dudok de Wit 2022). Despite the NFB's pronouncement that the reorganization "will reinvigorate and reaffirm the studio's national mandate to work with and support the animation community, a diversity of experienced and emerging filmmakers and wide-ranging digital artists across Canada" (Milligan 2022), it remains to be seen if this is an evolutionary step towards permanently securing the ongoing production of English-language interactive works at the Board or a signal that the profile of new media projects is now diminished at the institution. Beyond the question of how new media production, and interactive documentary specifically, is valued at the NFB, existential threats to the work produced by the Digital Studio remain. While the Rhizome partnership sought to "ensure sustainability and accessibility of [the NFB's] collection of 100 interactive web projects and 14,000 films, videos and born-digital productions" (NFB 2018), serious work remains in its pursuit of a stable, sustainable, public-facing repository of the Digital Studio's varied and valuable works.

Acknowledgments

Thank you to everyone who spoke to me directly, participated in correspondence, spoke on the record to publications in the past, shared materials or otherwise offered their endorsement and support of this project. Thank you again to Monique Simard, Cindy Witten, Hugues Sweeney, Robert McLaughlin, Loc Dao, Jimmy Fournier, Martin Viau, Ingrid Kopp, and Shari Frilot for sharing your time and your experiences.

References

Canada. 2009. Transcript of Proceedings before the CRTC: Canadian Broadcasting in New Media. Ottawa, 25 February 2009. https://crtc.gc.ca/eng/transcripts/2009/tb0225.html.

Dao, Loc. 2018. Interview with the author, 26 November 2018.

Dudok de Wit, Alex. 2022. "National Film Board of Canada Merges English

Animation and Digital Studios." *Cartoon Brew*, 10 February 2022. https://www.cartoonbrew.com/studios/national-film-board-of-canada-merges-english-animation-and-digital-studios-213266.html.

Frillot, Shari. 2018. Interview with the author, 17 December 2018.

Haynes, Kathryn. 2010. "Other Lives in Accounting: Critical Reflections on Oral History Methodology in Action." *Critical Perspectives on Accounting* 21 (3): 221–31.

Houpt, Simon. 2014. "National Film Board of Canada Appoints 11-Year Veteran Claude Joli-Coeur as New Chair." *Globe and Mail*, 2 December 2014. https://www.theglobeandmail.com/arts/film/national-film-board-of-canada-appoints-11-year-veteran-claude-joli-coeur-as-new-chair/article21891191.

International Internet Preservation Consortium. 2021. "Jimmy Fournier and Humbert Hardy: End to End Integration of NFB's Web Interactive Works Archive with WebRecorder." 12 August 2021. Conference proceedings, 14:50. https://youtu.be/AH1vdhNYJq8.

Kahana, Jonathan, ed. 2016. *The Documentary Film Reader: History, Theory, Criticism*. New York: Oxford University Press.

Kopp, Ingrid. 2019. Correspondence with the author, 19 January 2019.

McLaughlin, Rob. 2018. Interview with the author, 29 October 2018.

Milligan, Mercedes. 2022. "NFB English Program Combines Animation and Digital Studios." *Animation Magazine*, 10 February 2022. https://www.animationmagazine.net/shorts/nfb-english-program-combines-animation-digital-studios.

National Film Board of Canada. 2010. *Report on Plans and Priorities 2010–2011*. Ottawa: Government of Canada.

– 2015. "National Film Board of Canada Completes Its Four Golden Rules of Archiving with ASG-Digital Archive." Ottawa: Government of Canada, 11 September 2015. https://www.canada.ca/en/news/archive/2015/09/national-film-board-canada-completes-four-golden-rules-archiving-asg-digital-archive.html.

– 2018. "National Film Board of Canada and Rhizome Collaborate to Broaden the Technical Capabilities and Impact of Webrecorder, Rhizome's Leading-Edge, Easy-to-Use Tool Set for Web Archiving." Ottawa: Government of Canada, 18 December 2018. https://www.canada.ca/en/national-film-board/news/2018/12/national-film-board-of-canada-and-rhizome-collaborate-to-broaden-the-technical-capabilities-and-impact-of-webrecorder-rhizomes-leading-edge-easy-to.html.

– 2020. "New Ways of Storytelling for New Ways of Seeing: 2020–2023 Strategic Plan." Ottawa: Government of Canada, 4 April 2020. https://www.canada.ca/en/national-film-board/corporate/publications/plans-reports/strategic-plan.html.

NFB English Programming. 2009. "Digital." Ottawa: National Film Board of Canada, 15 April 2009, internal memorandum.

Perks, Robert, and Alistair Thomson. 2015. *The Oral History Reader*. 3rd ed. New York: Routledge.

Rosenthal, Alan. 1980. *The Documentary Conscience: A Casebook in Filmmaking*. Berkley: University of California Press.

Simard, Monique. 2018. Interview with the author, 26 November 2018.

Sweeney, Hugues. 2018. Interview with the author, 2 November, 2018.

Taylor, Katie. 2014. "Departure Leaves NFB Searching for Focus." *Globe and Mail*, 28 February 2014. https://theglobeandmail.com/arts/film/departure-leaves-nfb-searching-for-focus/article17163046.

Waugh, Thomas, Michael Brendan Baker, and Ezra Winton, eds. 2010. *Challenge for Change: Activist Documentary at the National Film Board of Canada*. Montreal and Kingston: McGill-Queen's University Press.

Witten, Cindy. 2018. Interview with the author, 6 November 2018.

2

NOTES ON IMPACT

THE CASE OF THE INTERACTIVE DOCUMENTARY *GDP*

Frédéric Dubois

Introduction

Digital forms of documentary, including long-form multimedia reportage, documentary games (Charles et al. 2017), interactive documentary (O'Flynn 2012), and, more recently, non-fiction virtual reality (Rose 2016), have all contributed to expanding our understanding of what – to take the expression of late Canadian documentary filmmaker Peter Wintonick – "docmedia" is (Wintonick 2011). Discussions on the "digital turn" in documentary practices have mainly focused on how authorship evolves to embrace multi-vocal approaches (Aufderheide 2014), how linear storytelling is being joined by fragmented narrative structures (Nogueira 2016), and how audiences are increasingly being assigned a role within a story (Dubois 2017). What has been critically under-researched and under-theorized in the Canadian context, among others, is the long view of how the social impact of interactive documentary might depart from that of traditional, linear documentary. Time and attention must be invested to ensure that the i-doc stories of today – and, by definition, the social histories, microhistories, and/or *Alltagsgeschichte* (Lüdtke 2003) of tomorrow – might have a sustained impact on society.

This chapter offers perspectives on the social impact of interactive documentary over time, and the ways in which this impact is potentially supported and undermined. I draw lessons primarily from the 2010 Canadian interactive documentary *GDP* (Hélène Choquette), a project in which I was directly involved. *GDP* is best understood as a "living documentary" (Gaudenzi 2013) – a project with frequent releases that expands, shifts, and lives on through the constant interaction between protagonists, the audience, and the makers. The lessons I draw illustrate three aspects of impact. First, that microhistory – understood here as local history (Ginzburg 1993, 10) – finds its value over time and that, with digital media in particular, the preservation of microhistory is not guaranteed. Second, that production constraints silence living documentaries over time and thereby curtail the ideal of expansion. Third, that the discussion of interactive documentary impact should not be limited to audiences but, rather, should acknowledge the broad effects of the production process itself.

My work is built upon a range of methodologies, including literature review, primary document research, and action research inquiry, in the context of my own direct involvement in the interactive documentary under consideration. These methodologies are complemented by personal observations stemming from the different roles I played in i-doc production, including web-coordinator for *GDP: Measuring the Human Side of the Canadian Economic Crisis* (Hélène Choquette, 2009); co-author of *The Hole Story Interactive* (Frédéric Dubois, Audrée Lapierre, and Akufen, 2011); game master of *Fort McMoney* (David Dufresne, 2013); co-author and producer of *atterwasch* (Marco del Pra' and Frédéric Dubois, 2014); and co-author and interactive producer of *Field Trip* (Eva Stotz and Frédéric Dubois, 2019). Finally, this chapter draws on three interviews with GDP producer Marie-Claude Dupont conducted in 2009, 2010, and 2019, respectively; online news sources to triangulate observations; and informal conversations across a range of professional and academic contexts.[1]

The Great (Canadian) Recession

If we go back in time, many of us will remember that there was something called "The Great Recession," which, according to the US-based Economic Policy Institute (2015), "officially lasted from December 2007 to June 2009." It started with a housing crisis in the United States fuelled by dubious mortgage loans and other financial instruments. It pulled many people out of their homes and employment, especially in the United States, and had a ripple effect on many sectors of the world economy. By early 2008, signs of a recession were starting to make daily headlines in Canada, too.

At that time, a new spirit at the National Film Board of Canada (NFB) was spreading even more rapidly than the recession. It was that of the "digital transition," as evidenced by the language used in NFB strategic planning documents (see, for instance, NFB n.d.). The NFB had already amassed homegrown digital production experience with pioneering programs such as *CitizenShift* – a curated web-portal project for engaged filmmakers, groups, and communities launched pre-YouTube in 2004 – and the Filmmaker-in-Residence cross-media project documenting life inside Toronto's St Michael's Hospital.[2] Yet it wasn't until 2009 that the first projects calling themselves "interactive documentaries" were released. Four notable i-docs from this early period include *GDP* (team including director Hélène Choquette 2010); *Waterlife* (team including director Kevin McMahon 2009); *Capturing Reality: The Art of Documentary* (team including director Pepita Ferrari 2008); and *Out My Window* (team including director Katerina Cizek 2010). At this time, the NFB established proper interactive studios under the guidance of Loc Dao and Rob McLaughlin in Vancouver and Hugues Sweeney in Montreal (see Baker, chapter 1, this volume).[3] These studios were instrumental for making major contributions to the expansion of the sub-genre of interactive documentary worldwide. Here, I revisit one early living documentary for the purpose of considering the long view on impact evaluation.

In late 2008, the fear of an economic and social meltdown was growing in Canada. Stories of serious hardships linked to the recession on Canadians were trickling in. The heads of the NFB's English and French programs, Cindy Witten and Monique Simard, respectively, came together in December of that year and decided that the NFB had a duty to capture what was growing into a major crisis of capitalism and to do so in an innovative way. The result was *GDP*, a one-year bilingual web documentary project meant to "document the effects of the recession in communities across Canada" (Canadian Broadcasting Corporation 2010). The exact form of the project was still to be decided, but the initial inspiration arrived in early 2009 in the form of a master class by Alexandre Brachet, CEO and interactive producer of the French production company, Upian. He presented *Gaza/Sderot*, an interactive documentary series that Upian co-produced with Arte France and Bo Travail! between 26 October and 23 December 2008. To this day, *Gaza/Sderot* remains a reference point in interactive documentary production circles, in large part – but not exclusively – due to its innovative split-screen interface and quick-fire tempo.

GDP's output comprised some 220 films – 167 documentary shorts divided into 17 series, 53 photo essays, 143 blog posts, and more than 300 comments by the audience – all generated between the months of

Figure 2.1
The split-screen interface is an innovative feature of the *Gaza/Sderot* project

September 2009 and September 2010 by some 14 field directors and 19 photographers (St-Jacques 2010; Pitzer 2010b). Importantly, this burst of activity and output coincides with what the *Columbia Journalism Review* and other outlets have described as the decline of long-form journalism and the in-depth reportage of institutional structures and their failures (among other things) (Starkman 2013); this "meltdown" was a consequence of dwindling ad-revenue for print media as a result of online news aggregation and the proliferation of news sharing via social media, all further compounded by shrinking online engagement with resource-intensive, word count-heavy articles (De Visé 2022). Over the course of that year, the series documented the evolution of fifteen protagonists scattered across Canada. The characters ranged from cranberry growers in Newfoundland and young drop-outs learning a trade at a metalworking school in Montreal to stock traders in Toronto's financial district, carwash employees in Calgary, and a real estate agent in Vancouver. Some were reinventing themselves, while others had to put up with job losses or

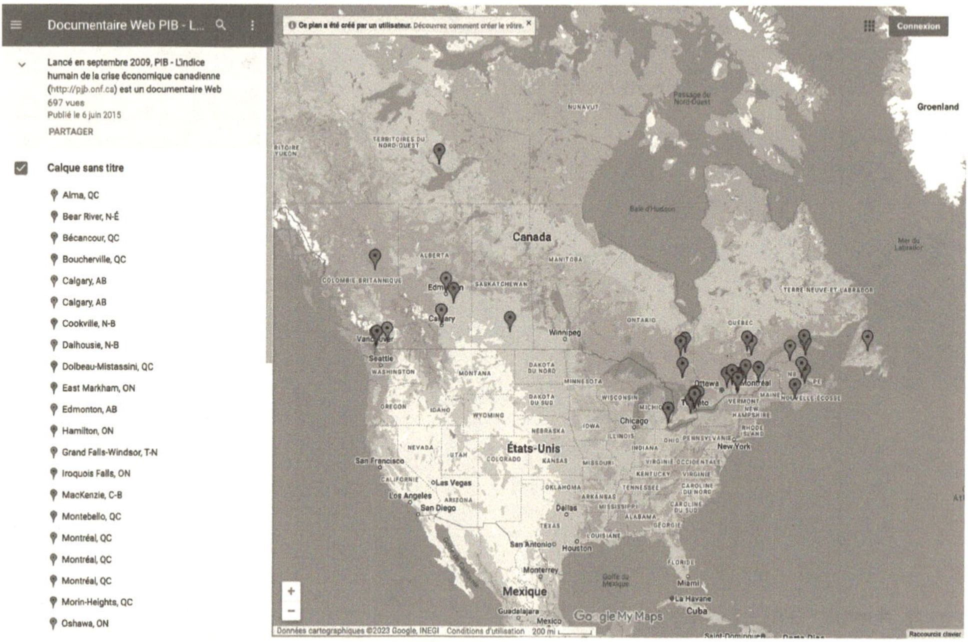

Figure 2.2

An interactive map of Canada marked the locations of user commentary to the *GDP* project

diminished financial resources; a small few were, in fact, profiting during the recession. The photo essays, captured by photographers sent to locations not covered by the video series, gave *GDP* a chance to more spontaneously react to recession-driven transformations in the lives of people and communities. The user comments, most of them in text form, were essentially reacting to the NFB-produced content and featured prominently on an interactive map of Canada.

On 20 September 2010, the NFB completed the project by releasing a twenty-three-minute linear film synthesizing fourteen hours of material published within the interactive documentary over the year of the project; this digital artefact stayed "alive" for five years.[4]

The *GDP* Production Process

For the production of *GDP*, the NFB hired a small team of web designers, filmmakers, writer-researchers, and a producer, all located at the NFB headquarters in Montreal. Documentary filmmaker Hélène Choquette came on board as the director in January 2009, kickstarting research. Marie-Claude Dupont, a media executive, hopped on next as the producer of the project. I was hired as the "web coordinator" several months later.[5] In June 2009, the team was almost complete, ramping production to full speed.

Contrary to conventional films, where filmmakers gather material in the field, assemble an edit, and complete production in a room far away from the public's eye over a long period of time, the process behind *GDP* meant, as Dupont rightly puts it, "experimenting with narrative on the fly" (Pitzer 2010b). One of the main challenges for the team and many departments at the NFB (e.g., IT, legal, marketing, etc.) was to establish a fast-paced digital production workflow that could accommodate the release of one short video or photo essay every working day of that year. For each filmmaker on the ground, this meant delivering one to two rough-cut episodes for their series every month. As there were thirty-three field directors and photographers, lead film editor Miguel Raymond would receive a digitally transferred file every day of the year. Together with Choquette, Raymond would transform these into video shorts and photo essays. In a compressed timeframe, writer-researchers Annie Richer and Philip Lewis, also in Montreal, would receive the final-cut media file, subtitle it, come up with a title, add a short description, and pass it on for publication. They would also generate "witty" human-centred stats about the recession to add an editorial voice to the films on the *GDP* website. Such a fast-paced production workflow was daunting on the film side.

On the web side of things, the team worked with the Montreal-based digital companies Turbulent and TOXA to generate mood boards, develop wireframes, and initial website designs to be integrated into a proprietary content management system. We spent a considerable amount of energy in the start-up phase expanding and modernizing the NFB web-player, adding options on video qualities, subtitling, and the option to visualize other episodes in a series within the player. Today, such features are standard on common players such as YouTube, but this was not the case a decade ago. The interactive map and user-generated content upload options also required extensive discussions around design and legal considerations.

While getting things started, it was my remit to create a project blog to document the creative process as well as to feature information about the recession in general and our protagonists in particular. In conjunction with the bilingual blog, we started conversations with our audiences on the social networking platforms Facebook and Twitter in both official languages.[6] We used the now-defunct social bookmarking web service Delicious to keep track of other interactive documentaries developing in parallel and used the NFB's YouTube channel to create a *GDP* playlist, which, as of this writing, includes twenty-seven entries. Internally, I kept track of the conversation around the project by using Netvibes, a social networking dashboard. More important, I was the main person responsible for – in the words of the producer – outreach to, and networking with, "blogger communities, social groups, and naturally, the citizens in the towns in which our protagonists live" (Boucher 2009).[7] This role was instrumental in documenting our efforts, in defining interaction on and around the *GDP* platform, as well as drawing target publics into the project. The browser-based documentary *GDP* finally launched in September 2009 with just enough stories and user content to tease the audience and set the stage for what was to come. The launch was accompanied by traditional press relations work, including the publication of a press release and outreach to targeted journalists.

Connecting with the Audience

Sean Flynn's graduate thesis, "Evaluating Interactive Documentaries: Audience, Impact and Innovation in Public Interest Media" (2015) – completed under the supervision of William Uricchio and Ethan Zuckerman at the Massachusetts Institute of Technology (MIT) – discusses some of the characteristics of impact that can be drawn from interactive documentary productions completed at the National Film Board, the US public broadcaster PBS, as well as the *New York Times*. For one, Flynn's work is useful for situating the notion of the impact of non-fiction storytelling historically. He looks at the main stakeholders, including "government agencies, foundations, non-profits and corporate sponsors" that have put social impact on the agenda (Flynn 2015, 20). Nash and Corner (2016, 227) expand on Flynn's genealogy of "impact," looking more precisely at "the emergence of a new kind of documentary making that marries documentary storytelling and the principles of strategic communication."

Flynn (2015, 143) argues, "Most of the social impacts attributed to public interest media – whether raising awareness, stimulating discourse or inspiring action – rely on connecting their work with audiences, typically on a national or international scale." In *GDP*, the "social impact" was firmly engrained in the original concept. We made every effort in trying to connect with target communities, even going as far as getting mayors of villages on the phone, e-mailing local media and civic groups, and engaging with individuals via social media and in person. This was particularly true with the presence of documentary directors and photographers in the field as they could keep up the continuous face-to-face connection with protagonists and their entourage.

Almost ten years after *GDP*, Marie-Claude Dupont spoke specifically to the question of impact: "Relating to *GDP*, the true impact is not for us to say, but for the protagonists. We would need to revisit them. Social impact was limited in time, since the production was replaced quickly. Impact was therefore diluted over time. *GDP* was a one-year-long project. Once the work was archived and no new content was added, the impact was diminished" (Dupont 2019). In quantitative terms, *GDP* and its French sister website, *PIB*, reached approximately fifty thousand unique visitors to its website in April 2010 (number drawn from Pitzer 2010a).[8] There are fragmented figures available for the amount of people that followed the project and the engagement rate across social media platforms (such as the compounded amount of Twitter followers that numbered over two thousand during the project's accessible phase), but the overall number of users across these platforms was negligible.

It is difficult to extrapolate anything specific from impact metrics for *GDP* as, by all accounts, these numbers are very low by today's standards. On broader terms, authors such as Jerry Z. Muller (2018) have already addressed some of the most harmful consequences of quantitative measurement on a granular level. Based on my personal experience as a maker of interactive documentary, however, I would argue that one cannot and should not ignore quantitative measures, and keeping an eye on analytics should not distract us from *thick* descriptions (Ragin and Becker 1992; Stake 1995) and rich qualitative impact evaluation. In our "big data society" (Ulbricht and Grafenstein 2016), quantity and measurability are often privileged over more in-depth and telling specifics of a case. For the sake of context, the *GDP* audience metrics are comparable to those of similar NFB and Arte Digital productions of that time (e.g., *Alma*, *Bear 71*, *Fort McMoney*, *Gaza/Sderot*).[9] However, it is hard to compare output in terms of metrics without considering input in terms of financial and human resources, especially when it comes to outreach efforts. While my efforts here are not based on a quantitative (or comparative) study, it should suffice to say that *GDP* did not perform negatively within the larger field of work.

In the contemporary media industry, especially in journalism, collecting audience metrics and demonstrating a strong user base is an obligation. A culture of accounting, linked in part to the growing role played by cultural foundations and other forms of philanthropy that support not-for-profit media production, demands detailed numbers to justify ongoing investment. For most media makers and journalists, delivering a "return on investment" (ROI) has become the new normal, although what matters for society is something else entirely. Konieczna and Powers (2018) provide a useful state-of-play of the academic discourse around impact in not-for-profit journalism, stressing the importance of measuring impact on democracy instead of a profit-focused ROI. When it comes to interactive documentary, from a producer's perspective, I would argue that selecting the right metrics for discussion and contextualization, as well as using longitudinal qualitative evaluation, best highlights the impact of projects on individuals, communities, and society. Both within and outside of the NFB, there is a history behind taking up such a position. As Flynn (2015, 155) explains: "Video activists in the Challenge for Change generation approached new technology like the Portapak camera in this way. While their work did not reach mass audiences and create impact in the Griersonian tradition of public education, it did create tactical, observable (but harder to quantify) impacts by activating local communities and creating new channels of communication between citizens and their government." With regard to *GDP*, specifically, Dupont (2019) explicates: "Expectations were ambitious and our marketing budget was low. The impact that was sought after was interactions: comments and engagement by Canadians. It was too early. Social media use was growing but not there yet. We were dependent on third parties such as Facebook and Twitter that were not ready yet. In terms of community, I think we had impact, but I'm not sure about the results. We tried to find multipliers, people locally who could put a spotlight on the phenomenon." So, what other longitudinal qualitative impact indicators might apply specifically to *GDP*? The most evident qualitative success indicator in the film industry is that of peer recognition. In other words: awards.

Awards remain the one currency that filmmakers brag about, often to attract the attention of distracted onlookers but also to justify their raison d'être. In terms of prestige, GDP collected three national awards recognizing its innovative character on two counts – website and documentary storytelling – and two "official selections," including one from the esteemed Webby Awards.[10] Awards have a use value but are often misunderstood and do not necessarily have a long-lasting impact. In the short term, awards and distinctions remain a motivational factor for the production team and a formidable public relations instrument internally and externally. Victor Ginsburgh (2003, 1) argues that "expert opinion given shortly after the work has been produced (Oscars, prizes, rankings in musical competitions) may influence success, though it does not always recognize talent and does often not survive the 'test of time' considered by many art philosophers, since Hume, as one of the possible measures of fundamental aesthetic quality." Ginsburgh reminds us of the need to take the long view on appreciating art, particularly its aesthetic component. Awards work against that because they are most often (except career and certain honorary recognitions) focused on the short term.[11] The prizes and commendations that GDP collected are now gathering dust, so to speak. They were won, but they are static. Did other elements of the project and recognition of its success survive Ginsburgh's "test of time"?

It's the Story

One of the main difficulties the GDP team tackled during production is today one of the stronger features of the project: its theme. In our outreach efforts, we quickly realized that, while we were looking at the economic slump from a human perspective – trying to take the pulse of a selection of Canadians across the categories of social class, gender, economic sector, and region – asking Canadians to "watch the economic crisis" unfold before their eyes was not how they preferred to spend their time online. However, putting a face on the recession, breaking it down in human terms, was our mandate. It might have been a hard sell in terms of attracting and growing an audience, and it was certainly compounded by an interface that (in my subjective and self-critical view) might not have been compelling enough to fully engage users; ultimately, it was the result of many compromises. Dupont (2019), however, sees the net benefit of the approach: "The content was much stronger than the format. At the end of the day, people will talk about a character, not the form. In the traditional media, in news for instance, we give the facts. In GDP, we went into the family, we went deeper.

We asked tough questions. The content is still valuable today, since it is based on sustainable [French: *pérenne*] questions." Looking back at that time of uncertainty and the many communities that we documented, I tend to agree with Dupont that the true value of the project over time is the microhistory that we managed to capture. However, the fact that GDP was a participatory, living documentary (Gaylor 2012) lends the content a very specific flavour:

> Our fifteen main characters (those we're following throughout the year) are involved in a very unusual reflexive experiment, i.e., they can watch their "testimonial" almost instantly on our Web site [*sic*] and can also notice afterwards what's written or posted by the users with regard to the films in which they're being featured. Since they don't have any clue about what's going to happen next in their lives or what's to be filmed, they deal with a great deal of uncertainty as well as their own judgment on their "appearance" online, what they say every month and agree to share with the "audience." The character is here being a character and a spectator at the same time. We're not in reality TV though, because this project stands on strong documentary ethics. (Dupont, as quoted in Pitzer 2010b)

It can be inferred from Dupont's exchange with Pitzer that protagonists may have expressed themselves in a more "media conscious" or dialogic way than if they had participated in a traditional linear documentary. This would be an unconventional and "innovative" feature of GDP that, in terms of impact, would require a more fulsome assessment.

Process versus Product

In the conclusion to his thesis, Flynn (2015, 146) writes, "to fully evaluate the impact of interactive documentaries – in the broadest sense of the word – it is necessary to separate social impacts, audience development and innovation." Flynn privileges a definition of impact "that goes beyond the social, looking at the various ways that the process of making documentaries – particularly emerging genres of interactive documentary – can contribute to long-term processes of institutional transformation and the development of new artistic forms" (21). In reference to workshop-generated documentaries, media scholar Max Schleser (2018) also pleads for a stronger focus on process when assessing digital documentaries (see Cammaer and Schleser, chapter 4, this volume). *GDP* producer Dupont (2019) reinforces placing such a focus on process when she offers: "It's okay that the project didn't survive. But I wonder what is left in terms of production approaches." She highlights the contribution of the *GDP* project in terms of coming up with the very first "fluid production flow at NFB," which challenged other studios at the NFB to match its innovation in the areas of "fast production speed, short formats, [and] archiving." Such an iterative process enabled production workflows to be refined over time. I would like to echo Dupont and suggest that, on an institutional level, *GDP* made an impact through its pragmatic trial-and-error approach, which confronted the status quo of other department workflows. The approach and the compact production schedule enabled the NFB's Digital Studios, especially the one in Montreal, to rapidly take note of and draw lessons based upon empirical evidence generated in real-time within the NFB institutional frame.

One aspect of the *GDP* experience that Dupont does not expand on, however, is the long-term living character of the documentary. A living documentary aims, in part, to "stay alive." However, as a result of budget limitations and rapid changes in technology, interactive documentaries in general – and *GDP*, in particular – are shelved quickly, turning these briefly formidable cultural artefacts into ephemeral ones. In the early 2010s, for example, Adobe's Flash was still the dominant technology for creating web interfaces (see Keyes and Robbins, chapter 3, this volume). Since then, HTML5 frameworks have taken over and Flash has been deprecated, rendering obsolete many early interactive documentaries. As a result, the documentary community and institutions that adopted the now obsolete format face one of their greatest challenges: How are living archives to be preserved on the web? Only in exceptional cases are projects previously reliant on old digital technologies refurbished to remain available to new audiences, as was the case when the Flash-based interactive documentary *Bear 71* was redesigned as a web VR project several years after its initial launch (Paura and Resnik 2017). In the case of *GDP*, the digital project was "unplugged" for another technical reason. As confirmed in an e-mail exchange with the author in April 2019, the NFB's technical director for interactive productions, Martin Viau, acknowledged that the content management system upon which *GDP* was built ran on an Ubuntu 9 server. Ubuntu 9, a Linux-based operating system, has not been supported since 2017 and there are no longer security updates available; therefore, the website had to be removed from the NFB's public-facing government servers for security reasons. Fading out discrete aspects of a digital project seems only logical; in *GDP*, the participatory component more or less came to a natural halt once the active production phase ended. However, offlining interactive projects completely and indefinitely raises many issues, not least any obligation the project and its producers might have to fulfill a public service mandate. For a legacy public service institution such as the NFB, this issue could become a time bomb, though steps have already been taken to archive and perhaps resuscitate presently unavailable projects in the near future.

Long-Term Impact

In a paper on participatory photography and participatory arts and media more broadly, Tiffany Fairey (2017, 618) argues: "In recent decades, participatory arts and media initiatives are increasingly agency-led rather than community-led, their value assessed using linear evaluative models and framed in terms of short-term, measurable, results … [T]hese tendencies impede the potential critical contribution of participatory photography to social change processes and fail to capture important aspects of the psychosocial, political and subjective impact of projects."

Although it could be argued most interactive documentaries – including *GDP* – are not community-led, the proposition by Fairey to reconfigure "how we understand, capture and attribute the impact" is, I would argue, of great value. Fairey draws on Paulo Freire's (1973) concept of critical consciousness. Freire, Fairy reminds us, speaks of the goal of any impact endeavour as that of creating critical consciousness, defined here as engendering a critical way of looking at the world (Fairey 2017, 627). Did *GDP* create such a thing? "In certain respects, yes," answers Dupont (2019). "The multiplicity of points of view gave a critical dimension to the piece," she explains, "[and] this is different from single author documentaries. There was a vision, but the choices were made in a collective fashion."

One might be tempted to say that the community referred to by Dupont has little to do with local communities empowering themselves in Fairey's sense (as inspired by Freire). Returning to our focus on interactive documentary production, the larger team of creators involved in *GDP* can be understood as a *community of practice*. In that sense, Dupont's perspective offers great insight. The critical consciousness developed by individuals within GDP's community of practice needs to be factored into a larger consideration of *civic impact*, wherein journalistic impact is stratified and its functions are detailed (Simons et al. 2016). Fairey's true interest would, in this general sense, mean evaluating the impact of the project on local communities in Canada. In the specific case of GDP, that would require consequent resources to support a multi-year investigation. But how might one capture what Fairey refers to above as the "important aspects of the psychosocial, political and subjective impact of projects"? One important way, as proposed by Dupont, would be to systematically interview the protagonists in the field and the team behind GDP.

Looking to the future while keeping an eye on the community of practitioners of interactive documentary, I see value in co-opting Fairey's far-sighted contribution to the middle-term impact assessment measures that have already been dynamically negotiated and renegotiated within the context of interactive media projects. There are plenty of practical impact guides that help one think through and act upon the question of short- and middle-term impact.[12] From a practitioner's point of view, many are useful to plan strategically and prioritize on short- and middle-range impact objectives. The Europeana Impact Playbook can best account for impact in open culture projects and is oriented towards such things as remixes and open licences for items such as historical artefacts. The BRITDOC field guide speaks the language of documentary filmmakers and provides quite a few case studies from which interactive documentary makers can learn. The Social Impact Navigator, meanwhile, is introductory and easy to use, with a clear focus on making a difference in local communities. While Nash and Corner (2016) have made a point of debunking the neoliberal bias that often comes along with impact assessments (and discuss the specific political context within which the BRITDOC guide is embedded), they remain useful tools and I recommend their use in addition to other methods, including case studies, research literature, and peer-to-peer collaboration.

Conclusion

In her work on audience and the NFB's interactive documentary *Bear 71*, Nash (2014, 233) argues that "understanding how audiences respond to the call to interact and participate is likely to become increasingly important [to practitioners and scholars alike]." Such an empirical inquiry of how audiences – including the protagonists themselves – reacted to the GDP "product," in combination with deeper qualitative research into the GDP process by way of in-depth interviews with the production team, would be one way of generating knowledge about the impact of this interactive documentary over time.

In this chapter, I aim to carve out the key characteristics of the production and distribution of the living documentary GDP, thereby offering a succinct case study of a significant interactive documentary in Canadian new media history. By discussing impact and documentary literature in relation to the project, I hope to challenge the dominance of short-term impact narratives. I could draw further on GDP to put into perspective the fixation upon audience-only impact metrics. These limitations in the mainstream discourse around impact result in challenges for digital media producers, including poor assessment of process-specific impact and the long-term accessibility of their works. Formulating a full impact evaluation model adaptive to interactive documentary is outside the scope of my contribution here. However, my hope is that the consideration of a single case offered here will trigger the right questions upon which we might build such a model. Accurately and holistically measuring the impact of living documentaries will always be a challenge as they are hybrid forms sitting smack in the middle between art, design, journalism, and community development. Each of these categories plays by different rules. The true challenge, therefore, is to come up with an impact assessment model ample enough to encompass these categories but also precise enough to create meaningful impact.

Acknowledgments

This work was co-funded by the European Union through the ERASMUS+ program under grant agreement 2018-1-DE01-KA203-004282.

Notes

1 The encounters include the i-docs conference in Bristol, UK, in March 2018; the docmedia workshop in Potsdam-Babelsberg, Germany, in June 2018; a workshop on media innovation and social change at the University of Oslo, January 2019; and ongoing discussions at the Film University Babelsberg, especially with my doctoral supervisors Susanne Stürmer and Björn Stockleben.

2 For an account of *CitizenShift*, see Levine (2010); the author of this chapter was the project manager of the French language sister website *Parole citoyenne* in 2008–09.

3 In historical terms, it is worth mentioning that many of the interactive projects and programs that came out of the NFB in the 2010s – as the public institution was undertaking its "digital transition" – explicitly mention the pioneering NFB program Challenge for Change (French: *Société nouvelle*) as an inspiration. Challenge for Change, which ran from 1967 to 1980, is examined in detail by Waugh, Baker, and Winton (2010).

4 The active phase of the interactive project – 2008 to 2009 – terminated with the web-accessible phase of the *GDP* i-doc site, which ended sometime around 2015. Since that time, the *GDP* website has not been accessible.

5 In 2009, I was already working at the NFB's headquarters in Montreal, heading the small team behind the *Parole citoyenne* digital project. My background was in media activism (see Skinner et al. 2009; Langlois and Dubois 2005; Sénécal and Dubois 2005) and creative journalism (Dubois et al. 2007).

6 Twitter accounts of the *GDP* project remain available in English (https://twitter.com/gdpproject) and in French (https://twitter.com/projetpib).

7 Translation by the author.

8 The official NFB unique visitor figure for *GDP* (excluding its French sister site *PIB*) for the period 20 September 2009 to 10 June 2010 is 34,528. We were not able to find compounded figures for both language websites, but it can be inferred that the total number of unique visitors during the active phase of *GDP* has not passed the 100,000 mark.

9 By similar projects, I mean relatively large browser-based documentary projects with similar production budgets and team sizes released between 2008 and 2012.

10 *GDP* was recognized with the Prix Boomerang for Information Website; the Digi Award for Best Online Program, Series or Film; and the Prix NUMIX for Original Production, Information and Magazine. It was an Official Selection at both the 2011 Webby Awards and the 2010 Gemini Awards.

11 For a critical foray into the reasons this is so, and to understand the economy of "prizes, awards and the circulation of cultural value," see English (2005).

12 See the Europeana Impact Playbook, "designed for cultural heritage organizations to assess the impact of digital resources" (Verwayen et al. 2017); the BRITDOC Impact Field Guide aimed at makers of "social impact

documentary" (BRITDOC n.d.); and the PHINEO Social Impact Navigator addressing civic organizations seeking social change (Kurz and Kubek 2017).

References

Aufderheide, Patricia. 2014. "Ethical Challenges for Documentarians in a User-Centric Environment." In *New Documentary Ecologies: Emerging Platforms, Practices and Discourses*, ed. Kate Nash, Craig Hight, and Catherine Summerhayes, 237–50. London: Palgrave Macmillan. https://doi.org/10.1057/9781137310491.

Boucher, Michèle. 2009. *En primeur, entretien avec Marie-Claude Dupont, productrice de PIB/GDP*). Blogue ONF. https://blogue.onf.ca/blogue/2009/08/12/en-primeur-entretien-avec-marie-claude-dupont-productrice-de-pibgdp.

BRITDOC. n.d. "Impact Field Guide and Toolkit." http://impactguide.org.

Canadian Broadcasting Corporation. 2010. "NFB Series Explores Human Side of Recession." https://www.cbc.ca/news/canada/montreal/nfb-series-explores-human-side-of-recession-1.918897.

Charles, Mathew, Brad Gyori, Sven Wolters, and A.U. Julián Peñuela. 2017. "Target BACRIM: Blurring Fact and Fiction to Create an Interactive Documentary Game." Paper presented at the 10th International Conference on Interactive Digital Storytelling – ICIDS, Funchal, Madeira, Portugal, 14–17 November 2017, 349–52.

De Visé, Daniel. 2022. "Is Long-Form Journalism Dead? A Five-Minute Read." *The Hill*, 4 December 2022. https://thehill.com/homenews/media/3760391-is-long-form-journalism-dying-a-five-minute-read.

Dubois, Frédéric. 2017. "Interactivity as a Key Feature Redefining Documentary Reality." *Images: The International Journal of European Film, Performing Arts and Audiovisual Communication* 21 (30): 31–44. https://doi.org/10.14746/i.2017.30.03.

Dubois, Frédéric, Marc Tessier, and David Widgington, eds. 2007. *Extraction! Comix Reportage*. Montreal: Cumulus Press.

Dupont, Marie-Claude. 2019. Interview with the author, 14 January 2019. Transcript in Frédéric Dubois, "Interactive Documentary Production and Societal Impact: The Case of Field Trip," PhD diss., Film University Babelsberg KONRAD WOLF.

Economic Policy Institute. 2015. "The State of Working America." 15 January 2015. https://www.epi.org/research/state-of-working-america.

English, James F. 2005. *The Economy of Prestige: Prizes, Awards and the Circulation of Cultural Value*. Cambridge, MA: Harvard University Press.

Fairey, Tiffany. 2017. "These Photos Were My Life: Understanding the Impact of Participatory Photography Projects," *Community Development Journal* 53 (4): 618–36. https://doi.org/10.1093/cdj/bsx010.

Flynn, Sean. 2015. "Evaluating Interactive Documentaries: Audience, Impact and Innovation in Public Interest Media." MA thesis, Massachusetts Institute of Technology.

Freire, Paulo. 1973. *Education for Critical Consciousness*. New York: Seabury Press.

Gaudenzi, Sandra. 2013. "The Living Documentary: From Representing Reality to Co-Creating Reality in Digital Interactive Documentary." PhD diss., Goldsmiths, University of London.

Gaylor, Brett. 2012. "What Is the Living Docs Project?" Livingdocs. Viewed 9 June 2019. http://livingdocs.org/about. URL now defunct.

Ginsburgh, Victor. 2003. "Awards, Success and Aesthetic Quality in the Arts." *Journal of Economic Perspectives* 17 (2): 99–111.

Ginzburg, Carlo. 1993. "Microhistory, Two or Three Things That I Know about It." *Critical Inquiry* 20 (1): 10–35.

Konieczna, Magda, and Elia M. Powers. 2018. "What Can Nonprofit Journalists Actually Do for Democracy?" In *The Routledge Handbook of Developments in Digital Journalism Studies*, ed. Scott A. Eldridge II and Bob Franklin, 198–210. London: Routledge.

Kurz, Bettina, and Doreen Kubek. 2017. *The Social Impact Navigator*. Berlin: PHINEO gAG.

Langlois, Andrea, and Frédéric Dubois. 2005. *Autonomous Media: Activating Resistance and Dissent*. Montreal: Cumulus Press.

Levine, Reisa. 2010. "CitizenShift and Parole Citoyenne: The Democratization of Media." In *Emerging Digital Spaces in Contemporary Society*, ed. Phillip Kalantzis-Cope and Karim Gherab-Martín, 50–2. London: Palgrave Macmillan.

Lüdtke, Alf. 2003. "Alltagsgeschichte - ein Bericht von unterwegs." *Historische Anthropologie* 11 (2): 278–95. https://doi.org/10.7788/ha.2003.11.2.278.

Muller, Jerry Z. 2018. *The Tyranny of Metrics*. Princeton, NJ: Princeton University Press.

Nash, Kate. 2014. "Strategies of Interaction, Questions of Meaning: An Audience Study of the NFBs Bear71." *Studies in Documentary Film* 8 (3): 221–34, https://doi.org/10.1080/17503280.2014.958904.

Nash, Kate, and John Corner. 2016. "Strategic Impact Documentary: Contexts of Production and Social Intervention." *European Journal of Communication* 31 (3): 227–42.

National Film Board of Canada. n.d. "Report on Plans and Priorities, 2008–2009." https://www.tbs-sct.gc.ca/rpp/2008-2009/inst/nfb/nfb01-eng.asp.

Nogueira, Patrícia. 2016. "Participative Interactive Documentary as a Fragmented and 'Deterritorialized' Archive." *Cinergie: il Cinema e le altre Arti* 10: 156–64.

O'Flynn, Siobhan. 2012. "Documentary's Metamorphic Form: Webdoc, Interactive, Transmedia, Participatory and Beyond." *Studies in Documentary Film* 6: 141–57. https://doi.org/10.1386/sdf.6.2.141_1.

Paura, Angelo, and Max Resnik. 2017. "VR Gives New Life to an Interactive Documentary." *Medium*, 22 December 2017. https://medium.com/journalism-innovation/bear-71-vr-experiment-4265f8e69904.

Pitzer, Andrea. 2010a. "Canada's GDP Project: Documenting the Economic Crisis, One Story at a Time." *NiemanStoryboard*, 9 April 2010. https://niemanstoryboard.org/stories/canadas-gdp-project-documenting-the-economic-crisis-one-story-at-a-time.

– 2010b. "Marie-Claude Dupont on Canada's GDP Project: 'We're Trying to Show How These People Reinvent Themselves.'" *Nieman Storyboard*, 9 April 2010. https://niemanstoryboard.org/stories/canadas-gdp-project-documenting-the-economic-crisis-one-story-at-a-time.

Ragin, Charles C., and Howard S. Becker, eds. 1992. *What Is a Case? Exploring the Foundations of Social Inquiry.* Cambridge, UK: Cambridge University Press.

Rose, Mandy. 2016. "The Empathy Machine: Hype, Hope and Immersion in Non-Fiction VR." Paper presented at the i-Docs Symposium 2016, Bristol, UK, March 2016. https://idocs2016.dcrc.org.uk/abstracts/the-empathy-machine-hype-hope-and-immersion-in-non-fiction-vr.

Schleser, Max. 2018. "24Frames 24Hours: An Emerging Form of Workshop-Generated Documentary." In *Digital Media and Documentary*, ed. Adrian Miles, 101–10. London: Palgrave Pivot. https://doi.org/10.1007/978-3-319-68643-1_7.

Sénécal, Michel, and Frédéric Dubois. 2005. "The Alternative Communication Movement in Quebec's Mediascape." In *Converging Media, Diverging Politics: A Political Economy of News Media in the United States and Canada*, ed. David Skinner, James R. Compton, and Michael Gasher, 249–66. Oxford: Rowman and Littlefield.

Simons, Margaret, Rodney Tiffen, Doug Hendrie, Andrea Carson, Helen Sullivan, Denis Muller, and Brian McNair. 2017. "Understanding the Civic Impact of Journalism." *Journalism Studies* 18 (11): 1400–14. https://doi.org/10.1080/1461670X.2015.1129284.

Skinner, David, Scott Uzelman, Andrea Langlois, and Frédéric Dubois. 2009. "Independent Media Centres in Canada: Three Case Studies." In *Making Our Media: Mapping Global Initiatives toward a Democratic Public Sphere*, ed. Dorothy Kidd, Clemencia Rodriguez, and Laura Stein, 275–93. Cresskill, NJ: Hampton Press.

Stake, Robert E. 1995. *The Art of Case Study Research*. Thousand Oaks, CA: Sage.

Starkman, Dean. 2013. "Major Papers' Longform Meltdown." 17 January 2013. https://archives.cjr.org/the_audit/major_papers_longform_meltdown.php.

St-Jacques, Sylvie. 2010. "PIB : l'après-crise, un jour à la fois." *La Presse*, 27 September 2010. https://www.lapresse.ca/arts/201009/27/01-4326926-pib-lapres-crise-un-jour-a-la-fois.php.

Ulbricht, Lena, and Max von Grafenstein. 2016. "Big Data: Big Power Shifts?" *Internet Policy Review* 5, no. 1. https://doi.org/10.14763/2016.1.406.

Verwayen, Harry, Julia Fallon, Julia Schellenberg, and Panagiotis Kyrou. 2017. *Europeana Impact Playbook*. Den Haag, NL: Europeana Foundation. https://pro.europeana.eu/what-we-do/impact#download-the-playbook.

Waugh, Thomas, Michael Brendan Baker, and Ezra Winton, eds. 2010. *Challenge for Change: Activist Documentary at the National Film Board of Canada*. Montreal and Kingston: McGill-Queen's University Press.

Wintonick, Peter. 2011. "Webdocs, Docmedia and Doctopia." In *Webdocs A Survival Guide for Online Film-makers*, ed. Matthieu Lietaert, Brussels: Not so crazy! Productions.

3

FORT McMONEY

THE CHALLENGE OF MAINTAINING INTERACTIVE DOCUMENTARY

Daniel Keyes and Mike Robbins

Between 2008 and 2014, the National Film Board of Canada (NFB) created forty-one interactive documentaries on the Adobe Flash platform (Steele 2019). In 2017, Adobe announced that sometime in 2020 it would no longer upgrade its Flash plugin for web browsers, thus rendering these i-docs inaccessible (Lardinois 2017; Warren 2017; LaForge 2017). On 1 January 2021, Flash ceased to operate on all internet browsers, seeing a whole generation of Flash-based websites disappear (Fox 2021). Since 2018, the NFB has worked to conserve and keep these i-docs accessible (NFB 2018).

Fort McMoney (David Dufresne, 2013) (hereafter *Fort*) is an i-doc focusing on the unsustainability of Fort McMurray, a resource boomtown in northern Alberta. Ironically, as a digital boomtown of sorts, the Flash-based *Fort*, along with many of the other Flash-based i-docs, became inaccessible in 2021. In June 2022, the NFB made available – to only one or two users at a time – the French version of *Fort* via a web emulator, while less complex i-docs like *Similkameen Crossroad* (Tyler Hagen, 2013) were converted into HTML5 to provide continued access to a general audience (Perrault 2022). The end of Flash means *Fort* has become an archival object rather than an accessible work of media art, its computer code preserved but otherwise a pale digital shadow of what former NFB head Tom Perlmutter (2014) envisioned in 2014. When launched in 2013, *Fort* was populated by 412,000 players (Flynn 2015a) and supported by a team of programmers in French, English, and German; it was feted in newspapers (Goldberg 2013; Goodfellow 2014; Reguly 2013; Wente

2013; Wohlberg 2013; Wohlberg 2014) and media savvy news websites (Toledano 2013; Jankovic 2014), and was winner of both a Gemini and Webby award (Dufresne, 2013–14) for its innovative gamified approach to documentary. Now *Fort*'s "About" page evokes a digital ghost town with its banner message reading: "Technology is moving fast, and we were no longer able to support this format. Because conservation is part of our DNA, we carefully archive our web experiences. Check out our most recent interactive works" (ibid.). The hyperlinked verb "archive" in the banner directs users to a press release touting the NFB's web archiving strategy, which, it states, will employ a web-recorder that is an "open-source web archiving platform used to collect, store and share interactive captures of web pages" (NFB 2018). The message's invitation to discover more recent i-docs suggests that the NFB is always moving forward and wishes to assure users that they should not fret about "lost" access to previous materials.

Fort, like so many other Flash-based i-docs, was built in the early 2000s when the NFB was primarily focused on innovation and impact. However, platform capitalism, or the accelerating obsolescence of proprietary software like Flash, frustrates backward compatibility and presents a challenge to the legacy of *Fort* and similar projects produced by the NFB. As such, *Fort* embodies a paradox of digital precarity: once widely available on the internet to anyone with a computer browser or smartphone, the project effectively disappears when the platform that supports it no longer communicates with the latest browser software.

Based on both textual research and interviews with key NFB employees – conducted in 2019 before *Fort*'s digital sunset – this chapter details the history and impact of *Fort* alongside the history of Adobe Flash and HTML5. In considering the archival challenges *Fort* and other Flash-based i-docs of its era face, it situates *Fort* as a precarious archival object with an uncertain digital afterlife. What is at stake when *Fort* and other Flash-based i-docs become less accessible and more archival (i.e., saved for future study and potential refurbishment but effectively no longer interactive)? Do we cede to the inevitability of change, as Heraclitus might advise, and accept Perlmutter's invocation to "drive forward relentlessly" without heed to what may be lost? This chapter wrestles with the conundrum that, while technological change and platform capitalism make loss seem inevitable, we might need an accessible version of *Fort* and the archival paratexts it spawned in our rear-view mirror to "drive forward." In more concrete terms, and writing at a moment when the world grapples with a carbon-based energy crisis and the increasing effects of climate change, users should ideally be able to return to *Fort* to think about how an earlier generation attended to the civic conundrum of extractive carbon economies and the looming consequences of climate change. It remains unclear whether the NFB will be able to deliver on this goal of restored and complete access or if *Fort* will remain in its archival limbo, in which access via emulation is limited to very few. This chapter suggests *Fort*'s full restoration as a game once played by thousands, while a laudable goal, might be impossible and that maintaining archival traces of the game via emulation might be most practical. *Fort*'s ephemerality offers a number of lessons for thinking about the longevity of i-docs.

A Brief History of Flash

To understand Flash's importance in the development of streaming and interactive video, it is first important to understand the evolution of HTML or Hyper Text Markup Language, a computer language that instructs a web browser how to behave. HTML is a non-proprietary code for structuring and presenting content on the internet. While initially launched in 1996 (Ankerson 2012, 393), it wasn't until the early 2000s that Flash emerged as a way to embed video content and other interactive elements into HTML, which otherwise lacked these functions. For over a decade, Flash was the dominant software for designers seeking to animate the internet; however, Flash was not backwards compatible and was developed with the intent that all makers and browsers were reliant on its proprietary software to render moving images and sound available online. Adobe's move to be the sole animation software on the internet was famously resisted by Apple's CEO Steve Jobs (2010) in an open letter, "Thoughts on Flash," that captures the sentiment that the internet needs to rely on open design. This sentiment, along with widespread support from browser developers for an open standard, resulted in the development of HMTL5 in 2014. "One of the big advantages of HTML5," notes Neil Thoms (2017), "is that it doesn't rely on proprietary third-party plugins to create complex and powerful web projects"; it contains simplified tags for audio, video, and applications program interfaces (APIs, the software that talks with other software as opposed to communicating with computer users). By 2014, HTML5's open standard was compatible with browsers from Google, Mozilla, Apple, and Microsoft (Stevens and Owen 2013, 7).

Writing in 2013, Luke Stevens and R.J. Owen see the ascendency of HTML5 as necessary and good for consistent web development, but they caution against the quirks of HTML5 and, like *Fort*'s chief programmer Dominic Mercier (2013), do not see it as dexterous as Flash (Stevens and Owen 2013, 81). Thus, *Fort*'s development occurs in a period during which makers like Mercier were accustomed to building in Flash and knew that it was not future-proof but were reluctant to adopt HTML5 (Mercier 2013). As mentioned above, this lack of future proofing for an i-doc designed to prick the environmental consciousness of its users seems particularly ironic. Game designer, activist, and professor Paolo Pedercini (2020) identifies the demise of Flash as emblematic of technology monopolies manoeuvring for control in a way that threatens "the entirety of our culture: TV, books, music, news, games," while noting that some emulation software can keep this material alive. While independent web designers were subject to platform capitalism, was the NFB equally held ransom?

In the early 2010s, the rapid increase in sales of smartphones that could use HTML5 – but not Flash – contributed to the quick decline of the Adobe product, prompting the company to signal Flash's impending demise in 2011; nonetheless, the NFB produced *Fort* and eight other i-docs requiring Flash following this decisive announcement. Sean Flynn (2015) notes that the first prototype for *Fort* appeared in April 2012, with Flash development beginning in January 2013. With the benefit of hindsight, head programmer Mercier admitted in 2013 that if *Fort* were undertaken again, he would have adopted HTML5 during production, but he offers three reasons *Fort* remained with Flash:

1. Developers were familiar with it as Flash offered a mature platform operating with all browsers.
2. Moving to HMTL5 might mean stranding older browsers like Internet Explorer 8 that would not be able to handle HTML5.
3. They could deliver the project on time.

Flash's ubiquitous use at the NFB in the early 2010s with *Fort* and other NFB i-docs prompts legitimate concerns about accessibility that, like many debates over why one technology is adopted over another technology, cannot easily be reconciled. One NFB project from this era, *Highrise*, directed by Kat Cizek, heeded Adobe's call and moved to the open platform of HTML5 in 2011 (Cucinelli et al. 2018). Perhaps designers at the NFB hoped that Adobe might develop a solution to make Flash-based files forward compatible but that was not to be the case: in 2015, Adobe's blog heralded a new era with the arrival of its cloud-based Animate software that would replace Flash (Lee 2015). However, Adobe later cautioned that importing files from Flash into Animate caused significant digital loss (e.g., "Sounds are not imported … Movie Clip timelines are not imported" [Adobe 2016]). The NFB eventually landed on the Webrecorder solution in 2018 and has since then made progress emulating *Fort* and other Flash-based i-docs (NFB 2018; Web Recorder 2019); in 2020, Webrecorder was renamed Conifer (Kreymer 2020). The NFB Digital Studios were aware of Flash's issues in the early 2010s but hard-pressed to develop solutions, so work on an emulation of *Fort* continued as recently as 2022.

Historian Ian Milligan (2019, 9) notes that digital archives have the challenge of "super-abundance." He argues that absences in web archives "are not necessarily bad" but simply the condition that historians and archivists must confront in making sense of the past (16). Accepting such digital loss as a norm for the archival prospects of i-docs makes sense if i-docs are considered performative texts subject to change with each experience, not unlike a live theatrical performance where performative loss is a given. The performative aspects of both i-docs and theatre are ephemeral. Perhaps there is a misperception that, since every mouse-click by an i-doc user can be logged (as Dufresne details with regard to Amazon's server support for *Fort*; Miller and Allor 2016, 67), i-docs can operate as over-abundant records (ignoring users' rights to be forgotten). Makers can capture and permanently record something more than a theatrical director might capture of an audience's reaction to a live performance.

I-docs, however, are proving more transitory than most media in terms of medium durability and not just in terms of performative loss. In terms of media, novelists do not worry four years after publishing their novel that every print copy will disappear when the publisher upgrades its production workflow, as is the case with software. Nor do novelists worry that readers will lose the seemingly intuitive ability to open the novel or understand the mechanics of turning a page in a sequential order. Perhaps for the next generation of digital natives who tap their phone screens to activate a hyperlink, clicking a computer mouse to activate a hyperlink may no longer seem intuitive. With interactive documentaries, the issue of an audience understanding and operating the required software and hardware persists. Clearly, digital longevity is a challenge for i-docs, which are dependent on software and hardware that is prone to upgrading and designed for obsolescence, not longevity, despite Milligan's sense that the digital leaves historians overwhelmed with abundance. *Fort* provides a lesson in how digital abundance can slip away and thus requires fulsome paratextual documentation, which in this case has gathered in various digital spaces like the NFB and MIT's Docubase hub (Flynn 2015a; Flynn 2015b) and the website Medium (Mercier 2013, 2014a, 2014b, 2014c, 2014d, 2014e, 2014f).

What Is *Fort McMoney*?

The northern Alberta tar sands project has inspired a range of documentary films, from the Greenpeace-sponsored experimental feature-length documentary *Petropolis: Aerial Perspectives on the Alberta Tar Sands* (Peter Mettler, 2009) to gritty sociological feature-length documentaries like *Oil Sands Karaoke* (Charles Wilkinson, 2013) and the NFB's *Limit Is the Sky* (Julia Ivanova, 2016) as well as fiction films like the mockumentary *Fubar II: Balls to the Wall* (Michael Dowse, 2010). These efforts highlight the contradictions of the tar sands' development in terms of climate change, environmental degradation, Indigenous land claims, and economic development. David Dufresne's *Fort*, while tilling similar thematic content, offers an innovative approach to petro-culture documentary via gamification that nonetheless has a precedent.

Pedercini's satiric Flash-based game, *Oiligarchy* (2008), offers a curious, decidedly low-budget precursor to *Fort* with its focus on demonstrating the false economy of oil extraction within the context of a videogame. *Fort*, with a budget of $870,000 (Wood 2014, 57) and funding from Canadian and European sources (Flynn 2015b), operates as an elaborate gamified social documentary in which online players engage with various interviews from the citizens of the region to negotiate, vote, and plan a future for Fort McMurray, Alberta, the urban epicentre of the tar sand development. In three different interviews with Flynn (2015a), Sandra Gaudenzi (2013), and Michael Toledano (2013), Dufresne explains that he models *Fort* on the videogame *Sim City* (Maxis, 1989–2014), wherein players try to build and sustain a virtual community. *Fort* blends videogame structure with a journalistic documentary focus in which players confront the testimonies of the citizens of *Fort* in direct address-style interviews. Flynn (2015b) writes: "In the game, players have control over a virtual city that starts off identical to the real-life Fort McMurray in terms of population, economic productivity and other variables. However, over the course of four episodes, players are able to debate and vote on a series of referendums that affect the balance between the social, economic and environmental health of the virtual city."

Thematically, *Fort* engages users with local issues faced by a single resource boomtown that, in turn, reflect national issues like Indigenous rights and global issues like climate change. According to Dufresne, *Fort*'s journalistic documentary conceit "does not want to moralise[;] it's players themselves who, through their actions, develop their critical sense" (as qtd. in Nash 2017, 14). Thus, *Fort* provides an educational resource and a valuable archive for analyzing the representations of these issues circa 2013. These issues continue to haunt Canadian and global politics, suggesting there is a social value in having *Fort* more widely available than is currently possible.

Fort's hybrid structure as part-game and part-documentary blurs boundaries, but Flynn (2015b) notes that *Fort*'s director Dufresne "doesn't see any contradiction between journalistic values and creating simulations that model hypothetical scenarios – in fact, he believes it's necessary." Dufresne explains: "It seems that most journalists only want to talk about the past and the present, never the future. But this is what Wall Street, the EU, the US government do all the time. They make projections. Journalism is not only about conveying facts. It's a tool for thinking" (ibid.). Dufresne's concept of *Fort* as a tool for planning a better future for Fort McMurray rubs up against the irony that this tool, within a few years of its initial release, is available to only a handful of persistent researchers in emulator form and no longer available for educators like Mike Farley (2019), an Ontario high school educator who from 2014 to 2019 had 625 grade 9 geography students play the game.

Despite the project's initial reception and enthusiastic uptake by users in Canada and Europe, it could not sustain a lively critical conversation on petro-culture and instead offers a lesson in media obsolescence. Looking beyond the issue of *Fort*'s use of the doomed Flash plugin, the resources and will to maintain *Fort* are well beyond the remit of the NFB's Digital Studios, which prefer to focus on discrete projects with finite funding timelines; thus *Fort*'s splash page encourages users to seek other new i-docs rather than maintaining a "live" conversation about Fort McMurray and Canada's dependence on resource extraction. Ideally, as the NFB continues to work on emulating *Fort*, it might become more widely available as both an excessive and perhaps haunted archival object – excessive in that it represents a detailed and complex snapshot of Fort McMurray, weaving hundreds of hours of documentary footage, but haunted in that emulation lacks any "live" trace of the hundreds of thousands of original players who once participated within the game throughout 2013 and 2014. Moreover, today's prospective players can only step back into a 2013 version of Fort McMurray as shaped by Dufresne; it is not today's Fort McMurray. In emulation form, users cannot know how the original players voted on the games' various proposals and thus are left playing in a ghost town. The next section of this chapter explores the haunted version of the game as explored prior to Flash disappearing and demonstrates how the absence of any of the original participatory or performative traces of the project offers a solitary experience and a static snapshot of Fort McMurray circa 2013.

Fort McMoney: Assessing the Archival Object in 2019

In May 2019, working with a Mozilla web browser (as no other browser supported Adobe Flash) and the final update for the Abode Flash plugin, we landed on *Fort McMoney*'s home page to hear the looped howl of a northern Albertan wind. After listening to a short introduction acquainting us with the principles of the game, we toured a virtual boomtown. The i-doc invited the player to debate a series of questions with other players while virtually wandering around the town meeting with locals, listening to their stories, and learning to whom pre-selected questions could be posed that would determine progress through the game. Hovering a cursor over the image of a citizen or one of these special locations triggered a new window where the player could watch a short interview with the citizen before a prompt appeared with three choices: go to another location, start an interview with the citizen, or return to the first location (Mercier 2013). All or none of the questions could be selected and the choice guided the player's progress in a Boolean labyrinth of "if-then" conditional statements with the possibility of revealing new areas of gameplay. The game was structured upon influence points collected through these exchanges that displayed on an elaborate dashboard and tracked the player's progress in the game. All the above bring to mind Dufresne's claim that the player's point-of-view is not in the editing of these clips but in "the structure of database" (Flynn 2015b).

The spatial feel of *Fort* was somewhat like a static version of Google Map's "street view" with its little yellow homunculus avatar that allows a user to explore a space from a moving point-of-view that is fixed along an invisible axis. In *Fort*, the player did not appear as an avatar but shared the view of the probing camera searching space and citizens to learn more about *Fort*. Eco-critic P. Saxton Brown (2014, 391) refers to the point of view in *Fort* as being that of a "detective" working through the "procedural rhetoric" of the game. This lack of embodiment and fixed identity for the player within the framework of the NFB's platform generated a neutral identity (neither male nor female, poor nor rich, simply the camera's eye) for the player. Arguably, this perspective mitigated a settler-Canadian or European players' responsibility as one who benefited from petro-culture at the expense of Indigenous rights and the environment. Moreover, it obfuscated the ethical responsibility a real-world reporter or filmmaker would have if they were to approach someone on the streets of Fort McMurray, pose similar questions, and deal with the real-world consequences of their actions. As a game, players once debated and voted on issues facing the town, but in the ghost town version we played in May 2019, the experience was decidedly static with no rejoinders for our actions. The civics lessons were decidedly virtual, suggesting that, as an exercise in citizenship, *Fort* failed to mobilize the type of political action that it modelled. Instead, the game offered absent players an opportunity to virtually and safely experience a hinterland's ugly social issues; it was more schadenfreude tourism than a civics project in which they were directly implicated every time a furnace ignited or a car was filled up with gas.

As mentioned above, *Fort* charted players' progress via an elaborate dashboard hidden from view at the bottom of the screen. The dashboard appeared in two forms: a simple version that appeared as a small window allowing the player to continue watching interviews – this small window informed the player of the number of players currently online and the player's influence score – and a more complex dashboard, which took the player out of the game and offered a complete representation of the player's progress by way of a map of the town, news, discussion, debating propositions, and earned "influence points" based on their progress through the i-doc.

Playing the game in 2019, however, was a solitary affair. The dashboard might inform visitors of five current players on the site, but with little evidence of their activity – only notes posted by players some years ago.

It was, indeed, a digital ghost town. New users who are ardent gamers might not appreciate the once-sophisticated coding and innovation of *Fort*. Indeed, one German-language gamer review of the i-doc from 2013 judged *Fort* to be a failure as a game because of its overly coercive programming (Klingler 2013). It seems unlikely that in 2019 it would have attracted the hardcore player who would spend hours on the site debating issues that are no longer presented as "live" – and, therefore, pressing or relevant – despite the fact the social and environmental issues *Fort* sought to illuminate continue to persist. *Fort* as a documentary, Lachman (2016, 10) notes, precludes "changing [the] outcome of the events depicted"; players may perform "the role [of] an investigator, observing and interviewing," but they cannot "directly alter the events that unfold." Without updates that might, for example, reflect the spring 2016 mass evacuation of Fort McMurray when the city was threatened by forest fire (Public Safety Canada 2016), the i-doc offered an unpopulated but fixed synchronic slice of *Fort* from 2013. The lonely experience of *Fort* in 2019 was a pale and haunted representation of its original performance for thousands of users years earlier.

Archiving *Fort* as Excessive Archival Object

Without factoring in the demise of Flash, *Fort* operates as an excessive digital archival object that challenges archivists to determine what of an i-doc can and should be preserved. They might ask, does it make sense to preserve the game's complex dashboard design and navigation system when it might not make sense to future users who lack a computer mouse? Should attempts to preserve *Fort* in a (digitally) durable form consider obscure spaces that only a handful of active users ever encountered when the game was still active? Louis Richard Tremblay (2019), *Fort*'s NFB producer, admits that some of the nooks and crannies in *Fort* were only accessed by a handful of players. Are there some features of the game that are unique to Flash-type programming that the web emulator cannot adequately capture? There is no way, and perhaps little point in trying, to preserve the user experience of 2013 with its vigilant trilingual game masters and thousands of players in what is now a virtual ghost town. Is preserving *Fort* a case of preserving a version of the game that never really existed for most users back in 2013? *Fort* is an example of accelerated digital ephemerality into which players of today and the future cannot, as the ancient Greek philosopher Heraclitus theorized (Plato 2011), ever step back into the same stream (or tar sands).

Digital art preservationist Hanna Hölling addresses notions of the ephemera in electronic art by acknowledging change is the only constant and, despite such change, Heraclitus's metaphoric stream is still recognizable as a stream. She writes, "things retain their identity through time even if they change physically" (Hölling 2017, 138). Preservation for Hölling has too long relied on the fetish of preserving the physical attributes of an artwork that are bound up with an idea of an author-creator as final authority over the created object. As an ardent preservationist of media artist Nam June Paik, Hölling argues that preservation of the conceptual element is ultimately more important than the physical details. This rationale conforms with Tremblay's (2019) conclusion that perhaps letting go of the goal of "restoring" the digital object and retaining the production spreadsheet might be sufficient for future makers seeking to reboot a return to *Fort* or media anthropologists seeking to apprise a project.

Hölling's pragmatic view of preservation resonates with Brett Gaylor, maker of the NFB's *Rip: A Remix Manifesto* (2008) and *Do Not Track* (2015) at the NFB. He disputes the ethic that the main goal of archiving should be longevity. He counter-intuitively asserts, "smart archiving is how to properly let something die" (Gaylor 2017). The proper digital death for Gaylor involves planning projects that are mindful of digital precarity and will involve resources like the Internet Archive, a non-profit digital online library. He notes that the work of independent makers, who produce content on contract, means that makers typically do not plan a good digital death. Rick Prelinger, an archivist and professor at the University of California Santa Cruz, supports Gaylor's line of reasoning. Prelinger asserts that digital content challenges the traditional carceral archive that imprisons content. He argues that, since so much digital content is based on use and sharing, imprisoning such content in the archive to preserve it no longer makes sense (Prelinger 2017). He calls on makers to conceive digital projects with an archivist involved in the original design so that project planners consider longevity and sustained dissemination. He envisions an open digital archive not bound by copyright and corporate architecture, although he admits that "the preservation of the [digital] work falls far short of the experience, but I want to say loss can be transformative. The histories that we investigate most eagerly today ... are often histories of losses that we want to remediate ...We should never make peace with erasure; we might get better at accepting the inevitability of digital loss."

Gaylor (2017), like Prelinger, challenges the independent auteur documentary tradition that would see permanence as a virtue and ultimate goal. For Gaylor, a good death for an interactive project would involve working in an open-source format in which future makers can rework material using new digital tools. He readily admits that the documentary tradition is not one predisposed to open-source design, yet he sees open-source as the route for building durability into the i-doc. "Open source is about building it out in the open," Gaylor (2017) contends, "so the project lives because other people see it and want to use it and preserve it."

Unfortunately, the ability to build i-docs in open formats is frustrated by the desire to embrace closed technologies and corporate platforms that ensure a broad and varied audience that is reliant on platforms like Facebook. For example, a quick glance at the NFB Interactive page at the time of writing reveals five categories: web experiences, apps, installations, virtual reality, and social media. The i-docs in the virtual reality category rely on hardware like 3D Oculus goggles, while the social media i-docs operate as linear films on Meta's Facebook (NFB 2022). Tremblay (2019) explains that, in talking with makers, the NFB first asks how the choice of a particular medium might frustrate conservation efforts so that decisions about ongoing access are made up-front as opposed to what happened with *Fort*'s development.

Hölling's pragmatic view of conceptual preservation versus slavish restoration occurred with the first Flash-based i-doc to be remade by the NFB into virtual reality (VR): the 2017 relaunch of *Bear 71* (Leanne Allison and Jeremy Mendes, 2012). The VR reboot of *Bear 71*, *Bear 71 VR* is a testament to the type of maker logic that is less concerned with capturing the authentic experience of the original i-doc and more concerned with exploring how the original gains a new life with VR (Matlin 2017). As someone familiar with both versions, Tremblay (2019) argues the translation from i-doc to VR changes the experience for the users but maintains the core idea of *Bear 71*. Hölling, Gaylor, and Prelinger collectively offer strategies for negotiating and anticipating digital loss as inevitable and support any approach whereby conceptual art is transferred from one flagging digital container to another to keep the idea accessible and present.

The NFB's Slow Flash Rescue Mission

As recently as 2007, the NFB issued a press release championing digitization as the solution to the threat of losing its vast archive of brittle and aging celluloid (CP 2007). Digitizing film was meant to be the lasting, inevitable, and long-term solution for its archive. However, digital technologies like Adobe Flash, which are built primarily on corporately owned proprietary software platforms that require continual updating, often deliver content to a digital cul de sac. Present-day computing devices often cannot access a file coded for a computer a decade ago. In the 2010s, the NFB – which has a long tradition as an archive of Canadian images – began to seriously develop its digital archiving of linear film. By 2015, it articulated its Golden Rules for comprehensive archiving and has, in the late 2010s and early 2020s, slowly worked to remediate i-docs (NFB 2015; see Baker, chapter 1, this volume). The 2017 Update or Die Conference held in Montreal and co-sponsored by the MIT Documentary Lab and the Phi Centre brought together a range of makers, archivists, and academics to develop strategies for dealing with digital material and resulted – in collaboration with a non-profit archival organization called Rhizome – in the development of Webrecorder, a software program that captures the experience of Flash-based i-docs. The NFB aimed to make an emulated version of *Fort* accessible in 2020 and yet, in 2022, only the French version of *Fort* was available in its emulated form, and a limit of two simultaneous users makes it difficult to assess just how complete this version is in comparison to the original. This slow development of *Fort*'s emulation is, we suspect, due to its sprawling complexity; i-doc development seems best suited for complex design on varied platforms. Jimmy Fournier (2019), the NFB's director of research and development, indicates that, while the NFB has solved the issues of capturing Flash-based i-docs, HTML5 now poses numerous other technological hurdles in its efforts to archive (and make available on the web) simulations of the HTML5 experience. Change is permanent, and accelerated digital loss comes in many forms (e.g., loss of user experience, death of formats, shifting of affordances offered by media, copyright, etc.). Working with open software platforms that allow for backward compatibility is part of the solution but a tough sell for an auteur-driven industry working on short-term contracts to produce innovative experiences on a tight timeline. Media studies scholar Wendy Chun's (2008, 148) characterization of new media as racing "simultaneously towards the future and past, towards what we might call the bleeding edge of obsolescence" comes to mind as the type of digital limbo of not just *Fort* but many other i-docs that, post-launch, recede from memory, their maintenance impeded both by the flagging platforms upon which they were built and the ongoing cost (and human resources) required to keep them available.

Conclusion: What Are the Stakes of Losing *Fort*?

Despite this chapter's focus on *Fort*'s disappearance, detailed conceptual traces of its existence exist in places like MIT's Docubase website (Flynn 2015a, 2015b; Dufresne 2015), a detailed blog account by its head programmers on the *Medium* website (Mercier 2014, 2014a, 2014b, 2014c, 2014d, 2014e, 2014e), Dufresne et al.'s (2015) book *Brut*, and in scholarly materials addressing *Fort*'s potential as an agent of social change (Brown 2014; Miller and Allor 2016; Miller and Allor 2017; Lachman 2016; Nash 2017; see Mulvogue, chapter 11, this volume). Following the ethos of the University of Stanford's LOCKSS (Lots of Copies Keep Stuff Safe), decentralized governmental and non-governmental digital repositories might be the future of archiving born-digital material (LOCKSS 2022). Ironically, the paratexts for *Fort* may have more longevity than the actual i-docs as a live multiplayer game, which gives rise to the question: Are linear documentaries ultimately more stable and long-lived than costly and complex i-docs such as *Fort?* We do not have the answer to this question but suggest that *Fort* – as an ambitious, foundational i-doc – provides a number of lessons about i-doc ephemerality:

1. Beware the devil's bargain of choosing platforms with built-in affordances and complex vulnerabilities; where possible, strive for open architecture or embrace the ephemeral under platform capitalism, accepting loss as inevitable.
2. Assume performative loss is a given with an i-doc and document whatever can be documented, and do so in different forms distributed across different networks (e.g., NFB Interactive, MIT's Docubase: the Open Documentary Lab, Medium, IDFA, Sheffield's i-doc.org, the *Interactive Film and Media Journal*, etc.).
3. Develop i-docs with a view of the long game that includes a death kit (Gaylor 2017) and assumes technologies change but that key concepts and approaches will be documented (Hölling 2017).

We remain grateful for the efforts of Fournier and his team of coders to preserve and revive versions of *Fort* and other Flash-based i-docs in the NFB's catalogue. The emulated version of *Fort* is imperfect and does not match a player's experience of the project in 2013; but, following Hölling, it provides a conceptual representation of the experience when supplemented by other paratexts. We suspect, for a few passionate educators like Mike Farley, there is an appetite to see *Fort* fully restored so his students might continue to benefit from the conversations it provokes on the topics of petro-culture and climate change, among other things. We do not want to discount the performative elements of the project as a vehicle for social change, but we suspect *Fort* would today appear creaky to the current generation of Farley's students; moreover, in our contemporary, complex, attention economy, few students are likely itching to play an expansive educational game like *Fort*. Yet we suspect, for media archeologists, having access to *Fort* would provide a valuable text for thinking through the evolution of i-docs and, for historians, *Fort* would provide a snapshot of Canadian nationalism negotiating its dirty colonial extractive economic engine. For educators like Farley seeking to sustain civil and reasoned discourse, we dream someday that the NFB might launch a *Fort 2025* that leverages the conceptual legacies of the original to further engage users in a discussion about the local and global impacts, and the social consequences, of climate change and colonialism. With the knowledge that *Fort McMoney*'s original budget marked a high point in i-docs spending at the NFB, a full-blown reboot seems extremely unlikely. Yet, apropos of Heraclitus, we need to keep stepping into Alberta's tar sands.

References

Adobe. 2016. "Edit, Import SWF Film/Animate." 8 September 2016. https://helpx.adobe.com/animate/kb/edit-import-swf-file.html.

Ankerson, Megan Sapnar. 2012. "Writing Web Histories with an Eye on the Analog Past." *New Media and Society* 14 (3): 374–400.

Brown, P. Saxton. 2014. "The Garden in the Machine: Video Games and Environmental Consciousness." *Philological Quarterly* 93 (3): 383–407.

Chun, Wendy Hui Kyong. 2008. "The Enduring Ephemeral, or the Future Is a Memory." *Critical Inquiry* 35 (1): 148–71.

CP. 2007. "Lack of Technology Has NFB Library in Peril." *Moose Jaw Times Herald*, 17 September 2007.

Cucinelli, Giuliana, Émilie René-Véronneau, and Belinda Oldford. 2018. "Interactive Documentaries and the Connected Viewer Experience: Conversations with Katerina Cizek, Brett Gaylor, Jeff Soyk, and Florian Thalhofer." *First Monday: Peer Reviewed Journal of the Internet* 23, no. 5. https://firstmonday.org/ojs/index.php/fm/article/view/6182/7222.

Dufresne, David. 2015. "Fort McMoney: Oops … We Messed Up Again! A Post-Mortem Examination of Fort McMoney by Its Director David Dufresne!" *MIT Open Documentary Lab*. Trans. Damien Hébert and Grayson Fuller. https://docubase.mit.edu/lab/case-studies/fort-mcmoney-oops-we-messed-up-again.

Dufresne, David, Nancy Huston, Naomi Klein, Melina Laboucan-Massimo, and Rudy Wiebe. 2015. *Brut: La Ruée Vers l'or Noir*. http://www.davduf.net/brut-la-ruee-vers-l-or-noir.

Farley, Mike. 2019. "Using Fort McMoney." E-mail, 18 January 2019.

Flynn, Sean. 2015a. "Evaluating Interactive Documentaries: Audience, Impact and Innovation in Public Interest Media." PhD diss., Massachusetts Institute of Technology. https://cmsw.mit.edu/wp/wp-content/uploads/2016/06/291106711-Sean-Flynn-Evaluating-Interactive-Documentaries-Audience-Impact-and-Innovation-in-Public-Interest-Media.pdf.

– 2015b. Fort McMoney: Concept to Launch. MIT Docubase. https://docubase.mit.edu/lab/case-studies/fort-mcmoney-concept-to-launch.

Fournier, Jimmy. 2019. Interview with the authors, 4 March 2019.

Fox, Chris. 2021. "Adobe Flash Player Is Finally Laid to Rest." BBC News, 1 January 2021. https://www.bbc.com/news/technology-55497353.

Gaudenzi, Sandra. 2013. "David Dufresne on Fort McMoney: Challenges, Narrative and Budget." *I-Docs*, 25 November 2013. http://i-docs.org/fort-mcmoney-today-david-dufresne-tells-us-whole-story.

Gaylor, Brett. 2017. "401 vs 404: A Tale of Documentary Horror and Redemption." Update or Die: Proofing Future Emerging Digital Documentary Forms Conference, 5 May, Phi Centre, Montreal, QC. https://www.youtube.com/watch?v=YzdLPyKZnrM.

Goldberg, Harold. 2013."Where Film Marries Video Game." *New York Times*, 26 November 2013, C1.

Goodfellow, Melanie, 2014. "Doc-Game Fort McMoney Pulls 350k." *Screen Daily*, 27 January 2014. https://www.screendaily.com/news/doc-game-fort-mcmoney-pulls-350k/5065847.article.

Hölling, Hanna. 2017. *Paik's Virtual Archive: Time, Change, and Materiality in Media Art*. Los Angeles: University of California Press.

Jankovic, Jovana. 2014. "Fort McMoney – Inside the Game Round 2: Fort McMoney Is Back and Better Than Ever." *InteractiveNew*, 27 January 2014. http://blog.nfb.ca/blog/2014/01/27/fort-mcmoney-round-2.

Jobs, Steve. 2010. "Thoughts on Flash." April 2010. https://web.archive.org/web/20170615060422/https://www.apple.com/hotnews/thoughts-on-flash.

Klingler, Nino. 2013. "Fort McMoney – Kritik." *Critic.de*, 29 November 2013. https://www.critic.de/film/fort-mcmoney-6168.

Kreymer, Ilya. 2020. "A New Phase for Webrecorder Project, Conifer and ReplayWeb.page." *Webrecorder: Web Archiving for All*, 11 June 2020. https://webrecorder.net/2020/06/11/webrecorder-conifer-and-replay-web-page.html.

Lachman, Richard. 2016. "Emergent Principles for Digital Documentary." *View: Journal of European Television History and Culture* 5 (10): 1–13.

Laforge, Anthony. 2017. "Saying Goodbye to Flash in Chrome." *Chrome*, 25 July 2017. https://www.blog.google/products/chrome/saying-goodbye-flash-chrome.

Lardinois, Frederic. 2017. "Get Ready to Finally Say Goodbye to Flash – in 2020." *TechCrunch*, 25 July 2017. https://techcrunch.com/2017/07/25/get-ready-to-say-goodbye-to-flash-in-2020.

Lee, Rich. 2015. Welcome Adobe Animate CC, a New Era for Flash Professional." *Adobe Blog*, 30 November 2015. https://theblog.adobe.com/welcome-adobe-animate-cc-a-new-era-for-flash-professional.

LOCKSS. 2022. "What Is LOCKSS." Stanford University. https://www.lockss.org/about/what-lockss.

Matlin, Julie. 2017. *Bear 71 VR*. NFB. 9 February 2017. https://blog.nfb.ca/blog/2017/02/09/bear-71-vr-google-nfb-partner-expand-world-virtual-reality-storytelling.

Mercier, Dominic. 2013. "How I Built Fortmcmoney.com – Part 1 – Introduction." *Medium*, 31 January 2013. https://medium.com/@d.mercier84/how-i-built-fortmcmoney-com-part-1-introduction-af47836d29de.

– 2014a. "How I Built Fortmcmoney.com – Part 2 – Exploration." *Medium*, 14 February 2014. https://medium.com/@d.mercier84/how-i-built-fortmcmoney-com-part-2-exploration-9c5b98b9e6e9.

– 2014b. "How I Built Fortmcmoney.com – Part 3 – Assets Automation with Grunt." *Medium*, 19 February 2014. https://medium.com/@d.mercier84/how-i-built-fortmcmoney-com-part-3-assets-automation-with-grunt-3107508a264d.

– 2014c. "How I Built Fortmcmoney.com – Part 4 –Video and Audio." *Medium*, 24 February 2014. https://medium.com/@d.mercier84/how-i-built-fortmcmoney-com-part-4-video-audio-2f14b0fbbfc1.

– 2014d. "How I Built Fortmcmoney.com – Part 5 – Internationalization." *Medium*, 24 February 2014. https://medium.com/@d.mercier84/how-i-built-fortmcmoney-com-part-5-internationalization-4f2d8d034f05.

– 2014e. "How I Built Fortmcmoney.com – Part 6 – Dashboard." *Medium*, 10 March 2014. https://medium.com/@d.mercier84/how-i-built-fortmcmoney-com-part-6-dashboard-73853af14e8d.

– 2014f. "How I Built Fortmcmoney.com – Part 7 – Conclusion." *Medium*, 14 March 2014. https://medium.com/@d.mercier84/how-i-built-fortmcmoney-com-part-7-conclusion-e1c7ba502a7.

Miller, Liz, and Martin Allor. 2016. "Choreographies of Collaboration: Social Engagement in Interactive Documentaries." *Studies in Documentary Film* 10 (1): 53–70.

Nash, Kate. 2017. "I-docs and the Documentary Tradition: Exploring Questions of Citizenship." In *I-docs: The Evolving Practices of Interactive Documentary*, ed. Judith Aston, Sandra Gaudenzi, and Mandy Rose, 9–25. London and New York: Wallflower.

Milligan, Ian. 2019. *History in the Age of Abundance? How the Web Is Transforming Historical* Research. Montreal and Kingston: McGill-Queen's Univerity Press.

NFB. 2015. "National Film Board of Canada Completes Its Four Golden Rules of Archiving with ASG-Digital Archive." Government of Canada, 11 September 2015. https://www.canada.ca/en/news/archive/2015/09/national-film-board-canada-completes-four-golden-rules-archiving-asg-digital-archive.html.

– 2018. "National Film Board of Canada and Rhizome Collaborate to Broaden the Technical Capabilities and Impact of Webrecorder, Rhizome's Leading-edge, Easy-to-Use Tool Set for Web Archiving." 18 December 2018. https://www.canada.ca/en/national-film-board/news/2018/12/national-film-board-of-canada-and-rhizome-collaborate-to-broaden-the-technical-capabilities-and-impact-of-webrecorder-rhizomes-leading-edge-easy-to.html.

– 2021. "Archived: Fort McMurray." 3 January 2021. https://www.nfb.ca/interactive/fort_mcmoney.

– 2022. Interactive. NFB. https://www-nfb-ca.eu1.proxy.openathens.net/interactive.

Pedercini, Paolo. 2020. "Gone with a Flash (Talk Transcript)," MacKenzie Art Gallery, Regina, Saskatchewan, *Molleindustria,* 23 November 2020. https://www.molleindustria.org/blog/gone-with-a-flash-talk.

Perlmutter, Tom. 2014. "The Interactive Documentary: A Transformative Art Form." *Policy Options*, 2 November 2014. http://policyoptions.irpp.org/magazines/policyflix/the-interactive-documentary-a-transformative-art-form.

Perreault, Catherine. 2022. "Re: Follow Up on Progress of Flash i-Doc Conversion to Web Emulator Software." E-mail, 6 June 2022.

Plato. 2011. *Craytlus.* Section 402a. Perseus Project, Tuft University. Ed. Richard Whaling. https://www.perseus.tufts.edrtext?doc=Perseus%3Atext%3A1999.01.0172%3Atext%3DCrat.%3Asection%3D402a.

Prelinger, Rick. 2017. "Perishable Practices: Preserving New Documentary Forms in a Post-Archival Moment." In *Update or Die: Proofing Future Emerging Digital Documentary Forms*, 5 May, Phi Centre, Montreal, QC. https://www.youtube.com/watch?v=SOMHl3iCd2g.

Public Safety Canada. 2016. *Canadian Disaster Database.* https://cdd.publicsafety.gc.ca/dtprnt-eng.aspx?cultureCode=enCa&eventTypes=%27WF%27&normalizedCostYear=1&dynamic=false&eventId=1135&prnt=both.

Reguly, Eric. 2013."'Fort McMoney': Let the Game Begin – and the Debate Rage." *Globe and Mail*, 25 November 2013, A9.

Steele, Janine. 2019. "Request for List of the NFB's Flash-Based I-Docs." E-mail, 4 April 2019.

Stevens, Luke, and R.J. Owen. 2013. *The Truth about HTML5.* 1st ed. New York: Apress.

Thoms, Neal. 2017. "A Look Back at HTML5," *Fasthosts.* https://www.fasthosts.co.uk/blog/websites/look-back-html5.

Toledano, Michael. 2013. "There's a New, Interactive Documentary about Fort McMurray." *Vice*, 25 November 2013. https://www.vice.com/en_ca/article/gqk8kb/theres-a-new-interactive-documentary-about-fort-mcmurray.

Tremblay, Louis-Richard. 2019. Interview with the authors, 8 January 2019.

Warren, Tom. 2017. "Adobe Will Finally Kill Flash in 2020." *The Verge*, 25 July 2017. https://www.theverge.com/2017/7/25/16026236/adobe-flash-end-of-support-2020.

Web Recorder. 2019. "WR About." *Rhizome.* https://webrecorder.io/_faq.

Wente, Margaret. 2013. "'Fort McMoney': Let the Game Begin - and the Debate Rage: 1." *Globe and Mail*, 25 November 2013.

Wohlberg, Meagan. 2013. "Ideas Battle Online for Control of Fort McMoney:

Online Docu-Game Puts Fate of Fort McMurray in Players' Hands." *Northern Journal*, 3 December 2013, A10.
– 2014. "Environment 'Wins' in First Round of Fort McMoney Online Game-Documentary Raises Questions about Resource Economy." *Northern Journal*, 21 January 2014, A14.
Wood, Chris. 2014. "A Sheep in Wolf's Clothing Fort McMoney: David Dufresne, Canada: Toxa Inc. and the National Film Board, 2013. / Fortmcmoney.Com." *Alternatives Journal* (Waterloo) 40 (3): 57.

4

VIEWFINDERS

EXPLORING TRAVELLING AND LANDSCAPES VIA AUGMENTED REALITY

Gerda Cammaer and Max Schleser

Introduction

Viewfinders is an international collaborative creative arts research project that connects travel experiences with mobile creativity. The mobility and functionality of devices like smartphones means that audience engagement with content no longer needs to be a passive viewing experience but can involve interaction, participation, and even location aware and/or responsive content. *Viewfinders* is an online project that incorporates all these elements to create a navigable augmented landscape composed of places visited, generated by mobile users in the form of brief travelling shots. It aims to recreate and explore travelling, contribute to the study of mobile cinema, compare various forms of moving image media (with a focus on interactive and AR experiences), investigate the possibilities of collaborative and practice-based research, and examine working with peer-generated content (Cammaer and Schleser 2018, 70). The idea for this project was first presented and submitted for peer review at the 2016 MINA (Mobile Innovation Network Australasia) Conference and RMIT's Docuverse Conference, both in Melbourne, Australia. In 2017, the online curation platform was exhibited at the *Invisible Geographies* exhibition of FLEFF (Finger Lake Environmental Film Festival) and the *Mobile Utopia* exhibition at Lancaster University, UK. Finally, the *Viewfinders* AR prototype was launched at the 2018 i-docs symposium in Bristol and is discussed in detail in a chapter of an ebook, *Docuverse: Approaches to Expanding*

Documentary (Cammaer and Schleser 2018). This chapter aims to situate the project within a historical and theoretical context pertinent to the study of interactive documentary, linking it to various other forms of adventurous film practices, particularly those that speak to the Canadian experience and those that aim to expand the notion of documentary. In the context of documentary and the often-cited reference to its Griesonian definition of "the creative treatment of actuality," *Viewfinders* explores the creative components at the intersection of content creation and technology innovation, understanding documentary as an experiential medium more than a narrative one.

Augmenting Travel (Film) Experiences

Within a dynamic screen production environment, there are now new possibilities to expand cinematic space and representations of travel that can make them more interactive, inclusive, and immersive, to not just present images but to surround them with a world. *Viewfinders* tries to do this by creating an interactive travel experience for the audience that transcends linear narrative documentary and other cinematic representations of travel. It aims to present moving images of the world as a non-linear voyage on mobile devices that can be accessed anywhere and everywhere, expanding both the experience of travel *and* the experience of cinema. It moves away from linear storytelling, and it has no "meaning" in the conventional sense. If there is meaning to be derived, it comes from the relationship between the viewer, the various film clips, and how these are experienced. This is achieved in two stages.

The first part of *Viewfinders* is an online curation platform that allows participants to provide short (up to one minute) travelling shots captured on smartphones for an immersive documentary experience that both situates travel images in the world and creates a world around them. *Viewfinders* is built exclusively with travelling shots or tracking shots filmed on mobile devices and while literally "on the move" because they best represent the experience of movement and travel, the freedom to travel, different modes of travel, and the trajectory of travel. The mobile camera is part of a conceptual exploration. While film history is full of attempts to explore and expand screen space with various camera movements, thanks to mobile cinema this has become much easier. The screen itself has become mobile. By uploading one-minute travelling shots captured with mobile devices – video taken, for example, from moving vehicles – participants also contribute to an ongoing broader creative and conceptual investigation into the content and aesthetics of travel films made with these mobile devices. The video database serves as the basic material for the AR app and might later also be used in a more "conventional" linear travel essay film depending on the interests of users.

The second part of *Viewfinders*, the AR app (which is the focus here and is further explained in detail below), offers participants the opportunity to observe how others have experienced the spaces through which they travel and discover a new view that they see forming before them. *Viewfinders* allows the participants to be transported to different places on the spot and in the moment, inspired by the place where they are, and that place's specific landscape: using their screen as a viewfinder, they themselves become "view finders." The project builds on the tradition of travel essay films as it offers viewers an experience of space that "redefines the self within a constantly shifting elsewhere" (Corrigan 2011, 105). Its distinction from this prior history is that it does so literally: the space is no longer limited to what is presented on the screen (places travelled and filmed by someone else) but includes any place where the viewer is situated when they are using the app, and it connects this place to those other places travelled (insofar as they were filmed and submitted). In other words, user/participants can experience the different travelling shots, not in the form of a narrative story created for the screen that replaces reality with a constructed one, but by experiencing it *in* reality, on their mobile screen, interacting with it in situ and in real time (and with real sounds). As such *Viewfinders* is part of the next wave of AR applications, those that include context. Papagiannis (2017, 4) explains, "Contextual information transforms the AR experience and content, because it now moves from an experience that is the same for every user to one that is specific to you, your location, your interests and your needs." Besides comparing and exploring different perceptions of places from around the world, the AR app also allows the viewer to discover new places or to see known places from a new perspective. With *Viewfinders*, the goal is to contribute to a greater geographical awareness and connectedness.

As Corrigan (2011, 109) notes, cinematic space "has described a wide variety of representational geographies ranging across narrative organizations, experimental explorations, and documentary representations." *Viewfinders* has an affinity with a variety of other film genres that have

Figure 4.1
Viewfinders video stills

travel as their central theme and that use travelling shots in expressive ways. The most obvious link is with home movies and amateur travel films that display a similar spontaneous form of "snap-shooting" and "moment collecting" following an "impulse to collect the world and resist, sometimes defiantly, the systematic or the 'orderly' as it was being defined in classical cinema" (Orgeron 2006, 77). Home movies implicitly reflect the amateur's belief in the ability of small film equipment to capture the world. They show attempts to find more exciting ways to portray travel with an enthusiastic, almost reckless, and definitely unscripted use of travelling shots (Cammaer 2015). A first compilation of travelling shots submitted to *Viewfinders* provides a good example of this (online 2018).

Viewfinders also builds on a long tradition in Canadian art and experimental film, more specifically those works that have landscape and travel as their subject matter (e.g., Michael Snow, David Rimmer, Richard Kerr, Jason Britski, Dan Brown, and Steven Topping to name just a few). The project shares with these experimental films a similar interest in landscape iconography. It also has a similar aesthetic that combines formal abstractions, montage (which we termed "ludic montage" [Cammaer and Schleser 2018, 68]), and experimentation with film technology. But

Viewfinders differs from them as it offers a collective series of moving landscape shots and tries to create a different experience, one that is not focused on the solo artist's vision but on the combined vision of a group of participants/collaborators who are invited to contribute their own observations of the world. *Viewfinders* offers the possibility to understand and experience the world as a traveller, through the experience of movement and mobility, as mobile cinema, as well as to connect with other travellers.

International Collaboration and Co-Creation

As an expanded cinema project, *Viewfinders* enables one to make new connections with peers through exchange and co-creation, and possibly to interact with the entire world while being out and about. Rather than providing information à la *Lonely Planet*, Wikipedia, or via other narrative elements, the notion of travelling itself becomes the experience that is shared and interacted with. In the same way as graphical editing works, *Viewfinders* connects locations with other travelling shots that users or, rather, peer-creators decided to upload. Mobile devices and smartphone affordances engender mobility and a specific form of interactivity. "Smartphones as nodes in networked media have illustrated how local networks and visual communication structures are shaped and co-produced" (Schleser et al. 2018, 2). Co-production and co-creation are at the heart of the *Viewfinders* AR app as it augments the travel experience. While AR in its earlier version was a closed system, *Viewfinders* opens it up towards allowing users not only to be consumers but also to be contributors of the content. The project is by creatives for creatives that appreciate travel films and smartphone filmmaking. As a creative arts research project, it explores the intersection of immersive media and travel films, and addresses documentary issues beyond medium specific distinctions. Moreover, as creatives/researchers we are working within the liminal space known as "practiced-based-research" or "research-creation," as it is referred to in Canada (Cammaer, Fitzpatrick, Lessard 2018, 6). The project is thus collaborative on different levels and in multiple ways: first, the research team is international (Canada, Australia, New Zealand/Aotearoa) and interdisciplinary (documentary studies, mobile media, filmmaking, and interactive design); second, we worked together with peers – fellow mobile filmmakers, who were asked to contribute travelling shots and were asked for feedback and suggestions; and, last, as the project is launched on a larger scale, anyone with a smartphone will be able to contribute and help to further develop it as co-authors, editors, and observers of the work.

Beyond Story and towards Relational Assemblage

As a work of non-fiction about travelling and landscapes – particularly their relation to smartphones, technology, and form – *Viewfinders* "do[es] not concern [itself] so much with representing life-worlds as with issuing forth novel reverberations" (Vannini 2015, 12). In the context of AR, *Viewfinders* blurs the notion of digital and spatial travel experiences as a form of expanded cinema and puts to the test the possibility of making an interactive doc that is not about storytelling but about offering an opportunity to experience travelling landscapes in a way that allows us to be immersed in the real world and not in a (pre-constructed) story about the real world. Adrian Miles (2108, 301) rightfully observes how interactive documentary found itself caught by the narratological assumptions that underwrite many film and documentary studies: "These narratological assumptions rely, implicitly or explicitly, on the necessary presence of a story that audiences are then invited to interpret to understand in some way." But interactive documentary can do something different, particularly when one takes into account that new media, the technical substrate for interactive documentary, is not linear and sequential like film or video. As Manovich (2001, 218) argued two decades ago: "many new media objects do not tell stories; they do not have a beginning or end; in fact, they do not have any development, thematically, formally, or otherwise that would organize their elements into a sequence. Instead, they are collections of individual items, with every item possessing the same significance as any other." Miles (2018) turns to Bruno Latour's actor-network theory (ANT) to study the structure of interactive documentary from a different angle (see Fox, chapter 8, this volume). This is a logical choice as the interactive documentary, seen from the point-of-view of ANT, is a collection of things and relations that can describe the world without recourse to story or narrative. For ANT, the entire world is made up of things that are constituted by, and rely upon, their relations. As Miles explains:

> When we recognize multilinear interactive documentaries to be in themselves socio-technical assemblages that express actor-networks, then it is simple to see that these affordances mean we no longer

> need to rely on story as the architectural or epistemological backbone for non-fiction. Rather, we can seek emergence, autopoiesis, and productive and elegantly entangled relations. Therefore, when designed and performed as a socio-technical machine, that is as an actor-network, interactive documentary is a relational assemblage, which does not need to rely upon our species' bias for story and representation, yet can still do the work of nonfiction as it seeks an isomorphic intimacy between machines, media, form, and epistemology through their respective performance. (Miles et al. 2018, 315)

Following Miles's argument that multilinear and interactive media can do other things in relation to non-fiction that addresses the world, with *Viewfinders* we are exploring the possibilities of creating a "relational assemblage" of landscapes travelled, travelling shots of landscapes, and travellers, and what this can do to create a real-life experience for the viewers. For example, what does it do to someone filming Pukurua Bay in New Zealand from a driving car to have the AR app connect this view to a similar shot of the coast of Lichnos, Greece, followed by Saint-Girons beach in France, also shot from a driving car, and even a shot of Lake Ontario in winter shot from a train window? What if that same shot of Pukurua Bay filmed by a traveller is linked by choosing specific geographical entry points with a shot of the same bay filmed at a different place and time, or even a shot of entering Wellington station by train? (Both examples described here can be viewed as part of the promo video for *Viewfinders* on Vimeo, online 2018). The app allows viewers to alter the relationships between the different shots by choosing different tags (e.g., day/night, mode of transport, sky, water, busy/calm, etc.) and obviously also by what they are filming and what the app recognizes in the shot (thanks to the image recognition software Google Cloud Vision API). The app thus "assembles" different relationships between the various travelling shots and creates an "on-the-spot" ludic montage that is not meant to "explain" reality but, rather, to see it as a combination and interaction of elements – in this case, landscapes – or, as Corrigan (2011, 105) would call it, "a constantly shifting elsewhere." Although our goal is to create a greater geographical awareness and imagination, the AR app was developed as blue-sky research to speculate on creative futures and for an engagement with the world based on peer participation, a playful experiment in relational assemblage. Similar to ludic interface design, the montage aesthetic that we created

Figure 4.2
Image of *Viewfinders* AR app

is playful as it stimulates self-motivated exploration based on curiosity and wonder. This is why the term "ludic montage" is used to describe the experience embedded in both the collaborative creation and the viewing experience of *Viewfinders.*

Viewfinders: Creative and Futuristic Visions

While a number of applications, such as Wikitude and Layar, display the potential for the commercial application, the development towards story making illustrates how mobile devices and smartphones are embedded in storytelling approaches to engage peer groups of interested participants. While geography can impose borders on communities, we see the *Viewfinders* app bringing interested participants together to create a joined experience that is not a typical linear narrative but more of a joined graphical editing exercise based on the formal qualities of the shots (as stated earlier, more in the tradition of experimental filmmaking than that of typical travelogues). Through the website (online 2017) participants can upload travelling shots to an online database. The AR app uses the Cloud

Vision API by Google (online 2018) and identifies various characteristic qualities of these moving-images, such as dominant colours and direction of movement, to blend a video from the database with the experienced travelling shots. The research team understands the idealistic vision of this project and that a number of critical responses can be formulated in response to it. As creative arts researchers and experimental filmmakers we focused on abstract qualities to investigate the process that led towards hybrid journeys. We are more interested in what *Viewfinders* does with the viewer than in what it represents to them, what the viewer experiences rather than what he or she "understands" or what it means to them. The smartphone became a key part of the research project as the AR app only works once one is on the move. The idea of being transient, nomadic, and constantly moving proposed here is a direct reference to the Deleuzian concept of line of flight (Deleuze and Guattari 1980) as much as to the basics of expanded cinema. The project is based on a kind of feedback and interconnectedness that is not possible in conventional cinema. "The viewer is forced to create along with the film, to interpret for himself what he is experiencing" (Youngblood 1970, 65).

In order to experience or engage with an AR project, one needs a smartphone, a tablet, a wearable computer or pair of see-through digital glasses. We chose to focus on AR experiences that are accessible on iOS or Android platforms via smartphones or tablets rather than on Microsoft's AR headset HoloLens, Magic Leap, or similar devices. With the launch of Apple's AR kit (2017), developments by Adobe with the Project Aero (2019) and a number of other commercial applications such as Wikitude or Layer, this new technical hardware and software infrastructure provide interesting opportunities for creating new forms of documentary beyond traditional storytelling. Documentaries engage with the world. This normally happened in the cinema as a dedicated screening space. Over the last century, stories moved from the big screen towards smaller screens with TVs in the 1960s, desktop computers in the 1990s, and now mobile screens in the last decade. Images can now interact with the world. In order to explore participatory modalities (Zimmermann and De Michiel 2018) and developments towards story-living (online 2018), *Viewfinders* developed from an online curation platform (www.viewfinders.org) to an AR app. The *Viewfinders* research team explored a number of options (Rubery 2018 online) and opted for Google Cloud Vision API. The AR app overlays the travelling shots from peer-generated content. In the end, the *Viewfinders* AR project launched

Figure 4.3
Overview of *Viewfinders*

in 2018 and, at the time of writing, remains available for Android devices as a working prototype.

The *Viewfinders* app is an example of Helen Papagiannis's (2017, 7) definition of AR as a digital overlay on top of the real world, consisting of computer graphics and video, which is interactive in real-time, and basically embraces "a new mode of hybrid physicality and virtuality." Rather than focusing on generating a notion of reality that is obliged to "truth," *Viewfinders* is expanding or "augmenting" reality, specifically the experience of being on the move. While AR is not new, its accessibility via smartphone provides new opportunities to engage audiences. Taking this to the next level, we define audiences as co-creators and explore the concept of peer-co-production or co-creation. This development towards using peer content is influenced by social media. Rather than working for a typical broadcast mass audience, our method engages more equal connections and creates opportunities to make new connections. By means of overlaying different travel shots we are connecting the world through abstract parameters of the image and we use the smartphone as a sensor to augment perception. Writing in "Mobile AR – Creating Augmented

Experiences," Schleser and David (2013) argue for a greater consideration of user contributions to AR projects and point at the potential of open AR experiences: "Mobile devices are ubiquitous and it looks like they will not disappear for a while. MAR (mobile AR) can demonstrate prospects to unlock the potential of mobile media and amplify the digital experience of places and by these means broaden the shaping and understanding of them differently. A consideration for implementing the Web 2.0 community aspect into MAR could advance these notions even further."

Canadian Context: Creative Innovation at the Intersection of Creative Arts Research and Documentary Filmmaking

Viewfinders was funded by a Creative Fund Grant at Toronto Metropolitan University as part of a larger research project titled *Travelling Shots* within the Documentary Media Research Centre in the School of Image Arts (online 2018). Canadian universities support creative arts research and encourage projects that blur traditional division lines between moving image arts, storytelling, emerging media, and the creative industries. In order to demonstrate the developments in the last decade from web browser to mobile browser and/or app, one can point to several interesting projects created within the competitive context of Canadian university research funding and some of the ground-breaking work done at the National Film Board of Canada.

It is interesting to note the developments within the past decade that changed one's understanding of AR from a predominantly desktop-based experience to one of mobile story making. A comparison between *Viewfinders* and *SnapDragonAR* illustrates this. *SnapDragonAR* was developed by the Augmented Reality Lab at York University in 2011. The project was developed for non-programmers to create AR videos on Mac computers and a webcam via markers. A more contemporary approach would probably adopt the Merge Cube or HP reveal (formerly Assana), which makes the creation of mobile AR projects feasible for storytellers without any coding knowledge. With the launch of apps, the way that citizen users and creative professionals represent, experience, and share the everyday is changing (Berry and Schleser 2014). A great example of this is the NFB interactive documentary *Barcode* (2011), which "playfully disrupts the routine, inviting users to engage with familiar objects – and to see them in a whole new light."

The story platform hosts one hundred short films that offer insight into how we use everyday objects and simultaneously reveal something about us, the users. While the barcode or product code (UPC) dates back to the 1970s (Bryan 2011), this project demonstrates how barcodes and other existing commercial applications can be effectively used in creative documentary projects. Not unlike the development of text messaging from an engineering technical message system to the delivery of personal micro-narratives, or mobile camera phones from a marketing strategy to a filmmaking tool, AR in all of its technical facets and forms has the potential to shape new spaces and experiences.

It is interesting to note that the NFB website's interactive section features distinct categories: web experiences, apps, installations, virtual reality, and social media. While these categories are of course overlapping, and within a transmedia environment the boundaries between these media experiences are fluid, they point to some conceptual choices for types of browsers or apps. Responsive websites will make a seamless transition between any device choice, but for video/moving-image content the context might be quite relevant with regard to aspect ratio (i.e., 16:9 or 1:1) and framing (i.e., vertical video or standard, cinematic, horizontal format). An app maintains viewers within one experience, very much like a TV channel. While one can change between apps and/or TV shows, the content is framed as one particular experience. The affordances of a website or mobile website are rather to link to other content and expand this through hyperlinks to other videos or "rich media" content.

For example, while *Barcode* uses everyday objects as touch-points and triggers interactions with these objects as gateways to story worlds, *The Enemy* brings story worlds into the environment where one uses the app. Specifically, *The Enemy* AR app (Karim Ben Khelifa, 2017) brings characters from conflict zones to "your" environment and situates the user in the centre of the experience by interacting with these avatars. By moving the smartphone and thus one's body towards an opposing position, one engages in their story world as it merges with one's own environment. As such, if you explore the project in your living room, you can have a face-to-face experience with people of three different conflict zones – El Salvador, the Democratic Republic of the Congo, or Israel and Palestine – from the comfort of a domestic space. In this way, it conjures the televisual experience of witnessing dangerous footage without the consequence of physical danger (and, importantly, without any opportunities to intervene and effect change). In contrast, in order for the *Viewfinders* project to be successful, the activity of being out and about is a necessary component of the viewing experience.

All three projects augment reality with complex story environments. The digital layer thus creates new connections and expands on one's engagement with the real world. As a result, one is presented with a new frame within the world and of the world. One of the changing conditions of storytelling is described by Alexander Bryan (2011) writing about the project *[murmur]* as a way to develop "a new intimacy with places." This particular Canadian project makes audio files available to urban explorers via signs that participants or, rather, listeners call into. The *[murmur]* project ran from 2003 to 2008 and effectively demonstrated audio as another widely accessible tool for expanding documentary experiences through mobile phones; the project website explains that "the stories are as personal as the relationship people have with the spaces they inhabit. Secret histories are unearthed, private truths unveiled and tales as diverse as the city itself are discovered and shared. All members of a community are encouraged to participate and contribute." *Viewfinders* similarly creates a new intimacy with spaces, albeit by offering images and new combinations of images as something to experience rather than by stories.

According to Papagiannis, we are entering the second wave of AR, which she calls the "Entryway." In order to fully understand the immersive qualities that Papagiannis describes as new sensory awareness and heightened interaction with our world, we need to ensure that we let experimental work drive the conceptual understanding or, otherwise, makers, creatives, and producers might constrain the interactive documentary to satisfy more commercial aims. As with many technological innovations, there seems to be certain phases in their development and situations when the markets and consumers are ready (or not) to engage with new tools and technology on a large scale. While Google Glasses never really took off, there is now widespread anticipation for Magic Leap and other AR glasses. The Consumer Electronics Show in Las Vegas in 2019 revealed the massive investment in this technology, with the showcase of eyewear including Focals by North, Vuzix Blade, nReal, Realmax, Dreamglass, Aurora AR Glasses, Third Eye Enterprise, Digilens, and Lumus; simulated reality displays such as Dimenco SR; and 3D display project holograms such as

Hypervsn. But while we see new commercially driven investments in this technology, more experimental projects will always be required to break new ground and to develop a deeper understanding of the future of these formats as well as to further explore their potential as tools for creative and expanded forms of documentary.

Conclusion

Using the *Viewfinders* project as a practical case study, what we propose here is to define "interactive documentary" in the broadest possible way by building on the basic notions of expanded cinema and by using the dictionary definition of "interaction": a reciprocal action or influence, a form of communication or direct involvement with someone or something. Although technology played an important role in the development and creation of the project, the emphasis of the project is on creating a meaningful experience for the viewer. While many i-docs allow the user to modify their journey through the documentary material in response to carefully plotted prompts, with the *Viewfinders* app peer-participants are able to create their own journey and the documentary by submitting their own travelling shots and/or combining shots themselves, editing reality by (and while) interacting with it. The research team comprising Gerda Cammaer, Phillip Rubery, and Max Schleser is aware that *Viewfinders* as a creative arts research project is following a vision that colleagues might consider to be a mobile utopia. But we feel strengthened by the ideas of documentary scholar Adrian Miles, who argues for interactive documentary as a form of relational media that is less about telling a story than it is about preforming the world critically. Through demonstrating alternative applications of AR and exploring what is possible with imaginative interpretations and augmentations, the team behind *Viewfinders* hopes to contribute to developments at the intersection of creative arts, documentary and experimental film, and a more comprehensive understanding of interactive documentary in particular.

References

Berry, Marsha, and Max Schleser. 2014. "Creative Mobile Media: The State of Play." In *Mobile Media Making in an Age of Smartphones*, ed. Marsha Berry and Max Schleser, 1–9. New York: Palgrave Pivot.

Bryan, Alexander. 2011. *The New Digital Storytelling: Creating Narratives with New Media*. Santa Barbara: Praeger.

Cammaer, Gerda. 2015. "Sharing Mobile, Portable and Personal Travel Stories," *Journal of Creative Technologies* 5 (November). https://ctechjournal.aut.ac.nz/paper/sharing-mobile-portable-and-personal-travel-stories.

Cammaer, Gerda, Blake Fitzpatrick, and Bruno Lessard, eds. 2018. *Critical Distance in Documentary Media*. London: Palgrave Macmillan.

Cammaer, Gerda, and Max Schleser. 2018. "*Viewfinders*: A Collaborative Travel Film Project." In *Docuverse: Approaches to Expanding Documentary*, ed. Hannah Brasier, Nicholas Hansen, Kim Munro, and Franziska Weidle, online. https://zenodo.org/record/1211520#.XErBJM9KjOQ.

Corrigan, Timothy. 2011. *The Essay Film: From Montaigne after Marker*. New York: Oxford.

Deleuze, Gilles, and Felix Guattari. (1980) 2004. *A Thousand Plateaus*. Trans. Brian Massumi. London and New York: Continuum.

Manovich, Lev. 2001. *The Language of New Media*. Cambridge: MIT Press.

Miles, Adrian, Bruno Lessard, Hannah Brasier, Franziska Weidle. 2018. "From Critical Distance to Critical Intimacy: Interactive Documentary and Relational Media." In *Critical Distance in Documentary Media*, ed. G. Cammaer, B. Fitzpatrick, and B. Lessard, 301–19. London: Palgrave Macmillan.

Orgeron, Devin. 2006. "Mobile Home Movies: Travel and le Politique des Amateurs." *The Moving Image* 6 (2): 74–100.

Papagiannis, Helen. 2017. *Augmented Human: How Technology Is Shaping the New Reality*. O'Relly: Boston.

Schleser, Max, and Marsha Berry. 2018. "Creative Mobile Media II: Making a Difference." In *Mobile Media Making in an Age of Smartphones*, ed. Marsha Berry and Max Schleser, London: Palgrave Macmillan. https://doi.org/10.1007/978-3-319-76795-6_1.

Schleser, Max, and Gaby David. 2013. "Mobile AR: Creating Augmented Experiences." *Anti-podes Design Journal* 2 (August): 35–45.

Vannini, Phillip. 2015. "Non-Representational Research Methodologies: An Introduction." In *Non-Representational Methodologies: Re-Envisioning Research*, ed. Phillip Vannini, 1–18. New York: Routledge.

Youngblood, Gene. 1970. *Expanded Cinema*. E.P. Dutton: Boston.

Zimmermann, Patricia, and Helen De Michiel. 2018. *Open Space New Media Documentary*. Routledge: London.

5

ALWAYS ALREADY OLD

LOOKING BACK WITH THE KORSAKOW SYSTEM

Matt Soar and Monika Kin Gagnon

Introduction

It is now over twenty years since the Korsakow System software was first made available as a free download by its creator, Florian Thalhofer (Soar 2014). Korsakow is a deceptively simple piece of low-cost software with which users create interactive, non-linear films, without the need for programming skills. Usually comprising dozens of very short video clips or SNUs (smallest narrative units), these browser-based films are built using just two types of keywords: IN and OUT. An IN keyword describes the SNU to which it is attached; the SNU's corresponding OUT keyword searches for the matching IN keyword of any other available SNUs. Korsakow films are thereby algorithmic, database-driven narratives. This distinguishes them from almost every other kind of interactive narrative: unlike k-films, the vast majority of interactive narratives rely on *fixed* paths. (The most obvious "tell" in identifying fixed-path non-linear narratives is their dependence on incorporating a menu or "home" button so that the viewer can retrace their steps, especially when they reach the terminus of a particular path, in other words, a dead end.)

There are numerous rich descriptions of Korsakow offered by scholars and researcher-creators. The late Adrian Miles (2014b, 209), for example, notes that "Korsakow is software for authoring generative, associative, and processual films. These films are complex, possibly autopoetic systems that rely on patterns of relation to emerge for author and users." More recently, Anna Wiehl (2018, 33) underscores its algorithmic qualities: "Korsakow documentaries are generative, interactive, computational, database documentaries which follow the 'logic' of nonlinearity: in contrast to most plurilinear (yet still plotted) documentaries, Korsakow relies on an asymmetry of keywords of its narrative units (in general, short video clips) and complex algorithms of probabilities which determine the narrative units that are presented to the user-interactor. As such, both the author and the user-interactor have to relinquish control to the Korsakow system."

In this chapter, we revisit a significant period in the development of Korsakow to demonstrate how this software has quietly made a unique contribution to the brief histories of non-linear documentary in Canada.[1] We explore some of its distinctive qualities in relation to historical cinematic events – algorithmic procedures through keywords, spatial montage – and highlight particular Korsakow films through the words of their makers. We therefore emphasize how, during this time, Korsakow prompted scholars and researcher-creators to develop a uniquely generative vocabulary – patternmaking, pinchpoints, polyvocality, soft video, sketch film, database diary – that has arisen through a richly eclectic range of media-making contexts and projects. Addressing at least some of these neologisms, we argue that they collectively challenge narrow definitions of the documentary enterprise. We conclude by offering a selective mediography for readers' further exploration.

Academic Contexts

Between 2008 and 2016, Gagnon and Soar collaborated on a team-based research-creation project investigating digital non-linear storytelling, in association with established filmmakers and graduate students. This project was initially called the Concordia Interactive Narrative Experimentation and Research Group (CINER-G, as in "synergy"; supported by a Fonds de recherche du Québec grant) and, latterly, Adventures in Research-Creation (ARC; supported by a Social Sciences and Humanities Research Council of Canada grant). During this time, we generated a range of interrelated outcomes, most significantly, perhaps, our complete overhaul of the Korsakow System itself, in close collaboration with its inventor, Berlin-based artist and documentary filmmaker Florian Thalhofer, and gifted programmer David Reisch. This was augmented by ongoing feature development, networking, and user support, including extensive Korsakow documentation: a Quick Start guide, FAQ, Software Manual, Tips and Tricks, and short tutorial videos. Members of the team conducted interviews with scholars, teachers, and filmmakers, and contributed to multiple conference presentations, panels, and screenings, while Soar led dozens of associated workshops chiefly in Canada but also in the United States, Italy, and Australia.

A capstone event was our hosting of seventy participants for Database/Narrative/Archive: An International Symposium on Digital Nonlinear Storytelling (Montreal, 2011),[2] which led directly to scholarly publications, including *Database/Narrative/Archive: An Anthology of Seven Interactive Essays on Digital Nonlinear Storytelling* (Soar and Gagnon 2013). Several substantial Korsakow films were created by our collaborators – Philip Hoffman and the late Marian McMahon (*Racing Home*, 2014) and Midi Onodera (*My 8 Days as a War Artist*, 2017) – and thesis films by graduate students at Concordia. Our own films included *Archiving R69* (Gagnon, 2009), *Ceci N'est Pas Embres* (Soar, 2012), *Fibonacci Korsakow* (Soar, 2013), and *Les Enseignistes de Montréal/The Signmakers of Montreal* (Soar, 2019). These "k-films" were grounded in a fulsome "thinking + making" approach to critical inquiry formally identified in Canada as research-creation.

We were continually impressed with the quality of films being made by Korsakow users outside our team, some of whom had attended our workshops, others of whom simply sent us a link to their new film after it had been built with the redesigned software and published online. Themes included drag king communities in Los Angeles (Mayahara, 2013), the lives of queer refugee youth in Montreal (Miller et al., 2011), contemporary life in a First Nation in Canada's North (Radu, 2017), and the threat posed to local craft vendors in Brazil by cheap imports (Francischelli, 2013).

The time period covered by the CINER-G and ARC/DNA projects coincided with a burgeoning Canadian and international ecology of nonlinear documentary filmmaking. This was enabled by a number of fateful developments, such as the increased ease-of-use of software, evolving open web standards such as the nascent promise of HTML5, accelerated web-streaming (both in terms of speed and quality) in suburban and urban areas, advances in portable camera technology, the new proliferation of mobile screens, and stagnating funding for theatrical documentary projects. Here we describe two contrasting strands of this complex, turbulent ecology, beginning with the extraordinary flowering of new, technologically

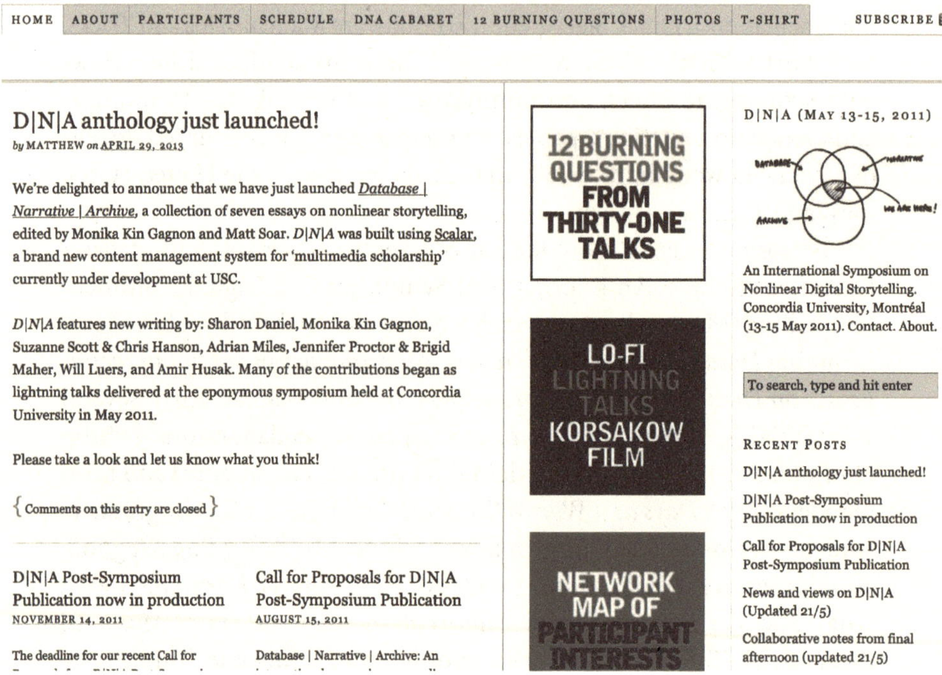

Figure 5.1
Website for the Database Narrative Archive Symposium

precocious "blockbuster" web docs (referred to by Adrian Miles as "Encarta model" projects). Most of these projects, such as the extraordinary non-linear oeuvre of Kat Cizek, NFB filmmaker-in-residence from 2008 to 2016, were entirely custom-designed and built with proprietary software libraries and tools, some with budgets on the order of six figures. Sadly, many of these works (and, indeed, unconverted Korsakow projects published prior to 2016) are now very difficult to view (and were only ever patchily playable on iPads) due to their reliance on Adobe Flash Player, a discontinued, formerly ubiquitous browser plugin associated with Adobe Flash software program (see Keyes and Robbins, chapter 3, this volume).

The second strand we identify in this ecology has been typified by low- and no-budget creators, relying largely on an ever-changing hodgepodge of free and low-cost software applications designed primarily for use by non-specialists. Prominent among these have been: 3W Doc (now defunct), Djehouti (superseded by RacontR), Klynt (no updates since 2018; website is now promoting Wonda VR), Storyplanet (now defunct), and Zeega (became GoPop; now defunct) (cf. Soar 2014). Thalhofer, meanwhile, released Version 6 of Korsakow in 2016 and switched to a pay model. While Klynt and Korsakow were by this point fully HTML5-compliant, films produced with either software still don't generally play well on mobile devices, inevitably limiting their appeal to makers and audiences alike.

A Prehistory of Non-Linear Narratives

For over twenty years, Korsakow films have been nothing more nor less than purposely minimalist exercises in spatial montage and algorithmic storytelling, most often created by individuals or communities with severely limited resources. In some senses, and with the benefit of hindsight, it may be that Korsakow films in particular have more in common with earlier, analogue media arts practices than with the recent historical moment of digital web doc production and consumption, referred to in this collection and elsewhere as "i-docs." In other words, *always already old*, to invert Gitelman's (2006) maxim in the title of her book *Always Already New* (itself adapted from the work of Stuart Hall and others in the development of critical cultural studies). It is therefore vital that we not treat Korsakow simply as yet another *digital* outcome of the "computerization of culture" (Manovich 2001, 32).

In December 2018, Netflix launched *Black Mirror: Bandersnatch*, its first interactive television show for adults (Roettgers 2018). Netflix was promptly sued for trademark infringement by Chooseco LLC, owner of the Choose Your Own Adventure brand of gamebooks (Jancelewicz 2019). The narrative principle underlying both of these media properties is not new, however. Argentinian author Julio Cortazar's book *Hopscotch* (1966; originally published in 1963 in Spanish as *Rayuela*), for example, is composed of 155 short chapters. Ninety-nine of them, he states, may be ignored "with a clean conscience." Cortazar calls this the first "book" ("of many") to be found in this single publication, and the "Table of Instructions" then describes a second "book" that can be read by beginning with chapter 73 and following the sequence indicated at the end of each chapter.

Kinoautomat (1967) by Czech filmmaker Raduz Cincera is often identified as the first interactive film (Huhtamo 2007). Presented in the Czech Pavilion at Expo '67 in Montreal (and occasionally confused with *Laterna Magika* and *Diapolyécran* in the same pavilion), *Kinoautomat* was presented in a custom-made theatre with seats built with "voting machines," wherein viewers could decide on the film's plot progression by pressing on a red or green button (another early example of "choosing one's own adventure," at least in aggregate, from the same era as Cortazar's *Hopscotch*). During successive breaks between screened segments, a live actor would comment on the narrative in the film and then invite the viewing audience to vote: the projectionist would apparently assess each ballot in order to select the next section of the film to be screened. (In this light, it is worth noting that Korsakow's inventor, Florian Thalhofer, has been experimenting for years with laser pointers, one per audience member, to advance his k-films, based on the greatest concentration of red dots on the previews visible on the theatre screen. As the "projectionist," Thalhofer stands at the lectern, counting dots over his shoulder and advancing the film via his laptop cursor.)

The Labyrinth Project began in 1997 under the direction of Professor Marsha Kinder at the University of Southern California. It marks a key contribution to the production and exploration of interactive narratives using digital technologies. Working in tandem with distinguished artists, the Labyrinth Project produced complex, sophisticated, exquisitely designed interactive narratives incorporating video, sound, text, and images (see Hight 2017, 88). Its work was a key inspiration for CINER-G: one of our first steps was to acquire most of the Labyrinth Project's back catalogue, all of it on CD-ROM or DVD-ROM. Alas, even as we received these works on disk, some of them wouldn't play properly due to incompatibilities with then-current operating systems. ("New" media, indeed.)

This is all to say that interest in, and the production of, interactive media has a long history. Indeed, media historian William Uricchio (2017, 191) invites us to rethink interactivity in film, suggesting that "continuities reveal long-term sites of fascination." The eighteenth-century panorama, twentieth-century stereoscope, twenty-first century 3D film, and Oculus Rift VR all reveal an ongoing fascination for immersion, for "being-there," invoking a tension between re-presentation and evocation/experience.

History also invites us to sort out disjunctures. As Uricchio (2017, 192) argues, algorithms radically reorder the binaries of maker and artefact, artefact and viewer. Algorithmic story generators introduce a third procedural programming element into the binary of a creator/user, he writes, introducing dramatic shifts (of author, argument, text) into our encounters with representation (201). It is here that we include "point-and-click" Korsakow films, not only because they now have the capacity to “link out” to other online media content but also because they introduce an element of purposeful *chance* (not to be conflated with *randomness*). Algorithmic editing forces the author-maker to relinquish *some* control over narrative sequencing and direction. Provocatively, Uricchio writes that “the reordering of the concept of agency common to these future systems does not fit easily with the notion of the subject as it has developed in the West since the fifteenth century” (203).

Technical and Aesthetic Characteristics of K-Films

What most i-docs have in common is that they are built on the premise of fixed paths. This is neatly captured in the book-cover design of Judith Aston, Sandra Gaudenzi, and Mandy Rose’s *I-Docs: The Evolving Practices of Interactive Documentary* (2017), which features an image of multiple, dividing train tracks. To roll with the metaphor, a railway system comprised, as it is, of fixed routes, will never lead a train somewhere unexpected, somewhere other than its prescribed destination, passing through (if not stopping at) each station, in strict sequence. In other words, in a fixed-path i-doc the choices available to the reader/viewer will always be the same with every encounter. In contrast, Korsakow films are database driven, meaning the content unfolds dynamically. (Other non-Korsakow examples exist, of course: Manovich and Kratky’s installation and DVD-ROM *Soft Cinema*; Canadian artist Stan Douglas’s film installation *Klaatsassin* [2006]; the Danish film *Switching* [2003], also distributed on DVD-ROM.)

The affordances of the Korsakow approach to designing and assembling a film – adding purposeful metadata (keywords) to a collection of pre-prepared media assets – are such that one could very easily (albeit pointlessly) assemble an entirely linear film in which each keyword is used only twice: once as an OUT keyword and once as an IN keyword, creating a singular chain of associations (or train stations). Similarly, one could also quickly put together an entirely random film (i.e., use one keyword for absolutely everything and give every SNU infinite lives). Neither option is desirable, of course. The point is that Thalhofer’s profound insight, manifested through his software, allows Korsakow filmmakers to explore *a truly vast range of possibilities between complete linearity and complete randomness,* even within a single film.

It must also be said that interactivity has never been the single defining feature of Korsakow films, hence our ongoing ambivalence about the term "i-doc." Miles and Hannah Brasier (2018a; 2018b) argue for the importance of the term "soft video" in the context of understanding web docs and, we believe, Korsakow films in particular. Note that this is distinct from Lev Manovich's "soft cinema" project, defined at the intersections of database software, cinema, and architecture (Manovich and Kratky 2005). Brasier (2018a, 16) defines "soft video" as follows: "I consider 'soft' to be an appropriate term to describe these works because there are variable degrees of pliable indeterminacy about what relations can take place between discrete audiovisual elements. A project is soft when new versions of the project can be made temporarily through each and every user interaction."

In her especially resonant consideration of Korsakow in the context of Marian McMahon and Philip Hoffman's k-film *Racing Home*, Anna Wiehl (2018, 34) favours the term "polyvocality" to highlight the unique affordances of Korsakow: "A central issue is the question of how far specific modes of editing in Korsakow affect the overall experience for both the authoring instances and the user-interactor. What role do polyvocality and algorithmic editing play? Furthermore, given Korsakow's specific embrace of contingency and its probing of non-linear narratives, the question arises whether configurations like *Racing Home* are more a methodology to explore complex matters of concern than a tool to present ready-at-hand answers." In this sense, the term "interactive" is too limiting. It may pinpoint a specific kind of user-film relationship, but it does not fully capture the fluidity, contingency, and openness at the heart of "soft videos" like those produced using the Korsakow software.

Another core quality of Korsakow films relates to their intrinsic embrace of "spatial montage" (Manovich 2001); in short, the deployment of *multiple frames within a single computer screen*. Spatial montage challenges common conceptions of film as a purely temporal experience structured by editing techniques that sequence images in time on a single screen/frame. Instead, it introduces a simultaneity of multiple images that each user will engage uniquely as their eyes scan multiple frames. In an uncanny evocation of the visual presentation of Korsakow films, Manovich describes the ways in which spatial montage "could involve a number of images, potentially of different sizes and proportions, appearing on the screen at the same time" (322). If Manovich emphasizes the computer screen, he does recognize some antecedents in the histories of cinema, including Abel Gance's *Napoleon* (1927) (created with six screens but presented with three), the film installations and projections of Stan VanDerBeek, and "the 'expanded' cinema movement of the 1960s" (271), such as an installation in the Czech Pavilion at Expo '67. This productively opens up a far broader context with which spatial montage might be productively engaged and mobilized in order to understand current media forms. To follow Uricchio, this would also lend continuity with other innovative film installations, for instance those at Expo '67 or the work of numerous filmmakers and video artists who have created multi-channel works over many decades, such as Nam June Paik's and Mike Macdonald's early video installations.

Indeed, film theorist Christine Sprengler (2014, 91) understands spatial montage beyond a single screen and in different material forms of film installation, for "what constitutes a frame … can be subject to a range of interpretation." Spatial montage, she continues, "may describe the edge of a screen onto which multiple images are projected. It may also describe the outermost edges of a series of monitors stacked on top of one another or placed in a row. It may even describe the physical limits of an installation" (ibid.). The National Film Board of Canada's multi-chamber, multi-screen *Labyrinth* (1967); Christopher Chapman's *A Place to Stand* (1967), which incorporated multiple smaller frames within a 70mm format; the Telephone Pavilion's nine-screen *Canada 67* (1967), created with Disney Circlevision (Gagnon 2014a); and IMAX co-inventor Graeme Ferguson's *Polar Life* (1967), which comprised a rotating audience surrounded by eleven screens (Gagnon 2019), all offer spectacular examples of spatial montage, suggesting an abiding fascination with the extraordinary creative possibilities of expanded cinema also achievable in Korsakow filmmaking.

Films Made in Korsakow

It is within this context of cinematic experimentation that the specific affordances of Korsakow can be effectively highlighted. This section provides an overview of a few notable Korsakow projects illustrating the participation, fragmentation, and contingency at the root of this software. These projects help us to think further about how to categorize k-films, a consideration which itself raises questions about the role of story in documentary and the ever-present conundrum of exhibition.

Fittingly, the most adventurous Korsakow films, in terms of project scale, conceptual sophistication, and visual innovation, are, without doubt, those of its inventor, Florian Thalhofer. *Planet Galata: A Bridge in Istanbul* (with Berke Baş 2010) and *Money and the Greeks* (2012), in particular, make rich use of the software's affordances. For example, the works offer audiences a hundred or more SNUs in each film, a great deal of visual variety in terms of spatial montage, and nuanced keywording. Additionally, they feature a heightened attention to graphic design (including the selection and arrangement of type, lettering, images, and text; the use of a thoughtful colour palette; an appreciation of scale and proportion) and usability (the logic of menus, buttons, rollovers, and information hierarchy).

In fact, Seth Keen (2014; 2018) has developed the concept of the "documentary designer," a role he distinguishes from a documentary maker due to their reliance on a "collaborative process of investigating suitable solutions relative to the particular requirements of each project" (Keen 2018, 65). As a provocation to illuminate his argument, Keen offers twenty-one propositions, including: appreciating the instability and ephemerality of web docs, understanding granularity, working iteratively, prototyping, and using sketches – all of which are routinely invoked both in Soar's Korsakow workshops and in the work of CINER-G/ARC.

Thalhofer's *Money and the Greeks*, made in collaboration with his life partner Elissavet Aggou and which explores the interminable, national economic crisis in Greece, is not only emblematic of the key role collaboration plays in the design of the work but also of the way in which participation has been embraced by Thalhofer within and beyond the film per se. As Soar (2013) has previously noted, *Money and the Greeks* "includes several innovations, including a community-oriented process for viewing and voting on potential SNUs. There are also several outcomes, including interactive installations, an online Korsakow film, and a Korsakow Show involving a panel of experts and a studio audience." The live "show" *Was ist. Geld.gr* was staged in Athens 2012 and is indicative of the eclectic ways in which Korsakow has been deployed beyond the confines of the screen. Of the participatory nature of his Korsakow Shows, Thalhofer explains: "In today's media it is all about having a competition between different opinions to find the winner, as if this winner then knows what to do. We all have to participate, listen and share and take some of the responsibility. I try to use computers to visualize and enable us to understand multiple realities. In this endeavor the brains of the people are of crucial importance. I don't want an audience that shuts up and listens. I want an audience that participates in the thinking process" (quoted in Soar 2013).

Figure 5.2
Screengrab from *Racing Home*

Regarding our own work, several k-films were created within the context of our research-creation group ARC, including works made by seasoned Toronto filmmakers Midi Onodera and Philip Hoffman, both of whom were invited to experiment with the platform. Their works exemplify the ways in which Korsakow can be put to use to express those aspects of reality that defy a linear narrative arc. In 2006, and again in 2007, Onodera created a series of 365 short online movies entitled *A Movie a Day*. Posted and hosted on her website, midionodera.com, these were followed by numerous other "calendar" films. In *My 8 Days as a War Artist* (2017), Onodera used Korsakow to assemble the various "fragments of footage, scores of digital files, a missing notebook, and excuses preventing me from making sense of the stories" that constituted her experiences in the official Canadian "War Artist" program. She was stationed at Camp Mirage in the United Arab Emirates, with a brief foray out to Kandahar, Afghanistan, in 2010. Onodera brought this material to ARC in order to make sense of her journey, through remembering, imagining, and the "unknown," as described in her opening SNU. Organized under the themes "Things I Don't Know," "Things That I Imagine," and "Things That I Remember," Onodera gathered and sifted fragments of still and moving images through her voice-over recollections. Her original proposal consisted of documenting the "domestic aspects of war," including meeting with cooks and cleaners. She discovered that these workers were civilians hired by the private engineering and construction company SNC-Lavalin. Further, she was given only restricted access – two hours in total. While her k-film explicitly documents her frustration and inability to adequately gain access to these workers, or to find a clear through-line for her film, it offers astonishing insights into the everyday activities, landscapes, and banalities of military life in proximity to a warzone. "No images can describe the unseen," as she states in one SNU. The k-film structure supports alternative forms of storytelling that may be formed from fragments and associations.

Philip Hoffman deployed Korsakow "to come to terms with issues that seemed to evade linear narration such as the working of memory, commemoration and counter-narratives" (Wiehl 2018, 34). In her nuanced and perceptive analysis of *Racing Home* (2014), the Korsakow film created by Philip Hoffman in "collaboration" with his former partner Marian McMahon, who died in 1996, Wiehl (2018, 34–5) describes its use of spatial montage:

> Let us return to the initial screen of *Racing Home* – the uncommented video displaying the figure passing the enormous columns of the Egyptian temple. This video frame, in which the short sequence is shown, does not fill the full screen, but runs in a small frame in the middle of an otherwise black screen. Below the screen, an excerpt from a text written by Marian McMahon appears in white letters – maybe an entry taken from her production notebook, or a passage from her personal diary, or a letter to a friend or to her partner Phil … Towards the end of this opening sequence, a small, still thumbnail image appears on the right-hand side of the screen. A hyperlink offers the option to activate this frame, which then moves into the large frame, substituting the former clip. This sequence, filmed by a shaky handheld camera in a first-person perspective, presents a slightly untidy room: the perspective is that of a person – Phil's, as one learns later –who explores a room in which the objects Marian bequeathed to him are kept. After a panning point-of-view shot, the

> still unsteady handheld camera sees some close-ups including a small figurine, earrings, a button and a timber box. As the protagonist – obviously Hoffman – picks these objects up, the narrating voice contextualises these actions.

Wiehl notes that *Racing Home* can be understood as a prime example of what Gagnon (2014b) describes as "posthumous cinema" and observes that "Korsakow frees the author from the pressure to create a documentary narrative" (Wiehl 2018, 34). Gagnon's own Korsakow film *Archiving R69* (2009) similarly exemplifies posthumous cinema and was likewise borne from working with an unfinished film. It is built on the archival fragments associated with a linear film that her father had begun in 1969 but had yet to complete at the time of his death in 2003.

The work and teachings of Miles have also been central to our thinking about Korsakow as a fragmented, non-fiction storytelling format. At the time of his sudden death in February 2018, Miles was senior lecturer in New Media and program director of the Bachelor of Media and Communication Honours Research Studio at the Royal Melbourne Institute of Technology (RMIT). He came to Korsakow via "a hypertext program called Storyspace" and LiveStage Pro (Rafla 2014). In an interview for the ARC-based Korsakow in the Classroom blog series, he wrote:

> I'm currently using Integrated Media One to expose students to less formal (but deeply informed) ways of making, using available tools of making, and then to stretch them in relation to multilinear video and network-specific ways of thinking and working … How are students adapting to non-linear storytelling? Is it a challenging experience for them? A liberating one? What are some of the observations/unexpected experiences that they encounter during and following the making of a Korsakow film? … The biggest step is that I try to steer them away from fiction storytelling. That's because there isn't enough time in a semester to do that well … politically, aesthetically, and ethically I'm more interested in work that shows us ways to engage with the world as peers/agents and lets us see, notice and discover what is already there, waiting, rather than teaching and building yet another layer that becomes my imposition of my will upon the world (through a story, casting, lighting, carting stuff around). (Rafla 2014)

This pedagogical rationale was fully embraced in the PhD project "ATTUNINGS: Multilinear Ways of Thinking about, Making with, and Sensing the World" made and written by Brasier (2018a) under Miles's supervision. "ATTUNINGS" consists of four essay films built in Korsakow – *I See You*; *Grey Skies/Blue Skies*; *Sunny, Rainy, Foggy*; *Sometimes I See Palm Trees* – alongside a substantial written component. All four k-films are intensely observational, allusive, and poetic, and all emphasize process over polish, reflexively foregrounding the trial-and-error of making without the perceived necessity of "finishing" the work.

Throughout her making and publishing, Brasier (2018b) returns repeatedly to "the list" as her principle organizing metaphor. She begins by asking: "Why and how does the online network invite a different approach to making and theorising audiovisual nonfiction?" (2). For Brasier, who successfully defended her PhD in August 2018, scholarship on interactive documentary did not provide a sufficient theoretical framework to understand the kinds of works she was making (4). Instead, she turned to the fields of posthumanism, new materialism, and ecocriticism, where "there is a call to consider the world and subsequently maintain the world in practice as: fragmented, relational, fluxing, dense, changing, and complex. As this research concludes and what the final half of *ATTUNINGS* narrates is how these particular affinities between multilinear making in Korsakow and the indeterminate world … have come to matter the most" (4). Brasier developed her own vocabulary to describe the kinds of films afforded by Korsakow: "I propose that in Korsakow fragments are the clips which show video content and soft relations are formed through a process of pattern making" (19).

It is true that, as Hight (2017, 88) notes in viewing a Korsakow film, "the user may be exploring material through a series of tangents, semi-random associational linkages and intended and unintended loops; all operations which would be confusing and even infuriating if the user were to encounter these as part of a promised narrative experience." Despite the potential for a perceived lack of dynamism or a discernible "through-line" in published k-films, we remain appreciative of its ease of access and conceptual malleability, its substantial contribution to the "politics of story" and against the "tyranny" of linear narrative. As Juhasz and Lebow (2018) write in their recent documentary manifesto:

> We are not against story per se. We are against the privileging of story as the most viable or supported organizing principle for

Figure 5.3
Screengrab from *Les Enseignistes de Montréal*

> documentary, especially at the very moment that documentary is poised to liberate itself from its narrative moorings. It is crucial to think beyond story; to learn from and/or imagine other organizing principles that may have a greater force. We urge filmmakers, funders, programmers, viewers, and scholars to look beyond story and to other forms of documentary; to ask why storytelling has become today's pre-eminent mode for documentary and what gets lost when storied structures prevail.

As we've shown, in moving away from linear storytelling, k-films embrace the "real" – complex, messy worlds – as necessarily in flux.

In a similar vein, there is a need for a rethinking of the modes of exhibition of "soft video" and, as we argue, the understanding of it in relation to other forms of media. In 2018, Soar completed work on his latest Korsakow film *Les Enseignistes de Montréal/The Signmakers of Montreal*. This project represented the convergence of two long-held research interests: database narrative, of course, but also signs and public lettering. (Soar is director and cofounder of the Montreal Signs Project, centring on a growing, permanent exhibition of commercial and civic signs in his department at Concordia University.) In the conclusion of Soar's essay for Nash et al. (2014, 169), he writes: "Today, scholars and makers of database documentaries, and associated software developers, routinely find themselves clubbed together on the 'new media' panel at documentary and cinema conferences or the 'new media' section of film festivals and competitions ... It would surely be one welcome indication of the 'arrival' of this medium if these particular scholars and makers were assigned to panels based more on the content of their work than exclusively on its form." Soar's experience with promoting *Les Enseignistes* suggests that we have not yet "arrived": choosing potential festivals based on thematic content (e.g., cities, architecture, design) led to at least three conversations with head programmers, all of which began with Soar being obliged to explain what constitutes a web doc and how one might screen it for a theatrical audience (see Klimek, chapter 6, this volume). (Conversely, to festivals focused directly on interactive content, it would perhaps be *just another Korsakow film*, or, as an NFB Interactive producer suggested in 2011, a mere "bucket for content.")

In this chapter we examined some of the recent, low-key histories of Korsakow as a non-linear storytelling platform and provided examples of unique k-films alongside the testimony of their makers. We considered Korsakow's distinctive qualities in relation to other experimental multi- and single-screen formats in order to highlight its particular affordances and the generative neologisms it has sparked. In doing so, we demonstrated that, while the Korsakow system has been central to the production of interactive non-fiction in Canada, the resultant projects also expand – and are sometimes at odds with – habitual understandings of the i-doc.

Acknowledgments

During the lifetime of the CINER-G and ARC grants – and for most of the time during which Korsakow 5 was being built, launched, and continually refined – we collectively grew a terrific network of makers and teachers using Korsakow in their classrooms and sometimes in their own work. Many of them commented on the ways in which Korsakow demanded or encouraged a shift in conceptual thinking for them personally and for their students, including disrupting received ideas about media production. We'd like to acknowledge as many as we can: Florian Thalhofer (Berlin), David Reisch (Montreal), Midi Onodera (Toronto), Philip Hoffman (York University), Adrian Miles (RMIT), Seth Keen (RMIT), Hannah Brasier (RMIT), Daniel Liss (ITP/NYU), Dayna McLeod (Montreal), Myriam Rafla (Dawson College), Michele Smith (Dawson College), M.E. Luka (University of Toronto), Steve Anderson (USC), Karen Kocher (UT Austin), Ben Miller (GSU), Hart Cohen (UWS), Liz Miller (Concordia), Mél Hogan (University of Calgary), Jenny Cool (USC), Grayson Cooke (Southern Cross University, Australia), Nicole Robicheau (Montreal), Brenda Longfellow (York University), Jen Proctor (University of Michigan-Dearborn), Morgan Tams (Victoria, BC), Steve High (Concordia), Giovanni Francischelli (São Paulo, Brazil), Nicole Miyahara (LA, USA), Giuliana Cucinelli (Concordia), Mo Engel (University of Alberta), Rod Coover (Temple University), and Bharath Haridas (Bangalore, India).

Notes

1 With the launch of Korsakow 6 in October 2016, much of the content on the previous (Korsakow 5) website became inaccessible, including the Showcase section, interviews, the Manual, FAQ, and so on. Fortunately, much of this content has been preserved via the Wayback Machine: https://web.archive.org/web/20150109161555/http://korsakow.org.

2 "D|N|A Anthology Just Launched!," Database Narrative Archive (Symposium), www.dnasymposium.com.

References

Electronic Sources

Note: (*) denotes Flash browser plugin requirement to play.

*7 Sons**. 2003. Florian Thalhofer and Mahmoud Hamdy. htttp://www.7sons.com.

*Archiving R69**. 2009. Monika Kin Gagnon. http://www.archivingr69.ca.

*Autonomy and Well-Being in the Cree Nation of Chisasibi.** 2017. Ioana Radu. https://chisasibi-healing.ca.

The Border between Us. 2012. Nicole Robicheau. https://www.theborderbetweenus.org.

Ceci N'est Pas Embres. 2012. Matt Soar. http://www.embres.ca.
*Digital Humanities in the Benelux Region**. 2014. Ben Miller. http://www.ehumanities.nl/web-documentary-digital-humanities.
*The End: Death in Seven Colours**. 2015. David Clark. http://theend7.net.
Les Enseignistes de Montréal. 2018. Matt Soar. https://www.lesenseignistes.ca.
Lost Leaders. 2012–. Matt Soar. http://www.lostleaders.ca.
Money and the Greeks. 2012. Florian Thalhofer. http://www.geld.gr.
*My 8 Days as a War Artist**. 2017. Midi Onodera. https://www.midionodera.com/8days.
Planet Galata: A Bridge in Istanbul. 2010. Florian Thalhofer and Berke Baş. http://www.planetgalata.com.
Racing Home. 2014. Philip Hoffman. http://www.racinghome.ca.
*Se Eu Demorar Uns Meses/If I Am a Few Months Late**. 2013. Giovanni Francischelli. http://doctela.com.br/se-eu-demorar-uns-meses.

Other Sources

Aston, Judith, Sandra Gaudenzi, and Mandy Rose, eds. 2017. *i-Docs: The Evolving Practices of Interactive Documentary.* London and New York: Wallflower.
Brasier, Hannah. 2018a. "ATTUNINGS: Multilinear Ways of Thinking about, Making with, and Sensing the World." PhD Diss., RMIT University.
– 2018b. "Moments of Noticing: 'I See You' as a Speculative Work towards an Essayistic List Practice for Interactive Documentary." In *Digital Media and Documentary: Antipodean Approaches*, ed. Adrian Miles, 13–28. New York: Palgrave Macmillan.
Cortazar, Julio. 1966. *Hopscotch.* Trans. G. Rabassa. New York: Pantheon.
Gagnon, Monika Kin. 2014a. "All-Embracing Circle-Vision 360: Canada 67 at Expo 67's Telephone Pavilion." In *Reimagining Cinema: Film at Expo 67*, ed. Monika Kin Gagnon and Janine Marchessault, 219–45. Montreal and Kingston: McGill-Queen's University Press.
– 2014b. "Posthumous Cinema and Creative Archiving: Charles Gagnon's R69 and Joyce Wieland's Wendy and Joyce." In *Cinephemera: Archives, Ephemeral Cinema, and New Screen Histories in Canada*, ed. Gerda Cammaer and Zoë Druick, 137–58. Montreal and Kingston: McGill-Queen's University Press.
– 2019. "The Two Lives of Expo 67's Polar Life (La Vie polaire)." In *Arctic Cinemas and the Documentary Ethos*, ed. Lilya Kaganovsky, Scott MacKenzie, and Anna Westerstahl Stenport, 191–206. Bloomington: Indiana University Press.

Gitelman, Lisa. 2006. *Always Already New: Media, History, and the Data of Culture*. Cambridge MA: MIT Press.

Hight, Craig. 2017. "Software as Co-creator in Interactive Documentary." In *i-Docs: The Evolving Practices of Interactive Documentary*, ed. Judith Aston, Sandra Gaudenzi, and Mandy Rose, 82–96. London and New York: Wallflower.

Huhtamo, Erkki. 2007. "Push the Button, Kinoautomat will do the Rest! Media-archaeological Reflections on Audience Interactivity." https://www.gebseng.com/media_archeology/reading_materials/Erkki_Huhtamo-Kinoautomat.pdf.

Jancelewicz, Chris. 2019. "Netflix Sued by 'Choose Your Own Adventure' Company Over 'Bandersnatch.'" Global News, 11 January 2019. https://globalnews.ca/news/4838835/netflix-sued-choose-your-own-adventure-black-mirror-bandersnatch.

Juhasz, Alexandra, and Alisa Lebow. 2018. "Beyond Story: An Online, Community-Based Manifesto." *World Records Journal* 2 (Fall). http://sro.sussex.ac.uk/id/eprint/103807.

Keen, Seth. 2014. "Netvideo, Nonvideo, Newvideo: Designing a Multilinear Nonnarrative Form for Interactive Documentary." PhD Diss., RMIT University.

– 2018. "The Documentary Designer: A List of Propositions for Interactive Documentary Practice Online." In *Digital Media and Documentary: Antipodean Approaches*, ed. Adrian Miles, 49–67. New York: Palgrave Macmillan.

Manovich, Lev. 2001. *The Language of New Media*. Cambridge: MIT Press.

Manovich, Lev, and Andreas Kratky. 2005. *Soft Cinema: Navigating the Database*. Cambridge: MIT Press. DVD set and book.

Miles, Adrian. 2014a. "Interactive Documentary and Affective Ecologies." In *New Documentary Ecologies: Emerging Platforms, Practices and Discourses*, ed. Catherine Summerhayes, Chris Hight, and Kate Nash, 67–82. Melbourne: Palgrave Macmillan.

– 2014b. "Materialism and Interactive Documentary: Sketch Notes." *Studies in Documentary Film* 8 (3): 205–20.

Rafla, M. 2014. "Korsakow in the Classroom: Adrian Miles." Korsakow 5 website. 12 February 2014. https://web.archive.org/web/20150104165133/http://korsakow.org.

Roettgers, Janko. 2018. "Netflix Takes Interactive Storytelling to the Next Level with 'Black Mirror: Bandersnatch.' The Latest Installment of 'Black Mirror'

Puts the Viewer in Control. Or Does It?" *Variety*, 28 December 2018. https://variety.com/2018/digital/news/netflix-black-mirror-bandersnatch-interactive-1203096171.

Soar, Matt. 2011. "Interview with Florian about His Korsakow Show 'Was ist. geld.gr' (Athens, Greece 10/22/12)." Korsakow 5 website. 6 January 2011. https://web.archive.org/web/20150104165133/http://korsakow.org.

– 2014. "Making (with) the Korsakow System: Database Documentaries as Articulation and Assemblage." In *New Documentary Ecologies: Emerging Platforms, Practices and Discourses*, ed. Catherine Summerhayes, Chris Hight, and Kate Nash, 154–73. Melbourne: Palgrave Macmillan.

Sprengler, Christine. 2014. "Spatial Montage, Temporal Collage and the Art(ifice) of Rear Projection." In *Hitchcock and Contemporary Art*, 91–117. Basingstoke: Palgrave Macmillan.

Uricchio, William. 2017. "Things to Come: The Future of Documentary – From a Historical Perspective." In *i-Docs: The Evolving Practices of Interactive Documentary*, ed. Judith Aston, Sandra Gaudenzi, and Mandy Rose, 191–205. London and New York: Wallflower.

Wiehl, Anna. 2018. "Beyond 'Toolness': Korsakow Documentary as a Methodology for Plurivocal Interventions in Complexity." *Alphaville: Journal of Film and Screen Media* 15 (Summer): 33–48.

6

I-DOCS AND LIVE PERFORMANCE

HIGHRISE: UNIVERSE WITHIN AT HOT DOCS

Caroline Klimek

The interactive series *Highrise* is the crown jewel of the National Film Board of Canada's (NFB) interactive documentaries. Created by filmmaker Kat Cizek and executive producer Gerry Flahive, it explores vertical living around the world. The project began in 2009 and includes five interactive documentaries – *The Thousandth Tower* (2010), *Out My Window* (2010), *One Millionth Tower* (2011), *A Short History of the Highrise* (2013), and *Universe Within: Digital Lives in the Global Highrise* (2015) – as well as more than twenty related projects such as public art exhibits and live performances. The *Highrise* series "solidif[ied] the NFB as a leading player in digital interactive storytelling" (Mulvogue 2019, 410). It received international acclaim, was shown at Mozilla Fest, SXSW, the International Documentary Film Festival Amsterdam (IDFA), the New York Film Festival, and Sheffield/Doc Fest and won multiple Canadian Screen Awards, Webby Awards, the IDFA DocLab Award for Digital Storytelling, an Emmy, and a Peabody Award. In 2015, Cizek and the NFB teamed up with Hot Docs Canadian International Documentary Festival (Hot Docs) to premiere the final instalment of *Highrise: Universe Within* as a live performance. For Hot Docs, including *Highrise* within its festival programming was an experiment in how a festival could program documentaries that fall outside the traditional black box while still retaining the festival experience for its audiences. Translating an intimate, single-user experience into a collective one was an unfamiliar but attractive challenge.

By examining the Hot Docs live performance of Kat Cizek's *Highrise: Universe Within* that took place on 29 April 2015, this chapter attempts to examine the following questions: How are film festivals responding to the inclusion of interactive works? How does a festival program a one-on-one experience for a collective audience? How does a live performance extend the power of an interactive documentary and encourage discussion and discourse? This event is an important case study as it commemorated the end of the *Highrise* series and marked a shift in the NFB's focus from interactive documentaries to new and emerging technologies such as virtual reality (VR). At the same time, it set a precedent for how film festivals could exhibit an interactive documentary for their festival audiences.

In her essay, "The World Navigated: Interactive Documentaries in Canada," Jessica Mulvogue ties i-docs to the long-standing tradition of documentary filmmaking in Canada and within the NFB. The NFB became involved in creating interactive documentaries with the launch of its Digital Studios – opened in Vancouver in 2008 and in Montreal the following year – where it could focus, Mulvogue (2019, 410) notes, "solely on the production of creative works of the imagination that would use new platforms and technologies as an experimental canvas for interactive storytelling." Mulvogue adds, "with such strong institutional backing, the interactive documentary has been able to flourish in Canada in a way only comparable to France" (ibid.). Since establishing the NFB Digital Studios, the NFB has created more than eighty interactive documentaries and has won over 150 international awards and honours, including a Gold Medal at Cannes Cyber Lions, over a dozen Webby Awards and Canadian Screen Awards (NFB 2023). After its Hot Docs premiere, the final instalment of the series *Highrise: Universe Within* would be exhibited at two other film festivals later in 2015: at IDFA DocLab (18–29 November) and at the Montreal International Documentary Festival (RIDM) (12–22 November, as part of its UXdoc program). However, by 2015, the popularity of interactive documentaries had already begun to decline as filmmakers turned to newer and more immersive technologies such as virtual reality. The NFB Digital Studios' shift away from i-docs to emerging technologies such as VR, augmented reality, and apps signals this decline.

Very few scholars have written about the use of live performance and the challenge of exhibiting i-docs at film festivals. Stefano Odorico's essay "Beyond the Screen: Interactive Documentary Exhibition in the Festival Sphere" (2020) and Judith Aston's chapter "Interactive Documentary and Live Performance: From Embodied to Emplaced Interaction" (2017) offer rare insights. Odorico (2020) turns to Francesco Casetti's (2011) notion of "re-location," which speaks to the ways in which the cinema experience is being repurposed outside of the black box experience. Film festivals, for Casetti (2011, 9), are largely events anchored in the past and therefore have difficulty adapting to new media: "the theatre that refuses new modes of vision in order to conserve, as much as possible, the traditional film watching environment (as happens particularly during ceremonial situations, such as festivals, a debut or a film series aimed at true cinephiles, during which the spectator is invited to see a film and nothing else)." Odorico looks at three different types of exhibitions that showcase interactive documentaries – traditional film festivals, those focused specifically on showcasing interactive documentaries and new media, and symposia/labs – to examine how they have adapted to programming and exhibiting i-docs. Taking a different approach, Judith Aston (2017, 233) focuses on the role of the audience and what she calls "emplaced interaction," which she defines as "the creation, manipulation and sharing of meaning through engaged interaction," a mode of interaction that brings "our bodies and minds into direct interplay with the wider world." Live performance, for Aston, holds the promise of reconnecting us to the physical world as life moves more online.

However, neither Odorico nor Aston discusses a specific live performance of an interactive documentary at a film festival. The *Highrise* event therefore offers a unique opportunity to explore how Cizek used the film festival setting – a traditional film viewing environment – to transform an individual encounter with an iPad or computer into a collective experience.

Hot Docs

Branded as a festival that programs "outspoken, outstanding" documentaries, Hot Docs is the largest documentary film festival in North America. It is held annually in late April and early May in Toronto, and its mandate is "to advance and celebrate the art of documentary, and to showcase the work of and create production opportunities for documentary filmmakers" (Hot Docs 2016). Locally, the festival stands alone in a city that hosts over ninety film festivals. Internationally, Hot Docs is frequently equated with other documentary film festivals such as the International Documentary

Film Festival Amsterdam (IDFA), Sheffield Doc/Fest, and the American Film Institute Documentary Festival (AFI Docs) held in Silver Spring, Maryland, and Washington, DC.

Hot Docs programs a wide spectrum of documentaries usually intended for television broadcast or theatrical distribution. Lyell Davies (2016, 90) notes how the festival "programs a heterogenous array of documentaries in a range of film categories, from serious social documentaries or observational-style studies of individuals or institutions, to quirky autobiography works." Similar to other film festivals, Hot Docs is classified as a charitable organization and relies on the sale of tickets and festival passes, sponsorship by corporate interests, and government funding to finance its operations. The festival is noted for having a very loyal and robust local audience who attend in record numbers: over 228,000 members attended Hot Docs screenings in 2019 (Hot Docs 2019, 2). An annual industry market complements the film festival. There, "over 2,600 delegates from around the world" attend "a series of passive and active networking opportunities to connect potential funding and creative partners" (14). Delegates who buy industry-level passes can attend networking events, workshops, and talks on the newest trends in documentary filmmaking at the Industry Conference. They can also pitch their film ideas to international broadcasters at the Hot Docs Forum.

To date, Hot Docs has exhibited only three interactive documentaries:[1] *Avatar Secrets* in 2014, *Highrise: Universe Within* in 2015, and *The World in Ten Blocks* in 2016. Hot Docs invited audiences to interact with a twenty-minute sneak preview of *Avatar Secrets* (directed by Ramona Pringle and produced with TVO, 2014) via two high-definition touch-screens in the main lobby of the TIFF Bell Lightbox. Pringle commented, "It was really important to us to retain that crystal clarity of the imagery and to use touch screens to translate the experience we're developing for the iPad to a live festival audience, and so we decided on large scale touch screen displays" (Gaudenzi n.d.). Interviews with Pringle suggest the installation was still meant for one-on-one interaction with the Hot Docs Festival audience. Its status at Hot Docs remained unclear, however: was *Avatar Secrets* premiering at the festival or was the installation intended as a bridge between the festival proper and the Industry Conference? Indeed, Ramona Pringle was also a panelist, along with Mickael Brock and Vincent McCurley, at the Hot Docs Industry Panel Tablet Strategies: New Directions of Interactive Documentary.[2] For the festival, this was an important opportunity to tie together the industry's focus on providing "transmedia" documentary workshops, conference sessions, and opportunities to pitch with exhibitions and programming. *Avatar Secrets* was mentioned as a "free event" in the festival schedule and was not part of any official film program.

Compared to other film festivals, Hot Docs came rather late to exhibiting interactive documentaries, which is somewhat odd for a festival that prides itself on staying abreast of current market trends. For example, the IDFA DocLab program emerged in 2007 and premiered its first interactive documentary that same year with *Thanatorama* (Julian Guintard and Vincent Baillais, 2007). The Sundance Film Festival premiered Nonny de la Pena's *Gone Gitmo* (2007) through its Sundance New Frontier program. And the following year, Sheffield/DocFest, SXSW, and IDFA showed multiple i-docs, notably *Journey to the End of the Coal* (Abel Ségrétin and Samuel Bollendorff, 2008).

Admittedly, before 2011 – when the production of i-docs exploded – film festivals did not have a wide selection of interactive documentaries to choose from (2011 marked the release of the NFB projects *Welcome to Pine Point*, *Highrise: One Millionth Tower*, and *The Next Day*). As well, to give attendees the experience of i-docs, film festivals generally used computers and iPads or offered live walk throughs (during which creators gave a running commentary as they showcased their project to an audience) of the interactive documentaries by filmmakers and producers. A few exceptions stand out: in 2010, for example, IDFA had an offline live event premiere of Kat Cizek's *Out My Window* in which Cizek "Vjed" the website in a cinema for audience members to "experience" the interactive documentary (Matlin 2010). Two years later, founder and curator of IDFA DocLab Caspar Sonnen commissioned a live performance of *Bear 71* (Allison and Mendes, 2012) with Jeremy Mendes orchestrating the event onstage to live music (Aston 2017, 227–8).

The *Highrise: Universe Within* live performance at Hot Docs was nonetheless unique in terms of its use of a hired host to create a conversation between the audience and the interactive documentary. Never again to be repeated at Hot Docs, this event provides a unique opportunity to examine how one of the largest documentary film festivals negotiated the exhibition of an interactive documentary.

Highrise: Universe Within

Highrise: Universe Within has been called Cizek's most ambitious and challenging project. It took four years and $628,000 to investigate the digital behaviour of residents in high rise apartments around the globe. "We knew that people worked there from around the world," Cizek states, "and that they must have really important relationships internationally, so how are they connecting and what tools are they using and how are they using these tools?" (Ravindran 2015a). While the project has the international focus of the previous chapters of *Highrise*, it is also rooted in community-based research in Toronto's inner suburbs. Cizek partnered with University of Toronto professors Deborah Cowen and Emily Paradis, whose methodology included conducting peer-to-peer research. Cizek hired fourteen residents to go door-to-door to ask their neighbours in their building about their access to the internet and their digital lives. The researchers found that 80 per cent of households in a Toronto apartment complex had internet access, despite living in one of the city's most precarious and low-income communities (ibid.). For Cowen and Paradis, "We learned people were sacrificing food so they could pay for their online time" (Ahmed-Ullah 2015). Based on the survey feedback, the team recognized that, for many residents, internet access was one of the first things they set up in their apartment, challenging previous assumptions about digital access. After conducting the research, Cizek commented: "That led us to thinking there's a real, invisible story here that we're not seeing in the media or even in academic literature about how the digital maps out in the vertical, so we went to over 20 locations around the world, to speak with [people] – through local journalists and photographers – and to find stories of how the digital and the vertical intersect in really intimate, personal and political ways" (ibid.). The result is an interactive documentary that asks participants to choose between seven different avatar hosts who discuss their own personal stories and then guide viewers through the narrative by asking questions about their own digital lives. Depending on how participants answer, they are presented with a profile on an individual from either Accra, Ghana; Seoul, South Korea; or Ramallah, Palestine.

Cizek has called this project "a whole larger than the sum" of its predecessors (Ravindran 2015a). Cizek teamed up with Toronto-based digital agency Secret Location to use 3D point cloud data to create the 3D digital avatars, resulting in a work much more technologically advanced than the docs that came before it. The avatars address the participant directly; for Cizek, these avatars are a way to create a conversation: "with *Universe Within* I wanted to hint at the idea of a conversation because the documentary form is so much about sharing stories" (NFB 2015). Some viewers have commented that interacting with the avatar is similar to a Skype call during which they thought they were talking to somebody real, a testament to the technology and how realistic these avatars look (ibid.).

Universe Within follows a more linear structure than the other i-docs in the series. Cizek says she "wanted to take people through the beginning, middle and end of the story," noting that "the entire experience is 70 minutes long, but it's broken into 12 to 15-minute-long units of storytelling" (NFB 2015). At the end of every storyline, users are prompted to start over and begin another conversation. If users choose the same host, the conversation progresses as more aspects of the avatar's story are revealed. Through these storylines, Cizek explains, *Universe Within* "challenge[s] our comfort in using digital technology to meaningfully engage with others – including those constructed solely of pixels."

Hot Docs included *Highrise: Universe Within* as part of the DocX program, which was introduced in 2015 as a small pilot project by then director of programming Charlotte Cook to see how Hot Docs could include non-traditional documentary formats within its festival line-up. According to Associate Director of Programming Sarafina DiFelice (2016), Hot Docs wanted to know if its festival audience was interested in this kind of programming and, more important, how the festival could include non-traditional documentaries within its main festival program. Hot Docs was hesitant to program i-docs because it did not know how to exhibit them. A live, one-night-only performance of an interactive documentary solved the challenge of how to program documentaries that are not considered traditional film to their festival audience, who enjoy a collective festival experience. The first iteration of DocX included four VR experiences and the one-night-only live performance of the NFB's final segment of *Highrise: Universe Within*.

The DocX program focused on "innovative documentary storytelling through new technologies and original experiences" (Hot Docs 2015a, 5). It was originally marketed as an opportunity for festival audiences to "witness the future creative and technical possibilities of documentary cinema" and to "immerse [oneself] in unforgettable documentary experiences" (ibid.). DocX encouraged audiences to prioritize the live performance of *Highrise:*

Universe Within as a singular experience that, unlike other screenings, would not be repeated throughout the festival. Tickets for the event were twenty-two dollars – a high price, considering attendees could watch the i-doc for free online a couple months after the event. However, DocX justified the ticket price as "once-in-a-lifetime" opportunity to witness the final instalment of the "acclaimed *Highrise* digital documentary project" (ibid.) and to showcase how i-docs can be commercially exhibited to a festival audience.

The Event

The live performance of *Highrise: Universe Within* took place on 29 April 2015 at Innis Town Hall, a cinema at the University of Toronto. The performance included musical accompaniment by Dafydd Hughes and Nick Storring. The production was set so that everyone – musicians Hughes and Storring, host/actor Misha Glouberman, director Cizek, and other NFB producers and technologists – shared the stage together, giving audiences a peek behind the curtain of this world-renowned interactive documentary and team. By hiring Glouberman to come in, connect with the audience, and interact with the documentary, Cizek added a unique element to this performance.

Cizek had workshopped her ideas for the live performance while a visiting artist at MIT's Open Documentary Lab. In an interview for the Arts at MIT website, she explained her aim "to take a web documentary and make it into a theatrical, meaningful, and cinematic experience on stage involving participatory elements with the audience" (Lacey 2016). Cizek also distinguished the live elements of *Universe Within* from the installations she had done for other parts of the *Highrise* series: "This is very performative; this has a host … on stage navigating us through the material in much the same way as what we're doing in the documentary. For sure there's a much stronger movement towards questioning the constructive nature of a documentary in this work" (ibid.).

The NFB hired popular host and communications expert Misha Glouberman to act as the evening's emcee.[3] Like a talk show host, Glouberman tried to create a conversation between himself and the audience, and to engage the audience with the world of the documentary. He posed questions to the audience for the entire performance, and – as envisioned by Cizek at MIT – the audience's answers drove the documentary forward. Glouberman asked the audience about its relationship with digital technology: "How many people have a Facebook and a Twitter account? How many have neither? How many people think Twitter is just stupid? How many people had a Facebook account but have since gotten off social media?" Through these questions, Glouberman tied together the major themes of the documentary while also uncovering the audience's digital choices. He encouraged audience members with opposing views to join him onstage to expand upon their answers and extend the conversation between audience and host. For instance, Glouberman asked, "Do you feel hope or despair about the Internet?" He then brought onstage one audience member who felt despair and another who felt hope to start a discussion. An older gentleman shared that he deactivated his Facebook account. When asked to explain why he felt the need to remove his account, he said he disliked the intrusion into his privacy and the amount of time he was spending online. Wanting to bring a younger perspective into the conversation, Glouberman asked if anyone born in 2001 or earlier would be willing to come on stage. When no one volunteered, Glouberman remarked that the younger generation lives online. A young boy piped up and said youth express themselves online rather than in person. This turned into a discussion about how the boy connects with his friends on Vine and how he had shared six-second videos with his school friends while on a family vacation. Glouberman asked the boy, "Is there anything notable that's different in how people older than you use technology versus how people your age use it?" The boy quickly answered, "They asked me how to use it a lot." By the end of the evening, Glouberman had interacted with a broad range of audience members, from senior citizens to a six-year-old.

A Microsoft Kinect device attached to Glouberman created 3D renderings of himself and the audience participants who joined him onstage. These renderings were then superimposed onto the backdrop of the website's interface and projected on the large screen above the stage. The use of the point cloud technology during the live performance seamlessly transitioned the world of the interactive documentary into the live performance. However, the setup was clunky and created a moment of levity when Glouberman had trouble getting onto the stage at the beginning of the performance: the contraption caused him to bump into things. Glouberman played off the embarrassment with a play on words, saying that the documentary was about connection and he was attached to a Kinect device.

By creating a 3D rendering of Glouberman, Cizek extended the feel and experience of the interactive documentary into the theatre. Glouberman's avatar joined the other seven digital hosts in *Universe Within*, blurring the lines between what was the i-doc and what was the live performance. Cizek integrated the performative and curated worlds of documentary, creating a collective experience. In this way, the audience could participate in an interactive documentary through a live performance.

Hot Docs has programmed participatory events before, such as the *Rocky Horror Picture Show* every Halloween at the Ted Rogers Cinema, to bring in audiences and create immersive experiences as part of its yearly programming. For Hot Docs, turning to event cinema allows it to create participatory cinematic experiences to better attract new audiences and "to respon[d] to the public's love for nostalgia and the power of fan engagement" (Atkinson and Kennedy 2016, 143). Judith Aston (2017, 230) aptly describes this kind of live performance: "This style of interactive performance relies heavily on the performer's skills as a storyteller, and is explicitly designed to encourage as much audience participation as possible. That said, the performance still has a set duration with a beginning, a middle and an end, very much predicated on the idea of a seated cinema-going audience with an onstage performer."

While the film festival and its audiences were seemingly fascinated with the new technology of the interactive documentary, Glouberman's role as the master of ceremonies was crucial to the shape of the event. It was the way Glouberman addressed the audience, how he posed questions and created a space for audience members to converse with one another that brought the message of *Highrise: Universe Within* to the forefront. Glouberman's hosting skills allowed audience members not only to experience the documentary collectively but also to learn more about the overall conversation that the documentary was trying to produce. Glouberman kept things light at the beginning by explaining what the audience was seeing and what would happen throughout this performance. The opening remarks helped to put the audience at ease by clarifying the expectations and etiquette for the event. Throughout the performance, Glouberman encouraged questions and debate, but he also knew when to move onto a different topic, especially when no one volunteered to go onstage. The most emotionally powerful story of the evening was the last one, motivated by the question, "How fulfilling is intimacy for you over the internet?" The audience member onstage selected the response "not at all," prompting the heart-wrenching story of a woman from Ramallah. For thirteen years, her parents, a mere one-hour drive away in Gaza, have been unable to secure Israeli travel permits to visit her, causing them to miss her wedding and the birth of her three daughters. The limitations of digital communication were on painful display as the audience witnessed the woman introducing her infant daughter to her parents by means of a shaky Skype connection. The whole theatre acknowledged that this digital exchange was a woeful substitute for the real thing.

Using Glouberman as performer/host, the live performance of *High Rise: Universe Within* harkens back to a practice found in early cinema, where narrators, or *benshi*, played a vital role in explaining or elaborating to the audience what they were seeing on screen.[4] We could also consider Glouberman's role in the event as something akin to a live television host but one that also evokes the tradition of documentary film narration. Guiding audience attention and framing the narrative during the live performance, Glouberman shaped audience understanding and emotional engagement with the content. He facilitated interactions between the audience and the documentary material and fostered a sense of community engagement within the cinema space.

The evening's performance emphasized the importance of conversations and its role within documentaries. Glouberman ended the evening by stating: "A lot of documentary filmmakers say if I can just change one person's mind, my work will be done. Well, we changed exactly one person's mind." The audience erupted into cheers, confirming the impact of the event. After a ninety-minute performance, the evening ended with Glouberman welcoming onstage the NFB commissioner Claude Joli-Coeur, who announced that *Highrise: Universe Within* would be online for all to see on 2 June 2015. Joli-Coeur praised the *Highrise* team for its work over the last six years. Kat Cizek then came onstage and provided a long thank you to all her team members before participating in a short Q&A. The evening ended with Glouberman inviting the audience to continue the conversation at the reception, where they could enjoy food and beverages and use a photobooth with the Kinect device.

Conclusion

The *Highrise: Universe Within* live performance was an experiment for Hot Docs in programming outside the black box, introducing a new mode of non-fiction storytelling to the festival stage. It marked the first time a new medium or technology took the main stage at Hot Docs, and, in doing so, it showcased the exhibition possibilities for other mediums outside traditional film, such as i-docs and virtual reality. While Hot Docs programming director Shane Smith acknowledged that "these interactive docs and hybrid forms of doc are the way of the future" (Ravindran 2015b), he also underscored the importance of maintaining the festival experience: "I think there are opportunities outside of the festival experience to enhance the brand and to work with other platforms, and explore other platforms as opportunities for doc filmmakers. I'm really interested in whatever we can do to enhance the *audience experience* and grow the Hot Docs audience, but also to provide a platform and opportunities for doc filmmakers ... *The festival experience will never die*" (emphasis added).

Since new technologies and platforms challenge the traditional black box, many film festivals, as Odorico (2020) argues, struggle to maintain the "festival experience" and to find ways of adapting to new modes of documentary filmmaking. While outside the scope of this chapter, these challenges also raise questions about what kinds of audiences this "festival experience" is for and what kinds of audiences it excludes. As an ever-evolving practice, Odorico ultimately thinks it is an exciting time for festivals; with interactive documentaries, the "boundaries are broken and the shift to new forms of exhibition is dynamic and fluid" (108). The live performance of *Highrise: Universe Within* offered an experience different from that of using a computer or iPad at home, opening up the potential for multiple ways of experiencing interactive documentaries, even those designed to be experienced individually. As Robinder Uppal and Marc Serpa Francoeur, creators of *The World in Ten Blocks*, state: "just as interactive documentary will never replace conventional linear documentary, likewise there is no reason to think that interactive docs intended for collective experience will replace those designed for individuals; these are not competing paradigms, but complementary forms, each with their own distinct narrative and communicative capacities" (Uppal and Francoeur 2015). They uphold the April 2015 performance of *Highrise* as a night where "the power of the transformation from passive consumption to active participation was striking" (ibid.).

Interestingly, however, the live performance of *Universe Within* marked the last time that Hot Docs would showcase an i-doc as a collective experience. The ephemerality of the *Universe Within* performance serves as a poignant reminder of the complexities involved in merging new media and technologies with traditional festival structures. While the live performance brought a sense of collective engagement, the audience was ultimately limited. The challenge lies in replicating such experiences beyond a single event. This, in turn, raises questions about the sustainability of collective encounters in the ever-evolving landscape of documentary storytelling.

The festival thus must critically reflect on the long-term impact of such experiments on audience engagement and the authentic festival experience. Striking a delicate balance between novelty and meaningful connection should remain at the forefront of Hot Docs' evolution as it continues to explore new horizons in the dynamic world of documentary filmmaking. The *Highrise: Universe Within* live performance at Hot Docs served as an experiment in pushing the boundaries of documentary storytelling. However, it also underscored the ephemerality of such events and the challenges in integrating interactive forms into a collective festival experience.

Notes

1 The three i-docs Hot Docs has screened are: 1) *Avatar Secrets* in 2014 as an installation at the TIFF Bell Lightbox; 2) *Highrise: Universe Within* at Innis Town Hall as part of the DocX program in 2015; and 3) *The World in Ten Blocks* at Hot Docs House as part of DocX in 2016. To read more about the story of *The World in Ten Blocks,* visit https://theworldintenblocks.com.

2 Watch "Tablet Strategies: New Directions of Interactive Documentary" panel online https://vimeo.com/117624863.

3 For more about Misha Glouberman, see his website http://www.mishaglouberman.com.

4 For more information about the history and impact of *benshi* on Japanese cinema, see: Jeffrey A. Dym, "*Benshi* and the Introduction of Motion Pictures to Japan," *Monumenta Nipponica* 55, no. 4 (2000): 509–36; and Hideaki Fujiki, "*Benshi* as Stars: The Irony of the Popularity and Respectability of Voice Performers in Japanese Cinema," *Cinema Journal* 45, no. 2 (2006): 68–84.

References

Ahmed-Ullah, Noreen. 2015. "How U of T Researchers Helped Shape HIGHRISE, the NFB's Interactive Documentary." *U of T News*, 5 June 2015. https://www.utoronto.ca/news/how-u-t-researchers-helped-shape-highrise-nfbs-interactive-documentary.

Aston, Judith. 2017. "Interactive Documentary and Live Performance: From Embodied to Emplaced Interaction." In *I-Docs: The Evolving Practices of Interactive Documentary*, ed. Judith Aston, Sandra Gaudenzi, and Mandy Rose, 222–36. London and New York: Wallflower.

Atkinson, Sarah, and Helen W. Kennedy. 2016. "Introduction – Inside-the-Scenes: The Rise of Experiential Cinema." *Participations: Journal of Audience and Reception Studies* 13 (1): 139–51.

Casetti, Francesco. 2011. "Back to the Motherland: The Film Theatre in the Postmedia Age." *Screen* 52 (1): 1–12.

Davies, Lyell. 2016. "Documentary Film Festivals as Ideological Transactions: Film Screening Sites at Hot Docs." *Canadian Journal of Film Studies* 25 (1): 88–110.

DiFelice, Sarafina. 2016. Interview by Caroline Klimek. Toronto, 27 May 2016.

Gaudenzi, Sandra. n.d. "From iPad to Installation: Interactive Documentary on Multiple Platforms." *I-Docs*. http://i-docs.org/from-ipad-to-installation-interactive-documentary-on-multiple-platforms.

Hot Docs Canadian International Documentary Festival (Hot Docs). 2015a. "2015 Screening Schedule." 23 April–5 May.

– 2015b. "Tablet Strategies: New Directions of Interactive Documentary." Hot Docs Film Festival. 23 January 2015. Vimeo video, 58:07. https://vimeo.com/117624863=.

– 2016. "About." https://www.hotdocs.ca/u/about-us.

– 2019. "2018/19 Annual Report for Hot Docs Film Festival." http://assets.hotdocs.ca/doc/HD19_Annual-Report.pdf.

Lacey, Sharon. 2016. "In the Making: Katerina Cizek." Arts Center for Art, Science and Technology at MIT, 13 January 2016. https://arts.mit.edu/in-the-making-katerina-cizek.

Matlin, Julie. 2010. "The NFB's Highrise Project Unveils Its New Unteractive Web Documentary, Out My Window." NFB Blog, 15 October 2010. https://blog.nfb.ca/blog/2010/10/15/the-nfbs-highrise-project-unveils-its-new-interactive-web-documentary-out-my-window.

Mulvogue, Jessica. 2019. "The World Navigated: Interactive Documentaries in Canada." In *The Oxford Handbook of Canadian Cinema*, ed. Janine Marchessault and Will Straw, 409–22. New York: Oxford University Press.

National Film Board of Canada (NFB). 2015. "Press Kit: Interview with Katerina Cizek" for *Highrise: Universe Within*. Media Space, NFB. http://mediaspace.nfb.ca/epk/highrise-universe-within/?_gl=1*1hr9bgw*_ga*ODk0OTA2OTg5LjE2MTg1MTE0OTY.*_ga_EP6WV87GNTYyMDA0MzM0OC42LjAuMTYyMDA0MzM0OC4w.

– 2023. "The NFB: Stories to Tell." Media Space, NFB. https://mediaspace.nfb.ca/epk/the-nfb-stories-to-tell.

Odorico, Stefano. 2020. "Beyond the Screen: Interactive Documentary Exhibition in the Festival Sphere." In *Documentary Film Festivals*, vol. 2, ed. Aida Vallejo and Ezra Winton, 93–111. Cham: Springer International Publishing.

Ravindran, Manori. 2015a. "Building the Final Story of the NFB's 'Highrise.'" *Realscreen*, 23 June 2015. https://realscreen.com/2015/06/23/building-the-final-story-of-the-nfbs-highrise.

– 2015b. "Hot Docs' Shane Smith on Shorts, VR and World Premieres." *Realscreen*, 21 August 2015. https://realscreen.com/2015/08/21/hot-docs-shane-smith-on-shorts-vr-and-world-premieres.

Uppal, Robinder, and Marc Serpa Francoeur. 2015. "The Power of Interactive Doc as Collective Experience." POV: *Point of View Magazine*, 7 May 2015. https://povmagazine.com/the-power-of-interactive-doc-as-collective-experience.

Vallejo, Aida. 2020. "IDFA's Industry Model: Fostering Global Documentary Production and Distribution." In *Documentary Film Festivals*, vol. 2, ed. Aida Vallejo and Ezra Winton, 23–53. Cham: Springer International Publishing.

PART TWO

Encounters with Others

Activism, Agency, and Ethics

7

COLLABORATIVE ENCOUNTERS

I-DOCS AND ENVIRONMENTAL PEDAGOGY IN AND BEYOND THE CLASSROOM

Rachel Webb Jekanowski and Elizabeth Miller

Introduction

We believe that one of the crucial places where interactive documentaries (i-docs) matter is in the classroom. In this chapter, we explore i-docs as both documentary form and method, as something that is uniquely suited for tackling "wicked problems" such as climate change, both in and beyond the classroom (Ferkany and Whyte 2011, 331). Judith Aston and Stefano Odorico (2018, 64) suggest that i-docs are well positioned to embrace the complexity of our contemporary world given that they incorporate both structures and production processes that permit multiple voices to be in dialogue with one another. Patricia R. Zimmermann and Helen de Michiel (2018) posit that interactives present an "open space" where communities and diverse forms of engagement can emerge. Building on these claims, we suggest that the polyvocal form of the i-doc is an ideal tool – even a method – for media literacy and comparative learning, and can reinforce issues key to critical pedagogy, such as environmental justice, by emphasizing multiple perspectives and positionalities. To reinforce our point, we use the environmental interactive *The Shore Line* (2017), a project to which we have both contributed, to demonstrate ways that interactives can hold complexity, challenge disciplinary approaches, and foster collaborative encounters through production processes and outreach efforts.

In *The Mushroom at the End of the World*, anthropologist Anna Lowenhaupt Tsing (2015, 19) proposes that we as scholars, educators, and engaged individuals need to tell more complex stories to help us "think about collaborative survival." Rather than resorting to "tales of progress [or] ruin" caught up in oppositional notions of technological salvation or apocalypse, we are inspired by Tsing to argue for more complex, "thick" narratives about climate change involving a density of voices, perspectives, and even contradictory notions about how we might move forward as a global society (ibid.). Environmental philosopher Timothy Morton (2013, 1) describes global warming as a "hyperobject," an entity that is "massively distributed in time and space relative to humans" and thus difficult to intellectually or emotionally grasp. For educators and concerned communities, this poses the challenge of how to connect the immediacy of individual experiences of disaster with the planetary scope of the problem. When confronting a seemingly intractable "wicked problem" like global warming, in which public consensus over clear solutions (or even formulations of the problem) is lacking (Ferkany and Whyte 2011, 331), how do we as cultural producers and educators find new ways of communicating that foster engagement and consensus-building? We believe this is where interactive and non-linear forms of documentary media come into play, as practices that can embrace multiple scales and voices and offer both analytic and affective connections to the messy, enormous complexity of global climate change.

The Shore Line addresses the combined threats of rising sea levels and unchecked development along our global coasts, asking users to contemplate how melting glaciers, resource extraction, and oil disasters on *one shoreline* affect communities on *another*. The objective of this i-doc was to explore how the open form of an interactive could connect individuals responding to these threats with creativity and resilience. The project includes maps, visualizations, soundscapes, data visualizations, educational resources, and over forty videos featuring individuals from nine countries. Miller spearheaded the project, developing a multifaceted collaborative approach that involved both directing and commissioning short videos and working with students, journalists, and non-profits to co-author teaching guides for the project. Fostering polyvocality within *The Shore Line* was largely intended to open spaces for proposing alternative, multiple "solutions" to grapple with the complexity of the climate change crisis. For example, the project features a sustainability architect in Bangladesh who designs floating schools, an Indigenous community organizer in Panama who coordinates the migration of his village from a low-lying island to the mainland, a science fiction writer imagining alternative futures for Vancouver, and a wide range of other people who are out there making a difference. Jekanowski got involved with *The Shore Line* as a curriculum designer, contributing her expertise in film studies and environmental justice to an educator's guide on speculative futures. She has since presented the project at academic and pedagogical events addressing environmental media and climate justice.

We draw on our experience creating, teaching, and distributing *The Shore Line* to explore how i-docs, and the forms of interactivity these productions enact, can help connect alternative modes of learning to interventions in the world around us. Environmental i-docs and other interactive media, like video games,[1] can target audiences who might not otherwise engage with environmental issues by reaching into the world of the screen to gesture back outwards. And yet we are also aware that these same media tools are frequently in conflict with the very purpose of the work: to think more critically about our impacts on the planet and to directly engage with local environments. Furthermore, digitally distributed media projects have an impact on our environment, relying on largely invisible but resource-intensive infrastructures like the internet.[2] We can't resolve these issues immediately but we can draw attention to the complex challenges we face in producing and circulating politically engaged media projects within mainstream networks.

While documentary has a long tradition of serving as a catalyst for political involvement, activism, and student engagement, there is an urgency to rethink how we are using documentary in our classrooms in this moment of climate disruptions and growing inequalities. As climate educator Bill McKibben (2017, 279) suggests, the "preoccupations of our society are starting quickly to shift – from endless expansion to strategies for survival. And in turn that should reshape the list of things we think are important to learn." This is true. We need to rethink *what* we teach, *how* we teach, what *materials* we use, and, specifically, how we might use documentary forms like i-docs to activate student involvement. Building on the tradition of using documentary to instigate student involvement, we propose that the interactive can be used as a method of environmental and climate change pedagogy in three, interrelated ways:

1 The interactive form permits diverse forms of learning and enacts polyvocality.

2 Interactivity permits interdisciplinary encounters that help to bridge existing divides.
3 Interactivity can be used to foster collaboration and build a politics of care for local environments.

These methods of interactivity can be applied to other socially engaged subjects, such as reproductive justice or mass incarceration. For the purposes of this chapter, however, we focus on climate change as one of the most pressing and pervasive issues the world is facing, which affects communities in unequal ways and which mandates a polyvocal, interdisciplinary, and activist approach.

Interactivity as a Method for Enacting Polyvocality and Addressing Complexity

> *The interactive method permits diverse forms of learning, flows of information, and of enacting polyvocality. Polyvocality can hold the complexity of our wicked problems like climate change and help us, to quote Donna Haraway (2016, 1), "live with the trouble" of our time.*

For many of us, the appeal of the interactive is the non-hierarchical curation of perspectives and media forms. A collaborative, non-linear form offers a welcome alternative to the exceptionalism of the single protagonist of many feature documentaries and puts diverse perspectives into conversation. Interactive scholar and documentary-maker Sharon Daniel concurs that most feature documentaries collapse complexity into a single narrative journey. In contrast, she claims interactive documentaries are well suited to address systemic injustices because they permit a "plenitude of voices speaking directly from a multitude of contexts about their own circumstances" (Daniel, Aston, and Odorico 2018, 95). This "polyphonic" approach of an i-doc can more appropriately speak to the complexity and scale of issues like mass incarceration or climate change, which Daniel describes as "a landscape or 'site' of socio-political and economic experience … a problem space rather than a narrative" (99). The promise of the interactive is an engagement with the breadth of the problem space, which defies any single perspective or voice.

Interactives can permit multiple paths through a project enabling users to explore and discover the interconnectedness of individuals,

Figure 7.1

Dreaming of Trees video pages featuring Safali and a coastal map of Maipith, India

societies, ecosystems, and educational resources. For example, with *The Shore Line* a user can choose to navigate through six structured chapters organized graphically like a storybook, or through the project's *Atlas*, which is spatial, or through a database organized by country, ecological disaster, and theme. Each "chapter" is composed of five to seven short video profiles that are placed on dynamic pages connected to maps and curated educational resources. For example, the chapter "Stormy Skies" begins with Safali, a fifteen-year-old who lives in the Sundarbans, the largest mangrove forest in the world.

On the reverse side of Safali's video page, users can find a map and a sea-level slider to explore what her community would look like with an influx of another six metres of water. Alternatively, a user can also access a "strategy toolkit" with additional videos related to youth empowerment, guiding questions, and community-based activities. The platform's structure helps to foster a method of listening and holding different perspectives about potential solutions at the same time.

When a user lands on *The Shore Line* site, they experience the sounds of the coast punctuated by crashing waves. When they select a chapter, this soundscape shifts to an eclectic mix of underwater mammals and ocean traffic, and selecting a video shifts the sound to the voices of human protagonists. Sometimes pleasant and at times discordant, this polyphony of sounds draws attention to the diversity of individuals, life forms, and industrial activity along coastal areas. In our experience, this type of polyvocality in *The Shore Line* and other interactives works well in a classroom, where students are asked to consider diverse media forms and platforms, comparative perspectives, frames of references, and situated experiences. When facilitated with care in an educational setting, polyvocality can foster engaged listening from a place of compassion, empathy, and critical analysis. In this respect, the *interactive method* permits students to value and embrace both the tension and possibilities of comparative perspectives.

The project also lends itself well to a deep engagement with the concept of environmental justice that foregrounds the power imbalances inherent in environmental struggles. Through curated educational resources and discussion questions, *The Shore Line* asks users to consider how race, class, gender, age, and geographic location influence how people perceive and respond to environmental problems. In the introduction of *Speaking for Ourselves: Environmental Justice in Canada*, the editors suggest that, rather than a fixed concept, environmental justice can be conceived of as an ongoing conversation to strengthen community understanding, advocacy, and mobilization against unequal power relations (Haluza-Delay et al. 2010, 19). Anishinaabe scholar Deborah McGregor (2010, 27) builds on this principle by suggesting that, while environmental justice concerns cultural dominance, environmental destruction, and power imbalances between people, it also addresses our relationships to other beings. In *The Shore Line*, because perspectives and voices are placed in conversation with each other, users (and students) are encouraged to engage with the spaces *in between*. These include the sonic spaces between underwater ecologies and the voices of human protagonists; the relations between sea life, humans, and industrial pollution; between the lived experiences of individuals from nine countries; and, we hope, between information and action.

By integrating diverse forms of media, i-docs can also serve as a unique resource to engage with new media literacies and the ethical issues that accompany emergent media forms. For example, what are the critical literacy skills we need to analyze or even to create data visualizations? How does the creation of non-human soundscapes shift our perception of ecologies? How are maps and modelling being used to project future scenarios? And how does placing diverse modes within a shared interface help us to embrace diverse modes of learning? By offering "spaces" for encounter, i-docs afford the possibility to address new media literacies in dialogue with, and in service to, methods of communicating complex structural issues like climate change.

Interactivity Bridges Diverse Disciplines and Modes of Address

Interactivity helps us move between diverse, polyphonic forms of storytelling and across disciplinary boundaries. The potential of the i-doc form includes the ability to hold past, present, and speculative (or future-oriented) perspectives within the same architecture, to facilitate the navigation of different temporalities and scales of inherent to wicked problems that exceed temporal or geographic borders. With the case of climate change in particular, such movement between geographic, temporal, and scalar registers necessitates the transgression of traditional disciplinary boundaries and engagement with diverse types of knowledge, from scientific evidence and traditional Indigenous knowledge to creative mediations of lived experiences.

Rachel Carson, a key founder of the American environmentalist movement, famously begins *Silent Spring* with what she calls a fable for tomorrow. Set in a mythical town within the American heartland, "where all life seemed to live in harmony with its surroundings," Carson (2002, 1–2) describes how a blight descends upon a community, silencing the hums of bees and songbirds and prompting illnesses among children and farm animals alike. Her account of the devastating effects of DDT and other pesticides on ecosystems and waterways, rooted in rigorous science, draws upon literary practices like nature writing to convey the urgency of this environmental problem and the poetry of the natural world. By traversing disciplinary and generic boundaries to bridge scientific evidence and literary forms, Carson makes science both lyrical and accessible. Her fable for tomorrow also moves between temporalities, positing, by extrapolating from data about the over-application of pesticides in her present, a speculative dystopian future.

Similarly, as a form of environmental pedagogy, i-docs like *The Shore Line* can be used to help educators and documentary makers foster conversations and practices of collaboration across a variety of boundaries: between the disciplines of science, the arts, and education; and between data sets and personal video profiles. In other words, the promise of interactivity is a movement across lived experiences and forms of knowledge, offering the potential to mobilize and translate scientific data in accessible ways and juxtapose multiple temporalities.

> *Interactivity functions as a form of bridge building across disciplines, modes of address, and knowledges.*

Transcending boundaries is all the more urgent in our current age, given the increasing polarization and political contestations around climate change. The necessity of fostering dialogue, especially across political divisions, is matched by a need to develop shared philosophical, ideological, and technological ways to survive and ameliorate these planetary shifts. Put simply, the challenge of climate change forces a reconceptualization of academic disciplines and regimes of knowledge. Just as climate change does not obey geopolitical boundaries, its implications for our health, ecosystems, infrastructures, and ways of thinking are not circumscribed by disciplinary limits. Literary scholar James Engell (2017, 27), echoing the perceptions of many working within environmental humanities and sciences, proposes the formation of a new field and methodological approaches that eschew disciplinary borders to emphasize "zones of contact, multiple interfaces." This may include, in Engell's view, bridging disciplines as disparate as atmospheric chemistry, oceanography, politics, history, economics, computer modelling, agricultural science, conservation biology, ethics, urban planning – and, of course, cinema and the arts (ibid.). Interdisciplinarity is not a luxury: it has become a necessary approach for our age. How, then, can we as educators trained within specific academic fields and frequently constrained by a limited time economy grapple with vastly different vocabularies, approaches, and methods that inform our teaching and research? Engels points to co-teaching and engaged conversation as one way to bridge these gaps. We suggest that interactives might offer another route for this work, by placing different types of disciplinary and embodied knowledge in conversation.

Making use of diverse media forms, *The Shore Line* places different types of knowledge about sea level rise and experiences of the coast in dialogue, creating multiple inroads to users to engage with the complexity of the problem. This includes videos about Western scientific ways of adapting to ocean acidification alongside videos about Indigenous archaeological

Figure 7.2
A street view of Hong Kong in the present juxtaposed against a speculative floodview

excavations of traditional clam gardens, and portraits of artistic and literary interventions, like the work of a sand artist from New Zealand and a science fiction author narrating a futuristic, flooded Vancouver. The project includes diverse forms of data visualization, including NASA datasets that put coastal population density in conversation with other sets mapping vulnerable and shrinking wetlands and mangroves. By toggling *between* these datasets, users might create meaning and educators can help students understand how data are open to interpretation and, in some cases, manipulation. Heather Houser (2017) suggests that climate visualizations, which she explains can range from basic line graphs to artistic renderings of climate data, are a meaningful way of representing climate change at different scales and through diverse media. As an educator, Houser helps her students see data as dynamic cultural artefacts that can produce varied responses rather than prescriptive or immovable facts. Drawing on Houser, interactivity similarly uses visualization and other modes of presenting information to activate data in relation to other forms of knowledge (142).

Dystopic *floodviews* offer another form of data visualization, appearing at the end of each thematic chapter of *The Shore Line*. By drawing on projected sea levels, each view depicts what one of the world's most densely populated cities might look like in the future if water levels continue to rise. Speculative renderings of New York, Hong Kong, Negoya (Japan), Manilla, Boston, and Miami function as a provocation or counterpoint to the forms of adaptation featured in the videos. Each of these six floodviews contains a relevant fact about sea level rise and a question for engagement, such as: "What are some ways to reduce our dependence on fossil fuels?"

Like Rachel Carson's fable for tomorrow, which moves between scientific and speculative modes of address, these floodviews enable viewers to literally toggle between imaginative renderings of these future cities. Serving as both documentary and wake-up call, these views mobilize movement between registers to prompt users to contemplate how we might shape a different future.

Collaboration and Building a Politics of Care

One challenge for the developers of interactive documentaries is how to use the form to facilitate grounded social engagement with the world around us. An i-doc on its own on the internet can be passed over quickly, but an i-doc in the hands of an educator or organizer has enormous potential. What we know from past social action documentaries is that media alone does not mobilize knowledge, communities, and alliances. There is a large amount of skill and creativity involved in the curation of partners, networks, and circuits of distribution to get a project into the hands of people who can use it. Educators and organizers can mobilize students' familiarity with digital media and make interactives relevant as a tool for fostering collaborative encounters between teachers, students, and ecosystems. However, environmental educators are also confronted by the overuse of screen technologies that can distance students from their local environments.

Through our experience with *The Shore Line*, we discovered ways in which we and other educators can help students to mobilize environmental knowledge to put knowledge into action outside the classroom. In the hands of educators, the interactive documentary and interactivity as a method have the potential to facilitate multiple levels of bridge building. They can foster the development of horizontal collaborative networks across disciplines building upon the expertise of colleagues and peers. They can also be used to develop avenues for student engagement with nature, to put environmental knowledge into action. Vital to this is the cultivation of a "politics of care" for the non-human world, which can be used to spark emotional and political engagement with potential solutions or ways of surviving the consequences of climate change.

> *Interactivity is not limited to the form of an i-doc; it is also a method for developing non-hierarchical forms of collaboration within classrooms as well as within the community. Interactivity can also help facilitate a "politics of care" for the natural world, a crucial aspect of environmental pedagogy.*

In the case of *The Shore Line*, we used the interactive form to develop collaborative networks in several ways. The first step involved the development of the site, an interactive infrastructure that would help us do *in-reach* or connect and link together the individuals featured on the site. The next step involved *outreach* with educators and groups who might use the interactive to foster new networks, relationships, and teaching resources. It is this integration of pedagogical approaches that can be used to develop a politics of care for environments beyond the confines of a classroom.

In an effort to design the site with teachers in mind, we utilized the open architecture of the project to embed collaboratively produced educational materials such as workshop cards and strategy toolkits. These downloadable cards address themes such as climate displacement, youth leadership, or speculative futures and were collaboratively written with various experts, teachers, and advocates, including an environmental journalist, the World Wildlife Fund, the Suzuki Foundation, Jekanowski, and others. Each card, featured in the database area of the site, includes learning objectives, a selection of *Shore Line* video portraits, and classroom activities for high school or university settings.

Following the completion of *The Shore Line*, we used the project to facilitate events, bringing together educators from different levels and disciplines. For example, in coordination with the project's launch in 2017, we hosted an evening soirée, inviting teachers from three universities and two local high schools in Montreal to think about how we might use interactive media within environmental education. As ecologists, geographers, social scientists, and film and communications studies educators, we exchanged class activities and discussed ways to further

speculative futures

LEARNING OBJECTIVE: To challenge students to imagine collaborative responses to future environmental and social challenges, and to consider how to enact these responses in the present.

Within the realms of literature, film, and gaming, science and speculative fiction have been used to imagine potential future societies and technologies—and to make us think about the present by representing it in unexpected ways. Afrofuturist, Indigenous, feminist, and environmental writers in particular have used the imaginative and political potential of speculative fiction to raise people's consciousness about social justice and environmental issues, and push for political change.
With rising water levels disproportionately affecting certain populations over others, some artists, scientists, and activists are creating scientific and creative ways to speculate about potential effects of climate change on future shorelines and societies. These future-orientated practices don't only offer tools to conjecture about the world as it might become. They also encourage us to imagine different ways of responding to environmental change in the present.

VIDEOS:

Glacier Nation (Chile) Matías Asun, Greenpeace director and activist, acts as a diplomat for the new Glacier Republic. Glacier Nation imagines a separate country to defend Chile's glaciers from mining companies when the Chilean state will not.

Game Changer (Vancouver) Dave Flanders, a landscape architect and computer modeler, has developed a video game with urban planners, engineers, and students to envision future scenarios for one of the lowest lying regions in British Columbia.

A Floating Future (Bangladesh) Mohammed Rezwan is a sustainability architect whose floating schools and gardens offer a practical solution to seasonal flooding in Bangladesh—and potential solutions to other regions faced with rising water levels.

An Acidifying Ocean (Vancouver) Robert Saunders, scientist and CEO of Island Scallops in British Columbia, explores genetic testing and other scientific solutions to adapt the shellfish industry to a future shaped by ocean acidification and climate change.

KEYWORDS:

speculative fiction, science fiction, storytelling, future imaginaries, environmental futures, social justice, art and data visualization.

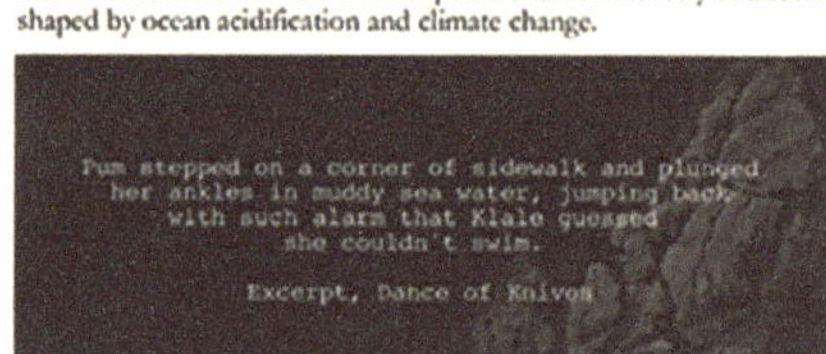

Science Fiction Futures (Vancouver) Science fiction writer Donna McMahon, depicts a future where intrepid characters must negotiate a flooded Vancouver.

1/3 theshorelineproject.org

Workshop by Rachel Webb Jekanowski, doctoral candidate in Film and Moving Image Studies at Concordia University

Figure 7.3 *Above and facing*
Examples of *The Shore Line* workshop cards

environmental journalism

LEARNING OBJECTIVE: To explore the potential for journalism and media to inform the public and shed light on issues that demand further action.

VIDEOS:

A Climate Reporter (Bangladesh) Hasan Kutubi, a local reporter on a remote island of Bangladesh, explains the urgency of building an adequate embankment to manage worsening floods.

Resisting Arctic Oil (Norway) Silje Lundberg, a youth activist, warns that oil drilling in Arctic Norway endangers the largest arctic coral reef in the world.

Forecasting Change (India) In the aftermath of two devastating storms Maharashi learns to forecast weather to help her fishing community in Southern India.

QUESTIONS:

Journalists can play a powerful role in steering public, social, and political agendas.

- How can this role—and the journalistic objective of impartiality—change in different settings or for different audiences? For example, how might a national or an international journalist cover a story differently than a local journalist?
- What different questions would they ask to frame the issue for their respective audiences?
- Is there a role for advocacy in journalism, and how would you describe this role? Use "A Climate Reporter" to inform this discussion.

KEYWORDS:

journalism; environmental journalism; community journalism; social media; alternative media; public service journalism

ACTIVITIES:

PROBLEM SOLVING:

- In Southern India, Maharashi is using media technologies to inform her community about important weather changes; discuss how her work fulfils a model of public service journalism and information dissemination.
- If you were to contribute to building a public information system like that seen in the video, what would you need to know about the media technologies that people in your community use?
- In class, sketch out: (1) an issue related to your community's safety and the environment, and why members of the public need to receive regular updates; (2) a series of questions about local media use that would inform your selection of a media platform for providing updates (i.e., who are you trying to reach? what media platforms do they use regularly?); (3) an outline of groups that could support or contribute to realizing a public information system (i.e., who might have the information that needs to be shared or resources available to support sharing this information? what organizations or institutions might also see a need for this information to be shared?).

SOCIAL MEDIA:

- In a group, discuss The Shore Line videos that have stayed with you. Why have these stories resonated? How were they told? What did they focus on? How do they connect with you or your community?
- List new questions you have about water, shorelines, or the environment.
- Share a link to a specific video with your social media community, express your thoughts, or send questions you want answered to a local politician, journalist, company, institution, or organization. Include us in your conversation by tagging us on Twitter (@theshorelinedoc) or Facebook (@theshorelineproject).

Workshop by Trish Audette-Longo, journalist and PhD candidate in Communications at Concordia University.

engage our students. This was the first of many in-class trainings and consultations. Taking advantage of the online nature of the i-doc, we also co-hosted a webinar with the educational non-profit Learn, inviting teachers along the St Lawrence River in Quebec to explore how we might use a shared water body to put our classes into conversation with each other. In both events, *The Shore Line* served as a vehicle to build conversations between teachers about how they are addressing climate concerns in their respective communities and to circulate resources we had discovered through our work.

Again and again, what surfaced in our pedagogical encounters around *The Shore Line* was a common desire to find ways that we might impart skills and values to encourage students to collaborate with each other and engage in the world around them. Matt Ferkany and Kyle Powys Whyte (2011) point to the need to integrate the development of what they call participatory virtues in environmental education. They argue that participatory projects often fail because of an absence of skills and virtues such as fairness, empathy, humility, judgment, negotiation, or compromise – skills that are required to manage complex issues. They explain that. while many of us may *know* of these values, we need to practise their application with students (331–2). This is where the interactive can serve as a tool and a method to encourage learning that emphasizes comparative perspectives and collaborative frameworks.

Within environmental education, there is a great deal of discussion about how to mobilize young people and communities to make the leap from learning *about* environments to directly engaging with it. Interdisciplinary researcher and educator Katie Kish (2018, 70), for instance, proposes that integrating emotion-driven learning and action-oriented learning into an environmental curriculum offers an important strategy for cultivating student agency "to make change in their communities" and "understand the complexity of multiple perspectives." Central to this is, in her view, "establishing a love of nature" through field trips so students can interact with the physical world multi-sensorially (ibid.).

Nature, however, is everywhere. Whether we are teaching in a rural community, a newly constructed suburb, or the inner city, our local surroundings are always already entangled with local ecosystems, climates, and watersheds. Yet, for most of us, our local environments are also human-disturbed, especially for those of us living close to industrial plants, in extractive zones, or in communities surviving colonial government policies.

Global warming exacerbates these conditions of inequality and ecological precariousness. Our challenge, then, is how to inspire in our students what Michi Saagiig Nishnaabeg scholar, artist, and writer Leanne Betasamosake Simpson calls "a politics based on love" with all local environments, especially "non-pristine nature" (Klein 2013). Developing such a politics of love and care can help students re-engage with damaged or human-altered landscapes, to see not only the damage but also the beauty in these places (ibid.). Such authentic relationships can only be built by moving from the virtual spaces of an i-doc into the world, by extended education beyond the classroom. Following Simpson's (2014, 18) articulation of "visiting" within Nishnaabeg intelligence, visiting is to get into the world, to "[share] oneself through story," learn from others, and nurture "relationship building." Thinking through interactivity, both as a non-linear form and as a mode of collaborative engagement and outreach, affords us an opportunity to broaden our toolkits for relation-building around environments. Developing a politics of care, enacting visiting as land-based pedagogy, and creating opportunities for collaboration between educators and across disciplines can all be used to enact environmental justice.

Conclusion: Teaching as if It Matters

This chapter is premised on our personal belief that in this era of massive environmental, social, and economic shifts, we need to teach as if it matters. Interactive documentaries like *The Shore Line* – which incorporate polyvocality, embrace the interdisciplinary urgency of our time, and offer the potential to spark different modes of environmental learning and practice beyond the classroom – offer an important tool for doing this. Our work as educators within media, film, and communication studies extends beyond the cultivation of creative production or critical thinking in our students, as crucial as this is. We believe that preparing our students for life after university includes equipping them to listen across difference, to engage in collaboration, and to participate in creating positive social change. As Bill McKibben (2017, 280) writes, one of the biggest parts of our work as teachers "comes after office hours and on weekends. It's the work of being citizens, of building movements." We can do this by helping to create avenues for both in-reach and outreach, as we argue in the last section of this chapter. We hope that this chapter can offer a collection of tools and resources for other educators within film and media studies to strategically bring environmental thought and action into the discipline and our own pedagogical practices. By asking students to engage with interactives, to explore the power of collaboration, and to help foster the values that could feed these relationships, we can help students develop both the skills and resilience for our collaborative survival.

Appendix:
Further Resources for Engaged Environmental Pedagogy

→ Andrejs Kulnieks, Dan Roronhiakewen Longboat, Kelly Young, eds., *Contemporary Studies in Environmental and Indigenous Pedagogies: A Curricula of Stories and Place* (Rotterdam: Sense Publishers, 2013). An edited collection for incorporating environmental and Indigenous pedagogies and eco-justice into curriculum, includes critical discussions and model curriculum.

→ Green Teacher. A non-profit organization dedicated to environmental education for children and teens that also publishes a quarterly magazine. https://greenteacher.com.

→ Indigenous Environmental Network (IEN). Based in the United States, the IEN was founded as a grassroots organization "to address environmental and economic justice issues." http://www.ienearth.org.

→ Kate McCoy, Eve Tuck, Marcia McKenzie, eds., *Land Education: Rethinking Pedagogies of Place from Indigenous, Postcolonial, and Decolonizing Perspectives* (New York: Routledge, 2018). This edited collection offers a useful guide for thinking about teaching-in-place on Indigenous land and incorporating intersectional and anti-colonial perspectives into curriculum.

→ Julian Agyeman, Peter Cole, Randolph Haluza-DeLay, and Pat O'Riley, eds., *Speaking for Ourselves: Environmental Justice in Canada* (Vancouver: UBC Press, 2010). A collection of essays offering insights into environmental justice in Canada.

→ Stephen Siperstein, Shane Hall, and Stephanie LeMenager, eds. *Teaching Climate Change in the Humani ties* (London and New York: Routledge, 2017). An edited collection about how to teach climate change within the arts and humanities, with practical resources, theoretical interventions, and reports from the field.

Notes

1 For more on environmental games, see Chang (2011).

2 *The Undersea Network* (Starosielski 2015) and the edited collection *Sustainable Media: Critical Approaches to Media and Environment* (Starosielski and Walker 2016) offer two insightful accounts of media's entanglements with telecommunication networks and physical landscapes.

References

Aston, Judith, and Stefano Odorico. 2018. "The Poetics and Politics of Polyphony." *Alphaville: Journal of Film and Screen Media*, no. 15: 63–93.

Audette-Longo, Trish. 2017. "Environmental Journalism." The Shore Line. http://theshorelineproject.org/media/workshop_cards/EnvironmentalJournalism.pdf.

Carson, Rachel. 2002 (1962). *Silent Spring*. Boston: Mariner Books.

Chang, Alenda Y. 2011. "Games as Environmental Texts." *Qui Parle: Critical Humanities and Social Sciences* 19 (2): 57–84.

Daniel, Sharon, Judith Aston, and Stefano Odorico. 2018. "Polyphony in Practice: An Interview with Sharon Daniel." *Alphaville: Journal of Film and Screen Media*, no. 15 (Summer): 94–105.

Engell, James. 2017. "Climate Disruption Involves All Disciplines: Who Becomes a Mentor?" In *Teaching Climate Change in the Humanities*, ed. Stephen Siperstein, Shane Hall, and Stephanie LeMenager, 24–30. Oxford: Routledge.

Ferkany, Matt, and Kyle Powys Whyte. 2011. "Environmental Education, Wicked Problems, and Virtue." *Philosophy of Education* 67 (February): 331–9.

Haluza-DeLay, Randolph, Pat O'Riley, Peter Cole, and Julian Agyeman. 2010. "Introduction – Speaking for Ourselves, Speaking Together: Environmental Justice in Canada." In *Speaking for Ourselves: Environmental Justice in Canada*, ed. Julian Agyeman, Peter Cole, Randolph Haluza-DeLay, and Pat O'Riley, 1–26. Vancouver: UBC Press.

Haraway, Donna J. 2016. *Staying with the Trouble: Making Kin in the Chthulucene*. Durham, NC: Duke University Press.

Houser, Heather. 2017. "Climate Visualizations as Cultural Objects." In *Teaching Climate Change in the Humanities*, ed. Stephen Siperstein, Shane Hall, and Stephanie LeMenager, 136–45. Oxford: Routledge.

Jekanowski, Rachel Webb. 2017. "Speculative Futures." The Shore Line. http://theshorelineproject.org/media/workshop_cards/SpeculativeFutures.pdf.
Kish, Katie. 2018. "School of Thought." *Alternatives Journal* 43 (3–4): 66–70.
Klein, Naomi. 2013. "Dancing the World into Being: A Conversation with Idle No More's Leanne Simpson." *Yes! Magazine*, 5 March 2013. http://www.yesmagazine.org/peace-justice/dancing-the-world-into-being-a-conversation-with-idle-no-more-leanne-simpson.
McGregor, Deborah. 2010. "Honouring Our Relations: An Anishnaabe Perspective on Environmental Justice." In *Speaking for Ourselves: Environmental Justice in Canada*, ed. Julian Agyeman, Peter Cole, Randolph Haluza-DeLay, and Pat O'Riley, 27–41. Vancouver: UBC Press.
McKibben, Bill. 2017. "Afterword." In *Teaching Climate Change in the Humanities*, ed. Stephen Siperstein, Shane Hall, and Stephanie LeMenager, 279–80. London: Routledge.
Morton, Timothy. 2013. *Hyperobjects: Philosophy and Ecology after the End of the World*. Minneapolis: University of Minnesota Press.
Simpson, Leanne Betasamosake. 2014. "Land as Pedagogy: Nishnaabeg Intelligence and Rebellious Transformation." *Decolonization: Indigeneity, Education and Society* 3 (3): 1–25.
Starosielski, Nicole. 2015. *The Undersea Network*. Durham, NC: Duke University Press.
Starosielski, Nicole, and Janet Walker, eds. 2016. *Sustainable Media: Critical Approaches to Media and Environment*. London: Routledge.
Tsing, Anna Lowenhaupt. 2015. *The Mushroom at the End of the World: On the Possibility of Life in Capitalist Ruins*. Princeton, NJ: Princeton University Press.
Zimmermann, Patricia R., and Helen de Michiel. 2018. *Open Space New Media Documentary: A Toolkit for Theory and Practice*. New York: Routledge.

8

THINKING IN NETWORKS

THE INTERACTIVE DOCUMENTARY AS A TOOL FOR SOCIAL CHANGE

Laura Ann Fox

Introduction

One aspect of the i-doc that is ripe for investigation is its vast potential to serve as a tool for activism. Regardless of the exact structure and content of a particular i-doc, the form consistently functions as a *network* – of nodes, links, videos, images, and other media elements, all of which are connected to create a whole. It is this existence as a network that gives the i-doc unique relevance within the realm of social engagement. To illustrate this potential, this chapter looks at a specific web-doc that was created in support of Sackville Schools 2020 (SS2020),[1] a grassroots educational movement in the small town of Sackville, New Brunswick.

The web-doc, titled *Sackville Schools 2020: A Web Documentary* (Laura Fox, 2017), is the practical outcome of a theoretical framework rooted in actor network theory and Bruno Latour's (1987) conceptualization of "network thinking." Through the creation of the web-doc, this network thinking emerged as the core component to understanding both the SS2020 movement offline and the functioning of the web-doc online. The concept of the (offline) "hybrid forum" is also crucial to understanding the potential of this network thinking in furthering a social cause. Introduced by Michel Callon, Pierre Lascoumes, and Yannick Barthe (2001) as they apply Latour's theoretical analysis to practical, real-life situations, hybrid forums act as real-world networks. They bring together experts and ordinary citizens to discuss the core issues of a particular social context (or what Latour terms "controversies") from all sides. Approaching a social issue by thinking in networks means putting an emphasis on the *connections* that exist between people, ideas, and things in order to find collective solutions.

Using the case of the ss2020 web-doc, this chapter situates Latour's network thinking and the concept of the hybrid forum within our current media environment. The structure of *Sackville Schools 2020* presents the movement not as one specific idea but, rather, as a network of people, physical environments, events, and ideas that are all related, interconnected, and valuable in creating change. Thus, understanding this web-doc through network theory is a means to address the complexities and nuanced perspectives within the ss2020 community movement.

Drawing on media ecology theory and the field of software studies, this chapter also suggests a need to extend the scope further, to recognize the connections between digital objects, software systems, hardware systems, and the human environment as networks increasingly shape our realities, both on- and offline. For it is at the intersection of documentary storytelling and computational, digital systems that the i-doc emerges. Software systems in particular are increasingly important in the shaping of culture and society; Yuk Hui's (2012; 2016) "digital milieu" helps to explain why we must acknowledge and appreciate the networks that bridge the virtual and the real. Indeed, these networks have had a significant impact on the ways in which activists and community leaders tell stories. The i-doc has evolved from media and systems that are constantly in flux, but its potential remains particularly important for filmmakers employing documentary practices in the hopes of sparking positive social change.

Sackville Schools 2020: A Community Movement

In 2015, in the town of Sackville, New Brunswick, a group of concerned community members came together to discuss the state of their public schools. The elementary, middle, and high schools were all decades old and required extensive maintenance and repairs. As the group began to meet regularly, their initial concern about the physical spaces of the schools grew into a larger conversation about how the school curriculum could be updated and improved as well. Along with their desire for a new, more environmentally and financially sustainable school infrastructure, the members of the group started discussing how their schools could develop a more modern education model that would give children the skills they need for the twenty-first century.[2]

The initial group of parents from the community established themselves as SS2020, a grassroots committee dedicated to updating both the spaces and curriculum of the town's K-12 schools by the year 2020. After a period of research into the issues within their schools, they began by hosting several public discussions with other educators, parents, students, and general community members. Now in its fifth year, at the time of writing, the SS2020 movement continues its push for change through an innovative public-private partnership. This means that a private architecture firm could finance and construct a new environmentally sustainable school – or what SS2020 terms a "community learning campus" – and lease it to the New Brunswick provincial government over a period of twenty to thirty-five years. There have indeed been broader criticisms of public-private partnerships as an approach to building public infrastructure, suggesting that it can result in the private sector influencing and, ultimately, profiting from public spaces or resources. However, these types of school building partnerships exist across Canada and the world, and their benefits include a faster build and more regular maintenance as compared to schools built through the traditional process of securing funding from a provincial department of education. These partnerships also potentially allow for more local input into the design, location, and management of school buildings.

Having sparked a complex and nuanced public debate, the SS2020 committee continues to strive for consensus within a divided community, where viewpoints diverge between those who seek change and those who would like to maintain the status quo. At the same time, the group is navigating a shifting political landscape at the local, provincial, and federal levels; as governments change, so, too, do their priorities for public education.

Sackville Schools 2020: The Web-Doc

Having attended middle school, high school, and university in Sackville, I have experienced the town's school system first-hand and feel a personal connection to the SS2020 cause. As I watched the movement grow, I wanted to contribute to it. I also wanted to connect it to my research on documentary media in Canada and the shift of traditional forms towards digital interactivity. In particular, I was seeking a useful format that could communicate SS2020's core mission while also presenting larger issues within public education, in New Brunswick and across Canada. The result of this exploration was the SS2020 web-doc, which examines the SS2020 movement through interviews with members of the committee as well as other parents, teachers, former students, and community members. It was built on the third version of Klynt (2019), a Paris-based interactive storytelling software. As I had no formal training in film production prior to creating the web-doc, this process was largely how I learned about camera and sound equipment as well as how to interview subjects and craft a story. The filming and building of the web-doc was, therefore, an intense process of learning by doing, embodying one of the core values of the SS2020 movement in itself: experiential learning.

Upon entering the web-doc, viewers are met with a landing page that shows a short opening video of children at the elementary school boarding a bus. This page orients viewers by introducing the title of the web-doc and providing brief instructions for viewing and interacting, as well as other functionalities such as the full screen button and the community page, which introduces all interview participants. After clicking the start button, viewers watch a short introductory video. Narrated by children from the community, this video introduces viewers to the town and to the key issues of the movement, including the neglected school infrastructure and the somewhat outdated curriculum. At the conclusion of this video, viewers are taken to the main menu page, which features an image of colourful tangram pieces, with a child's hand adding in an additional shape to complete the whole. The titles of four categories of videos appear on the tiles: *Our Spaces*, *Our Education*, *Our Region*, and *Our Movement*, which are also the core thematic "elements" (or "actors" to borrow Latour's term) within the SS2020 movement. The image is reminiscent of an elementary school math class and is a visual metaphor for the larger meaning of these elements connecting to one another to form a whole, a network.

As viewers choose a broad theme to dive into, they are met with another menu that presents various videos related to this theme, which they can watch in any order they choose. If they choose *Our Spaces*, for example, they find a series of videos that involve SS2020 teachers reflecting on the physical state of their K-12 schools, students giving tours of these schools, as well as information about the town's other civic educational buildings, such as the university in Sackville's downtown core (Mount Allison University), the pre-schools, and the seniors' college. There are also videos in which participants share ideas of how to create new school

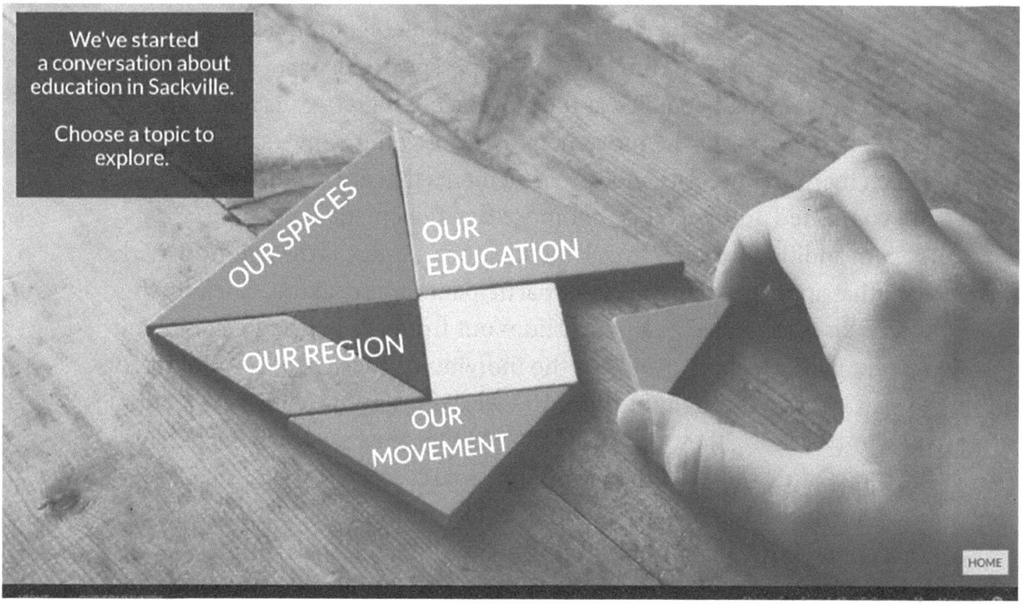

Figure 8.1
Sackville Schools 2020 web-doc menu

spaces that would be more environmentally and financially efficient, making it easier to integrate different age groups and learning styles. If viewers choose to enter the *Our Region* piece, they land on a menu of three videos with participant reflections on what makes the town of Sackville special, the challenges the school district faces on a regional level, as well as the current state and reputation of education in the province of New Brunswick. These videos are also accompanied by external links to additional media elements, including PDF reports such as the province's ten-year education plan as well as links to external websites.

Sackville Schools 2020 works as what Judith Aston and Sandra Gaudenzi (2012) refer to as "the hypertext mode," a closed database or archive of media that gives viewers the agency to explore. Rather than presenting certain people, elements, or ideas in a hierarchical storyline, or as a structured path, the web-doc conveys the overall network of all core themes of discussion – inviting viewers to watch at their own pace and according to their primary interests. As we see later on, the web-doc's non-linearity and exploratory mode are what make it a useful tool for communicating the SS2020 movement. It acts as an online reflection of the offline conversation taking place in Sackville; it is tailored to complement the ss2020 website by providing a range of interconnected perspectives, encouraging more community discussion offline as the movement progresses. Its non-linearity presents the story of the movement as an ongoing conversation, one in which there are multiple and varied elements that are of equal value; they are connected and, together, compose the movement as a whole.

An additional interactive element of the web-doc is the question mark icon that appears while interview participants are speaking. Clicking this icon pauses the video as a panel slides out from the left-hand side of the screen, giving a short profile of the individual. These profiles are linked to participants throughout the entire web-doc and provide information on who is sharing their perspective – whether they are teachers, parents, students, or those who inhabit multiple roles.

One of the key messages of the ss2020 movement is that education affects the Sackville community in many different ways: parents could be school volunteers, teachers are often former Sackville students, and university professors may be parents. Therefore, the interviewees bring multiple and varied perspectives to the different themes within the movement, an important factor to consider when representing a social movement as a network; in a network, all actors – whether ideas, people, or things – are equal and valuable. First, however, we must dig deeper into Latour's original concept of network thinking to further understand the significance of how networks shape our daily realities.

Network Thinking and the Hybrid Forum

In his seminal work *Science in Action* (1987), Latour expresses the foundational ideas of actor network theory, demonstrating the equal significance of social relations and technical instruments in science and technology. He challenges the notion of scientific "facts," which he suggests do not simply exist as something to be discovered but, rather, develop into being through a continuous process of decision-making by scientists and wider audiences: "the fate of a statement, that is the decision about whether it is a fact or a fiction, depends on a sequence of debates later on" (Latour 1987, 27). Latour shows the various ways in which scientific research works to convince readers that a statement is true in order for them to play their part in the process, which is to accept it as objective fact.[3] The construction of our objective reality is, therefore, always a *collective* process; it is inherently social. A fact can only emerge as truth through this ongoing process of decision-making, which creates networks between objects, people, and ideas. These elements are linked in multiple and varying ways, with equal influence on objectivity; all actors within the network play a valuable role in constructing reality. It is because of this that Latour claims no person, object, or idea can be fully understood without understanding the whole network of which it is part.

How do we apply this network thinking then not only to the natural sciences but also to civic engagement? Callon, Lascoumes, and Barthe (2001) successfully carry Latour's conceptualization of the network into real-life social and political contexts. They apply network thinking to realms such as public health, detailing several examples of a hybrid forum, in which French citizens, politicians, and scientists came together to discuss issues such as nuclear waste, asbestos, or avian flu. Named "forums" "because they are open spaces where groups can come together" and "hybrid" "because the groups involved … are heterogeneous," the hybrid forum is a space where researchers and ordinary citizens meet and discuss (18). They combine what the authors refer to as "secluded research," or scientific expertise, with "knowledge in the wild," or the lived experiences of citizens, challenging the divisions between groups (which they argue are outmoded).

Decades later, thinking in networks remains significant in bringing together the knowledge of experts, institutions, and citizens. By applying Latour's theoretical understanding of networks to social or political issues, we can begin to break down these long-standing barriers in order to value more varied types of knowledge and experience, and to imagine alternative solutions for our collective reality. As a global population, if we desire to move in the direction of strengthening democracy, fairness, and universal human rights, it is essential that we close the traditional gaps between what is considered expertise – scientific or otherwise – and the knowledge that is gained through the everyday lived experiences of our citizens. Instead of acting in silos, all actors within a network must be valued as having equal influence; we should not only be acknowledging the networks that shape our understandings of reality but also further developing and strengthening these connections as we move forward.

SS2020 is an example of a hybrid forum in the contemporary Canadian context. The core SS2020 committee consisted of parents who originally came together out of a growing concern for their crumbling public schools, though the maintenance of these buildings is the responsibility of the New Brunswick provincial government. In 2015, these parents heard rumours that the Anglophone East School District was planning an official assessment of all three Sackville schools. They assumed this would lead to the destruction of the middle school and the transfer of those young students into the dark, mouldy, vacant basement classrooms of the high school. Rather than waiting for this decision from the district, the group wanted to be proactive and come up with a healthier, more sustainable, and more cost-effective option for how to transform their schools. As the SS2020 committee continued to meet, the original issue of the school infrastructure grew into a broader discussion around education. The group wanted to develop a more modern, intergenerational, and community-based education model for the town – one that puts greater value on experiential and life-long learning. It also started to explore ideas for strengthening the connections between the K-12 schools and the town's pre-schools, the adult and family literacy programs, the not-for-profit seniors' college, and the university.[4]

At the heart of the movement is the recognition that the physical space of the school is inherently linked to the learning that happens within that space; more modern facilities enable the teaching and learning of more modern, twenty-first-century skills (Milton 2015). Here, we see the foundational principles of actor network theory at play, as both objects and ideas are assigned equal value in improving the town's education system. Within this is the understanding that community members who might normally be considered "outside" the school system can (and should) play an active role within it by joining the discussion about public education. The SS2020 committee has also made significant progress in connecting with traditional decision-makers, including the District Education Council, the minister of education and officials in the Department of Education and Early Childhood Development, and the Sackville mayor and council. There is a need to work with politicians as well as with those who are considered experts in the area of education: teachers, principals, vice-principals, professors, and other school administrators. What SS2020 also recognizes, however, is the vast potential that exists in "outside" resources beyond the classroom and within the community – the knowledge in the wild. In fact, SS2020 makes a point of acknowledging that these actors actually are *already* part of the Sackville educational network, engaging with education in various ways.

By starting this collective conversation, the SS2020 hybrid forum is reducing divisions between politicians, educators, school administrators, parents, students, and community members. They are consciously acknowledging that specialist knowledge is not the only valuable knowledge and valuing "the richness and relevance of knowledge developed by laypersons" (Callon, Lascoumes, and Barthe 2001, 9–10). This division between experts and laypersons seems particularly pertinent to Sackville as it reflects the class divisions that run deep within the town and the distinct divide between the university and the community (the "town/gown" divide). The Sackville educational network is indeed built upon various types of knowledge, as well as non-human physical spaces, and any creation or formalization of a community-based education model requires the strengthening and further development of these connections moving forward. These connections become even more relevant to our perceptions of social reality when we pivot to the digital.

Network Thinking in a Digital World

Our world has seen rapid changes in science and technology since Latour's 1987 publication, and even since Callon, Lascoumes, and Barthe's in 2001. If we are to understand the myriad social and political challenges facing our society today, we must consider our changing media environment and the growing significance of our lives online. In particular, we are seeing a growing reliance on software as it shapes both our material and immaterial society (Fuller 2005; Fuller 2003; Manovich 2013; Peters 2015). Lev Manovich (2013, 2) claims that we are now in a "software society" or "software culture." He notes that any investigation into society through a media lens must take software into account: "What electricity and the combustion engine were to the early twentieth century, software is to the early twenty-first century" (ibid.). The internet is, after all, one giant network to store and spread knowledge, a web of information comprising nodes, pathways, and links. With even more recent developments in smart technologies and the semantic web, these networks are only getting stronger and more intuitive (Hui 2016); it is becoming increasingly important to consider how networks shape our understandings of reality, both on- and offline. And, to understand the potential of the i-doc as an online form, we must examine our current media environment, in which film scholars note "documentaries become like software" (Dovey 2014, 26; Gaylor 2012).

Our online lives are now just as important as our offline lives with regard to how we perceive and understand our reality. Sherry Turkle (2015,

12) claims that both our understandings of self and "most relationships are a blend of on and offline interaction. Courtships take place via text. Political debates are sparked and social movements mobilize on websites." We must study the invention and growth of software if we are to understand our reality, particularly in terms of social and power relations – hence the rise of software studies as a theoretical field (Manovich 2013). However, applying the lens of network thinking, we must also connect this rising significance of software back to Friedrich Kittler's (1999) understanding of technical networks in order to consider the *whole* of technical systems. Kittler's theory on technical media is essential to understanding the current role of media in creating the real, that is, how we use media to logically create, order, preserve, spread, and interpret information. This includes the relationships between software and hardware systems, and their place within larger networks. John Durham Peters (2015) drives this claim home with examples of how our media networks have the ability to change our real-life experience in the world: the loss of identity and essential information if a student loses their phone; news media do not simply report the news but, rather, create the news; a change in romantic status on Facebook can somehow make a relationship real.

These examples further demonstrate the symbiotic relationship that now exists between the "virtual" and the "real" – a relationship that has been developing and growing over decades. What is necessary now, however, is a focused recognition of the networks that increasingly bridge these on- and offline spaces, thus shaping how we understand our social and political realities. As Hui (2013, 381) argues, "we know that the world consists of atoms, but to think only in terms of atoms won't help us to explain the world." Borrowing from Martin Heidegger's approach to understanding relations through *Dasein* (existence as a thing) and Gilbert Simondon's concept of the "milieu," Hui's "digital milieu" is the space where connections and links exist – where a network is formed. Hui suggests we approach digital objects through the concept of relations, including relationships to the human environment, which is precisely the type of network thinking theorized by Latour. Hui agrees, "an object is meaningful only within a network" (390).

The digital milieu is perhaps most easily understood with the example of social media networks. If you are tagged in an image on Instagram, for example, the significance of the image cannot be understood as the singular digital object; rather, it can only be understood by its existence within the network of Instagram's algorithms that instruct actions (such as sending you a notification of the tag or appearing on your friend's feed) as well as the physical hardware of your phone, which exists within the larger material network of cell service, and even the human-object connection between your finger and the app interface. The image as a digital object, therefore, does not exist alone but, rather, within multiple networks, both material and immaterial. It is precisely these connections within networks that give that particular image meaning.

Hui's digital milieu also relates back – as media theory often does – to the work of Marshall McLuhan, who recognized the significance of networks in media, culture, and society decades ago. As McLuhan (2003; 1964) correctly predicted, we have shifted into the "electronic age" or "post-mechanical age" and away from the mechanical, which favoured a more linear interpretation of reality. As a result, we are witnessing the breaking down of traditional dichotomies not only between on- and offline worlds but also in many realms of public life. McLuhan's most notable theory, that "the medium is the message," reflects this understanding of networks as essential to any changes in society and culture: "So 'the medium is the message' is not a simple remark, and I've always hesitated to explain it. It really means a hidden environment of services is the thing that changes people. It is the environment that changes people, not the technology" (McLuhan 2003, 242). McLuhan (1964) uses the figure-ground concept to illustrate the milieu, or "space between" where connections exist, which creates meaning. Hui (2016, 249) also speaks of the figure, or form, and its relation to the ground while introducing the digital milieu: "Forms are at the front, but they also need a ground, because it is the ground that carries them. Without the ground, forms cease to be." It is not the singular actor that creates an effect but, rather, the actor within its larger network; it is not the technology that creates a change in society but, rather, the environment within which the technology exists and operates.

Media and technology scholars note that, in our current media environment, the traditional dichotomies between consumers and producers, between audiences and creators, are breaking down (Arvidsson 2013; Hearn 2010; Jenkins 2006; Jenkins, Ford, and Green 2013; Jenkins et al. 2009; Dijck 2013). We see the effects of this breaking down in our offline lives, as these changing systems give rise to terms such as the "attention economy" or "reputation economy" (Hearn 2010; Terranova 2012), "convergence" (Jenkins 2006), and "participatory culture" (Jenkins et al. 2009). "With collaborative, that is, 'bottom up' processes, each and every person suddenly becomes able to participate in the production of metadata" that previously was "the principal activity of those in power" (Stiegler 2012, 14). Regardless of whether these changes are positive or negative, what is important to note here is their significance in facilitating a whole new way of thinking in networks. Latour argues that the construction of our reality has always been a social or collaborative process, but this has become much more visible online.

We are increasingly thinking in networks in essentially all areas of our reality: on- and offline worlds, data and metadata, media producers and consumers, experts and laypersons. The disappearance of oppositions that McLuhan speaks of is what Callon, Lascoumes, and Barthe (2001) argue actually must occur in order to benefit from any controversies that arise. This blurring or breaking down of boundaries is and has already been happening, but it must be acknowledged and embraced as a key first step in creating any sort of social change, or to "democratize our democracies." By reducing traditional dichotomies and embracing a more non-linear way of thinking that appreciates networks, we can uncover connections within our social realities that are perhaps unexpected. It is by facilitating this network thinking that the i-doc can assist activists in communicating the complexities of their cause.

The i-Doc: An Online Hybrid Forum

In this current software society, where consumers become producers of content, Thomas Austin and Wilma de Jong (2008) wonder about the relevance of documentary film. Just over a decade ago, they questioned whether we were moving into a "post-documentary moment." The continued importance of documentary as a genre, however, lies in its "special provenance with truth" (Juhasz 2014, 37), making it a particularly valuable genre for activism and social engagement.

Documentary films have historically been concerned with the question of how to depict reality (Barnouw 1993; Nichols 2001; Nichols 1991; Stallabrass 2013; Ward 2005), which has made the process of finding a concrete definition of the term difficult (Nichols 2001; Stallabrass 2013). It is important to consider this relationship to the real as we witness the continued evolution of documentary into online forms, looking not only at what a documentary is saying but *how* it is saying it. Through software systems, the i-doc offers new opportunities for how filmmakers can communicate a need for change. In the case of the SS2020 web-doc, the i-doc form posed a unique ability to reflect and strengthen both a filmmaker and a viewer's ability to think in networks. This was due to both its non-linear story structure and its interactivity through exploration.

Non-Linearity

The i-doc can offer a more non-linear version of a story by embodying a network; rather than a linear storyline with plot points along the way, the story can exist as a network, with different story elements connected through links. In the SS2020 web-doc, for example, the various controversies of physical space, education in the twenty-first century, the SS2020 human actors, and the regional and provincial political contexts all form a larger network. In the web-doc's backend, this network is presented visually as connecting menus and widgets that are linked to videos, images, PDFs, and outside websites. In the i-doc, it is often the connections between elements that produce meaning. In addition to the filming and editing that are typical of linear documentaries, there is also the design of the interface, which sets up connections between story elements, as well as the act of browsing by the viewer, which can create richer meanings (Gaudenzi 2014).

Presenting a documentary story in this way, as a network, allows separate pieces of information to be presented on equal footing or as equal actors within the overall story network. It therefore asks viewers to understand the *whole* of what is being conveyed to them rather than understanding one element at a time. This echoes Ted Nelson's (1987, 42) early philosophy on information technology, in his claim that "everything is intertwingled." A bizarre term, yes, but fitting for Nelson's belief that there are no singular subjects; rather, there is simply knowledge as a whole, which means it is wrong to ignore the connections between subjects by dividing them up. The i-doc's potential for non-linearity allows for a presentation of elements that together create a whole, encouraging viewers to engage with a story or social issue from all sides to form a deeper understanding of the myriad complexities within.

Interactivity

The i-doc is also unique in that it assigns a certain control or responsibility to viewers that is normally not possible in more traditional forms. They are prompted to interact with the story by clicking and scrolling, choosing or navigating content, and sometimes even contributing content themselves. Interactivity is the primary distinguishing element between traditional and newer forms of documentary as it changes both the role of the viewer and the story format itself (Nash 2014a, 50).

In the case of the SS2020 web-doc, the closed database exploration style means that interactivity is fairly simple but still inherently tied to the story. One of the main priorities of the SS2020 movement is to update and improve the curriculum to keep pace with our changing world as jobs today require different skills than they did in previous decades. A more modern education system means more autonomy for teachers in the classroom as well as more experiential, hands-on learning for students, and taking a "transformative" view of education with a student-directed approach. Allowing students to pursue questions and topics that stem from their own curiosity creates a learning experience that is more stimulating and memorable, therefore increasing student engagement. In a similar sense, the web-doc facilitates a viewer-directed approach, whereby viewers guide their own learning about the SS2020 movement. They have an active role in uncovering information by navigating the story through their personal choosing of topics – moving through videos and listening to speakers at their own pace and based on their own curiosity.

Creating the Web-Doc: The Challenges of Sense Making

One of the largest challenges in post-production was the question of how to make sense of the narrative, a concept that is central to the i-doc. Klynt, unlike other software programs such as Korsakow, relies less on algorithms to create connections between story elements and more on the filmmaker who creates the path for the story. However, what was challenging was presenting all of the elements of the SS2020 movement – space, curriculum, community, life-long learning – into a logical order that also conveyed a core message that audiences could understand without a linear storyline. Interactivity and non-linearity allow filmmakers to apply network thinking to a story. However, if the documentary is to make some sort of argument, the connections established between media within the i-doc must still be consciously created. This is particularly important for i-docs that include a call to action, as in my project, which was very much in support of the SS2020 movement. Although non-linearity might be necessary to facilitate a more nuanced understanding of a reality, the need to convey a specific message remains; to deliver a message effectively, the connections between media elements must be consciously structured. Thus, the role of the author or creator, in this case the filmmaker, cannot be taken for granted. In the i-doc, even if a story is non-linear, the author still chooses content to film in the real world and to upload into the software system; we cannot ignore the digital milieu and the relationships that exist between user and computer, human and hardware (Hui 2016; 2012). As in McLuhan's (1964) age-old argument that "the medium is the message," the master of the story and the story itself are always inherently linked, even if the creation of connections is left to automated systems.

Therefore, in creating the SS2020 web-doc, there was a need for the conscious structuring of digital objects as the connections themselves are what produce meaning. Managing the connections between media within an i-doc is how filmmakers can shine a light on the links that exist between ideas, people, and things in the real world. This is what led me to divide the videos, images, and texts in the web-doc into the four themes on the main menu, the four main concepts that I uncovered during my interviews and research into the offline movement. These choices, of course, reflect my role as both a creator and a researcher in this project. As I grew up in Sackville, I still consider myself part of that community, which is the community for which I created it. Furthermore, the participants featured within it are also part of the work's target audience; it is about the community, for the community. I wrote several of the texts within the web-doc, which is where my voice as the creator and as a member of the Sackville community reaches audiences directly. By creating the web-doc, I entered into the network and transformed it, therefore establishing my role as an actor within it. The i-doc "should not be seen as the uneventful evolution of documentaries in the digital realm but rather as a form of non-fiction narrative that uses action and choice, immersion and enacted perception as ways to construct the real" (Aston and Gaudenzi 2012, 125). It reflects the always social, collective process of constructing reality, which involves creators, participants, and audiences.

An Activist's Tool for Network Thinking

In the case of the SS2020 web-doc, the aspects of non-linearity and interactivity work together to facilitate the kind of network thinking that Latour, Callon, Lascoumes, and Barthe, as well as Hui, suggest we need in order to understand the complexities of our reality. The i-doc represents the concept of a hybrid forum online as different media and information are organized as a network, in which it is the connections that create meaning. Of course, we must be careful in assuming that giving viewers choice and an active role will result directly in their "empowerment" as this might not always be the case. There is a risk in assuming that *interactivity* automatically means there will be *interaction*. It is important to remember the 90-9-1 principle of the internet, "which suggests that there is participation inequality … with only 1 per cent of people creating content, 9 per cent editing or modifying that content, and 90 per cent viewing content without actively contributing" (Aston and Gaudenzi 2012, 131). Therefore, rather than creating a collab-doc or an online participatory mode, the web-doc is tailored to complement the SS2020 website and encourage more community discussion offline.

We must also remember that, while the i-doc gives filmmakers new opportunities for ways to reflect reality, it is still an art form that consists of both objective and subjective truths. We therefore cannot assume that an i-doc is entirely more beneficial to audiences because of its non-linearity and interactivity. As Neil Postman (1992, 18) reminds us, "a new technology does not add or subtract something, it changes everything." In this case, a new form in documentary does not render the linear, feature-length documentary obsolete. It does, however, offer filmmakers new ways to present their arguments about reality. It is particularly helpful for activists looking to highlight the complexities of a social issue. Non-linearity and interactivity are helpful for reflecting the interconnectedness of people, events, and ideas that produce a particular social reality. As is the case with the SS2020 web-doc, this form can provide a visual representation of a hybrid forum online. The i-doc invites audiences to recognize and appreciate the connections between elements as it can facilitate the network thinking that is necessary to do so; it gives filmmakers an ability to communicate a conversation and the nuances of our realities, which sometimes cannot be showcased through a linear storyline.

In our current media environment, we must consider the new role that documentary audiences have now as we find ourselves operating in vast networks of software, hardware, the virtual, and the real. As we continue as a software society, in which our on- and offline worlds converge, Latour's network thinking can also be applied to the genre of documentary itself as these new forms require filmmakers to work with others in the creative

Figure 8.2
Sackville Schools 2020 web-doc education page

process, such as graphic designers, user experience and interface designers, and web developers; we may need to think in "ecosystems" or "ecologies" to look at big pictures (Nash, Hight, and Summerhayes 2014).

The i-doc exists at the intersection between traditional, linear storytelling and the non-linearity and interactivity of software systems. By creating the SS2020 web-doc, I set out to investigate this intersection through both theoretical and practical means. This case demonstrates the unique opportunities that the i-doc form provides specifically for advancing social engagement. With its non-linearity and interactivity, the i-doc can present an issue or story as a network of ideas, people, and objects that are connected, therefore conveying the complexities of our realities and suggesting multiple entry points for creating change.

Notes

1 SS2020 recently rebranded as Sackville 20/20 to allow for federal funding, but this chapter uses the movement's name as it was during the time the web-doc was created in 2017.

2 The SS2020 committee drew much of its inspiration from the work of C21 Canada, Canadians for 21st Century Learning and Innovation. This non-profit educational organization outlines seven core competencies for the twenty-first century: creativity and innovation, critical thinking, collaboration, communication, character, culture and ethical citizenship, and computer and digital technologies. C21 Canada stresses a need for the integration of teaching practices such as student-centred or inquiry-based education, which generally lead to more engaging and memorable learning.

3 According to Latour, all scientific facts rely on a "black box," a network of decisions and links that are established and then repeatedly accepted as fact. The scientific research that follows builds upon these previously agreed upon facts, which are usually never questioned again. "Controversies" arise when these black boxes, or networks, are broken apart and previously established facts are questioned or disputed. He demonstrates this decision-making process with examples from both scientific literature and lab work, noting the various ways in which a statement or discovery is established as fact: the addition of multiple authors stating the same fact, references to other scientific articles, footnotes that anticipate a reader's possible counter-argument, or visual displays that rely on other facts.

4 This means integrating the schools into the community, both in terms of educational content and space. Currently, the schools are physically disconnected from one another. In particular, the high school is located across the Trans-Canada Highway on the outskirts of town. A community-based model would see the new school infrastructure built in a central location in town. This would encourage teachers to incorporate more field trips and school projects that allow learning outside the classroom and within the community while facilitating more experiential, hands-on learning.

References

Arvidsson, Adam. 2013. "The Potential of Consumer Publics." *Ephemera* 13 (2): 367–91.

Aston, Judith, and Sandra Gaudenzi. 2012. "Interactive Documentary: Setting the Field." *Studies in Documentary Film* 6 (2): 125–39.

Austin, Thomas, and Wilma de Jong. 2008. "Introduction." In *Rethinking Documentary: New Perspectives, New Practices*, ed. Thomas Austin and Wilma de Jong, 1–10. Berkshire and New York: Open University Press/McGraw-Hill Education.

Barnouw, Erik. 1993. *Documentary: A History of the Non-fiction Film*. 2nd ed. Oxford: Oxford University Press.

Callon, Michel, Pierre Lascoumes, and Yannick Barthe. 2001. *Acting in an Uncertain World: An Essay on Technical Democracy*. Cambridge: MIT Press.

Dijck, Jose van. 2013. *The Culture of Connectivity: A Critical History of Social Media*. Oxford: Oxford University Press.

Dovey, Jon. 2014. "Documentary Ecosystems: Collaboration and Exploitation." In *New Documentary Ecologies: Emerging Platforms, Practices and Discourses*, ed. Kate Nash, Craig Hight, and Catherine Summerhayes, 11–32. UK: Palgrave Macmillan.

Fuller, Matthew. 2003. *Behind the Blip: Essays on the Culture of Software*. Brooklyn, NY: Autonomedia.

– 2005. *Media Ecologies: Materialist Energies in Art and Technoculture*. Cambridge: MIT Press.

Gaudenzi, Sandra. 2014. "Strategies of Participation: The Who, What and When of Collaborative Documentaries." In *New Documentary Ecologies: Emerging Platforms, Practices and Discourses*, ed. Kate Nash, Craig Hight, and Catherine Summerhayes, 129–48. UK: Palgrave Macmillan.

Hearn, Alison. 2010. "Structuring Feeling: Web 2.0, Online Ranking and Rating, and the Digital 'Reputation' Economy." *Ephemera* 10 (3–4): 421–38.

Hui, Yuk. 2012. "What Is a Digital Object?" *Metaphilosophy* 43 (4): 380–95.

– 2016. *On the Existence of Digital Objects*. Minneapolis: University of Minnesota Press.

Jenkins, Henry. 2006. *Convergence Culture: Where Old and New Media Collide*. New York: New York University Press, 2006.

Jenkins, Henry, Sam Ford, and Joshua Green. 2013. *Spreadable Media: Creating Value and Meaning in a Networked Culture*. New York: New York University Press.

Jenkins, Henry, Ravi Purushotma, Margaret Weigel, Katie Clinton, and Alice J. Robison. 2009. *Confronting the Challenges of Participatory Culture: Media Education for the 21st Century*. Cambridge: MIT Press.

Juhasz, Alexandra. 2014. "Ceding the Activist Digital Documentary." In *New Documentary Ecologies: Emerging Platforms, Practices and Discourses*, ed. Kate Nash, Craig Hight, and Catherine Summerhayes, 33–49. UK: Palgrave Macmillan.

Kittler, Friedrich. 1999. *Gramophone, Film, Typewriter*. Stanford, CA: Stanford University Press.

Latour, Bruno. 1987. *Science in Action: How to Follow Scientists and Engineers through Society*. Cambridge: Harvard University Press.
Manovich, Lev. 2013. *Software Takes Command*. New York and London: Bloomsbury Academic.
McLuhan, Marshall. 1964. *Understanding Media: The Extensions of Man*. New York: McGraw-Hill.
– 2003. *Understanding Me: Lectures and Interviews*. Ed. Stephanie McLuhan and David Staines. Toronto: McLelland and Stewart.
Milton, Penny. 2015. "Shifting Minds 3.0: Redefining the Learning Landscape in Canada." C21 Canada. http://c21canada.org/shifting-minds-3-0-redefining-the-learning-landscape-in-canada.
Nash, Kate. 2014. "Clicking on the World: Documentary Representation and Interactivity." In *New Documentary Ecologies: Emerging Platforms, Practices and Discourses*, ed. Kate Nash, Craig Hight, and Catherine Summerhayes, 50–66. UK: Palgrave Macmillan.
Nash, Kate, Craig Hight, and Catherine Summerhayes. 2014. "Introduction." In *New Documentary Ecologies: Emerging Platforms, Practices and Discourses*, ed. Kate Nash, Craig Hight, and Catherine Summerhayes, 1–7. UK: Palgrave Macmillan.
Nelson, Ted. 1987. *Computer Lib/Dream Machines*. Redmond, WA: Tempus Books/Microsoft Press.
Nichols, Bill. 1991. *Representing Reality: Issues and Concepts in Documentary*. Bloomington: Indiana University Press.
– 2001. *Introduction to Documentary*. Bloomington: Indiana University Press.
Peters, John Durham. 2015. *The Marvelous Clouds: Toward a Philosophy of Elemental Media*. Chicago: University of Chicago Press.
Postman, Neil. 1992. *Technopoly: The Surrender of Culture to Technology*. New York: Vintage.
Stallabrass, Julian. 2013. *Documentary (Documents of Contemporary Art)*. London: Whitechapel Gallery.
Stiegler, Bernard. 2012. "Relational Ecology and the Digital Pharmakon." *Culture Machine* 13: 1–19.
Terranova, Tiziana. 2012. "Attention, Economy and the Brain." *Culture Machine* 13: 1–19.
Turkle, Sherry. 2015. *Reclaiming Conversation: The Power of Talk in a Digital Age*. New York: Penguin.
Ward, Paul. 2005. *Documentary: The Margins of Reality*. New York: Columbia University Press.

9

INTERACTIVITY AS ETHICAL ENCOUNTER IN *THE SPACE WE HOLD*

Freya Wright-Brough

Author Chimamanda Ngozi Adichie (2009) asserts that "power is the ability, not just to tell the story of another person, but to make it the definitive story of that person." Totalizing representations in art and media use stereotypes to define and homogenize diverse groups of people, and thus contribute to the oppression of marginalized peoples all over the world. In contrast, those who are part of dominant groups are often afforded the privilege of being represented in art and media in heterogeneous ways, contributing to perceptions of those people as complex individuals. The attempt to produce stories that resist these definitive narratives is a task incumbent on all practitioners producing publicly accessible representations of people. However, negotiating issues of totalization is a complex undertaking. For documentary scholars and practitioners, examining how totalization plays out – and might be resisted in practice – has become a rich site of investigation and debate (see Nichols 1991; Renov 2004; Cooper 2006; Saxton 2007; Nash 2011; Baek 2016; Colusso 2017). As both Bill Nichols (2017) and Kate Nash (2011) point out, different documentary modes raise different ethical questions. This chapter seeks to contribute to this growing area of debate by examining how interactive documentary practitioners are attempting to negotiate and resist totalization in their practice. To do this, the Levinasian concepts of the transcendent face-to-face encounter and infinity are employed as frameworks to analyze the interactive functions of the Canadian i-doc, *The Space We Hold* (Tiffany Hsiung and Christopher Kang, 2017).

While Emmanuel Levinas's ethics have been used by many scholars to explore documentary practice, his philosophy is not as commonly employed in i-doc scholarship. Brian Winston (2017, 29) is an exception: in his examination of the impact of digital technology and i-doc practices on ethics in documentary, however, he concludes that "documentary ethics in the digital era are fundamentally unchanged by technology." There are also scholars whose explorations of citizenship and politics in i-doc practice intersect with questions of ethics. For instance, Nash (2017) examines how interactive functions in i-docs encourage self-representation and resist totalizing portrayals of communities and places. Rather than focusing on self-representation or how digital technology affects ethics in documentary, this chapter seeks to contribute to the area of ethics in i-docs by examining another angle: I consider how filmmakers foster encounters in which the audience is made aware of its responsibility for the documentary subjects and thus show how these practitioners are working towards Levinas's notion of "infinity" through the application of interactivity. Before delving into analysis of *The Space We Hold*, further contextualization of Levinasian ethics is necessary to understand how the notions of face-to-face encounter and infinity might apply to the creation of interactive documentary.

Infinity in Documentary

Emmanuel Levinas's work is useful for those attempting to negotiate issues of totalization in documentary (and narrative more broadly) because he provides an alternative to the act of reducing and defining others. This alternative is the notion of infinity, something he describes as "the absolutely Other" (Levinas 1969, 49). According to Levinas, the Other "escapes my grasp by an essential dimension, even if I have him [*sic*] at my disposal. He [sic] is not wholly in my sight" (39; n.b., male pronouns in Levinas quotes hereafter changed to third person plural). For him, "to know amounts to grasping being out of nothing or reducing it to nothing, removing from it its alterity" (44). This suggests that attempts to know the Other absolutely are acts of totalization insofar as they subsume the Other's alterity into what Levinas refers to as "the same." Levinas positions the Other as the central figure within infinity rather than the self, and he warns that the "alterity of the Other does not depend on any quality that would distinguish [them] from me," adding that this sort of thinking "nullifies alterity" (194).

Levinas (1969, 26) presents the alternative to acts of totalization as that of "welcoming the Other, as hospitality" within which "the idea of Infinity is consummated." He elaborates on how this welcoming of the Other might work by stating: "To approach the Other in conversation is to welcome [their] expression, in which at each instant [they] overflow the idea a thought would carry away from it. It is therefore to receive from the Other beyond the capacity of the I, which means exactly: to have the idea of Infinity" (51). "Transcendence" and "infinity," for Levinas, is precisely this welcoming of the Other's expression and the acceptance of the Other's alterity (41). It is in this peaceful, face-to-face encounter with the Other that an ethical relation is formed, one that I argue the creators of *The Space We Hold* are pursuing through the construction of specific interactive functions.

Levinas's notion of responsibility also provides a useful way of thinking about how i-docs can produce opportunities for these peaceful encounters between spectator and the subjects on screen. He argues that ethics is born during the face-to-face relation with the Other, suggesting that "since the Other looks at me, I am responsible for [them]" (Levinas 1969, 96). In the following analysis of *The Space We Hold*, the ways in which the creators draw attention to the audience's responsibility to the documentary subjects are identified.

While this chapter presents a case for why Levinas's notion of infinity might be a useful way of thinking about the resistance of totality in i-doc practice, his stance on art's relationship with infinity must be recognized. Levinas touches on art only a handful of times throughout *Infinity and Totality*, but his assessment of whether art could facilitate encounters with infinity is decidedly negative. In one such instance Levinas (1969, 140) writes, "the world of things calls for art, in which intellectual accession to being moves into enjoyment, in which the Infinity of the idea is idolized in the finite, but sufficient, image. All art is plastic." In this statement, he paints art as stagnant, material, and purely representational. Levinas locates transcendence in the saying, rather than in the said, and is wary of any completed product such as a finished artwork: "a separation opens between the producer and the product. At a given moment the producer no longer *follows up*, remains behind. [Their] transcendence stops midway" (227, empahsis in original). Levinas's position on art does not seem to change vastly when he touches on the subject again in "Reality and Its

Shadow" (Levinas 1989). Jolanta Nowak (2010, 265) describes this essay as an argument that posits "that art's representational and rhythmic nature will always distract us from ethics"; she states that "Levinas's understanding of art's relationship with ethics is widely understood to be iconoclastic."

Given Levinas's position that art is a finite product and therefore it cannot facilitate encounters with infinity, it would seem that Levinasian concepts would be of little use to documentary scholarship and that arguing that an i-doc practitioner could work towards encounters with infinity would be a futile exercise. However, there are many scholars who have not only critiqued Levinas's position on art but also illustrated connections between art and the ethical encounter. For example, Jill Robbins (1995, 61) begins her essay, "Aesthetic Totality and Ethical Infinity: Levinas on Art," with the question, "does the work of art give access to the ethical, as Levinas understands it?" Though she notes that the "answer that Levinas most often provides to this question *in his work* is a resounding *no*" (61 [emphasis in original]), she concludes, "there is also the possibility of thinking the ethicity [*sic*] of poetry, or of thinking the ethical and aesthetics together" (77).

Nowak takes a similar approach, arguing that Levinas's position on art is not so damning. She points out the contradictions in his work, stating that he occasionally refers to artwork as something that has the "capacity to lead us to the Other," though he also argues that representation is "always a danger for ethics" (Nowak 2010, 274). Nowak reconciles this tension between infinity and a finite representation by contending that "ethics may at times involve representation which takes us away from the Other, while at the same time that same representation may refer us to that which is beyond representation" (ibid.). She ends her argument by stating, "art is no longer necessarily exiled, but may serve as an instrument for ethics" (276). As we will see, *The Space We Hold* aligns with Nowak's statement as the i-doc uses a finite medium to refer to that which is beyond representation and thus creates opportunities for an encounter with infinity.

Tom Burvill (2013) and Michael Balfour (2013) bring the question of performance into the debate about art and the Levinasian ethical encounter. If a performance is constructed as an "interactive event," Burvill (2013, 203) argues, then it need not be subjected to Levinas's objection to art for the interactive event becomes a dialogue between two subjects. Burvill goes on to make an argument for performance as uniquely situated to "embody and facilitate" Levinasian ethical encounters (212). However, attempting to facilitate ethical encounters in performance is complex.

Caroline Wake warns that the line between "witness" and "spectator" is thin and often invisible. Performances, therefore, risk re-creating and entrenching a relationship between audience and performer in which "'they' are there to be looked at and 'we' are here to look, appraise, and perhaps accept" (Wake 2010, 177). This danger for art to recreate and entrench power relations is particularly evident when examining *The Space We Hold*. Nevertheless, Burvill's argument that interactive events are uniquely situated to facilitate ethical encounters seems to open opportunities not only for theatre practitioners to move towards infinity but also for i-doc practitioners employing interactive functions as well. I show that interactivity can provide opportunities for encounters with infinity; however, it is not simply the presence of interactivity that facilitates such opportunities, but the way in which these interactions are constructed.

There are also a significant number of scholars who have linked Levinasian concepts to documentary specifically, and their work provides valuable ways of thinking about how *The Space We Hold* constructs opportunities for encounters with infinity. For example, Michael Renov (2004, 195) suggests that autobiographical documentary can include encounters between the self and the Other and that these encounters are "ethically charged in profound ways." In one instance, he argues that the film *Everything's for You* (Abraham Ravett, 1989) "serves as a locus for the teachings and insights of Emmanuel Levinas," illustrating a belief that transcendent encounter can occur in some capacity through factual screen content (Renov 2004, 195). Contending that Levinas's work "has much to offer to the visual arts," Sarah Cooper (2006, 92–3) argues that documentaries can suggest "that others are never fully knowable through the filmic image" and that this creates a "selfless encounter through which we might begin to see differently both in the cinematic space and beyond." Libby Saxton takes up a similar position, using the case study of *Shoah* (Claude Lanzmann, 1985). She argues that the film "constantly frustrates our desire to see, know and understand by refusing to allow the other and his or her history to take shape as objects under our gaze," thus "ethical relations are accorded precedence over questions of being and knowledge" (Saxton 2007, 12). *The Space We Hold* uses this technique, outlined by Saxton and Cooper, of suggesting that the subjects of the documentary are not fully knowable, something that I argue is a key part of constructing i-docs that provide opportunities for encounters with infinity.

Finally, Nash and Enrica Colusso investigate the ethical relationship between filmmaker and subject. Nash (2011, 238) argues that when "filmmakers acknowledge the contribution of the other and the limits of their own understanding, when they become vulnerable in the relationship and admit the limits of their own power and knowledge, the ethical encounter becomes possible." By analyzing her own practice, Colusso (2017, 155) concludes that documentary practitioners are "capable of precipitating the ethical encounter with the film subject, of raising awareness of the responsibility towards the other." While Nash and Colusso investigate the importance of responsibility in the relationship between filmmaker and documentary subject, my analysis of *The Space We Hold* demonstrates how the audience's responsibility to the subject can be fostered in a similar way through the construction of interactive functions in i-doc practice.

Negotiating Interaction in Analysis

Before embarking on an analysis of how the use of interactivity can engender responsibility to documentary subjects, the controversial nature of the notion of interactivity must be addressed. One of the first articulations around interactive text comes from Roland Barthes (1975), who delineated two types of texts: "readerly" texts, which require little effort to interpret; and "writerly" texts, which require the reader to interpret ambiguous messages in order to finish the story. These distinctions assert the importance of a reader's intellectual engagement with a text, and I argue, through an analysis of *The Space We Hold*, are highly relevant for i-doc practice.

As digital technology began to develop, there appeared to be new opportunities for film practitioners to increase the audience's role in creating the meaning of texts. However, as "interactivity" became linked with digital technology, a plethora of questions and critiques was elicited. For example, Espen Aarseth (1997, 48) suggests the term "interactive" is a buzzword used to promote technologies and should thus be used with caution. Alec Charles (2014, 90) warns that, if texts that invite audience participation "offer only an *illusion* of interactivity, then – rather than promoting participation – they may in fact serve entrenched structures of power by sublimating our desires for active, participatory citizenship" (emphasis in original). Lev Manovich (2001, 61) questions the outcomes of digital interactivity, arguing that when following a series of pre-programmed links, "we are asked to mistake the structure of somebody else's mind for our own." Acknowledging that interactivity is not a singular, watertight notion, the following analysis of the i-doc *The Space We Hold* uses Nash's (2012, 197) framework for "analyzing the meaning of interactivity in the context of specific texts."

Nash (2012, 198–9) acknowledges that interactivity is a complex notion that can differ in both kind and degree. She argues that "technology, while an important factor in discussions of interactivity, cannot in isolation help us to grasp the contribution that interactivity makes to documentary discourse" (200). Instead, Nash proposes that we "must be sensitive to the webdoc text as a whole and the place of interactivity within it" because the "same feature, clicking on a link, for example, may be technically identical but have very different impacts when used in the context of different webdocs" (200–2). To accomplish this sensitivity to the text as a whole she proposes three dimensions to consider when analyzing an i-doc: "the form of interactivity, the purpose or motivation for interactivity, and the context of interactivity" (196). The form of interactivity examines the relationship between audience, text, and author (although in this case I argue we recognize the relationship between audience and documentary subject as well), while the analysis of purpose refers to how the interactive functions support the goal of the documentary (201). Finally, the context refers to "the way in which interactive opportunities are presented to the user" (ibid.). These three dimensions are utilized as a framework for analyzing *The Space We Hold* in conjunction with the notion of ethical encounter from Levinas.

The Space We Hold

The Space We Hold is a Canadian i-doc created by Tiffany Hsiung and Christopher Kang and co-produced by the National Film Board of Canada and Cult Leader. It presents three testimonies of sexual violence told by women who were among the 200,000 girls and young women kidnapped and forced into sexual slavery by the Imperial Japanese Army during the Second World War. Seventy years after their imprisonment, Grandma Gil in South Korea, Grandma Cao in China, and Grandma Adela in the Philippines reflect on their decades of silence and shame. The i-doc begins by addressing the audience directly: the title page changes from stating "The Space We Hold" to "The Space I Hold" and finally to "The Space

You Hold." The shifting title is the first instance in which the filmmakers attempt to make the audience aware of its responsibility to the subjects of the i-doc. The title alludes not only to the physical act of holding down the space bar on the keyboard (which the audience must do to witness the grandmothers' testimonies later) but also to the responsibility both audience and filmmaker have to hold political space for the subjects so that they can speak. Throughout the work, *The Space We Hold* addresses the audience only in relation to its responsibility to the subjects of the documentary. It is this form of address, present throughout the work, that I argue aligns with Levinas's (1969, 51) notion of welcoming the Other's expression "beyond the capacity of the I."

The work adopts elements of documentary's participatory mode. Nichols (2017, 139) describes the participatory mode of documentary as one in which "what happens in front of the camera becomes an index of the nature of the interaction between filmmaker and subject." He also states that this mode "inflects the 'I speak about them to you' formulation into something that is often closer to 'I speak with them for you'" (ibid.). *The Space We Hold* continually foregrounds the filmmakers' presence throughout the work. For example, the first video component begins with the voice of Tiffany Hsiung, who states: "in the summer of 2009, I travelled to China, Korea and the Philippines to hear the stories of the comfort women." She then contextualizes her position as an outsider in relation to the subjects by stating: "growing up Asian in Canada, I knew very little Asian history." While Hsiung's presence recedes to make way for the grandmothers' voices during the interviews, she occasionally appears in the frame and her vocal responses to the grandmothers can sometimes be heard offscreen.

However, Hsiung is not satisfied with the audience passively viewing encounters between her and the grandmothers, as is common in traditional participatory documentaries. Nichols (2017, 139) observes that many interactive documentaries that engage in participatory filmmaking have "come to embrace the spectator as participant as well." Hsiung is an example of Nichols's observation as she not only uses her participatory role in the documentary to create a sense of intimacy during the video interviews with the grandmothers but also uses her role to address the audience members directly in order to engage them in these intimate encounters. For example, after the initial video plays, a second introductory video uses Hsiung's voice-over to introduce the grandmothers and situate their imprisonment within a larger history of using rape as a weapon of war.

The i-doc then returns to directly addressing the audience when Hsiung states, "they [the grandmas] still need us to listen and to respond." Here Hsiung uses her role as participatory filmmaker to directly engage with the audience and situate herself and the audience as part of the same group of people who need to listen and respond to the subjects of the i-doc. In making it clear that she as the filmmaker has a responsibility to welcome the expression of the subjects, Hsiung exemplifies the effort to create ethical encounters between filmmaker and subjects, as discussed by Nash and Colusso. However, Hsiung also positions the audience as having the same responsibilities through the interactive components of the work.

Directly after Hsiung's dialogue, a text component reads: "You are about to encounter the stories of the three grandmothers, some of the oldest living survivors of militarized sexual violence. Their stories are difficult to hear but even more difficult for them to tell." In this text, the filmmakers contextualize the political implications of listening to subjects who have been silenced. It is also another example of the way the work encourages the audience to welcome the expression of the Other "beyond the capacity of the I" by addressing the audience only in relation to its responsibility to the subjects (Levinas 1969, 51).

The documentary then poses the question: "Will you listen to the grandmothers' stories?" The audience is presented with two options, "yes" or "no." The ethical implications of this interactive function are significant and complex. As stated earlier, Wake warns that the line between witness and spectator is thin and often invisible. The power to listen or to silence the subjects of the documentary is risky. To some extent, the i-doc sets up a relationship between audience and subject in which "'they' are there to be looked at and 'we' are here to look, appraise, and perhaps accept" (Wake 2010, 177). This tension appears to be impossible to escape as it is part of the very nature of the face-to-face encounter. Nash (2011, 230) reminds us that when encountering the Other there is a choice to be made "between violence and responsibility." The choice to silence or to listen to the grandmothers in *The Space We Hold* mirrors this choice between violence and responsibility. Without the option to silence, the weight of the choice to listen to the subject cannot be fully comprehended.

If audience members choose to listen to the grandmothers, they are prompted to "hold the space bar to listen." Holding the space bar prompts a video interview of one of the three grandmothers to play. If the spectator lifts their finger from the space bar at any time, the story pauses and they

Figure 9.1
The choice to listen to the grandmothers

are prompted to hold the space bar to continue being able to access the story. Underneath this prompt is a second hyperlink option labelled "I choose not to listen," which takes the audience out of the story.

It is constructive here to return to Barthes's (1975) notions of "readerly" texts, which require little effort to interpret, and "writerly" texts, which require the reader to interpret ambiguous messages to finish the story. The function of holding the space bar, paired with the language used for the alternative option not to listen, constitutes a metaphor and is thus emblematic of a writerly text. The creators of *The Space We Hold* do not rely on digital technology to construct interactivity in their work; instead, they construct the space bar function as a writerly text to create interactivity. The members of the audience are invited to interact with the work in a way that demands the interpretation of a message about their own privilege in being able to silence the subjects of the documentary (by taking their hand off the space bar) and how this mimics the historical silencing of the subjects in the documentary. Through this metaphor, the creators attempt to make the audience more aware of its responsibility to the Other and its responsibility to welcome the documentary subject's expression by listening until the end of video.

If the audience chooses to hold the space bar, Allison Meier (2017) suggests that they participate in an act that encourages "an engaged listening experience." Because the interaction centres on the audience's ability to actively engage in listening, the space bar function also encourages the audience to welcome the expression of the "absolutely Other" without interruption or distraction. Thus, the filmmakers attempt to construct a digital space where infinity might be encountered. When the video is over, the spectator can stop holding down the space bar. The documentary then prompts the audience to respond using a comment function. In the background, behind the comment box, the creators make sure the face of the subject is visible. For example, when responding to Grandma Cao's video, the audience is faced with a meditative clip of Cao at home. She smokes and looks out the window just past the camera. I argue that this functions as a way to remind the audience of who it is responding to and thus its responsibility to the grandmothers. Once the comment is submitted, an audio clip from the filmmaker plays. The filmmaker takes this opportunity to remind the audience that it is inextricably linked to the subjects by stating that "we have all been a part of this story, the story of how we respond to sexual violence." This reminder that the audience is linked to the subjects of the documentary mirrors the notion that "I am 'in myself' through others" (Levinas 1981, 112). This is also further evidence that not only can documentary filmmakers attempt to be aware of their responsibility to their subjects to create a more ethical encounter, as Nash and Colusso have argued, but that they can also extend this awareness to their audience.

The spectator's response then joins thousands of other anonymous responses from other audience members. These responses are represented by a constellation of glowing dots, each of which is programmed to display the response text on a mouseover command. An analysis of the comments shows that *The Space We Hold* has constructed a space where audience members have experienced moments of infinity. Many of the responses, for example, demonstrate the audience's difficulty in "understanding" or coming to "know" the experiences of the subjects. For instance, one spectator responds, "Almost unimaginable, but here it is," while another adds, "I couldn't even for a second imagine what you and your fellow women had to go through." That the audience acknowledges the subjects' experiences cannot be understood by another illustrates Levinas's (1969, 194) notion that the "alterity of the

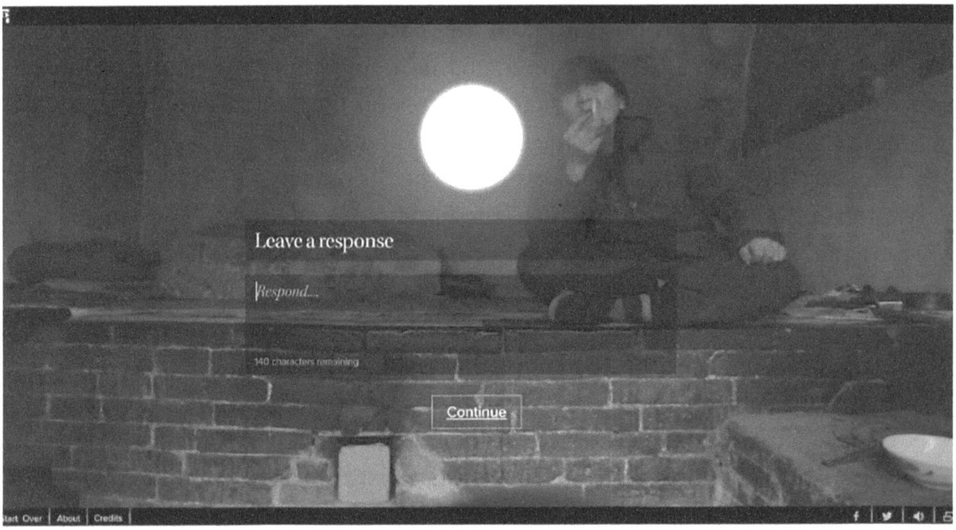

Figure 9.2
Grandma Cao sitting while the audience responds

Other does not depend on any quality that would distinguish [them] from me." By constructing its subjects as not fully knowable, *The Space We Hold* attempts to represent the subjects as complex persons rather than simply as vehicles for a narrow story about sexual violence. This, I argue, is a strategy to avoid constructing totalizing representations of women who have been marginalized and oppressed.

Another common response among audience members is a struggle to respond at all. For instance, one respondent writes, "There is no proper response to leave here, my heart breaks for them," while two others add, "There are no words" and "I'm sorry, and I know that's not enough." These responses imply an awareness that there is no finite statement that could articulate the infinite alterity of the documentary subjects. They suggest that spectators are able to encounter the infinity of a documentary subject through an i-doc and illustrate Nowak's (2010, 274) assertion that "ethics may at times involve representation which takes us away from the Other, while at the same time that same representation may refer us to that which is beyond representation."

A commitment to welcoming the expression of the Other was also a common theme in responses. For example, one audience member responds with "I am listening" while another responds, "I hear you and will continue

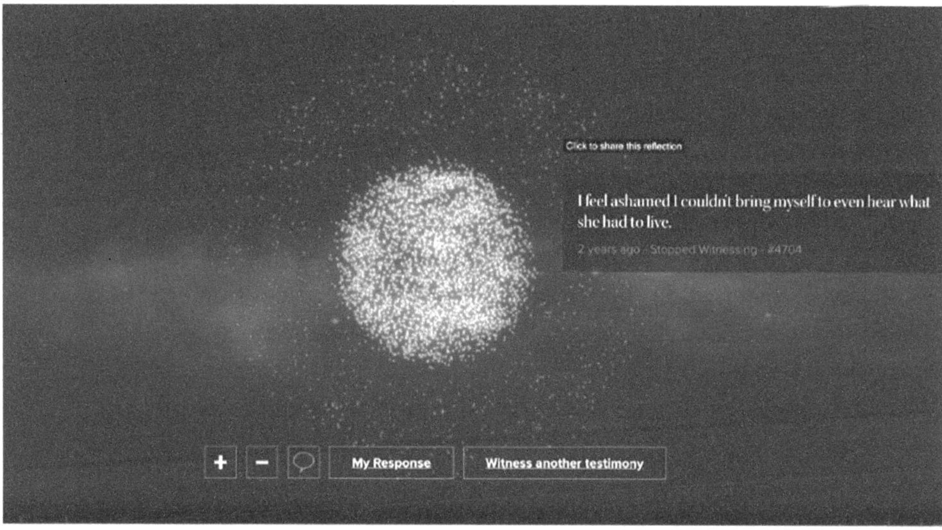

Figure 9.3
Respondent who stopped witnessing

to listen." These commitments to listening provide further evidence that this i-doc is successful in producing an audience that embraces the responsibility to welcome the expression of the documentary subjects.

Though the subjects and the audience are not directly in conversation, the design strategy of first welcoming the expression of the Other through the physical action of holding the space bar and then responding through a comment function mirrors Levinas's (1993, 15) notion that "the problem of knowledge and truth must ... be put in relation to the event of meeting and dialogue." Audience responses also illustrate a will to enter into conversation. In many instances, audience members directly respond to specific lines of dialogue from the grandmothers in their comments. For example, Grandma Adela states in her video, "If you expose yourself then what for? To be a hero? When in fact you are a society outcast?" One spectator responds to this by stating, "She's a hero." In another instance, Grandma Gil states, "People hear our stories, think about it for a few days and forget because it didn't happen to them." Many people respond with a commitment not to forget what they have heard, such as "I won't forget" or "You won't forget, neither will we." Through direct response to specific lines of dialogue the audience and documentary subjects enter into a quasi-conversation that assists in fostering an ethical encounter.

The creators of *The Space We Hold* do not ignore or attempt to hide those who choose to stop listening. Using the zoom out function on the response map, the audience can see a pattern. Those who witnessed video testimonies in their entirety are positioned within a globe formation in which the glowing dots overlap each other. Orbiting this globe are a sparse smattering of dots. Each dot represents an audience member who "stopped witnessing" during a video testimony. The below image is an example of an audience member who stopped witnessing. In the process of stopping the video, the audience member leaves the comment, "I feel ashamed I couldn't bring myself to even hear what she lived." While most audience members who stop witnessing do not leave comments, this audience member appears to be aware of the kind of violence enacted by choosing to stop listening to the expression of the documentary subject.

Conclusion

In closing this chapter, I return to Nash's three dimensions to analyze the meaning of interactivity in i-doc practice: form, purpose, and context. The form of interactivity in *The Space We Hold* is twofold. First, the documentary restricts users' access to content unless they actively engage in a listening process by holding the space bar. Second, the users are repositioned to speak and contribute to the encounter through the use of a comment function. Users also move from the position of an individual engaging in an intimate experience with the grandmothers to a collective experience of responding to sexual violence. This form of listening before speaking is constructed for a specific purpose that supports the goal of the documentary, that is, to construct opportunities in which the audience welcomes the expression of the documentary subjects "beyond the capacity of the I" and to encourage audiences to consider their responsibility to the subjects when responding (Levinas 1969, 51).

Finally, the context of the interactions is one of direct engagement. The i-doc uses audio, text, hyperlinks, and comment functions to directly address the viewer and request their interaction. The creators also take into account the historical and political context of the documentary subjects as people who are often silenced and embed metaphor into the interactive functions of the i-doc that encourage the audience to resist replicating and consequently entrenching this political and historical context. Instead, they construct a digital space wherein the subjects' recounts of violence are positioned as "testimonies" and the audience is encouraged to "witness" these testimonies. This is not to say that the creators of *The Space We Hold* have managed to evade totalization completely. Audience members can still enact the violence of totality by choosing to "stop witnessing," and the use of a finite medium to represent infinite subjects remains a tension here, regardless of the interactive components. However, as I argue, the creators of *The Space We Hold* have taken an active role in working towards infinity by seeking to design interactive functions that reveal the audience's responsibility to the documentary subjects, thus fostering genuine opportunities for ethical encounters.

In its eighty-year history, "the NFB has innovated countless contributions to the aesthetics of documentary film, often in tandem with – and often inspired by – technological developments" (Waugh and Winton 2013, 144). *The Space We Hold* is part of this continuity. Hsuing and Kang recognize their power as filmmakers to tell a definitive story about their documentary subjects and the power they engender in their audience to interpret messages about the documentary subjects. The filmmakers therefore devise innovative strategies to negotiate the totalization of people not only through their filmmaking practice but also through the design of interactive elements that prompt the audience to recognize its responsibility to the subjects on screen. These strategies attempt to shift traditional power dynamics between documentary subject and audience.

This method is not unique to *The Space We Hold*. The use of writerly interactive functions that highlight the responsibility the audience has to the subject can also be seen, for instance, in the i-doc *My Grandmother's Lingo* (McKeon 2016) from Special Broadcasting Service (SBS) in Australia. These approaches to i-doc practice constitute a step towards more sophisticated negotiations of totality in documentary, and it is therefore valuable to unpack how this step was achieved. As i-doc practitioners continue to negotiate totality, these methods for moving towards ethical encounters are likely already evolving and expanding. Using Levinas's notions of the face-to-face and infinity to continue mapping and critiquing these methods constitutes a vital area of investigation if i-docs are to continue advancing towards more ethical practices.

References

Aarseth, Espen J. 1997. *Cybertext: Perspectives on Ergodic Literature*. Baltimore: Johns Hopkins University Press.

Adichie, Chimamanda Ngozi. 2009. "The Danger of a Single Story." TED Talk. 7 October 2009. https://www.youtube.com/watch?v=D9Ihs241zeg&t=9s.

Baek, Jiewon. 2016. "Turning toward the Other: The Face of Humans, the Face of Things and the Face of Language in the Documentaries of Sylvain George." *Studies in French Cinema* 16 (1): 61–77.

Balfour, Michael. 2013. "Refugee Performance: Encounters with Alterity." In *Refugee Performance Practical Encounters*, ed. Michael Balfour, 213–28. Bristol: Intellect.

Barthes, Roland. 1975. *The Pleasure of the Text*. New York: Farrar, Straus and Giroux.

Burvill, Tom. 2013. "'Politics Begins as Ethics': Levinasian Ethics and Australian Performance Concerning Refugees." In *Refugee Performance Practical Encounters*, ed. Michael Balfour, 199–212. Bristol: Intellect.

Charles, Alec. 2014. *Interactivity 2*. 2nd ed. Oxford: Peter Lang.

Colusso, Enrica. 2017. "The Space between the Filmmaker and the Subject: The Ethical Encounter." *Studies in Documentary Film* 11 (2): 141–56. https://doi.org/10.1080/17503280.2017.1342072.

Cooper, Sarah. 2006. *Selfless Cinema? Ethics and French Documentary*. London: Legend.

Levinas, Emmanuel. 1969. *Totality and Infinity: An Essay on Exteriority*. Trans. Alphonso Lingis. Dordrecht: Martinus Nijhoff Publishers.

– 1981. *Otherwise Than Being*. Trans. Alphonso Lingis. Dordrecht: Martinus Nijhoff Publishers.

– 1989. "Reality and Its Shadow." Trans. Alphonso Lingis. In *The Levinas Reader*, ed. Sean Hand, 129–43. Oxford: Basil Blackwell.

– 1993. *Outside the Subject*. Trans. Michael B. Smith. Stanford: Stanford University Press.

Manovich, Lev. 2001. *The Language of New Media*. London: MIT Press.

McKeon, Gina. 2016. "My grandmother's Lingo." Special Broadcasting Service. https://www.sbs.com.au/mygrandmotherslingo.

Meier, Allison. 2017. "Interactive Documentary on 'Comfort Women' Asks You to Listen to Victims of Sexual Violence." *Hyperallergic*, 20 October 2017. https://hyperallergic.com/389794/the-space-we-hold-interactive-documentary-on-comfort-women.

Nash, Kate. 2011. "Documentary-for-the-Other: Relationships, Ethics and (Observational) Documentary." *Journal of Mass Media Ethics* 26 (3): 224–39. https://doi.org/10.1080/08900523.2011.581971.

– 2012. "Modes of Interactivity: Analysing the Webdoc." *Media, Culture and Society* 34 (2): 197. https://doi.org/10.1177/0163443711430758.

– 2017. "I-docs and the Documentary Tradition: Exploring Questions of Citizenship." In *i-Docs: the Evolving Practices of Interactive Documentary*, ed. Judith Aston, Sandra Gaudenzi, and Mandy Rose, 9–25. New York: Colombia University Press.

Nichols, Bill. 1991. *Representing Reality: Issues and Concepts in Documentary*. Bloomington: Indiana University Press.

– 2017. *Introduction to Documentary*. 3rd ed. Bloomington: Indiana University Press.

Nowak, Jolanta. 2010. "Out from Behind the Shadows: Levinas and Visual Art." *Philosophy Today* 54 (3): 265–78.

Renov, Michael. 2004. *The Subject of Documentary*. Minneapolis: University of Minnesota Press.

Robbins, Jill. 1995. "Aesthetic Totality and Ethical Infinity: Levinas on Art." *L'Esprit Créateur* 35 (3): 66–79. http://dx.doi.org/10.1353/esp.1995.0049.

Saxton, Libby. 2007. "Fragile Faces: Levinas and Lanzmann." *Film-Philosophy* 11 (2): 1–14. https://doi.org/10.3366/film.2007.0007.

Wake, Caroline. 2010. "Performing Witness Testimonial Theatre in the Age of Asylum, Australia 2000–2005." PhD diss., University of New South Wales. https://www.unsworks.unsw.edu.au/entities/publication/1eabb960-0792-422e-a72c-fa74c8422a21.

Waugh, Thomas, and Ezra Winton. 2013. "Challenges for Change: Canada's National Film Board." In *The Documentary Film Book*, ed. Brian Winston, 138–46. London: British Film Institute.

Winston, Brian. 2017. "'Le Rapport De Face à Face' in Digital Documentary." *Post Script* 36 (2): 12–30.

10

FISH LOVE

DIGITAL TECHNOLOGY AND PASSIVITY IN NETTIE WILD'S *UNINTERRUPTED*

Chelsea Birks

Nettie Wild's *Uninterrupted*, which ran every night in Vancouver during the summer of 2017, is part nature documentary, part environmentalist call to arms, and part art installation that immerses viewers in the life-cycle of BC salmon through a dazzling array of images projected onto the underside of the Cambie Street Bridge. The experience is difficult to categorize or define: by billing itself as a "cinematic spectacle," *Uninterrupted* acknowledges its unusual mode of viewership, which involves multiple digital projectors and requires an active spectator. This study explores the ways that *Uninterrupted* uses digital technology to investigate the ethics of agency and participation in documentary cinema. Although *Uninterrupted* is only an interactive documentary in a limited sense, its engagement with these issues usefully contributes to recent scholarship focusing on the intersections between documentary and digital media. I argue that it is precisely through its ambivalent engagement with interactivity that *Uninterrupted* takes an ethical stance: though it uses digital projection and transmedia content to push the boundaries of the traditional cinematic apparatus, it also emphasizes a feeling of passivity or even surrender in relation to the subaqueous world of BC salmon. While Aston, Gaudenzi, and Rose (2017, 2) describe the interactive documentary (or "i-doc") as highlighting a "humanistic approach to agency," *Uninterrupted* instead evokes a thoroughly *posthumanist* attitude to the spectator's engagement with reality. As an interactive documentary, it asks human audiences to consider themselves as co-creators of reality, but it also suggests optimistic possibilities for more passive forms of interaction.

Through this posthumanist approach to human relationships with the environment, *Uninterrupted* also provides a unique intervention into recent conversations about cinema's ability (or lack thereof) to evoke non-anthropocentric perspectives. These discussions ask us to reconsider humanity's position in relation to a reality that may be indifferent or hostile to us, especially given the increasing risks of climate change;[1] *Uninterrupted*, on the other hand, offers a more optimistic environmental ethics. The following section considers these ethics in the context of the interactive documentary by examining *Uninterrupted*'s transmedia content and participatory modes of engagement. I then analyze the screening experience itself, which maintains the idea of humans as co-creators of reality but also – and more important – urges the spectator to view salmon as agents and to adopt a more passive relation to the environment. I conclude by theorizing *Uninterrupted*'s movement between passivity and activity as a form of love, referring to Anat Pick's (2011) idea of a "creaturely poetics," founded on mutual vulnerability. *Uninterrupted*'s use of transmedia content and digital technology pushes the boundaries of both the cinematic apparatus and human subjectivity; in doing so, it endorses a dynamic new way of considering the relationships between humans, animals, and the environment.

Transmedia Content and Interactive Agency

Uninterrupted began as an NFB short in 2012. The central idea of the short – that the lifecycle of BC salmon is a massive and unending process stretching back millions of years – was then expanded into the ambitious installation project shown throughout the summer of 2017. In the 2012 short the screen is split into pieces, fragmenting the viewer's perspective on a process that far exceeds the timeline of human history: this non-anthropocentric vision interrupts the unified position of mastery usually associated with the cinematic apparatus.[2] The 2017 version of *Uninterrupted* expands on the idea of a partial view of natural processes by further pushing the limits of the apparatus. Director of photography Athan Merrick and cinematographer Nic Teichrob used Phantom Flex 4K cameras in underwater housing to shoot footage over three years during the Adams River salmon run, which takes place in the traditional lands of the Little Shuswap Lake Indian Band from the Secwepemc Nation. They shot additional footage in False Creek in the traditional territories of the Musqueam, Squamish, and Tsleil-Waututh Nations.[3] The eighteen-month editing process then used virtual reality to map how images from eight projectors would appear on the multiple three-dimensional surfaces of the Cambie Street Bridge.

Uninterrupted was promoted as part of Vancouver's Canada 150+ celebrations and was widely advertised throughout the city, resulting in crowds of thirty thousand people (around five hundred a night) throughout the summer of 2017. Advertisements directed viewers to the website, Uninterrupted.ca, where they could learn about the show and complete the interactive journey to see their names projected under the bridge. The website also emphasizes *Uninterrupted*'s environmental concerns by citing troubling statistics and directing visitors to charities and conservation efforts (the screening experience, which I discuss in the following section, is far less didactic). Like many interactive documentaries, the goal of *Uninterrupted*'s transmedia content is *action*: it uses digital technologies to alert the public to an issue and propose ways to help. In this way, it aligns with Aston, Gaudenzi, and Rose's (2017, 1) "deliberately open ended" definition of the i-doc as "any project that starts with the intention to engage with the real, and that uses digital interactive technology to realise this intention." The transmedia experience of *Uninterrupted* explicitly aims to engage audiences with the real situation facing BC salmon and to recognize themselves as agents capable of effecting change.

A number of i-docs similarly use interactive technologies to foster a sense of agency around social issues. Ryan Watson (2017, 601), for example, argues that i-docs like *Public Secrets* (Sharon Daniel, 2006) and *Points of View* (Zohar Kfir, 2014) belong to a longer tradition of radical politics in documentary filmmaking and that the use of digital technologies allows for a new kind of "multifaceted encounter" with marginalized groups (Californian female prison inmates in the former example, Palestinians in Israeli-occupied territory in the latter); Mandy Rose (2017) discusses i-docs about African American men and argues that co-creative strategies allow documentary subjects to take control of their representation, so that "media about" becomes "media with"; Paolo Favero (2013; 2017) argues that i-docs provide a means of "getting our hands dirty" in that they work against the distancing effects of cinematic modes of vision and promote more direct forms of interaction with the real world. Rose, Watson, and Favero all discuss i-docs focused around what Rose (2017, 52) calls "counterpublics," referring to "groups contesting hegemonic discourse or power structures," and they are all interested in exploring optimistic possibilities of the form by arguing that the user's agency over the computer system empowers them to effect change in broader social discourses or systems of power. Though *Uninterrupted* troubles notions of agency and participation in a number of ways, it shares this optimistic outlook on digital technology and similarly encourages users to actively engage with an emerging piece of art rather than passively receive it as a prescribed perspective on reality (Aston and Gaudenzi 2012, 132).

While *Uninterrupted* tests the boundaries of the cinematic medium in general and documentary form in particular, it only offers limited possibilities for co-creation and participation. Kate Nash (2012, 199) writes that, for i-docs, interactivity is "most often understood in terms of the user's ability to exert control over content." This can take several forms, ranging from a viewer's ability to choose the order in which they view the i-doc to more participatory models that allow participants to actively contribute content. While watching *Uninterrupted* and exploring its associated website is a more interactive experience than one provided by a more conventional documentary, it is less participatory than some of the more innovative examples of the i-doc genre: it lacks the elaborate network of online content in a work like *Hollow* (Elaine McMillion Sheldon, 2014), which allows users to click through thirty short films about the residents of McDowell County, West Virginia (Nash 2017), or the co-creative possibilities of something like *RiP: A Remix Manifesto* (Brett Gaylor, 2008), a collaborative open-source documentary featuring remixed content from hundreds of participants.

If interaction in the i-doc is restricted to changes effected within a user-computer interface, then only three major features of *Uninterrupted* might be categorized as such. These features are: the interactive journey, the making-of featurettes on the website,[4] and the projection of participant names on the bridge before the nightly show. In the interactive journey, visitors can click through the various stages in the lifecycle of the salmon, from fry hatching in rivers and streams to young salmon finding their way to the Pacific Ocean to mature adults swimming back to their birthplace to spawn. The timeline is supplemented by video clips, animations, games, and a quiz, as well as a number of opportunities to share information through social media platforms. Other parts of the website feature video that supplements the information highlighted in the interactive journey: the making-of videos feature interviews with the project's crew and volunteers, in which they describe the intensive processes required to shoot, edit, and screen *Uninterrupted* as well as its innovative new media technologies, such as the use of Oculus Rift VR headsets to map footage onto the bridge. Though *Uninterrupted*'s online content in many ways resembles previous i-docs – like *Hollow*, for example, it requires viewers to scroll through video clips, photographs, quotes, and animations – the interactive journey takes under fifteen minutes to complete and most of the videos on the website are under two minutes long. While users can click through the online journey in any order and have the freedom to skip or expand content, it makes the most sense if navigated in a linear, chronological fashion, from salmon egg to spawn to death.

This relative lack of depth suggests that *Uninterrupted* primarily uses transmedia content as a promotional tool rather than as a way of exploring new possibilities for interactive digital technologies. Marketing fuels the most participatory of *Uninterrupted*'s interactive features, which gives visitors the opportunity to fill out a form after completing the online journey to see "your name projected with others in a visual projection before the nightly viewings." The projection of audience names is the only way that spectators can co-create the experience in any concrete sense – though, as I discuss in the following section, they are encouraged to view themselves as agents in other ways during the show – since it makes for a slightly different viewing experience each night. After this pre-show, however, *Uninterrupted*'s screening experience emphasizes immersion: though the cinematic installation is more active than a conventional documentary in that spectators have to move around to see the whole image, it is passive in that the audience has no control over the content being projected. The fact that online content is secondary to the screening experience – the former promotes the latter – suggests that *Uninterrupted* favours the more passive mode of engagement between spectator and screen over participatory interactions between computers and users.

If the interactive possibilities of *Uninterrupted* are so limited, then why consider it under the framework of the i-doc? The primary reason is that *Uninterrupted* navigates the ethical issues around agency and digital technology at stake in the i-doc in a new way by emphasizing passive reception over participation or agency. This emphasis on passivity may help resolve some tensions within the scholarship on interactive documentary. While Nash, Rose, Walton, and Favero insist on interactivity as a positive, others are more sceptical about the i-doc's ability to encourage audience participation: Charles Forceville (2017) argues that the more interactive a documentary becomes, the less likely it will be to reach a wide audience since immersion and argumentation are key to the appeal of documentary cinema; Patricia Aufderheide (2015, 77) explores the limitations of a number of recent i-docs (including *Hollow*) and argues that they function more as media experiments than as successful public outreach since "possibilities for user immersion in the experience cross-cut with opportunities for choice." Both suggest that the i-doc has yet to find reliable strategies for balancing audience immersion and user control, and that form in the i-doc is continually contested and in search of more optimal modes of participation. While some have argued that the interactive documentary is a radically new media form,[5] the above discussions suggest that the i-doc is better understood as a dialectic between passive and active modes of viewership since some degree of passive immersion seems necessary keep users interested in interactive content.

Uninterrupted provides a new way of balancing the equation by exploiting the interactive possibilities of new media while also recognizing the immersive power of traditional linear storytelling. While Wild (2017) states in interviews that she sees herself primarily as a storyteller, producer Rae Hull (2017) explains that she, Wild, and co-producer Betsy Carson saw a need to connect Wild's immersive narrative with "the larger 'salmon' network – i.e. scientists, researchers, First Nations, communities, local streamkeepers." *Uninterrupted* is therefore designed as a conversation between old and new media forms, one that balances the need for broad public engagement with opportunities for further interaction. The following section explores the screening experience of *Uninterrupted* with a particular focus on how it pushes the boundaries of the cinematic apparatus. While i-docs with activist intentions often assume that agency is a de facto moral good – which makes sense given that they aim to empower marginalized voices – *Uninterrupted* uses cinematic and new media technologies to explore the ethical potential of passivity. By limiting audience control over the image, the apparatus of *Uninterrupted* deprioritizes the human and makes space for other perspectives and relationships to emerge.

Passivity and the Apparatus

Uninterrupted was screened in Cooper's Park, a busy playground underneath the north side of the Cambie Street Bridge in Vancouver's Yaletown district. Volunteers at the entrance of the park directed spectators towards the best vantage points, but viewers were given free reign of the park: they could stand at the back directly against the abutment, or perch on the playground equipment in the middle of the park, or sit on blankets or festival chairs on the ground. Though most spectators sat facing the piles in the water directly in front of the park, the screening experience does not prioritize any one viewing position, and some chose to lie flat on the ground facing directly overhead or even to sit closer to the water looking towards the abutment. Editor Michael Brockington (2019) explains that, during the editing process, "at any given time we're making decisions about what the screen should be because it's not a fixed thing, it's something that is dynamic and changing from second to second." The shifting parameters of the screen affect not only the filmmaking process but also the viewing experience: the spectator also makes decisions about where to look throughout *Uninterrupted* since it is often impossible to view the entire image at once.

The screening begins with an animated fish skeleton projected against the black backdrop of the bridge; a chime sounds as the skeleton transforms into the opening title. Blue water then gradually flows up the south piles before an image of the Yaletown skyline gradually appears on the span overhead. This nighttime city scene is a reflection of the surrounding environment, but the spectator's perspective is inverted: the flooded pillars give the impression of looking upwards at the surrounding glass condo and office towers from under the surface of False Creek.[6] These opening images give the impression of a fish-eye view, simultaneously speaking directly to its Vancouver audience and unsettling their perspective on a familiar space. The music, which continues the percussive chiming from the title sequence, evokes a sense of curiosity or awe and guides the audience through more images and sounds of downtown Vancouver:[7] a train passes by, and then the sparkling dome of the Telus World of Science – visible just east of the screening location – floats up overhead.

Nature is immediately presented as something that intersects urban space: it is not "out there," apart from human structures of civilization, but flows around, through, and under our anthropocentric modes of perception. This paradoxical view of False Creek – simultaneously familiar and strange – then transitions to more conventionally "wild" spaces as spectacular underwater shots of swimming salmon are intercut with images of bright red maple leaves and flowing underwater grasses. A fish's eye emerges from the piles to the south, identifying the bearer of the gaze in these sequences as it looks upwards towards the surface of the river. An enormous salmon then floats overhead before the bubbles in the flowing water turn into shimmering points of light, reminiscent of the Yaletown skyline in the first city sequence.

After establishing these parallels between urban and wild spaces, *Uninterrupted*'s narrative then echoes the structure of the interactive journey by loosely following the lifecycle of the salmon. Bright red sockeye males compete with each other using their hooked snouts; clear eggs wobble on a long fern and begin to turn bright vermillion; salmon carcasses float to the bottom of the river bed; and tiny fry emerge from their eggs. Shots are scaled to the fish, ranging from long shots of schools swimming to close-ups of faces and tails to extreme close-ups on amber eyes and wriggling roe, all looming enormous on the black screen of the bridge. Though the interactive journey is largely linear, depicting the salmon lifespan as a progressive process from birth to death, the screening emphasizes circularity. A number of round motifs – bubbles, eggs, eyes – play off the circular structure of the film, which begins and ends with the Vancouver skyline. After the sequence depicting the final stage of the salmon lifecycle, in which carcasses lie submerged in the Adams riverbed after successfully spawning, a blue artificial glow brings us back to urban Vancouver. Suddenly we are seeing through the windows of a condo tower, and time lapse images of people moving around their apartments are superimposed with train sounds and the rushing lights of city streets. Witness to this is a large hazel salmon's eye that again appears on the south piles. Finally, an orange egg floats up amid the sparkling lights of the Vancouver skyline. The embryo inside stirs, and the image cuts to black.

The image of the fish egg against the city lights looks something like the Star Child in *2001: A Space Odyssey* (Stanley Kubrick, 1968), and I always find this final sequence very moving without quite being able to explain why. It seems transcendental but at the same time deeply personal, as though it brings some mysterious cosmic insight right into the intimate spaces of high-rise Vancouver homes. Though previous sequences had positioned salmon as bearers of the look, this sequence fully reverses the gaze: we are no longer sutured into the world of the salmon, witness to processes that stretch back 6 million years. Here, the salmon looks with curiosity at *our* world, and the bustle of city life is framed as a very recent phenomenon against a much longer natural history. While animals are frequently represented in cinema, they seldom return our gaze and generally appear as mere objects to be looked upon or, worse, instruments to be handled or used. Here, it is the *human* that is represented as an object of curiosity, and this reversal of the look asks spectators to consider themselves as alien phenomena in a familiar landscape.

The affective experience of this final sequence is overwhelmingly positive as the film's pervasive sense of wonder is accentuated by the accelerating pace and rising score. Given *Uninterrupted*'s explicitly environmentalist aims, the choice to emphasize positive affect and to omit images of environmental degradation is significant: there are no smoke stacks, oil spills, or plastics clogging waterways. While the interactive journey does provide sobering statistics – for example, that only one or two out of every two thousand eggs will survive to reproduce, and that rising water temperatures and human infrastructure make the journey upstream increasingly difficult – the screening experience presents human-salmon relations in starkly optimistic terms. This optimism is not based on complacency or a denial of responsibility but, rather, on a particular configuration of the apparatus that encourages a sense of passivity in relation to the image. As discussed in the previous section, discourses on interactive documentary tend to argue that the traditional cinematic apparatus encourages a comparatively passive spectator and that digital technologies by contrast can provide a sense of agency or choice. In *Uninterrupted*, however, it is precisely the use of digital technologies – including the user-computer interface in the interactive journey as well as virtual reality, digital projection, and 4K imagery in the production and screening processes – that undermines the spectator's mastery over the image.

The complexity of *Uninterrupted*'s apparatus, which uses eight digital projectors and required the use of virtual reality to map the footage onto the three-dimensional surface of the bridge, *does* require the spectator to make choices, but these are often made at the expense of other possibilities. In my own recording of one of the screenings,[8] for example, I keep my phone as still as possible facing the south piles, thereby missing the images that frequently appear on the abutment and the span behind where I was sitting. This is a subtle deviation from more conventional modes of cinema viewership: unlike interactive documentaries in which users can interact with and control the content being presented on their computer screens, with *Uninterrupted*'s screening experience the spectator still sits in a darkened space with very little actual control over the content being presented. But the fragmentation of perspective here can help us see new possibilities for reshaping viewership using digital technologies. *Uninterrupted* is not the first installation to make use of multiple projectors or to map itself onto three-dimensional structures: urban projectionists and expanded cinema artists often encourage participatory relationships between spectators and screens by projecting films to and from unusual places such as bicycles, moving vans, and public buildings (see Youngblood 1970). What makes *Uninterrupted* important in the context of interactive documentary is how it uses digital technologies to encourage a more passive response from its audience.

Uninterrupted also reveals an aspect of *all* interactive documentaries that has yet to be fully theorized. By granting the spectator/user agency over the experience, whether by allowing them to choose the sequence of the narrative or encouraging them to actively contribute content, interactive documentaries work against the totalizing gaze of the traditional apparatus. Something like *Hollow* presents quite a fragmented view of reality: visitors to the site stay an average of five minutes (Aufderheide 2015, 75), and even if one watches all thirty short films, the experience is far less unified than a traditional feature. While scholars like Aufderheide and Forceville largely see this as a failure of the interactive form to properly engage spectators, I would argue that it is perhaps not an abundance of choice that prevents immersion but rather – somewhat paradoxically – a perceived *loss* of control. Apparatus theory would argue against the contention that the cinematic spectator is passive: Baudry (1986b, 286) argues that the apparatus functions precisely to grant an illusion of mastery by positioning the spectator as the "*active* centre and origin of meaning" (emphasis added). For Baudry, devices such as single-point perspective direct themselves towards the subject facing the screen and obscure other positions from which meaning might be proposed or derived. The spectator feels mastery over the cinematic image precisely because the image is limited to the confines of the frame and presented directly towards them; with interactive documentaries, by contrast, the user is asked to navigate through a series of images that may not come together in a comprehensible whole. Images are no longer directed towards the singular perspective of the spectator and, therefore, present a more fragmented and less totalizable view of reality. This sense of relative powerlessness in the interactive documentary can result in a loss of viewer engagement, but *Uninterrupted* suggests that it might also be embraced as a new and productive aesthetic strategy.

Uninterrupted is able to embrace passivity because the spectator's loss of control over the image is a crucial aspect of its environmental ethics. Anat Pick (2011) argues that it is not a common capacity for thought or reason that allows humans to empathize with animals but, rather, a shared sense of vulnerability. Pick's ethics are derived from external, corporeal similarities rather than from subjective identification: we relate to non-human animals not through a common psychology but because we are all embodied and therefore vulnerable to physical suffering. Compassion is therefore not an effect of reason or agency but comprises a more passive relationship, one that Pick (via philosopher Simone Weil) frames explicitly in terms of love: our responsibilities towards non-human animals are determined by "the interchangeability between vulnerability, reality, and beauty. That which exists must be loved, and loved because it exists" (3). Pick argues that film can oppose anthropocentric views of reality not only by calling attention to the animal but also by "grappling with what is inhuman in us" (6). What is inhuman is precisely a shared inability to act against or control all aspects of our environment, or what Weil (1998, 142–3) calls "the pitiless necessity of matter." By framing human existence in relation to a much longer natural history, *Uninterrupted* makes Vancouver city life seem impermanent and fragile, and therefore calls attention not only to the corporeality of salmon but also the creaturely aspects of the human.

Understood in the context of Pick's "creaturely poetics," *Uninterrupted*'s emphasis on passive reception and wonder over any specific call to action is not a failure to recognize the potential of new media for creating a sense of agency in the audience; rather, it is a deliberate strategy for undermining anthropocentrism and fostering compassion, even love. Because I am sceptical of our ability to entirely break from anthropocentrism – we are human, after all – I do not think *Uninterrupted* offers a radical disruption of humanist modes of perception. The camera sees much the same way we do and, as Baudry argues, cinema inherits the representational strategies and associated (emphatically humanist) ideological baggage of its Enlightenment technological progenitors. What *Uninterrupted* offers instead is a subtler reorientation – or even disorientation – of our usual ways of perceiving and relating to our non-human others. *Uninterrupted* does not entirely undermine human agency as the interactive journey and projected names of audience members offer opportunities for spectators to view themselves as co-creators of an emerging reality. The final sequence of the film, in which we see Vancouver city life as a recent phenomenon in the longer history of BC salmon, also recognizes the human tendency to actively change our environment. Crucially, however, *Uninterrupted* places this tendency towards action within the context of a larger, more primordial relationship with the environment. This relationship is not framed through identification, which, as Pick (2011, 5–7) argues, tends to reduce non-human others to humanist conceptions of thought or consciousness, but a shared receptivity to a common reality – specifically, the BC waterways inhabited by humans and salmon alike.

Conclusion

Interactive documentary practitioners and theorists tend to see active modes of engagement in utopian terms. Digital technologies, in this view, are a means of disrupting the didacticism of traditional documentary, which "can be defined as a monologue between the production and the audient" (Galloway, McAlpine, and Harris 2007, 331). As Giuliana Cucinelli, Émilie René-Véronneau, and Belinda Oldford (2018) argue, however, i-doc theorists also recognize the need for a specific definition of interactivity "in light of Lev Manovich's argument that all art is interactive at some level." The relationship between the computer-user interface in the interactive documentary is therefore privileged as a form of interactivity in which the human user and computer effect changes on each other as well as the artwork that emerges from their interactions. I argue, however, that the interactive documentary has yet to explore passivity as a desired mode of engagement with digital technologies. *Uninterrupted* is only a place to start in this respect since its engagement with interactive documentary form – defined as the "human computer interface, going beyond the act of interpretation to create feedback loops within the digital system itself" (Aston and Gaudenzi 2012, 126) – is quite limited: visitors to the website can only alter the artwork by completing the interactive journey to view their names projected under the bridge. *Uninterrupted*'s use of transmedia content is nevertheless significant because it provides a new way of thinking about the dialectic between agency and passivity that, I argue, characterizes the interactive documentary.

Uninterrupted's use of digital technologies beyond the computer-user interface – digital projection, 4K imagery, and virtual reality – promotes a *more* passive response from the spectator than does the sense of mastery usually engendered by the cinematic apparatus. This suggests that interactivity and passivity should not be viewed in binary terms, the former as a quality of new media technologies and the latter as an effect of traditional cinema. Further, *Uninterrupted*'s emphasis on passivity as an ethical response to our environment – a way of recognizing our shared vulnerability with animals – suggests that agency is not necessarily an optimal viewer response. In the context of posthumanism, which seeks non-anthropocentric modes of thinking and coexisting with nature, passivity can be a productive way to counter humanist pretenses and illusions. *Uninterrupted* does not want its spectators to avoid action, of course, and its online content aims to harness the positive affect encouraged by the screening experience to promote conservation efforts within the community. Its emphasis on affect over reason in the screening experience, however, suggests that we should feel before we act. *Uninterrupted* encourages a new kind of interaction between humans and salmon mediated by an innovative use of digital technology; simultaneously, it frames this contemporary moment within the context of the non-anthropocentric timescale of natural history. If, as Simone Weil suggests, shared vulnerability is an opportunity for love, then *Uninterrupted*'s emphasis on human fragility can help us to see our shared conditions of existence as beautiful and worth protecting.

Notes

1 Film ecocriticism is a growing body of scholarship that explores ways that cinema can present alternatives to anthropocentrism. For general overviews

of film ecocriticism, see Ivakhiv (2008); Pick and Narraway (2013). For works that focus specifically on the representation of animals, see Burt (2002); McMahon (2019); Molloy (2011); Pick (2011).

2 I am referring to Jean-Louis Baudry's classic apparatus theory, to which I return in more detail in the next section. See Baudry (1986a; 1986b). I argue elsewhere for posthumanist applications of Baudry's apparatus theory. See Birks (2018).

3 At the opening night of *Uninterrupted*, a welcome ceremony was performed by representatives of the Musqueam, Squamish, and Tsleil-Waututh Nations for partners and visitors from Secwepemc Nation: "the bones of a single Coho salmon were lowered into False Creek, in keeping with Coast Salish tradition." "First Nation's Tradition Launches Spectacle," Uninterrupted.ca, http://uninterrupted.ca/first-nation-tradition-launches-cinematic-spectacle/.

4 These videos were available on the website while it was promoting the 2017 screenings, but at the time of writing the website is changing in preparation for new screenings of the film in summer 2019. The videos can still be viewed through *Uninterrupted*'s Vimeo account at https://vimeo.com/uninterruptedca.

5 Dale Hudson, for example, argues that interactive documentary has a radically refigured conception of space in comparison to the linear structure of conventional documentary cinema. In *The Act of Documenting*, Brian Winston, Gail Vanstone, and Wang Chi discuss filmmaker Peter Wintonick's contention that documentary has become "docmedia" and that new media results in a "new species of communicative object." See Hudson (2014); Winston, Vanstone, and Chi (2017, 60). See also Cucinelli, René-Véronneau, and Oldford (2018).

6 False Creek is the short inlet running through downtown Vancouver. It passes underneath the Burrard, Granville, and Cambie Street Bridges and ends at the Telus World of Science east of Cooper's Park.

7 The score is similar to that of Wild's previous film, *Konelīne: Our Land Beautiful*, which also promotes a feeling of wonder towards British Columbia's landscape.

8 Taken on 21 September 2017. Recordings and non-flash photography were permitted.

References

Aston, Judith, and Sandra Gaudenzi. 2012. "Interactive Documentary: Setting the Field." *Studies in Documentary Cinema* 6 (2): 125–39. https://doi.org/10.1386/sdf.6.2.125_1.

Aston, Judith, Sandra Gaudenzi, and Mandy Rose. 2017. "Introduction." In *i-Docs: The Evolving Practices of Interactive Documentary*, ed. Judith Aston, Sandra Gaudenzi, and Mandy Rose, 1–3. London and New York: Wallflower.

Aufderheide, Patricia. 2015. "Interactive Documentaries: Navigation and Design." *Journal of Film and Video* 67 (3–4): 69–78. https://doi.org/10.5406/jfilmvideo.67.3-4.0069.

Baudry, Jean-Louis. 1986a. "The Apparatus: Metapsychological Approaches to the Impression of Reality in Cinema." In *Narrative, Apparatus, Ideology: A Film Reader*, ed. Philip Rosen, 299–318. New York: Columbia University Press.

– 1986b. "Ideological Effects of the Basic Cinematographic Apparatus." In *Narrative, Apparatus, Ideology: A Film Reader*, ed. Philip Rosen, 286–98. New York: Columbia University Press.

Birks, Chelsea. 2918. "Objectivity, Speculative Realism, and the Cinematic Apparatus." *Cinema Journal* 57 (4): 3–24

Brockington, Michael. 2019. "The Editor." *Uninterrupted* on Vimeo. https://vimeo.com/229154214.

Burt, Jonathan. 2002. *Animals in Film*. Chicago: University of Chicago Press.

Cucinelli, Giuliana, Émilie René-Véronneau, and Belinda Oldford. 2018. "Interactive Documentaries and the Connected Viewer Experience: Conversations with Katerina Cizek, Brett Gaylor, Jeff Soyk, and Florian Thalhofer." *First Monday* 23, no. 5. https://doi.org/10.5210/fm.v22i5.6182.

Favero, Paolo. 2013. "Getting Our Hands Dirty (Again): Interactive Documentaries and the Meaning of Images in the Digital Age." *Journal of Material Culture* 18 (3): 259–77. https://doi.org/10.1177/1359183513492079.

– 2017. "The Travelling i-Doc: Reflections on the Meaning of Interactive Documentary-Based Image-Making Practices in Contemporary India." In *i-Docs: The Evolving Practices of Interactive* Documentary, ed. Judith Aston, Sandra Gaudenzi, and Mandy Rose, 237–54. London and New York: Wallflower.

Forceville, Charles. 2017. "Interactive Documentary and Its Limited Opportunities to Persuade." *Discourse, Context and Media* 20: 218–26. https://doi.org/10.1016/j.dcm.2017.06.004.
Galloway, Dayna, Kenneth B. McAlpine, and Paul Harris. 2007. "From Michael Moore to JFK Reloaded: Towards a Working Model of Interactive Documentary." *Journal of Media Practice* 8 (3): 325–39. https://doi.org/10.1386/jmpr.8.3.325_1.
Hudson, Dale. 2014. "Undisclosed Recipients: Database Documentaries and the Internet." *Studies in Documentary Film* 2 (1): 89–98.
Hull, Rae. 2017. "An Interview with Rae Hull from *Uninterrupted*." Interview in *Vancouver Is Awesome*, 11 September 2017. https://www.vancouverisawesome.com/2017/09/11/an-interview-with-uninterrupted-producer-rae-hull.
Ivakhiv, Adrian. 2008. "Green Film Criticism and Its Futures." *Interdisciplinary Studies in Literature and the Environment* 15 (2): 1–28.
McMahon, Laura. 2019. *Animal Worlds: Film, Philosophy, and Time*. Edinburgh: Edinburgh University Press.
Manovich, Lev. 2001. *The Language of New Media*. Cambridge: MIT Press.
Molly, Claire. 2011. *Popular Media and Animals*. London: Palgrave.
Nash, Kate. 2012. "Modes of Interactivity: Analysing the Webdoc." *Media, Culture, and Society* 34 (2): 195–210. https://doi.org/10.1177/0163443711430758.
– 2017. "I-docs and the Documentary Tradition: Exploring Questions of Citizenship." In *i-Docs: The Evolving Practices of Interactive Documentary*, ed. Judith Aston, Sandra Gaudenzi, and Mandy Rose, 9–24. London and New York: Wallflower.
Pick, Anat. 2011. *Creaturely Poetics: Animality and Vulnerability in Literature and Film*. New York: Columbia University Press.
Pick, Anat, and Guinevere Narraway, eds. 2013. *Screening Nature: Cinema beyond the Human*. New York: Berghahn.
Rose, Mandy. 2017. "Not Media About, But Media With: Co-Creation for Activism." In *i-Docs: The Evolving Practices of Interactive Documentary*, ed. Judith Aston, Sandra Gaudenzi, and Mandy Rose, 49–65. London and New York: Wallflower.
Watson, Ryan. 2017. "Affective Radicality: Prisons, Palestine, and Interactive Documentary." *Feminist Media Studies* 17 (4): 600–15. https://doi.org/10.1080/14680777.2017.1326560.

Weil, Simone. 1998. "Epilogue." In *Simone Weil*, ed. Eric O. Springsted, 142–3. New York: Orbis.

Wild, Nettie. 2017. "An Uninterrupted Conversation with Artist Nettie Wild." Interview by Nancy Lanthier. BC *Alliance for Arts and Culture*, 27 June 2017. https://www.allianceforarts.com/blog/2017/6/27/uninterrupted-conversation-nettie-wild.

Winston, Brian, Gail Vanstone, and Wang Chi. 2017. *The Act of Documenting: Documentary Film in the 21st Century*. New York and London: Bloomsbury Academic.

Youngblood, Gene. 1970. *Expanded Cinema*. New York: Dutton.

11

PLAYING WITH EXTREME OIL

SLOW CATASTROPHE AND THE MELANCHOLIC IMAGINARY OF *OFFSHORE* AND *FORT MCMONEY*

Jessica Mulvogue

Introduction: Twenty-First-Century Fossil Fuel Narratives

Frederick Buell (2012) suggests that nineteenth- and twentieth-century stories of coal and oil are characterized by the twin motifs of exuberance and catastrophe. Looking at how these motifs emerge in literature, Buell follows William Catton (1982), who describes the energy culture of the twentieth century as an "age of exuberance." Such exuberance spoke to the sense of profuse growth and never-ending possibilities that fossil fuel energy seemed to promise. It was seen as inciting a new vitality for the wondrous progress of modernity and for a humanity that was gaining extraordinary power. Quoting Catton, Buell (2012, 276) adds that fossil fuel energy in particular helped to galvanize "a faith in progress so strong that 'the idea that mankind could encounter hardships that simply will not go away' was not just unlikely but in fact 'unthinkable.'" Such views "play a powerful role in sustaining the prevalent mode of capitalist production in the face of its environmental consequences" (Keary 2016, 7). Fossil fuel energy came to represent an expansion of the human knowledge of, and power over, nature (Marx 1997, 965).

For Buell, this faith in progress provided a pretext for that which underpinned the exuberance of fossil fuel culture: catastrophe. As he puts it, the exuberance of fossil fuel culture is always "haunted by catastrophe" (Buell 2012, 276). Catastrophic accidents at coal mines due to unsafe labour practices and exploding oil wells that alighted villages of makeshift barracks: these are just a couple expressions of twentieth-century fossil fuel culture. Buell asserts that "exuberance and catastrophe materialized as historically specific forms of capitalist triumph and oppression, of environmental domination and destruction, and of human liberation and psychic and bodily oppression" (280). While most of his article focuses on twentieth-century literature, Buell begins to muse on how catastrophe has become more prominent in culture of late. We could think here of the rise in post-apocalyptic or disaster novels, films, and television shows. For Buell, these artefacts combine exuberant narratives with post-apocalyptic milieux, expressing the curious combination of excitement for high-tech culture alongside anxieties about civilizational collapse (292). However, Buell also notes near the end of his essay a new kind of narrative, one that eschews the spectacular exuberance seen in many of the stories of climate catastrophe and narratives of post-oil worlds. He names Cormac McCarthy's *The Road*, Kazuo Ishiguro's *Never Let Me Go*, Sarah Hall's *The Carhullan Army* as examples of works that, in contrast to the above, feature "narratives of slow, painful, on foot struggles" and stifle the "fantasies of post-physical acceleration and quicktime [sic] metamorphosis" (ibid.). Buell is not yet clear on what the cultural significance of these artefacts is, but what they do make clear is that "the old faith in stability is gone" (293).

This chapter situates two i-docs – Brenda Longfellow's *Offshore* (2013) and David Dufresne's *Fort McMoney* (2013) – within this framework of new twenty-first-century oil narratives. Both are docu-games, a subcategory of the i-doc that adopts the aesthetic and structures of the first-person video game to lead the player through their respective oil worlds. While Buell's analysis of oil narratives focuses on fiction, his framework can be extended to these i-docs because they inhabit a space in between fiction and non-fiction. That is, most of the content of these works is documentary – based in factual evidence and testimony – but their interactive form invites the viewer into a fictional framework in which the players are characters within the story worlds. Both works take the player to sites of extreme oil extraction: deep offshore rigging in the Gulf of Mexico and the tar sands of northern Alberta. Such extreme oil practices represent a new stage in the history of fossil fuel extraction. Thus, if, as Buell thinks, there is a new kind of oil narrative emerging, it may be precisely because the landscape of the oil world has shifted: both physically because of new methods of extraction and figuratively because of the widespread knowledge of the relationship between CO_2 emissions and climate change. As oil reserves run out, petrol industries are forced to look for oil in increasingly inhospitable places where the scale of environmental destruction is vast. Deep offshore rigging and tar sands extraction are "extreme" not only because they are found in difficult to reach locations or involve complex chemical processes and advanced extraction technologies but also because of the devastating scale of their effects on the surrounding environment. But this devastation is unlike the catastrophe that underpinned the exuberance of twentieth-century stories of oil; rather than sudden incendiary events, catastrophe in the era of extreme oil (and climate change) unfolds slowly over time, for example, through the steady poisoning of land due to toxic waste or the slow accumulation of CO_2 in the atmosphere. In their focus on these slower forms of catastrophe, I argue that the exuberance found in oil narratives of the past is in *Offshore* and *Fort McMoney* eclipsed by a melancholic imagination. I consider how this melancholic imagination emerges at the level of content, form, and in the affective, ludic interactive modes employed. I suggest that it has a productive function not only as a means of innovatively conveying this new kind of catastrophic situation but also as a tactic to resist the normalization of the continued reliance on oil.

The Slow Catastrophe of Extreme Fossil Fuel Extraction: *Offshore* and *Fort McMoney*

Rob Nixon's idea of slow violence provides means through which to understand this new kind of catastrophe as it relates to fossil fuel extraction. In *Slow Violence and the Environmentalism of the Poor* (2011), Nixon submits that the destructive consequences of human industry within neoliberal capitalism, such as the energy industries (and their pollution and toxic waste), are forms of violence. However, this violence does not play out, temporally or spatially, in the conventional sense of the word. Slow violence extends Johan Galtung's idea of structural violence, which sought to name those social institutions, systems, and structures that, due to their failure to meet people's basic needs, give rise to acts of personal violence. While Nixon (2011, 27) shares with Galtung a concern "with social justice, hidden agency, and forms of violence that are imperceptible," slow violence is not equivalent to structural violence. Slow violence, Nixon explains, "might well include forms of structural violence, but has a wider descriptive range in calling attention, not simply to questions of agency, but to broader, more complex descriptive categories of violence enacted slowly over time" (28).

The accumulation of the CO_2 in the atmosphere due to the burning of fossil fuels is a slow violent act. This is a violence that does not confront people "body-to-body but [plays] out over vast stretches of time through the medium of ecosystems" (Verges 2017). CO_2 accumulation in the atmosphere does not affect people directly; however, as it contributes to the warming of Earth, it slowly provokes a wide range of disasters – hurricanes, floods, droughts, rising sea levels, food shortages, species loss – that may incite mass involuntary migrations of people, wars, and other kinds of conflict. In fact, it is not a stretch to assert that the burning of fossil fuels can no longer be considered only violent: it is also catastrophic.

Offshore and *Fort McMoney* depict various kinds of violence, but the slow catastrophe of oil industries emerges as an overarching theme of both works. In doing so, and by situating the viewer as player through their interactive form, *Offshore* and *Fort McMoney* provide answers to Nixon's (2011, 2) question of how we represent, in images and narratives, a violence that is incremental and accretive, not spectacular or instantaneous. As we will see, they "bring home – and bring emotionally to life" a catastrophe that may "never materialize in one spectacular, explosive, cinematic scene" (31).

In Deep Waters: Offshore

Brenda Longfellow's *Offshore* is an interactive documentary that tells the story of the catastrophic consequences of deep offshore drilling. The i-doc was made in partnership with Helios Design Lab and in association with York University's Future Cinema Lab and is the final piece in Longfellow's trilogy of oil-themed films, which includes *Carpe Diem* (2010) and *Dead Ducks* (2012). *Offshore* takes the viewer to the Gulf of Mexico, where hundreds of offshore and deep offshore rigs pull oil from the ocean floor. In the prologue to the docu-game, the player is taken by helicopter over a dystopian landscape dotted with these rigs. Complete with a menacing score, statistics about the estimated reserves of oil in various parts of the world flash on screen alongside nightmarish images of an oil spill disaster. The helicopter lands on a CGI-created rig – the fictional *Spartan 208* – which is empty and ominous against a stormy sky and sea, and the game begins. The player adopts the character of an official who is here to investigate a disaster that has occurred on the rig and its aftermath.

The i-doc uses a 360-degree scrollable screen in which are embedded hyperlinked materials, such as video, audio, and textual documents. As you wander around the various levels of the rig you discover a variety of information on offshore drilling, the BP Deepwater Horizon spill, and frontier offshore operations in other areas of the world. While the focus of the i-doc is on the Deepwater Horizon spill, the i-doc, as Imre Szeman (2015) writes, "draws our attention to the larger system of oil extraction that makes a disaster possible even when it is introducing us to oil-rig workers and to fishermen who depend on the Gulf for their livelihoods."

On 20 April 2010, the Deepwater Horizon blowout killed eleven men working on the rig and injured seventeen more. Oil gushed from the rig into the Gulf of Mexico for eighty-four days, inundating it with 5 million barrels of oil. *Offshore* documents a range of people affected by the event, directly and indirectly. For instance, multiple fishers, whose livelihoods depend on the fish, shrimp, and oysters found in the Gulf, are featured. Most of them have seen a significant decrease if not outright disappearance of the species they depend on to support themselves and their families. In one video, we are aboard the trawler of Timothy "Blimp" Cheramie, who shows us that, years later, while shrimp are still to be found in the Gulf, many of them have oil clogging their gills. "I'm lost in the world right now," Cheramie laments. The shrimping business, however small scale, was his entire life.

Nixon (2011, 290) asserts that "the slow violence that underlies Deepwater Horizon long predates the out-of-control gusher." Indeed, the kinds of violence that the characters in *Offshore* experience are only partially a result of the actual blowout. Jennifer L. Lawrence (2017, 18) suggests that we consider what she calls the "flawed rationalities" and the problematic governance of the environment as constitutive of the disaster. Such energy extraction rationalities and strategies of governance are, she argues, manufacturing "both acute and chronic biopolitical disasters" (16). As a response, Lawrence proposes that, rather than focusing on the particular events that led to the disaster – the actions of workers, technicians – we pay attention to the ideological and structural issues that shape the oil industry (16–17). We could say then that the violence enacted on the bodies of Deepwater Horizon workers is not circumscribed by the event of the blowout. Such violence is found in the very corporate practices, operations, and rhetoric that preceded, and most definitely will succeed, it.

The controversial use of Corexit in the Deepwater Horizon case is exemplary of these kinds of catastrophic "rationalities" and one to which *Offshore* pays particular attention. Corexit is the chemical dispersant that BP claims breaks up the oil into small particulates that are then consumed by oil-eating microbes. Anne McClintock (2012) suggests that Corexit wasn't used *only* to clean up the oil in the Gulf. It was also used as an image dispersant to mask the amount of oil that had leaked. What is more, while the chemical does indeed break down the oil and disperse it, it has been shown to be much more toxic than undisturbed oil. The chemical is then consumed and absorbed by people and other wildlife who come into direct contact with it. *Offshore* documents how the locals, who were in proximity to the spill or who helped to clean up the waters and beaches, have since developed serious illnesses. One fisherwoman tells us she developed rashes, headaches, and dizziness after going out on her boat in the Gulf in the days after the accident. We also hear from a doctor who works in the area and who has been witness to dozens of people, mostly those who helped clean up beaches, complaining of similar illnesses. For some, these symptoms have affected their life to the point that they can no longer work. While *Offshore* provides statistics on the effect of Corexit in populations – human and otherwise – it may take many years for some violent effects to emerge. As Rosina Phillipe, a Grand Bayou resident who appears in the i-doc, states: "we're sitting on a time bomb."

Especially striking is the way *Offshore* combines computer-generated imagery alongside documentary, realist images. In documenting various kinds of violence emerging from the Deepwater Horizon spill and setting these against the fictional context of another offshore rig disaster, *Offshore* makes clear that the occurrence of another disaster is a matter of when not if. Moving between these two realms, one's encounter with the real people, who are situated within a historical time and space, extends in interesting ways. When you leave the documentary realm and find yourself again back on the CGI rig, there is a strong sense of having witnessed a past that continues in a new catastrophic (future) present. The documentary characters linger in the CGI plane almost like ghosts, reminding you that, as Nixon (2011, 25) says, "the past of slow violence is never past" and "the post is never fully post: industrial particulates and effluents live on in the environmental elements we inhabit and in our very bodies, which epidemiologically and ecologically are never our simple contemporaries."

Those entanglements across time are reflected in the documentary's database structure, which, unlike linear documentaries, opens up new configurations of narrative and new relations between the subjects featured. The significance of the narrative that the player constructs could emerge in stark variations when played by a different player; in other words, as different users move through the space in varying ways, the unique way they put the pieces together holds the potential for the creation of diverse meanings.

But while the multiple space-times of *Offshore* generate certain sites of potential and possibility, the framing of the CGI rig also evokes a sense of inertia. The characters seem trapped as lingering presences within this fictional rig. In a way, then, the i-doc moves the characters' real-life situation onto the formal plane of the work: just as they are trapped within the structures and systems that produce and perpetuate slow violence, so they are in the i-doc forever enclosed within the fictional world of another offshore rig catastrophe. The coexistence of multiple documentary times and places heightens the intensity of catastrophe as it spreads across multiple lives and diverse contexts, from the Gulf region across the world.

This situation of inertia extends to the viewers/players themselves. *Offshore* looks and feels like a video game, and this invites the viewer/player into a different space of spectatorship, one initially defined by that of gaming. The game-mode of this work situates the viewer as a participant in the unfolding of the narrative. While the documentary clips employ traditional techniques, one arguably approaches them in a different way because of the fictional framing. Here, you are not just viewers witnessing documentary evidence, you become part of the world in which the characters reside. And yet the game-mode that is referred to both formally and narratively – at the beginning of the work you are set up as an investigator – is ultimately undercut or denied. As you wander around the virtual environment, encountering the many stories and characters, you begin to become aware that the goal established for you at the i-doc's beginning is never fully realized in the actual game. There are many different places to explore on the rig, but the various bits of information you've gathered do not add up to any solution, revelation, or sense of completing the task. What was set up as a game-mode, investigative i-doc ends up being more of an open play-mode: a world created for the player to discover facts relating to offshore rigging, but one in which there is no "end." Later I discuss the distinctions between such modes and the significances of this shift in terms of the subject matter of the work. But first I turn to *Fort McMoney*, as I see in it a similar trajectory in which a game-based interactivity is ultimately denied.

Tarried Toxicity: Fort McMoney

Like *Offshore*, the NFB-produced *Fort McMoney* begins with a short prologue. Situated in a car, the player is driving down a highway set within a desolate snowy terrain. From the window, you see an abandoned car overturned in the highway's median strip as a narrator welcomes you to the "edge of the world." You pass huge factories, with smoke billowing from their many stacks, while the narrator stresses that you are entering a game in which your choices will not only affect your own experience but also the experience of others playing. Your task in this game is announced as reaching the impossible: the heart of the oil industry. The player is thus set up as a kind of investigative journalist, attempting to uncover the "truth" of the tar sands industry. The car stops in an unspecified location – a camp of some kind on the edge of town. You have arrived in Fort McMurray, the notorious tar sands town of northern Alberta.

The Albertan tar sands are the world's largest industrial project and are widely criticized for being one of the most destructive (Takach 2017, 3). This remote region of the world, which is the size of Florida in land area, contains the world's third-largest recoverable source of oil – approximately 315 billion barrels of oil, 170 of which can be extracted using current available technologies. However, 80 per cent of the area must be exploited by in-situ extraction, a method that involves the injection of high-temperature steam into the ground to reduce the viscosity of heavy oils, which then drain into a recovery well and are pumped to the surface. Beyond the CO_2 produced by the eventual burning of the oil obtained from the tar sands, the environmental costs of the extraction operations themselves are immense. The method requires the burning of coal, natural gas, and diesel, which combined produces more greenhouse gases than the extraction of conventional oil. In fact, carbon pollution in Alberta exceeds the combined totals of Ontario and Quebec, provinces of Canada that are home to more than 60 per cent of its population (Takach 2017).

In addition to emissions, massive destruction of land and the poisoning of water sources has greatly affected local human and non-human communities. The tar sands are located in an area that is home to what was once pristine boreal forest, "a verdant spongy bog [that] has been sucked dry of life" (Klein 2014, 326), and to numerous species, such as woodland caribou, fish, and countless birds, which are being threatened by both the scale of the operations and its toxic refuse. Additionally, Fort

McMurray sees many problems common to "frontier" towns, such as gambling, addiction, and homelessness.

Fort McMoney examines a wide range of the region's problems through three episodes: "Boomtown," which loosely considers social issues; "Black Gold," economic issues; and "Winter Road," environmental issues.[1] Each episode is organized as a "choose-your-own-adventure" narrative. At the beginning of episode 1, for example, the player is presented with two characters, each of which will open up different areas of town, new scenarios, and more characters. For the most part, information about the region is discovered through "interviews" with local inhabitants. In these interviews, the player assumes the role of the interviewer and must choose from a series of questions to pose to the interviewee. The game also contains extra-textual elements such as influence points, discussion boards, a newsfeed, and bi-weekly polls and referenda in which you can vote on issues. The points earned through meeting a variety of people and visiting different locations grants one greater access to the spaces and stories of each episode.[2] The game departs from *Offshore* in that it is almost entirely composed of documentary images. It is only the dashboard – which records your activity, provides a map, and is the interface through which you participate in polls – that is conventionally styled as a gaming interface. Since 2014, however, the polls, discussions, and newsfeed no longer operate as "live" interactions, and thus a major part of the original concept has ceased being a part of the game (see Keyes and Robbins, chapter 3, this volume).

Each episode of *Fort McMoney* provides an enormous amount of content, so much so that trying to cover all three episodes is well beyond the scope of this chapter. I thus focus on episode 3, "Winter Road," which deals mostly with environmental issues. Named after a five-hundred-kilometre ice road that is open only in the winter months because it comprises frozen rivers, lakes, and streams, "Winter Road" takes us from Fort McMurray to Fort Chipewyan on the Athabasca River. When you reach Fort Chipewyan in the game, you are welcomed to "the end of the world," a turn of phrase that points to the remoteness of the community but that takes on new meaning as the episode advances. The toxicity of the tar sands takes central stage in this episode.

One of the first characters we meet in "Winter Road" is Ray LaDouceur, an Indigenous fisherman who has lived and worked in the Athabasca

Lake region for fifty-five years. He provides a first-hand account of the environmental changes, discussing the loss of species that he has witnessed in the last few decades. Frogs, muskrats, and birds that inhabited the lake region have all but disappeared. He shows us a fish that has been deformed and talks about the strange smells in the air and the funny colour of the sky. Such deformities and species loss cannot be uncoupled from the decades of pollution and toxic waste that have reached Fort Chipewyan by river and air. Nor can, LaDouceur suspects, the fatal cancer of his mother and other illnesses afflicting the community. We accompany the fisherman to his late mother's house, where he discusses the cancer that killed her and her sudden, unexplained loss of mental capacity. Such unforeseen occurrences, he tells us, have become increasingly common in Fort Chipewyan.

His suspicions are corroborated later in the episode when we meet another character, Doctor John O'Connor. O'Connor reached a certain level of notoriety when, in 2006, he publicly brought attention to what he saw as abnormally high levels of auto-immune diseases, such as leukaemia, lymphoma, lupus, colon cancer, and Graves' disease, in the region. He suspected that the prevalence of such diseases was a direct consequence of the rising levels of carcinogens in the waterways that pass by tar sands operations.[3]

Another outspoken critic of the impact of the tar sands appearing within the i-doc is Allan Adam, Chief of the Athabasca Chipewyan First Nations, who has been labelled a "home-grown terrorist" by the oil industry. Such a label hardly fits his demeanour and argument as it is presented here. A despondent and cautious Adam tells us in "Winter Road" that his primary complaint is that the industry is allowed to be self-monitoring; the provincial and federal governments let it conduct its own environmental studies. Adams suspects that the governments refuse to step in because of the economic power of the oil corporations.

"Winter Road" betrays how the tar sands' polluting of the land and water is a "slow industrial genocide" (Huseman and Short 2012) and one that is advanced by a certain idea of progress itself.[4] For Kim Tallbear (2019, 24–5), it is not only "CEOs at the helm of resource-extraction companies who have accepted Indigenous elimination as the collateral damage of settler-state development" but all scientists, policy makers, and technological developers who continue the dream of the extractive nation-state. While the deaths caused by the various auto-immune diseases the communities are suffering come into play, the lives lost is only one part of such arguments. The vast destruction of the land is also a genocidal act as the land is central to Indigenous livelihoods, rituals, and traditions. According to Tallbear, extractivist practices continue to undercut "intimate relations with these lands and waters" and "memories relentlessly erased" (24–5).

Over the course of your journey in northern Alberta, you collect a massive amount of information. This information is not, however, organized into a neat narrative. By denying the player any stable or guiding perspective, the game perhaps acknowledges the complexity of the situation. In its stead, what is gained for the player is an emotional and affective attachment to the place and its inhabitants, which (ideally) drives them to continue returning to the work. Asking for the player's participation in polls and referenda, the game creates a sense of community. This attachment to the world is built slowly. Emerging from the accumulation of stories and places, it piles up as a palimpsest of encounters.

But like *Offshore*, *Fort McMoney* takes the player on a circuitous route that ends in a kind of inertia. In the last section of the game, a Syncrude spokesperson takes you on site to view the mining operations. The hope, which the game has encouraged, that we can reach the "heart" of the tar sands industry by reaching its centre of operation, is not fulfilled. While we do get on site, what we are granted access to is limited. Presumably knowing that the filmmakers are critical of the environmental impacts of the industry, the spokesperson, speaking solely in industry propaganda, shows us only areas that are undergoing the reclamation process. We are not taken to the actual mining sites. As such, there is ultimately a sense of incompletion with regard to the player's task set up at the beginning of the game.

In denying the fulfilment of the game-mode, *Offshore* and *Fort McMoney* instead, as I suggest above, position the player in a situation more akin to a *play-mode*. Bo Kampmann Walther (2003) explains the distinction: if games are "confined areas that challenge the interpretation and optimizing of rules and tactics," then "play is an open-ended territory in which make-believe and world-building are crucial factors." The i-docs begin as games – they look like videogames, they have confined spatial and temporal platforms as well as rules, goals, and, in the case of *Fort McMoney*, even points – but as you move through them, this game-mode is usurped by a more open-ended engagement, in which the player still moves through the platforms as a character but their trajectory becomes decreasingly circumscribed as they encounter more and more content. But, in that these are *documentary* films, the "magic circle" of the play-mode – this liminal space set apart from reality – is never fully maintained. Reality keeps intruding, creating an unstable, unsettling play arena as the player is connected to multiple people, places, times, and spaces that all converge.

I say "unsettling" because what these i-docs so frighteningly document are different kinds of losses: people, places, environments, species, cultures. These are losses that, the playing of these games tells us, not only have occurred but will continue to occur. This laces the experience of playing these works with a sense of despair. In their lack of resolution, the i-doc's moments of fear and outrage for a violence that, since it has already been unleashed, is hard to stop, are coupled with inertia. This combination gives these works an overwhelmingly melancholic tone.

Stephanie LeMenager (2011; 2016) outlines an emergent melancholy that follows from the love of oil, so deep-seated in American ways of life. Through the analysis of cultural artefacts and events, LeMenager discerns a "competition between emotional investments in modernity as we know it, through its fossil fuel infrastructure, and in ecology, as the network of human-non-human relations we theorize as given habitat" (27). If modern environmentalism is characterized by a melancholia for nature, LeMenager thinks it may be eclipsed in the twenty-first century by "an unresolvable grieving of modernity itself, as it begins to fail" (ibid.). She calls this "petromelancholia." However, I see melancholy operating in *Offshore* and *Fort McMoney* not as a grieving for a modernity built upon the burning fossil fuels but, rather, as an affective tone or horizon that attunes the spectator to the slow but catastrophic impact of the fossil fuel industry and a tactic that refuses to accept the continuation of this kind of capitalist exploitation in the name of "progress" and the various kinds of violence that accompany it.

The Political Potential of Melancholy

"Melancholy" has been used to describe a wide range of medical disorders throughout the ages, all of which were accompanied by a particular mental state characterized by sadness, fear, and withdrawal (Radden 2000, 5). The term comes from the Greek "melas" (black) and "khole" (bile); up until the eighteenth century melancholia was considered a disease of the spleen, which was thought to have produced black bile, one of the four humours, along with blood, phlegm, and yellow bile (Jouanna 2012). Dark, dry, cold, heavy, dense, gross and binding, black bile was cast as the metabolic agent of Earth, much like oil is today. Melancholia occurred when there was an excess of black bile in the body. Such thinking provides a useful metaphor for my argument: the excess of oil – and the relentless, destructive searches for more that *Offshore* and *Fort McMoney* depict – has given rise to a kind of melancholic imagination, one that is linked to the impossibility of mourning fully the losses caused by reliance on fossil fuels.

One of the most noted theorists of melancholia is Sigmund Freud, who, in his 1917 essay "Mourning and Melancholia," distinguishes between the psychological and physiological states of melancholia and mourning. The two are related as they are both responses to the loss of a loved person, object, or idea. But whereas mourning represents the healthy process involved in a painful loss, melancholia, for Freud, turns pathological. Freud notes that, while the mourner withdraws temporarily from the world, eventually the loss of the beloved object is accepted, and the libido attaches to another object.[5] The sufferer thereby "returns" to the world. But for the melancholic, it is the ego itself that becomes "poor and empty" (Freud 1953, 246). That is, the attachment to the lost object is not directed to another object but is instead directed inward; the lost object becomes associated with the ego itself, thus creating an inner division.

While the distinction between the "normal" processes of mourning and the "pathological" processes of melancholy are still commonly upheld, Srećko Horvat (2021) has recently attempted to recoup melancholy from its regressive meanings in order to provide a language for the effects of the destruction of the planet on human subjectivity. For Horvat, the knowledge of the destruction of the planet generates what he calls a pervading "post-apocalyptic melancholy." This is a sense of an ending "that is unlike any other endings before, an ending that is inevitable if we continue with our current world system, an ending meaning the end of the biosphere and mass extinction, whether it is rapid or slow, the feeling that everything changes and that the only thing that's certain is extinction" (19). This is an ending that is impossible to mourn because it is an ending impossible to accept for it is beyond human comprehension. Melancholy, then, for Horvat, seems to be a more appropriate term to describe the mix of present and anticipatory grief produced in the knowledge that we are on the path towards extinction.

However, Horvat shifts melancholy away from being either a reactionary longing for the past or an attitude of defeatism by reminding us of Walter

Benjamin's (1977) take on the matter. In his study of the German mourning play, *Trauerspiel*, Benjamin, unlike Freud, doesn't strictly distinguish mourning and melancholy (Horvat 2021, 22). Mourning/melancholy is neither a pathological response nor the full acceptance of the loss; it is, rather, something in between, a dialectical interplay between these two understandings of how human beings deal with loss. As Horvat explains: "Instead of 'pathologizing melancholy,' Benjamin rehabilitated the subversive potential of melancholy, showing that it always contains the possibility of its own undermining" (22). Benjamin does so by positing a dialectics of melancholy that can play (*spiel*) with mourning (*Trauer*). To play with and within mourning/melancholy suggests a possibility of coping with a loss in a constructive way, "turning mourning into a potential political tool" (ibid.).

The rethinking of melancholy as a political tool has precedents. What Patricia Rae (2007, 18) calls resistant or activist melancholia is a means of "keeping things unsettled." She refers back to the strategies of the Greek heroines Electra, Antigone, and Medea who use militant lamentation as a way to counter the state's attempt to circumscribe mourning. Not agreeing to "come to terms" with a loss is a means of disrupting social order. In the context of the AIDS catastrophe, Douglas Crimp similarly argues that completed mourning, the acceptance of loss, results in the restoration of the status quo (Takemoto 2003). As Rae (2007, 19) states, "consolations only serve to repress the full meaning of what has happened above all the question of who is responsible for the deaths."

My argument is that *Offshore* and *Fort McMoney* use *play* as a means to prevent a kind of "completed mourning," an acceptance of the status quo that is fossil-fuel culture. The dominance of a play-mode over a game-mode by their ends disrupts a clear progression or trajectory, leaving the viewer more in a "wandering" or exploratory state. By embracing inertia and a lack of closure, these works undermine or "play with" both traditional narrative and game-based form. In doing so, they open up a space to consider or rethink what we understand as "progress" or "endings" as such.

The undermining of the traditional flow of (narrative) time is discernible in the database structures of the works. We are given snippets of moving image documents embedded within a spatial platform and, thus, a simultaneity of different time(s); in other words, time is not related to cause and effect. It is, rather, fragmented and spatialized: multiple pasts exist on the same spatial plane in the architectures of these i-docs. While the works make the viewer choose one particular story at a time, the potential for simultaneity is always there. In *Offshore*, especially, the characters and their situations seem to "haunt" the present of the CGI rig. In both i-docs, the documentary content is hidden in the respective oil-related landscapes, mirroring the way in which slow violence is often unseen or concealed.

In embracing a "play-mode" and undermining the linear progress of traditional narrative, *Offshore* and *Fort McMoney* create an affective experience for the player that assimilates them into the aforementioned melancholic structures. Adrian Miles (2014) situates the interactive documentary within the tripartite structures of perception, affect, and action, or "notice, decide, do." He explains: "in interactive documentary something is presented to a user (notice), the user views this material more or less quickly (decide), and is then obligated to make a decision that is literally a motor action that effects some sort of change within, or to, the work (do)" (79). For him, affect emerges in the virtual encounter between the information on screen and the viewer/user insofar as it moves the viewer from their traditionally passive role into one of activity. While I think we should be sceptical of easy divisions and unnuanced understandings of passivity/activity in cinema spectatorship, there *is* a difference of intensity between watching a linear film and using an interactive documentary, at least in successful instances of the latter. Indeed, it is important to remember, as Brian Massumi (2008, 13) asserts, that "you may interact with a work is not enough." It is not interactivity as such that generates meaningful encounters. When interactive art *works* affectively and effectively, according to Massumi, it "[takes] the situation as its object" and "potentially 'open[s]' the interactions it affords" (ibid.). This "opening of interactions" involves going "into an existing situation, and [opening] it into a relational architecture" (14).

The designs of *Offshore* and *Fort McMoney* produce relational architectures of slow catastrophe, wherein the player not only learns about the effects of slow violence, but also, through the novel structures of interactivity – which both provide us with direct encounters with characters in the docu-games and undermine the perceived "activity" of interaction – situate the players within the situation of slow catastrophe, giving rise to a melancholic milieu. That is, the interactivity of *Offshore* and *Fort McMoney* is therefore best understood not just in terms of how it activates the viewer but also in how it creates relational encounters that generate affective forces within the indeterminate situation of slow catastrophe. The i-docs open up the potential not only for *seeing* the catastrophic but also for *feeling* it, putting the spectator into a new kind of situation, a novel relational mode with the subject and subjects of slow violence. And this, for Massumi, is what makes art political: "aesthetic politics is an exploratory politics of invention, unbound, unsubordinated to external finalities. It is the suspensive aspect of it that gives it this freedom. The suspension of the most available potentials, the potentials already comfortingly embodied, well-housed and usefully institutionalized, gives a chance for more far-fetched potentials to ripple up" (14).

Conclusion

The melancholic imaginary in *Offshore* and *Fort McMoney* undercuts the exuberance described by Buell as central to twentieth-century fossil fuel culture. In these works, the catastrophic is the defining motif and the melancholic its twin. If the exuberance of fossil fuel narratives betrayed an unrelenting belief in progress, in which catastrophe was just an unfortunate (but also sometimes exciting) side effect, perhaps the melancholic intimates a waning in the belief of progress, or at least that built upon the exploitation of Earth. For, melancholy, as it was discussed, is precisely a state in which progress is suspended. The social and environmental catastrophes shown in *Offshore* and *Fort McMoney* reveal the dark underbelly to modern "progress," and they problematize easy solutions for moving forward. Through the particular characteristics of their interactive modes *Offshore* and *Fort McMoney* innovatively find ways of expressing slow violence beyond the representational. The inertia, lack of resolution, and the disruption of linear time in *Offshore* and *Fort McMoney* produce a melancholic imagination that is not a longing for the past exuberance of fossil fuel culture. It is, instead, a mode of resistance, a refusal to accept the losses – human and non-human – that have resulted from the violence of the fossil fuel industries. It is a strategy to keep their stories aligned and "alive." And, moreover, it is a game plan that works to prevent "a catastrophe from becoming assimilated into the order of things" (Rae 2007, 18). That is, the way interactivity is employed in these i-docs gives rise to a melancholic imaginary that works to articulate the affective and emotional nature of slow violence, something that, due to its long duration, is difficult to represent. The i-docs open up the potential not just for seeing slow violence but also for *feeling* it.

In helping us to *feel* the slow violence of the fossil fuel industries, *Offshore* and *Fort McMoney* also point towards the affective facets of the slow catastrophe that is climate change. These works tell us that it is not the heart-pumping, adrenalin-fuelled fight or flight scenario we have felt or imagine would feel in the experience of a conventional catastrophe. It is instead something akin to melancholy: lethargic, heavy, slow, with moments of trepidation, a cold sweat. The "bodies" of these works stand firmly within the present catastrophe, embracing what it means to live and die in the now of climate change and slow violence; refusing to move on, to get on, with it or to come to terms, they implicate the spectator in this melancholic milieu through their interactivity as an effort to forge a kind of resistance to the relentless search for oil and its slow, violent destruction of Earth. Put differently, in creating platforms imbued with melancholy, *Offshore* and *Fort McMoney* ask us to resist accepting the inevitability of the systems and structures of slow violence and put us into relation with people, things, and contexts that are beyond our given temporal and spatial frameworks, just like the workings of slow violence itself. In doing so, they gesture to futures that we do not have to accept.

Notes

1 When *Fort McMoney* was released in 2013 a final episode was included that considered the post-oil era and offered users the chance to discuss and debate the possibilities of a post-oil world.

2 The participatory element of *Fort McMoney* was open only for the period in which the game was live, but the game continued to be playable when I was writing this chapter in 2019–20. However, the game requires Adobe Flash, which has since become obsolete, and *Fort McMoney* can no longer be accessed (for more on this, see chapter 3, Keyes and Robbins, this volume).

3 O'Connor's inference was questioned by the Alberta College of Physicians and Surgeons (ACPS), which lodged a formal complaint against him. And even though O'Connor's conclusions were eventually backed up by a series of scientific studies, in 2015 he was inexplicably fired.

4 Huseman and Short borrow this phrase form Mike Mercredi, who used it to describe the situation in Fort Chipewyan in a *Dominion* podcast (2009). See Mercredi (2008).

5 Freud in fact eventually changed his hypothesis on mourning and melancholia, rendering mourning more akin to the melancholic state. See Clewell (2004).

References

Benjamin, Walter. 1977. *The Origin of German Tragic Drama*. Trans. John Osborne. London: New Left Books.

Buell, Frederick. 2012. "A Short History of Oil Cultures; Or, the Marriage of Exuberance and Catastrophe." *Journal of American Studies* 46 (2): 273–93. https://doi.org/10.1017/S0021875812000102.

Catton, William. 1982. *Overshoot: The Ecological Basis of Revolutionary Change*. Champaign: University of Illinois Press.

Clewell, T. 2004. "Mourning beyond Melancholia: Freud's Psychoanalysis of Loss," *Journal of the American Psychoanalytic Association* 52 (1): 43–67.

Freud, Sigmund. 1953. "Mourning and Melancholia." In *The Standard Edition of the Complete Psychological Works of Sigmund Freud*, vol. 14, *1914–16: On the History of the Psycho-Analytic Movement, Papers on Metapsychology and Other Works*. London: Hogarth Press and the Institute of Psychoanalysis.

Horvat, Srećko. 2021. *After the Apocalypse*. Cambridge: Polity Press.

Huseman, Jennifer, and Damien Short. 2012. "'A Slow Industrial Genocide': Tar Sands and the Indigenous Peoples of Northern Alberta." *International Journal of Human Rights* 16 (1): 216–37. https://doi.org/10.1080/13642987.2011.649593.

Jouanna, Jacques. 2012. *Greek Medicine from Hippocrates to Galen: Selected Papers*. Trans. Neil Allies. Leiden/Boston: Brill.

Keary, Michael. 2016. "The New Prometheans: Technological Optimism in Climate Change Mitigation Modelling." *Environmental Values* 25: 7–28.

Klein, Naomi. 2014. *This Changes Everything: Capitalism vs. the Climate*. Toronto: Knopf Canada.

Lawrence, Jennifer L. 2017. "Manufacturing Biopolitical Disaster: Instrumental (Ir)rationality and the Deepwater Horizon Disaster." In *Biopolitical Disaster*, ed. Jennifer L. Lawrence and Sarah Marie Wiebe, 15–29. London: Routledge.

LeMenager, Stephanie. 2011. "PetroMelancholia: The BP Blowout and the Arts of Grief." *Qui Parle: Critical Humanities and Social Sciences* 19 (2): 25–56. https://doi.org/10.5250/quiparle.19.2.0025.

– 2016. *Living Oil: Petroleum Culture in the American Century*. Reprint. New York and London: Oxford University Press.

Marx, Leo. 1997. "Technology: The Emergence of a Hazardous Concept." *Social Research* 64 (3): 965–88.

Massumi, Brian. 2008. "The Thinking-Feeling of What Happens: A Semblance of a Conversation." *Inflexions* 1 (1): 1–40.

McClintock, Anne. 2012. "Slow Violence and the BP Oil Crisis in the Gulf of Mexico: Militarizing Environmental Catastrophe." *The Hemispheric Institute* 9, no. 1. https://hemisphericinstitute.org/en/emisferica-91/9-1-dossier/slow-violence-and-the-bp-oil-crisis-in-the-gulf-of-mexico-militarizing-environmental-catastrophe.html.

Mercredi, M. 2008. "Slow Industrial Genocide." Audio broadcast. Dominion Radio, November 2008. http://oilsandstruth.org/quotslow-industrial-genocidequot.

Miles, Adrian. 2014. "Interactive Documentary and Affective Ecologies." In *New Documentary Ecologies: Emerging Platforms, Practices and Discourses*, ed. Kate Nash, Craig Hight, and Catherine Summerhayes, 67–83. Basingstoke: Palgrave Macmillan.

Nixon, Rob. 2011. *Slow Violence and the Environmentalism of the Poor.* Cambridge, MA: Harvard University Press.

Radden, Jennifer, ed. 2000. *The Nature of Melancholy: From Aristotle to Kristeva.* London: Oxford University Press.

Rae, Patricia. 2007. "Modernist Morning." In *Modernism and Mourning*, ed. Patricia Rae. Lewisberg: Bucknell University Press.

Szeman, Imre. 2015."Art against Oil: Brenda Longfellow's *Offshore.*" *POV Magazine* 97 (Spring). http://povmagazine.com/articles/view/art-against-oil.

Takach, Geo. 2017. *Tar Wars: Oil, Environment, and Alberta's Image*. Edmonton: University of Alberta Press.

Takemoto, Tina. 2003. "The Melancholia of AIDS: Interview with Douglas Crimp." *Art Journal* 62 (4): 80–90. https://doi.org/10.1080/00043249.2003.10792186.

Tallbear, Kim. 2019. "Caretaking Relations, Not American Dreaming." *Kalfou* 6 (1): 24–41. https://doi.org/10.15367/kf.v6i1.228.

Verges, Françoise. 2017. "Racial Capitalocene: Is the Anthropocene Racial?" In *Futures of Black Radicalism*, ed. Gaye Theresa Johnson and Alex Lubin, 72–82. London: Verso.

Walther, Bo Kampmann. 2003. "Playing and Gaming." *Game Studies: The International Journal of Computer Game Research* 3, no.1. http://www.gamestudies.org/0301/walther.

PART THREE

Image and Sound beyond "the Real"

Media Pasts, Presents, and Possible Futures

12

NOSTALGIA, "OLD" MEDIA, AND *WELCOME TO PINE POINT*

Peter Urquhart

Introduction

"This was supposed to be a book." Thus begins the "About This Project" page at the conclusion of the 2011 interactive documentary *Welcome to Pine Point*, created, written, and designed by "The Goggles" (Paul Shoebridge and Michael Simons) and one of the first batch of i-docs produced by the then newly created Digital Studio of the National Film Board of Canada. The statement concludes by adding, "it could have been a book, but it probably makes more sense that it became this." This chapter argues that they're right: that it makes *much* more sense that *Welcome to Pine Point* became an interactive documentary rather than a book. Ostensibly about a mining town in the Northwest Territories (NWT) that no longer exists, *Welcome to Pine Point* is read here as an interactive documentary that uses its new media form to cast into sharp relief a series of claims about artefacts, memory, nostalgia, and possible futures through the mobilization of (and with reference to) an array of old and often defunct media forms, including but not limited to Polaroid film and other obsolete photographic formats, videotape, typewriters, and Web 1.0.

The interplay between the handmade Goggles aesthetic; the array of old photographs, videos, and other artefacts; and the behind-the-scenes coding and software that contains these vestiges of the past could be seen simply as exemplary of Bolter and Grusin's (1999) concept of remediation, but this chapter argues that there is more at stake here than new media enveloping and transforming the old: *Welcome to Pine Point* calculatedly collides "new" and "old" media to speculate on the nature of memory and media and on how nostalgia and media frequently influence or even dictate what we choose to remember or are able to remember.

Interestingly, despite the activist pedigree of the key creatives behind this i-doc, not to mention the activist pedigree of National Film Board documentaries since the beginning of the Challenge for Change program in the late 1960s (and, in some cases, even earlier), *Welcome to Pine Point* seems wilfully unconcerned with the political issues that surround its story.[1] In a work with resource extraction and northern development hovering over every single aspect of the world it depicts, the decision to focus almost entirely on nostalgia and memory through the consideration of both old and new media – and to ignore environmental destruction and colonialism – requires some examination alongside the areas of interest identified. *Welcome to Pine Point* fondly remembers a small town past when everybody in town was comfortable (thanks union wages!), when everybody pursued their hobbies and played as hard as they worked, and when there was no evidence whatsoever of Dene and Métis, the Indigenous peoples whose land the Cominco iron and zinc mines and the entire town of Pine Point occupied.

Interestingly, perhaps because of an institutional habit of expressing such concerns (even where they are not addressed in the work being discussed), the NFB portal (2011) introducing its various interactive projects describes *Welcome to Pine Point* as "an interactive documentary about what happens when you lose your job, when everyone you know loses their job, when your entire town is out of work, is shut down and dismantled, and completely disappears." But, as we know, *Welcome to Pine Point* is no such thing. It devotes not one iota of attention to such questions as these. Instead, this is a media project about *certain* ways of remembering *certain* aspects of the past.

The Project

Welcome to Pine Point is an online documentary that uses still photography, video, text, an old website, sound, and various handmade drawings and lettering in a nominally interactive Adobe Flash animation – all embedded in a webpage – to consider the question, "Imagine your hometown never changed … would it be so bad?" Using the real example of Pine Point, NWT, a mining town on the south shore of Great Slave Lake that existed only from 1964 to 1988, *Welcome to Pine Point* is actually much more interested in using this strange story to ruminate on the nature of memory and media. At the centre of this rumination is Pine Point Revisited, an amateur memorial website and online repository of hundreds of photos, videos, and written recollections submitted by former Pine Pointers and maintained by Richard Cloutier, himself a former town resident. Cloutier becomes a central character in the piece along with our narrator, co-creator Michael Simons, and former residents Kim Federoff ("The Beauty") and Wayne and Lyle Hryniuk ("The Brothers"). Framed by our narrator's reminiscences (not spoken but in faux label-maker on-screen text), the bulk of the piece is taken up with the reminiscences of the characters in Pine Point and a then-and-now juxtaposition of the characters of Pine Point in the past alongside what ultimately became of them. Generally, the Pinepointers reflect on what a really fine place it was and what good times they had there. These threads of the story are interspersed with some explanatory asides about how the town came to be, how it came to disappear, and – in one anomalous chapter – the crashing of a Soviet satellite in the area of Great Slave Lake in January 1978.

As The Goggles themselves have noted, *Welcome to Pine Point* is scarcely interactive at all, at least so far as interactive documentaries go. Furthermore, As Nabil Kashyap (2013, 95) points out, "while an experiment, the site is not experimental ... though nominally interactive, the purpose of the project is to tell a story, to disclose a fixed narrative." Simons himself puts this even more succinctly, noting: "It's not a website, it's not an interactive doc ... what is it? Coming from print, part of the process for us was minimizing the interactivity to only those elements that serve to forward the narrative" (Weldon 2011). The story told within *Welcome to Pine Point* is more or less strictly linear, and the opportunities it affords audiences to interact really amount to little more than choosing (or choosing not) to look at some or all of the artefacts it provides as visual illustration in each of the pages and chapters. Of course, this is of interest to us because one of the fears on the part of committed documentarians about too much audience choice or too much audience interactivity in new i-doc formats is that polemic, or even simply an argument with evidence, becomes diluted (and, in some cases, even impossible) due to the opportunities for audience choice provided by such work. That is, linear forms lend themselves to guided audience experiences in which creators are free to disclose facts, details, arguments, or any content at all, whenever and in precisely the context the creators choose. This problem exists not just for the arguments of a documentary but also for interactive dramatic narratives. Plots require that details be

Figure 12.1
The degraded video quality and cut-and-paste aesthetic of the *Welcome to Pine Point* opening page foreground some of the thematic concerns of the piece

revealed in a correct order so that they are comprehensible to audiences, hence the difficulties with some interactive forms of storytelling.

For an i-doc, *Welcome to Pine Point* sidesteps these potential difficulties with its strictly linear structure. It begins with a fuzzy and degraded video-transferred image (scan lines and all) of an airplane landing at the Pine Point airport sometime in the early 1970s. Text on screen explains that our narrator visited the town for a hockey tournament (his family lived in Yellowknife at the time), that he became curious about the place, and that one night he happened upon the memorial website Pine Point Revisited, an online compendium of photographs, reminiscences, and tools for reconnection for use by former "Pine Pointers." The opening page of *Welcome to Pine Point* also foregrounds some of the thematic concerns of the piece. The narrator tells us that he went to Pine Point when he was nine years old for a hockey tournament. He says he doesn't remember much about the journey except a couple of minor details, including the hockey rink's blue lobby. Later, when we learn that the hockey rink had been dismantled when the town was closed, moved, and re-erected in Fort Resolution (further north on the shore of Great Slave Lake), the narrator tells us that the lobby was not – and apparently never had been – blue; he confesses to remembering little about the trip and then reveals that one of his few memories turned out to be wrong. The narrator's subsequent confession – over the image of an airplane landing – that "that's not the plane and my team's not on it" is yet another instance of the opening page of the project signposting for audiences the thematic terrain upon which they wander, and it is presented in a largely linear fashion.

In addition to these stories and themes, the tone is accentuated by several notable formal choices. First among these is the decision to eschew a voice-over in favour of text-based narration. As creators coming to the digital realm from the tactile medium of print, it is unsurprising that The Goggles should choose words printed on the screen instead of audible narration, given the crucially important effect of this decision upon the pace of the experience. When audiences are confronted with words on a page or screen, they must read them at their own pace and may choose to linger, affording them all the time they need to dig a little deeper into the minimal interactivity a small number of the pages offer. You read the narration and decide whether to click on none, one, or perhaps twenty of the photos on offer in an album. Moving images generally dictate pace, but with the prevalence of printed text in this i-doc, it's the readers that do so. Furthermore, the absence of a voice-over affords the project many other sonic opportunities: *Welcome to Pine Point*'s rich soundtrack, in addition to a haunting score, includes distant, barely perceptible conversations, sound effects like clinking bottles, and other subtle "noise" that contributes an organic tactility to the experience of clicking through the piece. Finally, so many aspects of the hand-drawn and lettered aspects of the project – from animations and cut-outs to hand-lettered navigation tools on the site itself – further enhance this quite unclean, un-"new" media-like experience of something that is in practice a technological marvel. As Kashyap (2013, 105) pointedly observes, "coding something to appear ragged and handmade on the screen requires time, expertise and expensive software." All of these formal choices – the eschewal of voice-over narration to allow audiences to linger, the rich sonic environment, and the disavowal of the actual technological sophistication of the piece – make vital contributions to the way the project communicates its tone of wistful nostalgia for an unrecoverable past.

Nostalgia

Svetlana Boym tells us that the word "nostalgia" derives from two Greek words, *nostos* ("return home") and *algos* ("longing"). Elaborating on its meaning, she defines it as "a longing for a home that no longer exists or has never existed" (Boym 2001). In that *Welcome to Pine Point* is, on one level, an i-doc about a town that no longer exists and the nostalgia some former residents feel for the no-longer-existent place, it would seem that Boym's conception of "nostalgia" is dead-on for its encapsulation of the emotional pull of the project. There is a considerable literature, of course, on the relationship of nostalgia to cultural texts.[2] In what follows, I aim to demonstrate the formal and narrative means through which The Goggles accentuate the sensations of nostalgia their project seeks to generate. *Welcome to Pine Point* has a tone that is a combination of beautiful sadness but also of wonder, a sensation that suggests "you'll never believe this incredible story and what it means to the people who lived it."

Andrew Burke's monograph, *Hinterland Remixed* (2019), shares many concerns with *Welcome to Pine Point*, most especially its interest in the relation of memory to analogue media of the 1970s and 1980s. In it, Burke speculates on the sources and kinds of nostalgia that some feel for the defunct and deteriorating audio-visual styles and textures of Canadian media of the 1970s. He notes,"Svetlana Boym's distinction between restorative nostalgia, the kind that wants to return to or recreate the past based on conservative desires to restore and maintain a lost past, and reflective nostalgia, the kind that fully understands the past is past and was not perfect, yet nevertheless takes pleasure in the act of memory, is crucial in understanding that nostalgia is not, simply because of the presence of emotion itself, corrupt or contaminated" (Burke 2019, 7).

He goes on to observe that the "remembered plenitude" of the past is always partial and problematic" and how the 1970s "was deeply divided and contradictory, harbouring desires and ambitions for progress at the very same time that it held tight to fundamental exclusions and injustices" (ibid.). Cementing these contradictions, Burke first cites Walter Benjamin (2003) – "There is no document of culture which is not at the same time a document of barbarism" – before invoking Mark Fisher's claim that "the 1970s were in many respects better than neoliberalism wants us to remember them" (Burke 2019, 7).

One section of *Welcome to Pine Point* in particular illustrates this seemingly contradictory form of reflective nostalgia, one that is aware of the imperfections of the past being remembered but that nevertheless revels in the emotional pull of its memory. We see excerpts from a Cominco-produced memorial video entitled "Pine Point Memories" that was distributed to all the town's citizens, while the text on the screen tells us, "there is a concentrated sadness in mementos. They commemorate something that might never be again." The corporate PR tone of the mining company video, clearly intending to evoke a "remembered plenitude," clangs loudly in the face of the recognition of this company as one that failed to contribute to the local Indigenous communities and instead despoiled their forests, traplines, and lake. The nostalgia of *Welcome to Pine Point* is "reflective" insofar as it allows space for one to feel sad about a lost past without paying heed to whatever shortcomings this lost past might also have contained.

Even, or maybe especially, the Besnard Lakes soundtrack contributes to the nostalgic effect of the project. Perhaps it is because the Montreal-based band's founder, Jace Lasek, is more or less the same age as Simons, attended high school with him in Regina, and became acquainted with Shoebridge during their time in Vancouver attending Emily Carr University. The band is widely regarded for its nostalgia-driven, atmospheric sound, respectful of and indebted to the rock canon, endeared to the pop cultural cache and perceived authenticity of vintage analogue equipment and recording techniques such as reel-to-reel tape. As Shoebridge put it in an interview, "it [the music provided for the soundtrack] was a great fit. Their sound is somewhat haunting … sad and beautiful at once. Nostalgic almost." "Almost" is an understatement, especially since the most prominent and compelling of the tracks the Besnard Lakes provided for the soundtrack is a slowed-down, elegiac cover of Vancouver rock band Trooper's 1977 minor hit (but CanCon radio staple), "We're Here for a Good Time (Not a Long Time)." In fact, Lasek's wife and collaborator in the band, Olga Goreas, told Toronto's *Now Magazine* that the Trooper cover was the only thing The Goggles specifically requested of the band (Boles 2011).

"Old" Media

As demonstrated above, "nostalgia" is the best possible descriptor for the tone and subject of *Welcome to Pine Point*. Some will quibble that the section heading used here – "old" media – lacks the same precision.

It could be argued that "residual" media is the term that better explains *Welcome to Pine Point*'s use of defunct photographic formats and glitchy, degraded videotape. As is now widely agreed in media studies, terms like "old" and "new" media fail to take account of the considerable overlap in time and of the formal and cultural practices of various media technologies. While I agree completely with this assessment of, and approach to, a historiography of media – one that takes as its helpful and instructive premise Raymond Williams's (1977) explanation that the continuum of dominant, emergent, and residual cultural forms has enormous explanatory power – I choose to stick with "old" media (in quotation marks) because *Welcome to Pine Point* itself suggests reasons that this is the way it would like to be understood. To demonstrate, first let me point to remarks by the creators themselves. "It's about the death of a couple of things," Shoebridge explains. "Of analog media and about how we think the things that people of my generation react to, the digitization of things, newness, disposability, and the way to edit things has changed the way we perceive our media and the way memories are formed" (Shoebridge in Lofaro 2011). Shoebridge's own work shows how wrong he may be about the "death" of analogue media, though this quotation clarifies one aspect of the creator's intended aims. Second, we could point to aspects of the project's narration; specifically, a segment addressing the photographs assembled by Cloutier on the Pine Point Revisited memorial site. "The pictures are impossibly friendly," the narrator explains. "Even the colours and textures seem unselfconscious – wood panelling, perms, velour, deep shag – all enclosed in yellowing photos with rounded corners." The narrator concludes, "this isn't Facebook: the photos have scratches, wrinkles and dust – people awkwardly framed and with half-closed eyes. Just pictures taken with the hope that they might preserve a moment." Summarizing the communicative power of defunct or degraded forms and the design decision informing the project's reliance upon "old" media, Simons suggest: "the old photos and videos have an authenticity about them, an innocent, naïve, quality" (May 2014).

Will Straw provides some productive concepts for thinking about things like repositories of "old" media assembled in "new" media packages such as *Welcome to Pine Point*. He writes, "the Internet becomes a comfortable place, less because we are adept at handling its futuristic openness than because it has already rendered the already familiar all the more coherent and solid. Paradoxically, that coherence and solidity serve to naturalize

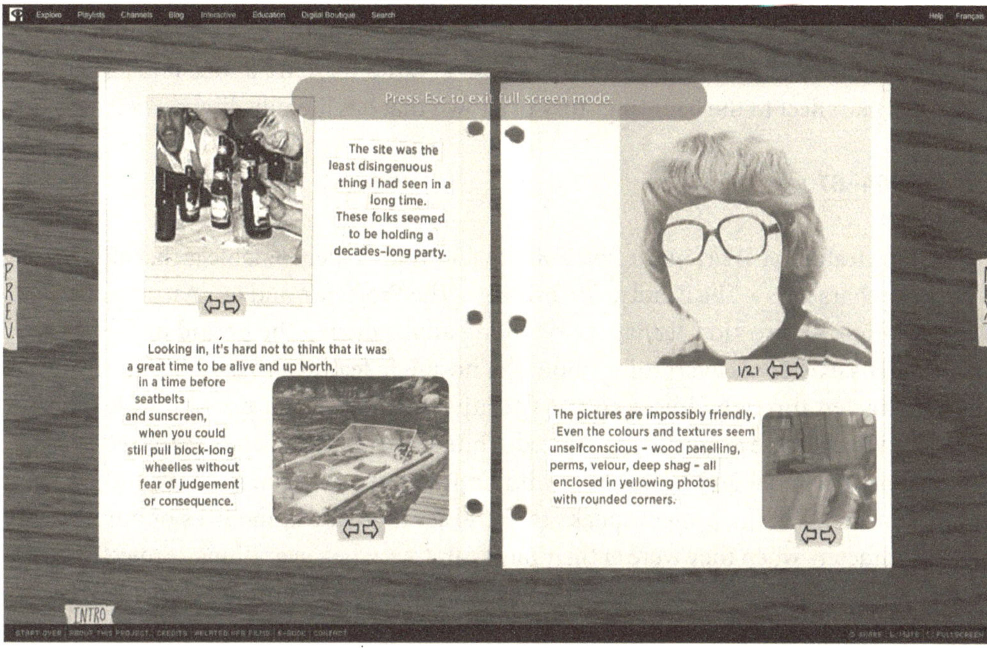

Figure 12.2
The Googles and the NFB technical team took the "old" media and assembled them in a masquerade of an even "older" media form through the artful application of the appearance of handmade craft

versions of the past, whose artifacts, we believe, the Internet has merely discovered" (Straw 2007, 4). The internet's "inspiration" for *Welcome to Pine Point* was Cloutier's vernacular and home-made website, Pine Point Revisited, which assembled the "old" media artefacts in the already outmoded but iconically "new" media form of Web 1.0 (with its clip-art and blinking buttons), whereas The Goggles and the NFB technical team took the "old" media and assembled them in a masquerade of an even "older" media form through the artful application of the appearance of handmade craft. As Kashyap (2013, 109) puts it: "In many ways, the original site Pine Point Revisited is more participatory and dynamic, reflecting these Web 2.0 aims more effectively than the newer project, which has every technological affordance at its disposal. At the same time, the critical success of *Welcome to Pine Point* suggests that a conventional text-based narrative structure can be the most effective strategy, even in new media contexts." Everything about *Welcome to Pine Point*, from the dust and patina, the VHS tape glitches and scan lines, signal noise, and even "old" musical selections such as a 1970s CanCon radio hit, lend a tone and an elegiac affect to the haunting story of a town that has literally disappeared.

1964–87

One feature of *Welcome to Pine Point* that is immediately notable is that all the characters – The Beauty, The Brothers, The Protector, and our narrator, Simons – were kids, teenagers, or young adults during the period of the town's existence. Everything about the nostalgic features of the piece are refracted through almost entirely positive memories of a period of life in which these relatively privileged white Canadians occupy a carefree time of wonder and exploration with limited responsibility. Every sound and image of the project speaks to the exact moment in the lives of our characters when they were at their most carefree, when everything seemed possible for them. As the narration explains over images mined from the Pine Point Revisited website, "these folks seemed to be holding a decades long party … looking in, it's hard not to think that it was a great time to be alive and up north. In a time before seatbelts and sunscreen, when you could still do block-long wheelies without fear or consequence."

The recollections of these characters, supported and reinforced by sounds and images faithful to the period of time they lived in Pine Point, are almost entirely nostalgic and positive. Both the characters' testimonies and their visual accompaniment make frequent reference to playing sports – Wayne Hryniuk says they played sports twelve months of the year, even singer Kim Federoff refers wistfully to the arena that housed the hockey and curling rinks, middle-class "suburban"-looking houses, and recreational accoutrements, including gymnasia and the hotel bar; these and other thing were all made possible because of well-paying mine work and Cominco's considerable profits, which economically supported the community. These aspects of life in Pine Point support my reference to Burke's invocation of Mark Fisher's (2014) injunction that the 1970s were in some ways not nearly as bad a time as the current economic moment, and certainly not for the working class. As well, as some of the characters note independently of each other, because the town of Pine Point was dismantled and removed from the map, all they have is these fond memories, suspended in amber, with none of the change and degradation that happens to a town over time; the narration reminds us, “[their] corner store never became a Taco Bell.” This was a town of about two thousand citizens at its peak (and about eighteen hundred for most of its existence) that had a new golf course, a shopping centre, libraries, a hotel, restaurants, churches, and schools. And so how, exactly, did it end?

Arn Keeling and John Sandles note in their comprehensive history, “Claiming the New North: Development and Colonialism at the Pine Point Mine, NWT, Canada,” that, throughout the 1950s, in part abetted by a Cold War demand for industrial minerals, a consensus emerged across political parties and in corporate Canada about the centrality of “northern development” and mining, specifically, in Canada’s future. The Consolidated Mining and Smelting Company – predecessor to Cominco – lobbied the federal government hard throughout the 1950s, encouraging the then newly minted Department of Northern Affairs and Natural Recourses (established in 1953 – a moment that has since been described by historians as “the effective beginning of colonialism in the region” [Keeling and Sandles 2012, 8]) to contribute to the mine at Pine Point. Large subsidies were paid for rail links, town planning and construction, and other infrastructure with the idea (genuinely felt, one has to assume) that generating economic development in the North would benefit the local communities, provide them with growth, and, perhaps, sustainable futures. And while the government, when asked, declined to offer subsidies for deflated fur prices in the region to local communities in 1956, the ideological demands of “northern development” allowed them to insist that subsidies for mining development were the way of the future. In Keeling and Sandles’s words, this “signaled the dawning of a new north” (12). Unfortunately, it was ultimately proven that resource extraction-based northern development policy had no net-positive impact on the local communities: Indigenous employment remained stubbornly low and the economic opportunities that previously existed in the form of hunting, fishing, and trapping were all negatively affected by the existence of a giant, open-pit iron-zinc mine on their territory. While over $400 million in net profit was exported from the mineral wealth of the region, local communities derived very little economic benefit (14). There was little reason to believe Pine Point would break from this pattern.

Towards the end of the 1980s, as the lead and zinc deposits around Pine Point were rapidly depleted, Cominco decided that instead of just closing the mine, in consultation and collaboration with government authorities, it would plan to decommission the entire town. *Welcome to Pine Point* goes so far as to reveal some of the documents the government and Cominco prepared in preparation to do so, citing the inevitable terminal decline of a mining town with no functioning mine. The likely increase of alcohol abuse, domestic violence, and other crime were cited in the studies arguing for the demolition of Pine Point and its considerable amenities. Noting a turn towards less pessimistic revisionism in cultural geography and environmental history examining such "mining imaginar[ies]," Keeling and Sandles (2012, 3) explain, "the abandoned mining landscape and town at Pine Point reminds us, however, that stories of environmental degradation and community collapse still have a place in the mining history literature." They emphasize that, while the "disappearance" of the town of Pine Point to avoid the community's inevitable post-mine social degradation was a unique situation, the other deleterious results of northern mining towns, even after Pine Point's eradication, nevertheless linger.

This detour away from the project through the town's history and the various contexts that surround it illuminate one of the key claims this chapter makes about *Welcome to Pine Point*, namely, that both its form and content suggest the i-doc is primarily concerned with the relationship between nostalgia, memory, and media, and the quasi-scientific positivism that drove the conviction that industrial development in the North was simply the sign of an advanced, properly functioning nation-state. It seems inevitable that the project should overlook the ideology at work and that there was, in fact, a better future imagined for the town – even if, in actual fact, it resulted in environmental destruction, no tangible benefits for the Indigenous communities in the vicinity of the mine, and the erasure of the town itself.

Towards the end of Burke's (2019, 21) introduction to *Hinterland Remixed*, he invokes Charity Scribner's *Requiem for Communism* and her observation that, although the social and economic experiment of the former Eastern Bloc was clearly a catastrophic failure in most ways, the art from the period is a reminder of the experimental attempts to "recollect ways of living and working that were imagined to be possible under the socialist alternative, but also to resuscitate the principal of hope that inspired much of the last century's social and cultural production." Burke uses this idea in defence of his project about the complicated and problematic visual culture of Canada in the (as many would say) socially regrettable 1970s, and it seems aptly applied to *Welcome to Pine Point*. While the project documents – and is itself a document of – ways of thinking about memory and media, it also directly sidesteps the obviously fraught political contexts of colonialism in Canada's North, widespread environmental destruction, and the place of both in the Canadian national imaginary. Nevertheless, I'd suggest that a town created with the genuinely felt assumption that "northern development" would have positive consequences for the communities that surrounded it, and a place where nearly all citizens not only made a living wage but also had access to all the recreational facilities they might desire, does offer us the ability to imagine better futures than the frequently grim present we face. *Welcome to Pine Point* captures and celebrates this optimism despite the town's fate.

"I suppose we all want a chance to edit our story. To keep the best stuff on top, to bury the rest. To decide how we'll be remembered by others." This is our *Welcome to Pine Point* narrator speculating on some of Richard Cloutier's motives for his Pine Point Revisited site. If, as Will Straw (2007, 4) explains, one of the internet's effects is to lend cultural weight and legibility to an endless array of disparate pasts, it is clear that the interactive documentary *Welcome to Pine Point* is engaged in the same practice to a degree. Individual memories and mediated "old" artefacts are curated with craft into a wistfully nostalgic reminiscence of the past, at once necessarily disregarding social catastrophes of environmental destruction and racism, thus allowing one, through that which one chooses to remember, to imagine possible futures of progress, stability, and comfort.

Notes

1 Shoebridge and Simons were, prior to *Welcome to Pine Point*, perhaps best known as the long-time artistic directors of *Adbusters Magazine*, a publication characterized by its unusual design and anti-consumerist bent.

2 Perhaps most influential among this work in the recent past is van Dijck (2007).

References

Benjamin, Walter. 2003. "On the Concept of History." In *Walter Benjamin: Selected Writings*, vol. 4: *1938–1940*, ed. Howard Eiland and Michael W. Jennings, 389–400. Cambridge, MA: Belknap Press of Harvard University Press.

Boles, Benjamin. 2011. "Besnard Lakes Score Pine Point." *Now Magazine*, 23 January 2011. https://nowtoronto.com/music/besnard-lakes-score-pine-point.

Bolter, Jay and Richard Grusin. 1999. *Remediation: Understanding New Media.* Cambridge, MA: MIT Press.

Boym, Svetlana. 2001. "Nostalgia." In *Atlas of Transformation.* http://monumenttotransformation.org/atlas-of-transformation/html/n/nostalgia/nostalgia-svetlana-boym.html.

Burke, Andrew. 2019. *Hinterland Remixed: Media, Memory and the Canadian 1970s.* Montreal and Kingston: McGill-Queen's University Press.

Fisher, Mark. 2014. *Ghosts of My Life: Writings on Depression, Hauntology and Lost Futures.* Winchester, UK: Zero Books.

Kashyap, Nabil. 2013. "Hometown Memories: Reading Memory and Materiality in *Welcome to Pine Point.*" *Topia* 29: 95–112.

Keeling, Arn, and John Sandles. 2012. "Claiming the New North: Development and Colonialism at the Pine Point Mine, NWT, Canada." *Environment and History* 18 (1): 5–34.

Lofaro, Tony. 2011. "'Liquid Book' on Demise of Mining Town Wins Pair of Webby Awards." *Ottawa Citizen*, 6 May 2011, 55.

Straw, Will. 2007. "Embedded Memories." In *Residual Media*, ed. Charles R. Acland, 3–15. Minneapolis: University of Minnesota Press.

Van Dyck, Jose. 2007. *Mediated Memories in the Digital Age.* Stanford: Stanford University Press.

Weldon, Carolyne. 2011. "Welcome to Pine Point: An Interview with The Goggles." *NFB Blog*, 3 February 2011. https://blog.nfb.ca/blog/2011/02/03/welcome-to-pine-point-an-interview-with-the-goggles.

13

ACOUSTIC PROFILING IN HOGAN'S ALLEY

MAPPING INTERSECTIONAL SOUNDWAYS IN THE LOST VANCOUVER NEIGHBOURHOOD OF STAN DOUGLAS'S iOS APP *CIRCA 1948*

Randolph Jordan

Stan Douglas's *Circa 1948*, an app for ios devices co-produced by the National Film Board of Canada's Digital Studio in Vancouver, presents a navigable 3D-modelled replication of two lost Vancouver spaces: the second iteration of the Hotel Vancouver and the Hogan's Alley district, home to Vancouver's Black community and point of intersection with Chinatown and the Italian quarter. In this chapter, I focus on Hogan's Alley, "an almost legendary neighbourhood … with a reputation for extraordinary music, no frills food, illegal liquor, a little pandemonium, sexual (mis)adventure, and sometimes violence" (Purvey and Belshaw 2011, 52). Before the westernmost section of the alley was razed to install the onramp to the new Georgia Viaduct in 1970, the Vancouver planning department took a detailed photographic survey of all the structures on the block (now open-access through the online database of the City of Vancouver Archives). This rich photographic record served as the basis for Douglas's painstaking visual reconstruction, a project very much in line with the artist's long-standing interest in staging large-scale photographic reconstructions of Vancouver's Downtown Eastside, challenging the area's notoriety as "Canada's worst neighbourhood" (Sommers and Blomley 2002, 19). On the level of the images in *Circa 1948*, Douglas attempts to remain faithful to the buildings and their decaying states of repair while also filling in the blanks to render it as a seamless 3D virtual environment, inviting users to investigate its nooks and crannies while activating narrative vignettes along the way. Of course, the app's meticulous visual realism raises an important question: In the absence of an equivalent sonic record of the area, how does *Circa 1948* present the auditory environment of Hogan's Alley?

Douglas approaches the sound component of *Circa 1948* quite differently than he does the image track. There are three distinct layers to the soundtrack that correspond with the conventional organization of film sound production: sound effects, music, and speech. In the app, however, the relationship between these elements is decided by the user's navigation of the environment and creates important relationships between and across them. Amidst the continuously shifting environmental sounds and wafts of music from various sources, there are key points in the alley where users can tap on glowing objects to reveal ghostly apparitions that float through the space while dialogue reveals the characters these people once were, offering pathways into narratives of the lives of figures that represent (stereo)typical residents of the alley. In acting style and auditory presentation, the dialogue sounds more like period radio drama than the realist street documentation of the images, extending from Douglas's play *Helen Lawrence*, a noir drama featuring elaborate projections of the animated environments of *Circa 1948*. The stage production premiered in Vancouver in 2014, the same year the app was launched. As Douglas puts it, *Circa 1948* presents us with these characters during the day, and *Helen Lawrence* takes us into their nights (Glassman 2016). The tension between sound and image reflects two important tendencies in Douglas's body of photographic work: documenting real-world spaces and staging moments of historical importance. These impulses sit at opposite ends of the range of documentary media's expressive modes, yet they inform each other in works like *Circa 1948* to emphasize the relationship between history and the present moment, spaces of the past lost to processes of urban renewal that we cannot escape today.

The intersection of *Circa 1948*'s narrative and the design of its gameplay reveals a predominant mode of experience for the user based on recognition of distinct regions of the alley, their points of intersection, and the tensions that live in the spaces of overlap. In *Circa 1948*, it is the sound that most connects the storyworld to the real world, but for reasons quite opposite to the documentary quality of the photorealistic images: it is the staged quality of the sound, highly contrived, that provides a template for a mode of listening that allows us to hear through the conventions of film sound to the realities with which they engage, even as they often obscure what might have been heard by any microphones in the region, were they present. I label this mode "unsettled listening," premised upon the practice of "acoustic profiling," two strategies for unpacking mediated sound that I have developed more fully elsewhere (Jordan 2017; 2018; 2023).

Drawing on the concept of the "acoustic profile" and how it maps "acoustic communities" in the field of acoustic ecology, the practice of acoustic profiling requires attunement to the ways in which the sonic fields of any source play out across geographical space, and how they map their own territories while overlapping with others. This mapping reveals points of contest in space, and I demonstrate how *Circa 1948* positions the user in the midst of these overlapping spaces that connect to points of narrative tension between characters in the alley whose interests both align and conflict. Charting how the navigation of the alley prompts ways of experiencing the space as already contested, I argue that the deployment of sound within the app's interactive navigational design offers useful ways of thinking about the costs of disrupting relationships between real-world communities with divisive infrastructure such as the viaduct and suggests pathways to correcting these problems in the face of the impending destruction of the viaduct and the City of Vancouver's current plans for renewal in the northeast area of False Creek.

I present my analysis along two fronts. First, I examine the formal qualities of the storyworld as activated by user navigation, which I theorize through the strategies of unsettled listening and acoustic profiling. Second, I connect these formal details with Stan Douglas's larger body of Vancouver-specific work in order to suggest a way in which the spaces opened up by the photographer's storyworlds can offer a template for thinking through the relationship between real-world space and audiovisual representation, and how this relationship can speak to the needs of renewal in the area once the present Georgia Viaduct comes down. Acoustic ecology was founded on the notion that better acoustic design creates better acoustic communities, and that urban planning should take this into consideration. Without the divisiveness of the traffic thoroughfare, what potential might there be to honour the legacy of the Black community and its historic overlaps with Chinatown and the Italian quarter? And how might renewal in the area be made to work without the trappings of gentrification that have threatened the long-term residents of Vancouver's Downtown Eastside?

Sonic Boundary Lines

Hogan's Alley stretched three blocks between Main Street on the west and Jackson Avenue on the east, bounded by Union and Prior on the north and south, respectively. The westernmost block between Main and Gore was demolished for the viaduct, and this is the area covered in the navigable storyworld of *Circa 1948*. Users can run the full perimeter of the block along the front sides of its buildings, but there is no action here. The soundtrack is dominated by the din of traffic with no sonic information regarding the alley's goings on and no access points to its spaces except at the east and west ends. The traffic fades as users turn into the alley, and the details of the area's activities take over. Here there are many discrete sound effects – birds, footsteps, horse hoofs, door knocking, dogs barking – each of which operates on independent loops, and independent variability in amplitude and stereo panning that depend on the location of the sound source relative to the user's position. Through these fluctuating yet generally repetitive elements, pieces of music emanate from radios and record players in many different spaces, often overlapping. And then there is the dialogue that users can trigger by tapping on golden props within the mise-en-scène, revealing the ghosts of denizens past embroiled in the day's negotiations over alley business, legalities, and political manoeuvring.

The closest thing to documentary sound evidence of Hogan's Alley that *Circa 1948* offers comes from the period music and vintage news broadcasts that extend from a multitude of radios and record players, one inside each navigable house on the block. These electroacoustically transmitted sounds float the most freely through the environment of any of the storyworld's sound elements, often overlapping into a dense soundscape reflecting various layers of the social realities of the space. At the western end of the alley there is a "T" intersection, the centre of which allows us to hear three of these sound sources at once, along with the various other sound effects. One of the houses at this intersection features a radio from which a news anchor speaks of housing shortages for veterans and the legalities of squatting, issues at the forefront in the Downtown Eastside for decades and that continue to define its resistance to encroaching gentrification (Sommers and Blomley 2002). This is also a direct reference to the Hotel Vancouver portion of the app, a space that was defined by its veteran squatting after the Second World War in the face of the city's general housing shortage. As the user moves through this small house, the mobility of sound becomes apparent, shifting in volume with proximity and stereo panning depending on the user's position in relation to the sound source. The sound's variability as a marker of the user's mobility also plays into the permeability of these spaces; other pieces of transmitted sound are audible here, which can be traced to other buildings. A quick jaunt across the alley and into the adjacent structure reveals a record player spinning some jazz, and from here you can still hear the news broadcast from the first house. After triggering these sources by entering the spaces that house them, movement back out into the intersection keeps these two going while a third source drifts in from further east. Users can repeat this pattern all the way down the alley, creating a mode of experiencing the space based on profiling interiors with their sound sources, then threading them together as one moves inside, outside, and down the way.

Then there is character dialogue. The app is structured around a series of locations based on known historical establishments of the alley, like Buddy's Beer Garden that sat across from a brothel, where you can trigger staged conversations with imagined characters that might have lived in the alley; these imagined characters are based on real-world figures like Buddy Black, a Black boxer who runs the beer garden and poker house, and Carl "Lungo" Marchi, the "King of Hogan's Alley," an Italian immigrant known for his homemade wine (Purvey and Belshaw 2011, 104). An Irish constable wanders in and out of houses, each ethnically coded through stereotypical accents, from the Italians at the east end of the alley to the Chinese madam May Liu and Buddy Black, her business partner. Italian opera, Chinese popular music, and American jazz populate these areas as the user moves in and out of conversations about the tensions held in balance between each of these characters.

These conversations take on the tone and delivery of radio drama productions, highly stylized performances in the tradition of film noir and mic'd according to conventions of American radio drama of the 1930s and 1940s. Neil Verma (2012) identifies two key styles in these period dramas, both of which are in play here: the "intimate" style, in which characters are followed closely, mic'd at the same close range that minimizes spatial details even as we follow them in movement – like tracking shots that maintain their subjects in close-up, allowing for heightened empathy on the part of listeners (61); and the "kaleidosonic" style that diminishes a sense of the individual by presenting a multitude of voices equally from a variety of different positions simultaneously, no longer locking onto the "audiopositions" of any one specific character at any one specific time (67). In *Circa 1948,* the duality of these two modes is enabled by the interactive component: the ability of the user to shift positions during the conversations. The recordings present intimate access to these characters, while the navigation allows for a kaleidosonic effect when moving around the space while listening. The kaleidosonic aspect of the user experience suits the episodic nature of the dialogue, offering the sense of larger narrative developments but with no plot to follow. We don't get closure on the characters, but we do get a closer sense of the people who populate the alley.

There are two useful ideas that I'd like to put into play here as indicators of what makes the interactive soundworld in *Circa 1948* productive for thinking through both the history of Vancouver and the city's present incarnation. First, in her collaborative project *Soundscapes of the Urban Past* (2013), Karin Bijsterveld uses the term "staging" to address the specific ways in which media sound can provide access to historical realities if we learn to navigate the complexities of how the sound has been constructed according the historical, political, cultural, and technical context of any given moment (Bijsterveld 2013, 6). Second, in *Figuring the Past* (2012), Belén Vidal offers the notion of period filmmaking as "figuration" of the past "through the prism of present stylistic choices, cultural concerns and imaginative retro-projections" (10). There are two different but related lines of questioning here: How do the media of the past stage their present? And how do media of our present stage the past?

These questions often overlap when a period piece makes heavy use of historical media, as is the case in *Circa 1948*. The sound effects provide a base layer of environmental realism to the alley, consistent with modern-day Foley work and game sound design. The music recordings and news broadcasts establish period authenticity in their content and also in their presentation on vintage media formats. Moreover, the presentation of the period dialogue draws on the authentic stylization of the era to develop points of narrative engagement, while the networked and episodic nature of the narrative itself is consistent with postmodern approaches to storytelling. Understanding how Douglas figures the past through his staging of the Hogan's Alley district, and what this has to tell us about present-day renewal in the area, depends on assessing how the three layers of the soundtrack in the storyworld establish distinct spaces while allowing users to map the relationships across both geography and politics. *Circa 1948* thus offers an interactive construction of the Hogan's Alley soundscape that speaks to the need for community participation in reimagining how this location will develop in the future. To assist with the process of unpacking these sonic relationships, I turn to two strategies that I have been developing for the analysis of location-based media: unsettled listening and acoustic profiling.

Unsettling Profiles

Across a variety of prior publications, I have been developing ways of thinking about "unsettled" forms of listening to works of sound and image as a way of using media representations of particular geographic locations to engage more deeply with the overlapping histories and patterns of use present in those real-world places (see Jordan 2014; 2017; 2023). I take a cue from a critical process that Nicholas Blomley (2004) calls "unsettling the city" in his book of the same name. With Vancouver as his example, Blomley reveals the city as a site of continual contestation and mobility across generations and cultural groups, and calls for an "unsettled" approach that can account for the multiple overlapping patterns of use that are concealed by "settled" concepts of bounded property. He advocates for ways of thinking about sites in the city through histories that have been obscured, a way to "re-place" them by revealing the places that they were and continue to be underneath the veneer of settlement (145). With that in mind, I propose "unsettled listening" as a way of experiencing the city from these multiple positions simultaneously, an especially effective strategy when listening to media representations of the city with attention to how they are staged according to historical position and production context. Unsettled listening asks of any piece of media: How can the soundtrack reveal how a particular location has been staged to foreground certain aspects of its geographical and social environment while concealing others, and what can hearing through these manipulations tell us about the real-world space represented on screen?

A key tool for unsettled listening is the practice of what I call "acoustic profiling." Here I combine the standard notion of profiling, as a means of extrapolating information about something based on its known characteristics with the loaded connotations of racial profiling, and tie these to acoustic ecology's use of the term "acoustic profile" (Truax 1978, 5) to define the area over which any given sound can be heard. Acoustic ecology engages with the idea of acoustic profile to define the spatial boundaries of acoustic communities (Truax 2001, 66), bound together by common experience of the same sounds, as in the way parishes of old have been defined by the auditory limits of the church bell. Barry Truax extends this idea of acoustic community to examine not only listening but also communication by way of sound, offering a model for exploring the rich interplay of sounds within the limits of the profile that defines the area in which community exists.

In his early writings within the field of acoustic ecology, R. Murray Schafer (1977, 90–1) holds the idea of "schizophonia" as a negative consequence of the electroacoustical transmission of sound, a threat to the viability of acoustic communities by disrupting the "natural" propagation of sound through artificial extension and displacement of its profile. The term has been roundly critiqued for its failure to account for the medial nature of human engagement with the world and for mobilizing ableist stereotypes around mental disability. Truax (2001, 207) later articulates how electroacoustic transmissions could be understood as important aspects of acoustic communities, while Andra McCartney (2002) calls for heightened attention to "electroacoustic ecology" as part of the field's purview. For present purposes, however, it is useful to consider another productive point of tension within Schafer's theorization: his notion of the "hi-fi soundscape" equates fidelity not only with a strong signal-to-noise ratio in the environment, which he borrows from the postwar consumer electronics industry (Sterne 2013), but also with the ability of sounds to travel a long way in an environment without being masked by density (Schafer 1977, 43). The greater the distance from which we can hear any given sound, the greater the fidelity of the sound environment. For film analysis, Michel Chion (1994, 87) uses the term "extension" to assess how far into the distance a film's soundtrack allows us to hear, the auditory equivalent to depth of field. For Schafer (1977, 207), the hi-fi soundscape is one in which sounds exist on a "human scale," which he associates with the principles of the non-human world: "There are few sounds in nature that interfere with our ability to communicate vocally and almost none that in any way pose a threat to the hearing apparatus." Though Schafer's claim here can easily be refuted, what is important to understand is his equation of high fidelity with what Jonathan Sterne (2003, 342) refers to as "the spatiality of the unamplified voice." For Schafer, the presence of electroacoustically transmitted sound creates an artificial sense of distance while in reality contributing to the density of sound that ultimately hinders long-range listening within the environment. As I argue elsewhere, this is an instructive conflation of fidelity, geographical range, and unamplified soundmaking when considering the value of the acoustic profile concept: fidelity, in this construction, can map community (Jordan 2023, 175). For my purposes here, this notion of fidelity can account for the way that *Circa 1948* deploys discreet sound events with particular acoustic profiles that can be used to articulate the community dynamics within Hogan's Alley, particularly when differentiating between amplified and unamplified sound sources within the storyworld.

When asking how faithful *Circa 1948* is with respect to the historical Hogan's Alley, the image and soundtracks provide differing standards. The archival photorealism of the image speaks to Douglas's penchant for detailing the excruciating minutiae of the environments he reconstructs in his photographic work. The sound offers another pathway in, a mode of understanding fidelity not by how realistically the sound elements reflect what would have actually been heard in those environments but, rather, by how the patterns of navigability through the various sound elements map the real-world relationships between communities that defined this area. So what do we learn if we apply acoustic profiling to the interactive storyworld of *Circa 1948*, and what can this knowledge tell us about the app's relationship with real-world Vancouver?

Profiling Hogan's Alley

Circa 1948 makes for an especially apt case study of how acoustic profiling can work. The conversations that Douglas stages between differing residents of the alley are deliberately coded with ethnic stereotypes, a knowing detail that he uses as part of his process of staging to call attention to how these stereotypes have functioned in our ideas of this area's historical past, and how these ideas might be unsettled to reveal more complex realities. Each conversation deals with some point of overlap, either cooperation or tension, between the various different parties that have set up shop in the alley. For example, the Irish constable visits Chinese brothel owner May Liu for his regular pay-off (after having collected a sum from the Italians up the alley) but is interrupted by Inspector Leonard Perkins, who is tasked with cracking down on police corruption. They argue about whether or not any money will change hands today, and the constable leaves empty handed while the inspector stays for a stint with one of May Liu's employees. Profiling issues of ethnicity is straightforward in dialogue like this, in which accents are heavily inflected with stereotype – Liu's choppy English and the constable's thick Irish accent – or coded neutral to the emerging standard for white settled Canadians, like Perkins. To this we can add the geographical element of acoustic profiling to listen for the audible range of their conversation. As they talk, users can pull out of the interior space of May Liu's house into the alley to test the limits of extension. Performing this exercise on any given conversation reveals a very specific line after which the conversations cease. The conversation between the constable and May Liu, for example, holds for only a few feet away from the door, about the width of the alley, which means that no conversation triggered inside a house can carry past the property line of any other. And the conversations cut off so abruptly at the threshold that this appears more a function of the limits of the software engine used to manage the sound elements than a design feature specific to the goal of the storyworld. However, it is clear that the acoustic profile of the conversations has been intentionally set to a more limited range than that which Chion (1994, 76) would call the "on-the-air" sources, positioned within the storyworld as being transmitted electroacoustically, which extend for a greater distance. Chion argues that such sounds "are not subject to 'natural' mechanical laws of sound propagation" and "enjoy the freedom of crossing boundaries of cinematic space" (ibid.). *Circa 1948* capitalizes on this convention of cinematic freedom to articulate territories and their points of overlap in the alley.

For example, once the conversation between Liu, the constable, and the inspector is done, a sound system in Liu's place begins playing Chinese music that can still be heard deep within the yard space in the beer garden across the alley, mingling with the sounds of the guitar and piano suggested from the instruments on the stage there. Liu's music is even audible within Buddy Black's house at the back of the beer garden, where one of the conversations you can trigger reveals Buddy Black teaching a neophyte how to play poker. Further still, Liu's music remains audible while the inspector argues with another party about the mayor's plan to make an example of Hogan's Alley in a new bid to rid the city of crime, warning of the danger in messing with May Liu – with whom Buddy is in business – because of her connections to powerful interests in nearby Chinatown. In this space there is yet another sound system that gets activated after these conversations are triggered, which can then carry out into other spaces down the alley.

A pattern emerges in which dialogue is bounded by property while on-the-air sound is not. The conversations are settled; the electroacoustic transmissions are unsettled. The radio and record player cues are used to thread the property-specific conversations into a broader network, connecting on points of narrative and theme in the dialogue and in the extension of their sound within the geographical deployment of the storyworld's acoustic profiles. Douglas has explained that the lack of narrative development or closure is by design (Glassman 2016). Through the dialogue, we get only partial access to the lives of these characters. What is clear through the formal implementation of these conversations within the broader sound world is that, through the user's navigation of the space, the boundaries and overlaps between specific locations are made manifest. Above all, I would like to emphasize how the broader profile of the on-the-air tracks, compared to the conversations, allows for a formal exploration of how the private conversations that happen in the interior spaces, largely inaudible from the street, nevertheless affect the other spaces in the alley directly. This phenomenon is suggested by the music that more freely floats through the space with greater extension and much greater overlap, each piece associated with a particular space and its corollary ethnic propriety.

In designing the variable acoustic profiles of the different layers of the soundtrack, *Circa 1948* poses important questions about how social integration can function within the domain of contested spaces like these. Here we might think of a bit of wordplay on the term "integration" itself as it serves the study of media sound. The idea of the integrated soundtrack is gaining popularity as an object of study, concerned as it is with how filmmakers dissolve boundaries between three traditionally divided areas of the soundtrack: speech, music, and sound effects (see Greene 2016). As I demonstrate here, these relationships are constructed in this storyworld to emphasize the threading of spaces that are divided and contested. In this way, *Circa 1948* makes a point about the traditional division of film soundtracks and how these divisions can be made to expose themselves on points of political importance. Here it is not the category of sound as traditionally divided that dictates its level of integration; rather, it is the status of the implied source that matters. Sound presented as on-the-air, or schizophonic, allows both speech and music to thread spaces together in ways that unamplified voices do not. Might there be a critique here of the theory of human scale as the foundation for community? It is the electroacoustic transmissions that speak more to integration across the boundaries of ethnic property and interest, and point to models of urban planning currently in place in the real-world space of Vancouver's Northeast False Creek.

Augmenting Reality

Douglas's initial vision for *Circa 1948* was as an augmented reality tool to be used on the present-day site of the old Hogan's Alley, "to use a smartphone like it's a window to the past. As you look up, down and around you'd see what would have been there in 1948" (Glassman 2016). However, the geographical area covered in the app is precisely that which was destroyed for the new Georgia Viaduct, with the onramp running through the main alleyway that users navigate in the storyworld, making it an effectively unusable space for pedestrians – especially ones glued to their mobile screens while walking. So the project became an "immersive art app" (as declared on the first screen when initiating the app), a mobile installation piece with a sister gallery installation that was featured in the *Storyscapes* section of New York's Tribeca Film Festival in 2014. However, aspects of the augmented reality vision live on in *Circa 1948*, which are revealed by considering its relationship to Douglas's larger body of work and how this work intersects with the discourse of the cinematic city, where the norms of filmic representation mesh with location-based research in critical geography and urban studies.

Douglas has long been interested in exploring issues of urban disenfranchisement in his other large-scale photographic works. In *Abbott and Cordova, 7 August 1971* (2008), Douglas staged a recreation of a pot riot in Vancouver's Downtown Eastside that resulted in substantial police brutality and marked a turning point in the city's hippie culture whereafter the bulk of its participants left central urban enclaves both downtown and on Fourth Avenue for the rural spaces of the interior and the islands off the coast. The photograph was composed in a series of takes then composited into a seamless whole. It is now installed permanently in the new downtown campus of Simon Fraser University, an architectural complex on the site of the old Woodward's building, once the centrepiece of the downtown shopping district but closed in 1992 and occupied for many years by squatters in protest over what vacating business was doing to the Downtown Eastside. Many believed the building should be used for low-income housing, an element that the new structure partially incorporated into its design though it primarily features commercial shopping and spaces for the university. Here, Douglas literally overlaps a tense historical moment of class conflict with the most current manifestation of such conflict in the area, an act of unsettling that serves as a continual reminder of the contested nature of the space (Proudfoot 2011, 90).

This site-specific installation is an example of the augmented reality impulse in Douglas's work, to impose unsettling views of real-world geographical space through artistic reconstructions of that space viewable on site. A similar impulse drives *Every Building on 100 West Hastings* (2002) in which Douglas photographs the titular buildings of this "worst block in Vancouver" (Sommers and Blomley 2002) individually, framed centrally for minimal geometric distortion, and then composites the images to create an impossible vantage point on this very real space that eschews the conventions of Renaissance perspective. Photographed in exposures long enough to erase signs of people moving through the scene, the image leaves the buildings glowing from inside but strangely empty, a quality that Denise Blake Oleksijczuk (2002, 110) suggests is an invitation for the viewer to contemplate the fate of dozens of Indigenous women who have gone missing from this area over the past several decades, a story that speaks to systemic failure on the part of governments, the police, and the general populace, all of whom contribute to maintaining this Vancouver neighbourhood as one that is intentionally neglected.

In both works described above, the seamlessness of the composites belies the fragmentary heart of the works, a quality that commentators like Denise Blake Oleksijczuk and Serge Guibault (2011) suggest is part of how they function to destabilize viewers and make us aware of the cracks behind the façade. This is a goal well in keeping with Blomley's goal of unsettling the city but is not without the possibility for critique. Jesse Proudfoot (2011, 90) questions Douglas's gesture in *Abbott and Cordova*, arguing that the victims of his photograph's injustice were the already-privileged class of white hippie culture with the leisure time to protest the smoking of their recreational drug of choice while obscuring the much longer-standing dispossession of the *lumpen* class, the poor viewed as "undeserving," often tied to Indigeneity. One could make a similar argument about *Every Building on 100 West Hastings* as the invisibility of the people deflects attention away from the implications of race, class, and gender that complicate this space. *Circa 1948* follows some of the formal characteristics of these earlier works while directly addressing the intersectional tensions that inform them, acting as a kind of augmented reality for the alley that can then be mapped onto the city at large.

In its treatment of present-day issues through a look to the past, *Circa 1948*, like Douglas's other historical reconstructions, serves as what Guibault (2011, 39) calls a "back to the future exercise," and the "exercise" is left to the users as we take part in staging our own figuration of how this space functions. Here, the interactive basis for the app reveals the seams between the composites that Douglas has presented as a whole and allows us to dig into the cracks in order to unsettle historical representations of these spaces in the present moment. Awareness of the process of staging is key here, and the tension between the photorealism of the images and the theatricality of the sound makes the staging explicit. What does Douglas's figuration of the past, then, tell us about present-day concerns in Vancouver's Downtown Eastside?

Back to the Future

The razing of Hogan's Alley for viaduct construction was at once a beginning and an end for a city in the process of reinvention. It was to be part of a larger freeway project that would have cut through the downtown core, a plan that ended up being shouted down through vigorous community protests, which led to a new political party, TEAM (The Electors Action Movement), gaining power in 1972 (Berelowitz 2005, 81). While the viaducts remain to this day as "constant reminders of the severe urban design problems that the completed freeway system could have posted," TEAM quickly drew a new vision for Vancouver development with its "Downtown Plan" begun in 1975 (Punter 2003, 25). Resisting the homogenizing impulse of globalizing cities after the Second World War, city planners engaged in a detailed study of the distinctiveness of Vancouver's existing downtown neighbourhoods, commissioning "character area descriptions" for distinct blocks and regions – separate from official zoning designations – and embarked on a plan to maintain the spirit of these while allowing for development and expansion (64). It was too late for Hogan's Alley, and the Downtown Eastside increasingly came to function as an intentional gutter into which fallout from renewal elsewhere would be swept. As a whole, however, the Vancouver project is intriguing in its commitment to maintain the traditional make-up of existing neighbourhoods without ghettoization. In other words, they aimed to build intentional overlap and cross-pollination between areas, one of the features of urban planning that has led to the moniker "Vancouverism" taking hold in international planning circles, and which continues with the city's plan to reconnect parts of the Downtown Eastside that were severed by the Georgia Viaduct (City of Vancouver 2016).

To plan well, planners have to imagine lived experience on the ground. What *Circa 1948* offers is a sampling of what this lived experience entails and how the relationship between distinct properties and points of communal overlap raises issues of conflict and collaboration. Now that Vancouver is poised to enact a kind of do-over for the Hogan's Alley district, imagining how to stage these points of overlap is key. With *Circa 1948*, Douglas takes the contentious histories and invisible victims of urban governance on display in his other works and allows his viewers and listeners to take part in the creation of the art. As we are all complicit in how our spaces function based on how we choose to use them, it behooves all of us to imagine different uses if we are to create spaces of inclusion while respecting the singularities that comprise diversity.

It is an illustrative juxtaposition that, just as Vancouver was coming into its own as a self-aware city embarking on a distinctive urban planning course that would win it international attention, the city also rose up as a major centre for filmmaking premised largely on runaway film production in which foreign producers would disguise Vancouver locations as other parts of the world. The city's distinctiveness, driving urban planning, was downplayed by filmmakers wanting the kind of genericism increasingly common to global urban spaces. One of the most intriguing aspects of *Circa 1948* is how Douglas reverses this scenario, using the generic language of film noir as a basis for which the location-specific particularities of Hogan's Alley could shine through, conducting his own character area study of the distinctive properties and proprietors of the neighbourhood. In turn, this invitation to become immersed in Vancouver's historical specificity is mirrored by the app's intriguing position with respect to the conventions of augmented reality design. I suggest that *Circa 1948* leans towards what Benjamin Koslowski (2016) identifies as the potential for screen representations of urban space to create a productive mise-en-scène in which social media interaction can take place. While typical approaches to augmented reality use mobile technologies to overlay real-world space with additional contextual information, the flipside is also possible: online interaction can be facilitated by placing users inside representations of real-world spaces (240). *Circa 1948* does not have a social media component as part of its interactivity. However, as mentioned before, nor does it function well as an augmentation tool for use on site. Instead, *Circa 1948* sits in the middle, offering a provocative potential model for urban planning in the twenty-first century. Rather than a Smart Cities approach to embedding urban space with interactive technologies, the experience of navigating the virtual world of Hogan's Alley provides an understanding of how social interactions take place within and across the boundaries of bounded property.

Conclusion

In *Circa 1948*, the integrity of Hogan's Alley is marked by its isolation from the surrounding neighbourhoods, the emphasis on internationality marked by spaces occupied within the alley. This treatment is an example of the figuration that Vidal argues is an unavoidable staple of any period piece: by design, *Circa 1948* presents a doomed location twenty years before its demise. Yet one of the features of its original manifestation was its ease of connection to surrounding neighbourhoods: to the waters of False Creek one block west, to Chinatown a little further, to Strathcona to the north. What *Circa 1948* achieves is a microcosmic presentation of the way that the whole of the Downtown Eastside area once functioned before being broken up by the viaduct and encroached upon by the forces of gentrification. Spaces were connected; they overlapped, even in their distinction according to ethnic orientation. In *Circa 1948*, this spatial form is rendered through the soundtrack. Each house serves as a neighbourhood, each conversation an uneasy participation between their residents, each radio a map of the realities of overlap between these spaces no matter how hard their residents attempt to stand their ground.

There are lessons in this presentation that can speak to both the benefits and harms of neighbourhood integration. Gentrification, on the one hand, encroaches on low-income space and pretends towards mixed use – playing friendly – before bulldozers inevitably wipe out the old neighbourhood and leave new social structures in its place. On the other hand, we have genuine renewal efforts that seek to maintain the integrity of existing spaces and make them function within the larger fabric of the city. With its Northeast False Creek plan, the City of Vancouver is speaking the language of the latter, removing divisive infrastructure and mapping out pathways between existing communities and new planned spaces, complete with nodes of intersection that will revive the spirit of Hogan's Alley and provide some reconciliation with not only the dispossessed Black community but also the Chinese community and the Musqueam, Squamish, and Tsleil-Waututh First Nations (City of Vancouver 2016, 21–3). As with any staging that seeks to refigure the past, we can ask how the city will interpret what has been lost and how it will attempt reconciliation for the present moment. Stan Douglas's *Circa 1948* lays a template for thinking through issues of boundary and flow. How navigable the renewed area will become remains to be heard.

References

Berelowitz, Lance. 2005. *Dream City: Vancouver and the Global Imagination*. Vancouver: Douglas and McIntyre.

Bijsterveld, Karin. 2013. "Introduction." In *Soundscapes of the Urban Past: Staged Sound as Mediated Cultural Heritage*, ed. Karin Bijsterveld, 11–28. Bielefeld: Transcript Verlag.

Blomley, Nicholas. 2004. *Unsettling the City: Urban Land and the Politics of Property*. New York: Routledge.

Chion, Michel. 1994. *Audio-Vision: Sound on Screen*. Trans. Claudia Gorbman. New York: Columbia University Press.

City of Vancouver. 2016. *Northeast False Creek Plan*. https://vancouver.ca/files/cov/northeast-false-creek-plan.pdf.

Glassman, Marc. 2016. "The POV Interview: Stan Douglas." *Point of View* 102 (Summer), 25 October 2016. http://povmagazine.com/articles/view/stan-douglas.

Greene, Liz. 2016. "From Noise: Blurring the Boundaries of the Soundtrack." In *The Palgrave Handbook of Sound Design and Music in Screen Media*, ed, Liz Greene and Danijela Kulezic-Wilson, 33–42. London: Palgrave Macmillan,

Guibeault, Serge. 2011. "Lightning from the Past: Police, Pot, Public, and Stan Douglas's *Abbott & Cordova*." In *Stan Douglas: Abbott & Cordova, 1971*, eds. Brian Lam and Robert Ballantyne, 26–45. Vancouver: Arsenal Pulp Press/Contemporary Art Gallery.

Jordan, Randolph. 2014. "Unsettled Listening: Integrating Film and Place." *Sounding Out! Blog*, 14 August 2014. https://soundstudiesblog.com/2014/08/14/unsettled-listening-integrating-film-and-place.

– 2017. "Unsettling the Soundtrack: Acoustic Profiling and the Documentation of Community and Place." In *The Routledge Companion to Screen Music and*

Sound, ed. Miguel Mera, Ron Sadoff, and Ben Winters, 590–602. New York: Routledge.
– 2018. "Re-placing the Urban Soundscape: Performative Documentary Research in Vancouver's False Creek." In *Critical Distance in Documentary Media*, ed. Gerda Cammaer, Blake Fitzpatrick, and Bruno Lessard, 257–78. London: Palgrave Macmillan.
– 2023. *Acoustic Profiles: A Sound Ecology of the Cinema*. New York: Oxford University Press.
Koslowski, Benjamin. 2016. "The Mediating City: Towards a Mise-en-scène for Interaction Online." In *Filming the City: Urban Documents, Design Practices and Social Criticism Through the Lens*, ed. Edward M. Clift, Mirka Guaralda, and Ari Mattes, 223–43. Bristol: Intellect.
McCartney, Andra. 2002. "Sharing Experiences towards the Possibility of an Electroacoustic Ecology." *Soundscape: The Journal of Acoustic Ecology* 3 (1): 22.
Proudfoot, Jesse. 2011. "The Derelict, the Deserving Poor, and the *Lumpen*: A History of the Politics of Representation on the Downtown Eastside." In *Stan Douglas: Abbott and Cordova, 1971*, eds. Brian Lam and Robert Ballantyne, 88–105. Vancouver: Arsenal Pulp Press /Contemporary Art Gallery.
Punter, John. 2003. *The Vancouver Achievement: Urban Planning and Design*. Vancouver: UBC Press.
Purvey, Diane, and John Belshaw. 2011. *Vancouver Noir: 1930–1960*. Vancouver: Anvil Press.
Schafer, R. Murray. 1977. *The Tuning of the World*. Toronto: McCLelland and Stewart.
Sommers, Jeff, and Nick Blomley. 2002. "The Worst Block in Vancouver." In *Stan Douglas: Every Building on 100 West Hastings*, ed. Reid Shier, 18–58. Vancouver: Arsenal Pulp Press/Contemporary Art Gallery.
Sterne 2003. *The Audible Past: Cultural Origins of Sound Reproduction*. Durham, NC: Duke University Press.
– 2013. "Soundscape, Landscape, Escape." In *Soundscapes of the Urban Past: Staged Sound as Mediated Cultural Heritage*, ed. Karin Bijsterveld, 181–93. Bielefeld: Transcript Verlag.
Truax, Barry, ed. 1978. *Handbook for Acoustic Ecology*. Vancouver: ARC Publications.
– 2001. *Acoustic Communication*. 2nd ed. Westport: Alex Publishing.
Verma, Neil. 2012. *Theatre of the Mind: Imagination, Aesthetics, and American Radio Drama*. Chicago: University of Chicago Press.
Vidal, Belén. 2012. *Figuring the Past: Period Film and the Mannerist Aesthetic*. Amsterdam: Amsterdam University Press.

14

A JOURNAL OF INSOMNIA

THE INDIVIDUALIZATION OF SLEEP IN A WIRED WORLD

Zoë Druick

Insomnia is a highly prevalent sleep disorder that has been estimated to affect between 30% and 50% of the general population. Insomnia is diagnosed by the following symptoms: difficulty initiating sleep, maintaining sleep, or having nonrestorative sleep that is also accompanied by daytime dysfunction despite adequate opportunity to sleep. These interferences in healthy sleep patterns typically coexist with a variety of comorbid conditions, such as a medical or psychiatric disorder, that can have a profound effect on the individual's functioning and overall quality of life.

C.L. Drake, S. Eklov, and T. Roth, *Encyclopedia of Sleep*

Illness is the night-side of life, a more onerous citizenship.

Susan Sontag, *Illness as Metaphor*

Given the common occurrence of sleep disruption in relation to the demands of a highly caffeinated, always-on digital culture, it may seem strange that very few films have explored in any depth the "onerous citizenship" of insomnia *as a normal experience*, usually focusing instead on drug addiction, automatism, and psychosis. A 1997 Norwegian film blanche (Erik Skjoldbjaerg) and its American remake (Christopher Nolan, 2002), both called *Insomnia*, are typical in this regard. In these films, a policeman investigating the murder of a teenage girl in the height of an

Arctic summer (Norway and Alaska, respectively) mistakenly shoots his partner and then loses the ability to sleep during the bright nights. The excessive light here signifies both nature-out-of-kilter (he is not from the Far North; the night should be dark) as well as his conscience, both of which prevent him from sleeping. Not only did he shoot his friend in error, but he also tries to frame the girl's killer for the murder. Insomnia here is both real and metaphoric as the protagonist's psyche and the environment bleed together.

Alan Berliner's essayistic documentary *Wide Awake* (2006) explores the ordinariness of insomnia in an age of anxiety, but it also pulls the viewer into the filmmaker's autobiography. The fifty-year-old American independent filmmaker crafts a story about his lifetime of insomnia, which braids together childhood memories of his parents' nocturnal fights and the relentless, unpredictable violence of the twentieth century with the birth of a son whom the filmmaker hopes will become a successful sleeper. The confluence of personal and social unrest is here collated into vertiginous sequences of news photographs, which flicker by at almost subliminal speed. But, ultimately, Berliner's obsession with twentieth-century violence and social foment, which he has organized into a personal archive so elaborate it almost seems like an analogue internet, is ultimately made to seem more like the result of his insomniac mind than the cause.

The collaborative, interactive documentary *A Journal of Insomnia* (Hugues Sweeney, 2013), produced by the NFB Digital Studio, by contrast, attempts to normalize insomnia, exploring the relationship between the internet and interrupted patterns of sleep. The i-doc combines a quartet of insomniacs speaking in stand-alone sequences about their disquieting experiences with a demand that viewers experience interrupted sleep themselves through an invitation to a night-time "appointment" with one of the project's subjects. In what follows, I situate *Journal* within the rich metaphoric field of illness in general and insomnia in particular. Insomnia's long connection to capitalist modernity is considered, as is the range of affects associated with the inability to sleep, such as guilt, shame, depression, and anxiety. I pay particular attention to the role of voices in the i-doc in terms of the creation of authenticity and intimacy in relation to narratives of dis-ease and consider the ways the text invites a mimetic response through its collaborative affordances.

A Journal of Insomnia

A Journal of Insomnia was initially designed as an interactive gallery exhibit in Montreal in 2012. Viewers were invited to enter a small dark tent where they could experience stories of insomnia on video screens as well as leave video responses. Of these, the stories of four Montrealers of different ages and ethnicities were chosen for the online version: Tina, Francis, Sarah, and Fatiha. The main interface for the project is a dark screen with an animated orifice, or "mouth," that is matched to the sound of a closely mic-ed female narrator, who remains an *acousmêtre*, only heard and never seen (Chion 1999). Her voice, untethered to a body, is unnerving and uncanny; she may possibly be the Siri-like voice of the computer itself. Viewers of the online version must make a nighttime appointment with the site, choosing one of the four characters to connect with in the small hours. Requiring you to leave contact information, your phone rings at the appointed hour and you are sent an e-mail with a link that reads in part "thanks for agreeing to surrender part of your night to collective insomnia." If you don't click through at the designated time, a follow-up e-mail will ask where you have gone and prompt you to connect. Produced at the tail end of the wave of "webby" i-docs made between 2010 and 2013 (Moskowitz 2017, 174), *Journal*'s digital architecture effectively produces a sense of having to make a conscious effort to connect to the world of the documentary and of foregoing sleep in order to do so. It also directly links the theme of insomnia with the relentless beckoning of the internet.

The home/interface site uses the image and sound of a ticking clock (a thin, white, analogue second hand against a black background), the clattering of keyboard keys, and other vaguely suspenseful sound effects to put the viewer into a zone of discomfort and premonition. White on-screen text is designed to evoke the numbers of 1970s flip clocks, with their characteristic split-flap display and black backgrounds. Each story of approximately ten to fifteen minutes in length (depending on the interaction) is related in a different style, but all of them are noticeably nocturnal and saturated with the ominous overdetermined objects familiar from dream states. For instance, the story of Sarah, a twenty-something anglophone, takes place in her shared apartment, which is filmed in a retro-glitchy video style. If you click on buttons that appear on the screen, the images will quickly rewind or fast-forward to the next sequence, evoking an amateur horror video-aesthetic, such as that used in *The Blair Witch Project* (Daniel Myrick and Eduardo Sánchez, 1999). As the camera cuts away from sync-sound interview sequences while Sarah speaks in voice-over of her late nights spent cruising the internet, her middle-of-the-night radio show, or the disruptive sounds and smells of the city, it pokes around in corners, peers into the toilet, and picks out eccentric elements of her apartment's décor, such as her roommate's collection of taxidermy specimens. The sequence effectively combines the ironies of old forms of "new" media with unsettling feelings of modernity's velocity.

Francis, the only man in the quartet, is filmed at work (wearing his uniform) in the firehall (by contrast, all of the women are filmed at home). For his story, the viewer is able to toggle back and forth between three intimate camera angles that simultaneously capture him in a reclined – almost analysand-esque – position (low side close-up, low side medium shot, and from above; eyes looking away from the camera) as he relates his fruitless attempts to use various techniques of sleep hygiene to mitigate his life as a shift worker. His feverish story, related in off-centre images and noirish lighting, gives a sense of dis-ease and guilt that parallels his frustration with the diminishment of his ability to be a good father and husband when he doesn't sleep well.

Each of the four subjects expresses elements of mental distress associated with their insomnia. Sarah, for instance, speaks about her struggles with depression and describes insomnia as a feeling of the mind spinning out of control, an affect that is matched by the architecture of her story, in which sections randomly repeat. Tina's insomnia story is tied up with her long history of manic behaviour and impulsive life changes, such as long-distance moves and drastic career changes. A woman in mid-life, Tina is never shown speaking; instead, her disembodied voice is heard jumping from crisis to crisis in her life story, precisely the kind of narrative that might cycle through one's head at night, if one had a tendency to feel shame when dwelling on past regrets. The viewer is able to trigger subsequent segments of her story by pressing an on-screen button that shifts the visual track to a different room in her house at night, where she appears in the dimly lit, though well-appointed, space as a still image, clearly not sleeping.

Fatiha reluctantly takes sleeping pills and anti-depressants to treat her insomnia, which began in mid-life. For Fatiha's interface, pressing an on-screen button leads to the fragmentation of her image and a sonic shattering that mirrors her fragile psychic state. Fatiha's inability to sleep is, according to her, connected to her gendered training in the art of self-sacrifice. This corresponds with the fact that gender is the greatest risk factor for insomnia.[1] At any point, one can exit from any of the stories and return to the ticking clock home page that invites you to continue to listen to serial stories of insomnia through the night – potentially indefinitely. In all of the stories, the night, with its oppressive, loud clock sound, presses in on the domestic spaces (and Francis's firehall couch), evoking an existential claustrophobia and leaving no sense of possible respite or escape. Tonight seems likely to be another one without the release of sleep. *Journal* thus inventively manifests many of the experiential elements of insomnia described by the subjects, creating feelings of frustration, anxiety, and even fatigue in the viewer through its fragmentary and sometimes unnerving interface encountered in the middle of the night.

Insomnia as Metaphor

Susan Sontag posits that night is itself often used as a metaphor for illness. Those up during the night are therefore doubly off-kilter and perhaps de facto ill. Thus, while sleep debt (and its precursor, chronic fatigue) is a real phenomenon, insomnia continues to operate as a rich metaphor for everything from the city and the internet to mental illness and death – often all at once. Like both the urban environment and the internet, insomnia is seen to be infinite and unmappable, at once alluring and disturbing. Eluned Summers-Bremner (2008, 111) likens cities to "laboratories of insomnia." Literary figures from Dickens to Benjamin have walked the streets when they couldn't sleep, the city operating as both tormenter and muse, though women walking the streets at night have had other associations to contend with (Solnit 2001). The internet invites a virtual *flânerie* in a "circumscribed infinity" (Summers-Bremner 2008, 111), algorithmic programming offering a trail of forking paths for those up for some digital wandering without a map.

Beyond isomorphism with the landscapes we inhabit, insomnia is commonly seen as a symptom – and often a harbinger – of mental illness. If sleep is one of the human drives that is closely shaped by culture, not sleeping in the nighttime is a figural way of being out of step with social norms. Moreover, becoming chronically fatigued can bring out anti-social behaviours, which, in turn, come to be read as forms of mental distress or illness. The close association between twenty-four-hour sprawling cities, the internet, and insomnia demonstrates the multi-directional pathologization of our environments, our sleeping habits, and our mental states.

Capitalism, Modernity, Insomnia

Though Sontag argues that illness is *not* a metaphor, insomnia has operated as one for as long as it has been available as a psychological diagnosis. As Kenton Kroker (2007, 349) points out, insomnia has "proven a crucial component of the medical knowledge of sleep" during the past two centuries. In the nineteenth century, it stood for nervous complaints, and in the first half of the twentieth it often stood for drug addiction; it has long been linked to the disruptions and excitements of the industrial city (ibid; Summers-Brenmner 2008). Pharmacological developments of the 1960s made sleep disorders into diseases of their own (rather than symptoms), and over time insomnia became the prototype – and metaphor – of modern disease itself, typically the product of a "psychopathological problem that the patient refused to recognize" (Kroker 2007, 376).

Communication theorist Sheryl Hamilton (2019) suggests that the best way to investigate disease is to ask not what it *is* but, rather, what it *does* in the social field. Seen that way, insomnia is a disease that refracts an ambivalent relationship between bodies and capitalist modernity. Simon Williams (2011, xii) calls sleep a prism "for a range of other fears, worries, frustrations and anxieties regarding contemporary life and living." Although this theme doesn't appear explicitly in any of *Journal*'s stories, which are essentially personal, the write-up on the NFB website locates insomnia squarely in a field of late capitalist sleep problems. "The internet is insomnia ... The more economically productive we become, the less we sleep ... the market value of time is decreasing ... [with] urban life synchronized to the cadence of the manufacturing, processing and service industries" (Braun et al. n.d.). The asymmetry between individual health concerns and inhuman structural conditions make insomnia a perfect lens for feeling, if not envisioning, capitalist modernity.[2]

In critical literature on capitalism and the body, insomnia is often linked to the affordances of the platforms made central in the digital economy. There is no way to engage with the "impossible temporality" of the 24/7 lures of the online world *except* by foregoing sleep (Crary 2013, 29). "Wakefulness and the wired world go together," argues Summers-Bremner (2008, 131);

indeed, insomnia may even be imagined as a twisted form of historical consciousness (148). Communicative capitalism, as delineated by Jodi Dean (2010), compels our never-ending participation in social media and the digital space by over-engaging our drives. Work on the computer seeps into leisure time and even sleep time (Gregg 2011). In this regard, digitally induced insomnia is an intensification of relations of global capitalism that began with the eighteenth-century slave economies that traded in stimulants, such as coffee, tea, chocolate, and sugar, and the associated anxiety-provoking relations of bondage and debt (Summers-Bremner 2008). Indeed, insomnia is a perfect metaphor for the encroachment of capitalism into human lives and may be seen as the unintended byproduct of the very stimulants that facilitate capitalist relations (Wolf-Meyer 2011). Yet, as in the film *Insomnia*, the insomniac is not commonly represented as responding to external conditions and is more often seen as, in some way, morally suspect. Being out of sync with both "biotemporal" and "sociotemporal" patterns reflects badly on the individual rather than on the society in which they live (Kroll-Smith and Gunter 2005). Rarer still are explorations such as the one found in *The Sleep Dealer* (Alex Rivera, 2008), an independently produced dystopic science fiction film in which the manipulation of workers' sleep is clearly associated with the exploitation of natural resources in relations of global capitalism (Jeffries 2014). More usually, sleepiness, like idleness, is represented as a personal pathology.

Other commentators have focused on the ways in which Western legal and knowledge systems based on rationality operate on the structural erasure of sleep, privileging an insomniac (usually masculine) subject who would rather work than sleep. In his research on the right to sleep, for instance, Jonathan Goldberg-Hiller (2019, 3) shows how the development of the concept of legal personhood so essential to Enlightenment political theory is predicated on the erasure of the fact of "daily unconsciousness" in a semi-delusional attempt to approximate the sleeplessness of the global markets. As Goldberg-Hiller puts it, the insomniac gives a figure to contradiction-ridden ontological condition of modernity (14). Similarly, Summers-Bremner (2008, 84) highlights the erasure of the knowledge of night that was foundational to the promise of illumination wrought by the Enlightenment. Modernity, she argues, is predicated on the repression of other ways of knowing and experiencing the nocturnal; the insomniac who fights against sleeplessness is therefore at once the perfect embodiment of "rational modernity" and a reminder of its limits (Williams 2011, xiii).

Though privatized, paradoxically sleep is best understood as a form of social relation; it permeates social institutions in assumptions about "its embodied agents … spatio-temporal arrangements and discursively constructed boundaries" (Williams 2002, 174). Subjects are obligated to sleep in particular ways (in a bed; at night) or risk social repercussions (182). Goldberg-Hiller (2019, 28) argues that sleep is "unevenly distributed through political arrangements." Yet, despite compelling arguments for the collective nature of sleep, most people likely experience sleep disturbances as individual issues and attempt to overcome them in the same way.

A number of theorists investigating the politics of sleep have noted its more recently elaborated biopolitical aspects, the close relationship between the regulation of sleep and the production of the "good subject" (Kroll-Smith and Gunter 2005), or what Simon Williams (2011, 44) calls the "dormative-normative." In the widespread popular discourse around health, of which sleep is a key part, personal responsibility looms large. Across "scientific studies, popular media, business ventures and non-profit organizations (e.g. National Sleep Foundation)" "somnolent bodies" are commonly figured as unproductive, out of control, and a threat to themselves and others (Kroll-Smith and Gunter 2005, 351 and 361). Sleep has been fetishized to the point of an "unhealthy obsession" (Williams 2002, 195). The need to govern our own sleep patterns is tied to the ascendency of Fitbits and other self-monitoring technologies that track and report on our sleep, overriding our experience with more authoritative data about our sleep. While many may report that they are insomniac, studies show that sleep debt is more common than true insomnia, which is still relatively rare (Summers-Bremner 2008; Drake et al. 2013). Nevertheless, daytime sleepiness stemming from poor sleep has become widespread enough to lead to the emergence of lucrative industries dedicated to the promotion of restful nights through special mattresses and bedding as well as bedroom appliances (such as white noise machines) and monitoring devices (Williams 2011).

Illness Narratives

A Journal of Insomnia uses the strategy of matching the experience of insomnia with evocative experimental styles. Stella Bloaki (2016) discusses "illness narratives" as expressions of the subjective experience of illness, often written as responses to medical interpretations of patient health. For the most part, *Journal* excribes medical experts from the text, gesturing to them only with a bibliography of reports and studies as well as with numbers for help lines for those suffering from depression. The focus instead is on subjective stories, with no attempt to shy away from the fragmentary, non-linear, and at times unstable aspects of the experience of illness (Bloaki 2016, 9). If anything, the use of interactive affordances – such as the encouragement to click on hot spots or buttons and the growing database of stories – interrupts the stories being told, accentuating and enhancing their fragmentary character. These are stories of struggles with inadequacy and failure, and there are no happy endings waiting to be revealed (19).

What the site does offer, alongside references and sources of support, is the possibility of adding your own illness narrative in a mimetic cycle. You are prompted to add your own answers as videos or drawings in response to a series of questions, such as:

→ What do you do at night that you don't do during the day?
→ What do you do on nights you can't sleep?
→ What does it mean to say someone is an insomniac?
→ What techniques help you get to sleep?
→ How can insomnia be treated?
→ How does not sleeping make you feel?
→ What do you like about being awake at this time of night?
→ Are you enjoying our conversation? I have more questions for you.

Those already added appear through a mosaic interface of faces and line-drawings that float against a black background, inviting you to click through.

Journal thus approaches the discussion of insomnia as an individual "psychic voyage," like any mental illness, and encourages a multiplicity of serial monologues on the topic (Sontag 1978, 34). Making use of the i-doc's compellingly layered architecture, *Journal* encourages users to mimic the "techno-analytics" (Renov 2004) of the longer segments with confessional self-disclosures of their own. While the medical profession has long since dispensed with the talking cure in favour of pharmaceutical treatments, *Journal* gestures at the intimacy of a technologically mediated therapeutic encounter. In addition, by meeting in the middle of the night, the i-doc evokes something of the sleep lab where sleep (rather than dreams) has been the favoured object of analysis studied since sleep emerged as a full-blown area of post-psychoanalytic investigation the 1960s (Kroker 2007, 350).

Haptic Listening

Given its focus on alienated embodiment, *Journal* effectively deploys a number of sonic strategies to create a feeling of authenticity, including haptic affordances particular to an i-doc experienced on a small, personal computer screen. From the first engagement with the text's outer architecture, one is introduced to the project's disembodied, or *acoustemêtric*, narrator. Speaking slowly with a low voice and (in the English version) a French accent, the narrator is a perfect example of the recalled intimacy of the maternal voice attributed to female voice-overs by psychoanalytic sound studies scholars (e.g., Chion 1999; Doane 1980; Silverman 1984). Spoken into a mic, without any reverb, her voice sounds extremely intimate, almost claustrophobia-inducingly close, emanating from the surface of the screen and enveloping the listener, especially if one is listening through headphones. The *acousmêtre*, according to Chion (1999), is neither inside nor outside the world of the film and, because it is never linked to a visible body, is easily associated with ubiquity, panopticism, omniscience, and omnipotence (23–4). The dryness and lack of reverb of the *acousmêtre* is what signals that it does not exist in space.

However, even if one resists appeal to the primordial maternal, *Journal* inarguably maintains focus on the material aspects of speech. Throughout, the i-doc invites what film scholar Irina Leimbacher (2017, 293) calls "haptic listening," asking us to focus not only on what is said but also on the textures of its saying – what Roland Barthes calls "the grain of the voice." The stories are enhanced with sound effects and music that emphasize the isolation of these lone voices in the night, the repetition of their stories built into the narrative architecture. Nevertheless, there is an authenticity to the stories that comes from the grain of each of the interviewees' voices, especially in comparison with the conspicuous artificiality of the *acousmêtric* narrator.

Many i-docs rely on strategies of polyvocality, braiding together multiple voices (FitzSimons 2009; Zimmermann 2018). In an influential essay on the use of confessional modes in video art, Michael Renov (1995, 90) observes that speaking to others by way of technological mediation can "turn out to be a more powerful facilitator of emotion." Yet, just as often, video can act as a machine of "self-encapsulation," drawing attention only to the subject's psychological situation at the expense of "bracketing out the world and its conditions" (Krauss 1976, 53 and 64). *Journal* treads a fine line in this therapeutic/narcissistic space, using the narrator and the bank of user-contributions to embed the four main stories within a larger "community of solitaries" (Summers-Bremner 2008, 112). Unlike with video art, the i-doc form implicates the viewer not in a gallery or public setting but likely in their own private space, watching on a small, intimate screen. *Journal* thus pairs its subjects' self-disclosures with its viewer-participant's technologically enhanced opportunity for empathy, if not political analysis.

Discussion and Conclusions

A Journal of Insomnia tacitly engages with a number of the issues associated with the disease of sleeplessness that are structural to the experience of what Zygmunt Bauman (2000) calls "liquid modernity," an individualized and privatized version of modernity. The subjects wrestle with moral discomfort about being unable to sleep, all seek sleep hygiene, and some resort to medications in order to function normally at work or in their families. Sarah identifies the city as well as the internet and other media as parallels to, if not causes of, her insomnia. Her apartment is full of gothic imagery of taxidermy and the faux-ironic horror of amateur, analogue media, gesturing at the residual image of the night as harbouring remnants of a repressed premodern, now denuded of its power. Francis's work in the firehall is represented as being full of loud, industrial sounds and an inhuman/heroic-masculine demand to stay up at night to protect others (thereby enabling them to sleep soundly while he cannot). Tina is represented as diving into life but becoming unstable and feeling buffeted by events beyond her control. Fatiha presents herself as having been too giving, putting her family's needs before her own requirement to replenish her body. The quest for sleep in her case is reluctantly tied to self-care as prerequisite for care of others. All of them have struggled with sleep problems for many years and are on the edge of sanity, desperate for some respite. Yet, although none of them directly links their personal plight to the historical moment in which we live, I posit that the form of *Journal* itself gestures in that direction.

The i-doc form is closely bound to digital capitalism through its reliance on the affordances of programming and networked computerization

(Hight 2017). Many i-docs attempt to excavate the humanistic potentials of interactivity while struggling with the mandates of the participatory economy, but i-docs also partake of a longer history of immersive media in which technologies are used to "evok[e] experience rather than merely representing it" (Aston, Gaudenzi, and Rose 2017, 2; Barney et al. 2016; Uricchio 2017, 192). *A Journal of Insomnia* deploys elements of the techno-confessional to tell illness narratives that obliquely connect to the social and biopolitical elements of insomnia and its range of allied spatial and epochal metaphors. It uses the affordances of the internet and communicative capitalism (interactivity, surveillance, drive, seduction) as structural parameters for the limits of the human ability to fulfil the demands of the digital economy. It also effectively evokes the experience of insomnia by focusing on affects such as fragmentation, interruption, frustration, unease, and failure. Even if not moved to include one's own stories of insomnia when prompted to do so, the viewer who spends time with the project may develop new insights into the way digital capitalism, in different ways, upends us all. However, given that many people are put off by appointment viewing and interactive "webby" i-docs, it's just as likely that many potential viewers will never be willing to give up their own precious sleep to make the connections on offer.

Illnesses have often been used to "enliven charges" against a particular society. "Any important disease whose causality is murky, and for which treatment is ineffectual tends to be awash in significance," writes Sontag (1978, 57). Insomnia has convincingly been presented as a disease central to our time. Yet it remains beguilingly linked to the dark places that lack representation and mapping: the night, the city, global capitalism, the internet. With its participatory features, *A Journal of Insomnia* gestures at the connected seriality required to begin to map these interrelated yet amorphous features. And, in the meantime, the narratives of *normal* insomnia it presents are a compelling place to start.

Notes

My thanks to Loc Dao, chief digital officer, and Martin Viau, technical director, Interactive Productions, both of the National Film Board/Office National du Film du Canada, for their invaluable help.

1 "Women have been found to be 40% … more likely to develop insomnia than men and this difference increases with age" (Drake, Eklov, and Roth 2013, 198).

2 Capitalist modernity is infamously hard to represent. See Jameson (1988) and Toscano and Kinkle (2015) on the concept of "cognitive mapping."

References

Aston, Judith, Sandra Gaudenzi, and Mandy Rose, eds. 2017. *i-Docs: The Evolving Practices of Interactive Documentary.* New York: Columbia University Press/Wallflower.

Barney, Darin, Gabriella Coleman, Christine Ross, Jonathan Sterne, and Tamar Tembeck, eds. 2016. "The Participatory Condition: An Introduction." In *The Participatory Condition in the Digital Age*, ed. Darin Barney, et al. vii–xxxix. Minneapolis: University of Minnesota Press.

Bauman, Zygmunt. 2000. *Liquid Modernity*. Cambridge: Polity Press.

Bloaki, Stella. 2016. *Illness as Many Narratives: Arts, Medicine and Culture.* Edinburgh; Edinburgh University Press.

Braun, Guillaume, Bruno Choinière, Thibaut Duverneix, and Philippe Lambert. "A Journal of Insomnia: Exploring Mental Health in the 21st Century." https://www.nfb.ca/interactive/a_journal_of_insomnia.

Chion, Michel. 1999. *The Voice in Cinema*. Ed. and trans. Claudia Gorbman. New York: Columbia University Press.

Crary, Jonathan. 2013. *24/7: Late Capitalism and the Ends of Sleep*. London: Verso.

Dean, Jodi. 2010. *Blog Theory: Feedback and Capture in the Circuits of Drive.* Cambridge: Polity Press.

Doane, Mary Ann. 1980. "The Voice in the Cinema: The Articulation of Body and Space." *Yale French Studies* 60: 33–50. https://doi.org/10.2307/2930003.

Drake, C.L., S. Eklov, and T. Roth. 2013. "Description of Insomnia." In *Encyclopedia of Sleep*, ed. Clete A. Kushida, 193–8. Amsterdam: Elsevier.

FitzSimons, Trish. 2009. "Braided Channels: A Genealogy of the Voice of Documentary." *Studies in Documentary Film* 3 (2): 131–46. http://doi.org/10.1386/sdf.3.2.131/1.

Goldberg-Hiller, Jonathan. 2019."Is There a Right to Sleep?" *Theory and Event* 22 (4): 951–83.

Gregg, Melissa. 2011. *Work's Intimacy*. Cambridge: Polity.

Hamilton, Sheryl. 2019. "Mediating Disease Cultures." *Canadian Journal of Communication* 44 (2): 151–6. http://doi.org/10.22230/cjc.2019v44n2e3611.

Hight, Craig. 2017. "Software as Co-creator in Interactive Documentary." In *i-Docs: The Evolving Practices of Interactive Documentary*, ed. Judith Aston,

Sandra Gaudenzi, and Mandy Rose, 82–96. New York: Columbia University Press/Wallflower.
Jameson, Fredric. 1988. "Cognitive Mapping." In *Marxism and the Interpretation of Culture*, ed. C. Nelson and L. Grossber, 347–57. Champaign: University of Illinois Press.
Jeffries, Fiona. 2014. "Cyborg Resistance on the Digital Assembly Line: Global Connectivity as a Terrain of Struggle for the Commons in Alex Rivera's *Sleep Dealer*." *Journal of Communication Inquiry* 39: 21–37. https://doi.org/10.1177/0196859914550689.
Krauss, Rosalind. 1976. "Video: The Aesthetics of Narcissism." *October* 1 (Spring): 50–64. https://doi.org/10.2307/778507.
Kroker, Kenton. 2007. *The Sleep of Others and the Transformation of Sleep Research*. Toronto: University of Toronto Press.
Kroll-Smith, Steve, and Valerie Gunter. 2005. "Governing Sleepiness: Somnolent Bodies, Discourse, and Liquid Modernity." *Sociological Inquiry* 75 (3): 346–71. https://doi.org/10.1111/j.1475-682X.2005.00126.x.
Leimbacher, Irina. 2017. "Hearing Voice(s): Experiments with Documentary Listening." *Discourse* 39 (3): 292–318. https://doi.org/10.13110/discourse.39.3.0292.
Moskowitz, Ben. 2017. "Look Who's Watching: What Storytellers Can Learn from Privacy and Personalization." In *iDocs: The Evolving Practices of Interactive Documentary*, ed. Judith Aston, Sandra Gaudenzi, and Mandy Rose, 170–86. New York: Columbia University Press/Wallflower.
Renov, Michael. 1995. "Video Confessions." In *Resolutions: Contemporary Video Practices*, ed. Michael Renov and Erika Sunderburg, 78–7. Minneapolis: University of Minnesota Press.
– 2004. *The Subject of Documentary*. Minneapolis: University of Minnesota Press.
Silverman, Kaja. 1984. "Dis-embodying the Female Voice." In *Re-Vision: Essays in Feminist Film Criticism*, ed. Mary Ann Doane, Patricia Mellencamp, and Linda Williams, 131–49. New York: American Film Institute.
Solnit, Rebecca. 2001. *Wanderlust: A History of Walking*. New York: Penguin.
Sontag, Susan. 1978. *Illness as Metaphor*. New York: Vintage.
Summers-Bremner, Eluned. 2008. *Insomnia: A Cultural History*. London: Reaktion Books.
Toscano, Alberto, and Jeffrey Kinkle. 2015. *Cartographies of the Absolute: An Aesthetics of the Economy for the Twenty-First Century*. London: Zero Books.
Uricchio, William. 2017. "Things to Come: The Possible Futures of

Documentary … from a Historical Perspective." In *i-Docs: The Evolving Practices of Interactive Documentary*, ed. Judith Aston, Sandra Gaudenzi, and Mandy Rose, 191–205. New York: Columbia University Press/Wallflower.

Williams, Simon J. 2002. "Sleep and Health: Sociological Reflections on the Dormant Society." *Health: An Interdisciplinary Journal for the Social Study of Health, Illness and Medicine* 6 (2): 173–200. http://www.jstor.org/stable/26646445.

– 2011. *The Politics of Sleep: Governing (Un)consciousness in the Late Modern Age*. London: Palgrave Macmillan.

Wolf-Meyer, Matthew. 2011."Natural Hegemonies: Sleep and the Rhythms of American Capitalism." *Current Anthropology* 52 (6): 876–95. https://doi.org/10.1086/662550.

Zimmermann, Patricia. 2018. "Thirty Speculations toward a Polyphonic Model for New Media Documentary." *Alphaville: Journal of Film and Screen Media* 15 (Summer): 9–15. https://doi.org/10.33178/alpha.

15

GOING DEEP

HYBRID CAPTURE IN DOCUMENTARY

Cindy Poremba and Amy Siegel

Hybrid captured images, blending lens-based and computational technologies, are increasingly pervasive in digital documentary. Current interest in augmented reality (AR) and virtual reality (VR) has given hybrid capture approaches like volumetric video a boost by driving demand and interest in the recorded 3D content that best showcases immersive experiences. As a matter of course, volumetric video has made its way into Canadian interactive documentary and VR projects, including *HIGHRISE: Universe Within* (Katerina Cizek, 2015), *Made This Way: Redefining Masculinity* (Irem Harnak and Elli Raynai, 2018), and *The Choice VR* (Infinite Frame, 2022). Such projects not only showcase the emerging potential for this mode of computationally hybrid capture but also present different ways in which such images can be approached, interpreted, and assembled within postmedia documentary contexts. These negotiations are prefigured by prior hybrid capture contexts, including rotoscoping and motion capture in documentary animation.

We are continually fascinated by what captured media brings us: immediacy, evidence, connection, and presence – no matter how ephemeral or unstable. Captured media promises discovery in its representational excess. It allows for phenomenological shifts in our relationship to images in ways that bring us closer to actuality (by grounding us in the world) and ways that alienate us (in never quite being the real thing). Digital media increasingly complicates these dynamics by working in the grey area between captured and created modes of representation. Increasingly, the ideals underpinning the terminology and the process are blurred (Wolf

2000; Rosen 2001; Bryant and Pollock 2010; de la Peña et al. 2010). Create and capture modes are converging, mutating into hybrid forms in which it is impossible to untangle recorded and reconstructed elements. This is accelerated by the increased prominence of digital capture technologies in both our media production and consumption. The ways in which these technologies affect areas like documentary make visible particular shifts in the way media are being mobilized and understood.

Nowhere is the impact from such hybrid image-making more visible than in relation to images still casually read as captured, particularly within non-fiction and documentary contexts. We continue to make presumptions about what it means to record, capture, or otherwise "take" an image from the world, often without reflecting on the extent to which these images are manufactured, increasingly by both human and non-human agencies. This work aims to examine the ways in which we stabilize an understanding of hybrid captured images within networks incorporating histories, desires, affect, human, and non-human agents, and, in doing so, negotiate our own understandings, desires, and expectations of such images: when we want and need to maintain transparency, prefer obfuscation, or to see behind the curtain. Using the work of Canadian interactive artists and documentary creators as a ground, it considers the ways in which volumetric video is materially (often using a combination of lenses, sensors, and algorithms) and discursively (embodying notions of presence, actuality, and virtuality) intra-acted between both human and machine agencies.

Volumetric Video as Hybrid Capture

Volumetric capture can be accomplished using several techniques: for example, the computational overlay of point cloud (a series of X, Y, Z coordinates in 3D space) and video images or the computational suture of arrays of photographic images. Some of these setups can involve hundreds of capture devices (commonly cameras) and involve sophisticated studio production. Others, like the volumetric video platform Depthkit (Scatter), rely on prosumer motion capture technologies like the Microsoft Kinect. Documentaries like *Blackout* (2017) and *Zero Days VR* (Oculus/Scatter, 2017) utilize the Kinect to build volumetric models onto which digital video images (captured either using digital cameras or directly using the Kinect) are mapped. The result is a hologram-like volumetric 3D image easy to read as captured – through both a digital SLR camera or on-board

Kinect camera and a digital sensor reading and interpreting an infrared projection – but one that is also, in a sense, highly constructed. Here, the computational back-end builds us a hybrid image, made to map to both human and computer vision, with motion fidelity and photographic iconicity courtesy of a traditional video camera and spatial depth courtesy of a depth sensor. Tools like Depthkit create a more accessible pathway for documentary creators who do not have a background in computational vision or creative coding to incorporate volumetric video into an increasingly wide range of projects, using equipment they may already have. At the time of this writing, the potential for creating volumetric images is increasingly entering the consumer realm, with cameras capable of supporting volumetric image creation now incorporated into commercial smartphones and, increasingly, integrated machine learning tools that synthesize missing volumetric "data."

This lowered and automated bar is also significant in that it creates a minimal-intervention method of producing this imagery that better fits with technological ideals of documentary capture. It obscures "the active mediation of hardware and software" (Wolf 2000) and evokes, to paraphrase André Bazin (1960), the ideal of limited intervention capture via a non-living agent. Holly Willis (2016, 66), speaking broadly about hybrid captured images, including volumetric capture, notes: "These technologies all serve to catalyse a transformation of cultural expectations related to the synthesis of data and images. Once occupying separate realms … the combined technical and conceptual apparatus (surrounding the technology) dissolves the distinction between these two, resulting in fully navigable 3D spaces that are not just 'photorealistic,' but are genuinely 'photographic.'" Where the computationally constructed and the photographically captured may once have been understood, and mobilized, as distinct entities, they are increasingly constituted simply as photographic. And while some of that networking occurs actively, other values, interpretations, and practices become drawn in under familiar paradigms, practices, and desires surrounding the captured image.

Anne Pasek (2015) suggests it is too simple to think of volumetric images solely in terms of the union of a depth camera and a traditional lens-based camera, or a human (conceptual) and machine (technical) apparatus, noting devices like the Kinect process images using machine learning elements, creating an emergent computational vision that learns and evolves. Through the process of capturing images, the sensor is learning to structure what it is capturing in accordance to its internal algorithm, exercising machinic agency within the capture process. William Uricchio (2011) reminds us that algorithmically enhanced seeing remains ideologically complicit in human-situated design decisions underlying said algorithms, although, of course, these biases are not isolated to hybrid capture. Capture technologies underlying volumetric images are taught how to see (often in reductive ways) and how to train continuously to capture a "better" image. It is also notable that the tangle of hybrid image technologies, the algorithms, sensors, lenses, and so on, draw in a number of devices and approaches that do not originate with documentary work in mind: the Kinect, for example, was designed as a gesture-capture peripheral for Microsoft's Xbox console, so the creative, technical, and ethical decisions underlying how it sees and understands material objects placed in its field of view are optimized for said context.

Tracing these component relationships is important because, while volumetric images are increasingly taking the shape of familiar documentary tools and participating in non-fiction practices, a closer look at this technology reveals a tangle of understandings, technologies, and agencies involving both human and computational/machine participants, in which such participation takes place. This tangle is easier understood under familiar paradigms, but this can obscure the ways in which hybrid capture challenges the technical presumptions and expectations we hold in relation to these images. Performing such an inspection necessitates an approach mindful of the various entities implicated in assembling volumetric video.

New Materialist Approaches to Volumetric Images

New materialism incorporates many different approaches found within what has been described as the "non-human turn" in interdisciplinary theory (Grusin 2015). Rather than one singular perspective, it is better thought of as a collection of movements and theories that bring together thinking from fields such as STS, feminist theory, affect theory, and environmental and political science to offer better ways to think about the emergent construction of being and meaning from a non-anthropocentric position. As Fox and Alldred (2019, 3) note, these approaches can be commonly characterized as posthumanist, materially embedded and embodied, relational and contingent, and capable of examining a material world that is "plural, complex, heterogeneous and emergent." It often serves as a corrective to the dominant positioning of language and human agency in poststructuralist and social constructionist thought, instead emphasizing material-discursive agencies, inclusive of non-human entities, within flat or semi-flat ontologies.

Karen Barad's work (2003; 2007) has been a key influence on this discourse. Barad offers what she terms an "ethico-onto-epistemology" that foregrounds the inseparability of ethics, materialities, entities, and meaning. She uses the term "intra-action" to describe the mutual constitution of entangled agencies (Dolphijn and Tuin 2012). Barad maintains agency is "not a property of persons or things; rather, agency is an enactment, a matter of possibilities for reconfiguring entanglements" (Dolphijn and Tuin 2012, 11). This framing resonates with Bruno Latour's actor-network theory (ANT), which has also had a significant impact on new materialist thought, particularly in its framing of the mutual and ongoing constitution of the social, technological, and the material. ANT emphasizes distributed agency (including, notably, the agency of non-human participants in networks) and the continuous mutual constitution of relational network entities (Latour 2005). Bringing both together, Belliger and Krieger (2014) use the term "networking" to describe processes of entanglement resulting from constructed actor-networks under the conditions of digital media.

It is important to note that from a new materialist perspective (notably in Barad), representation is not viewed in terms of signifier and signified (a relationship that presupposes a hierarchy privileging the signifier) but as separate entities in intra-active and co-constitutive relations. In the context of volumetric images, this is significant in that it recognizes that, while the volumetric image is produced by the materialities it captures, it is also a creator of these materialities and that this entanglement is further inseparable from the contexts in which these images come into being. Laurie Gries (2015, 335), in the context of new materialist rhetoric, encourages us to consider images more like virtual-actual events, both as dynamic networks in and of themselves, of "distributed, unfolding, and unforeseeable becomings," and as multiplicities "constituted by heterogeneous materializations with virtual-actual dimensions," including as agents in a network. Gries's approach can be useful in considering hybrid images like volumetric video as relational entities materialized in particular ways as part of particular entanglements that both perform their own agency and are affected by human and non-human agents within a network.

This occurs within a backdrop of digital postmedia (Manovich 2001; Weibel 2006; Corner 2002; Kim 2016; Kim 2022), in which each medium becomes subsumed within the logic (and materiality) of the digital, thus taking on its transformative quality. This accelerates and makes readily visible the reassemblies of form and affordances previously treated as medium specific. Postmedia has seen media forms detached (virtualized) from their technologies – a flat transformation in which the originary forms are no more real than the simulated ones – and reassembled in context. Such transformations have been prompted by both technological (notably the affordances of digital simulation) and cultural (a move away from formalism) factors. I would argue this postmedia context holds in large part what Belliger and Krieger describe in their framework as the conditions of digital media.

From this perspective, volumetric video can be described as a relationally constructed entity being networked within the context of postmedia. As such, it is being intra-acted with other entities within the network, commonly drawing upon entities (including values and technological ideals) common to photographic practices and taking the shape of familiar assemblages from epistemic cultures such as documentary. However, it is not always networked in the same way – and as an emerging technology we can observe an instability in relation to how it is used and understood, particularly in documentary contexts.

Volumetric Images and the Digital Subject

Volumetric images, while still technologically emergent, are already coalescing around some common conceptual and aesthetic affordances, particularly in relation to notions of "the digital," presence (perceptual and figurative co-presence), and embodiment. They are stabilizing some of the previously stated tangle into particular configurations drawn from the larger space of meanings and materialities surrounding this technology.

Universe Within: Digital Lives in the Global Highrise (2015) is part of Katerina Cizek's acclaimed *HIGHRISE* transmedia series. The online interactive documentary is one of a number of projects developed through the NFB's Digital Studio that experiment with volumetric filmmaking, including prototypes exploring physicality and presence in cultural performance.[1] *Universe Within* uses volumetric video to present "digitally embodied" avatars of its three "host" interface characters. A mouse click

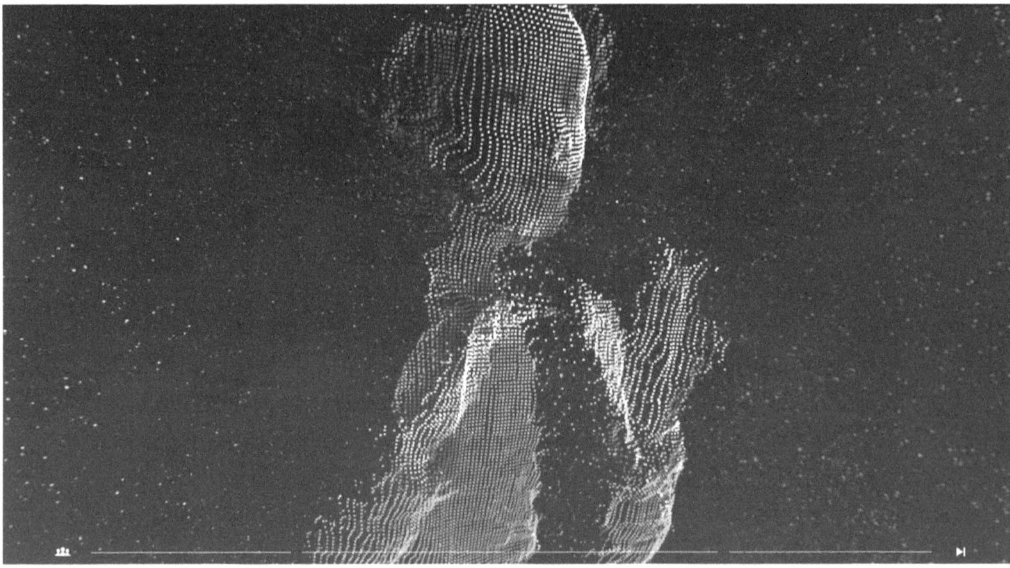

Figure 15.1
A mouse click on the *Universe Within* interface options dissolves the performers into a shower of pixels as you transition into the main body of the work; these hosts are explicitly framed as fictional within the work despite the presence of captured actors

on the interface options dissolves the performers into a shower of pixels as you transition into the main body of the work. These hosts are explicitly framed as fictional within the work despite the presence of captured actors; each host emphasizes that, while they are not "real," they are guides to the real stories presented through video with the web interface.

So why use volumetrically captured performers at all? NFB creative technologist Brandon Bratuhin notes that, in presenting the i-doc hosts in digital form, the creative team was able to reinforce their "born digital" characterization (NFB 2015): one that aligns with Cizek's exploration of the intertwining of online and lived experience for subjects living in highrise towers. This use of volumetric images echoes projects created by Scatter, including the imagery used in *Zero Days* and its VR experience. Alexander Porter (co-founder of Scatter) notes: "There's a great tradition of representing people in the network, of embodying ephemeral characters – 'I'm a character, made of code here to tell you about the internet and networked realities.' These are less about anonymity and more about liminal states (AI's, holograms, characters embodying algorithm, etc.) or states of coexistence with *the digital*."[2] In situating hosts within a navigable space, *Universe Within* further hopes to create a poetic alignment between one common conceptual thread in the work – seeing things from different perspectives – through an affordance of volumetric imagery (NFB 2015).

One affordance of hybrid images like volumetric video is the ability to negotiate the balance between the depth sensor and a video camera in the presentation of the image – in simple terms, how much the image reveals of the depth camera, and how much it presents of the video camera. This opens the door to the presentation of a more hybrid visual look – wireframes, scan lines, point-clouds – that can be interpreted as a signifier for "digitality" or computational hybridity. The characters captured with volumetric video in *Universe Within* are not rendered as flawless, photorealistic 3D images. While they are recognizable as video images, they appear closer to the Princess Leia hologram from the original *Star Wars* than a living, breathing human being. They are what Hito Steyerl (2009, 1) describes as poor images: "a visual idea in its very becoming": cut through with flaws from the production process, and reflective of the same unrefined quality of the bulk of our online images. In fact, a scan of volumetric video images demonstrates a significant number of projects embracing visible depth rendering, glitch effects and filters, and images replete with spikes and holes (errors from the depth capture). While in some cases the decision to present the images in a glitchy, filtered state represents simple time and budget constraints, often their presence represents an intentional choice to leave the image unrefined, reflecting what the images are thought to mean in the context in which they are being used. Embracing and obscuring visual artifacts through stylization adds an intentionality to revealing the computational structure underneath. In the case of host characters in *Universe Within*, fully photographic rendered images would not capture the ambiguity of a subject meant to be read as both material and computational.

Indexicality and Presence in Volumetric Images

Capture technologies have always mapped well, and are easily positioned, in relation to indexical effects and desires. In Peircian semiotics, an index is one of three types of signs, the other two being symbols (which hold a conventional relationship to the referent) and icons (which have a semblance to a referent). The index suggests a causal or existential relation to the world – indicating the necessary presence of the object that makes it. Indexicality holds a lingering but contested presence in captured media, due largely to the common (but messy) linking of Charles Sanders Peirce's framework to the photographic ontology of André Bazin (Wollen 1969; Gunning 2007; Dobbs 2013). Peirce's work is challenging to situate outside of realist ontologies, and the way it has been conceptualized within digital media practice is inconsistent at best. However, indexical effects serve several purposes in supporting understandings of actuality, and, as such, it enacts agency within networks and mobilizes effects. These network effects include transposing (where the media object is treated not as *like* the referent but *as* the referent), anchoring (providing a specific bond to the material world [Nichols 1991], and thus grounding interpretation not in *a* world but in *the* world [Ward 2008; Rosen 2001]), and warranting (providing evidence or testimony through a presumed causal link between the material world and its representation).

Desires for presence are also commonly part of these entanglements, a relation that precedes spatialized images. To paraphrase Tom Gunning (2007, 35) on the photographic image, capture puts us "in the presence of something" rather than simply indicating or providing evidence of it. Ideals of presence have a long (complex) history within documentary practice and are often interwoven with technocultural affordances – for example, the use of portable video equipment and "fly-on-the-wall" observational documentary styles. In the context of film, theorists such as Gunning, Christian Metz, and Mary Ann Doane have linked movement to perceptual reality and affect (Dobbs 2013). Similarly, Rose Woodcock (2003, 179) suggests that VR provides an important epistemological shift in moving from a pictorial rendition of objects and spaces to establishing a relationship between observer and environment that is perceptually real, as they succinctly explain, "from the representation to the *presentation* of perceptual spaces" (emphasis in original). A reality that contains a depth of space gives the observer a real-like world to explore, thus providing a temporary replacement for the "real" world by exploiting the innate perceptional knowledge of human vision. Mel Slater (2003, 2) claims that the more a system "preserves fidelity in relation to their equivalent real-world sensory modalities, the more it is immersive … [P]resence is a human reaction to immersion." Slater further suggests that presence is contingent on form and can therefore be assessed as "the extent to

Figure 15.2
In *Made This Way*, each subject is presented as an array of nearly identical photographically-rendered volumetric videos

which the unification of simulated sensory data and perceptual processing produces a coherent 'place' that you are 'in.'"

While *Universe Within* highlights aesthetic elements, resisting transparency and embracing the connotations of "computational" imperfect images, other projects network more closely around photographic fidelity and the potential for an immersive sense of presence these deep images, re-embodied and perceptually faithful, may provide. From Elli Raynai (Cinehackers) and Irem Harnak, *Made This Way: Redefining Masculinity* (2018) is a documentary VR work focusing on experiences of negotiating masculinity by non-cis men.[3] *Made This Way* demonstrates the use of volumetric video as a means to immerse audiences in encounters with captured subjects. In his discussion of the work, Raynai highlights the ability for volumetric images to "place" the viewer in a world, the better to explore personal subject matter with marginalized people: "What we attempted to do with this project is to share the relationship that Irem has with these subjects to the viewer. To put them in the same space and make them feel the openness that she felt when she was able to connect with them" (XRMust 2018). The images are described as visual holograms, existing in a constructed space designed to be warm, dreamy, and slightly surreal: a safe space mirroring Harnak's encounters with their subjects.[4]

Made This Way presents volumetric video testimony from two subjects: Elijah Miley, a transgender man from Toronto, and Devyn Farries, a non-binary artist based in New York City. Each subject is presented as an array of nearly identical photographically rendered volumetric videos, allowing the audience to select from different points of testimony while also giving the audience the ability to move freely through the container space, play with the spatiality of the images, and encounter the creative practices of the subjects (in the case of Elijah, a dance performance; in the case of Devyn, a spatialized version of their visual art constructed using another hybrid capture approach: photogrammetry). This allows not only for visceral moments of intimacy (e.g., when a character meets your gaze) but also for potentially monstrous positioning behind (where the capture is incomplete) or intrusively within the intimate space of the characters. Unlike *Universe Within*, *Made This Way* adopts a more photographic rendering style for the characters themselves, even as they are placed within spatially collaged environments including imagery from multiple sources and united through spatial sound. As a result, *Made This Way* more clearly trades on commonly entangled entities with photographic capture such as indexical effects and presence.

A more recent project, Infinite Frame's *The Choice VR*, also networks elements familiar to documentary contexts, including, again, indexical effects and presence. Co-creators Joanne-Aśka Popińska and Tom C. Hall chose to custom design their own volumetric capture software in order to achieve the immediacy afforded by filmic recording without the distracting computational artefacts of moderate- to low-end volumetric capture. Like *Made This Way*, their aim was to reinstantiate some of the intimacy shared in the capture of their subjects – individuals sharing deeply personal experiences with abortion. Even given the use of volumetric capture,

Figure 15.3
The creators of *The Choice* VR sought to re-instantiate some of the intimacy shared in the capture of their subjects, individuals sharing deeply personal experiences with abortion

The Choice VR is readily identifiable as a documentary work, embodying familiar elements such as recorded first-person testimony.

Feeling immersed and co-present with the subjects of *Made This Way* or *The Choice* VR is one of the primary ways in which the spatiality of volumetric video reinforces the experiential goals of these projects. Indexical effects, drawn in through desires and expectations surrounding capture, help stabilize the idea you are co-present with real people, despite visibly constructed spaces. Volumetric video provides a warranty that the testimony presented has occurred and anchors it to embodied experience: that what you are seeing is necessarily linked to a specific instance of what was recorded. Both conceptual assemblages are networked in the context of the documentary's goals to make visible lived experience, whether it be negotiations of masculinity for non-cis subjects or the emotional complexity of the abortion choice.

Hybrid Images in Rotoscoping and Motion Capture

Volumetric video images are not the first "hybrid" image forms we can examine, and taking a look at prior networking can reveal additional ways volumetric videos may yet manifest in practice. For example, the use of rotoscoping attempts to go beyond semblance to extend the indexical effects (or alternately "aliveness" through motion) of the original video image onto an animated form. Steve Fore (2007, 113) refers to rotoscope as "'a hybrid product' that combines technology and the human body," citing Mike Langer's observation of the "simultaneous presence" of animated (created) and photo-indexical (captured) modes in rotoscopy, in which an animated image is mapped to a human body. This blurring between indexical and "manufactured" (particularly animated) images is also prominent in discussions surrounding rotoscoping and, more recently, motion capture. The practice of mapping animation to a filmed object encompasses a number of techniques (Hébert 2006; Honess Roe 2013) but is commonly identified with the form popularized by Max Fleischer in 1917 in which filmic images are traced to create animated frames. Fleischer's work included capturing, on film, the performance of Samoan Indigenous dancer Miri and appropriating her movement for the character Betty Boop's "authentic" island dance performance (Bouldin 2001). This creates what Joanna Bouldin (2001, 50) calls "a reality effect bound to corporeality,"[5] often including nuances of movement that are otherwise unrepresented. Paul Ward (2008, para. 15) suggests that rotoscoping can also provide a sense of instrumentality: "a shift in modality, intended as a shift to sober discourse." Ward notes that this can change the reception of the image from cartoon to ontologically distinct rotoscoped animation, which lends it to use in scientific, technical, and other "serious" contexts. Ironically, the effect can appear too real, and Bouldin (2001, 50) notes: "the connection between real and animated body alters the ontology and shifts our phenomenological understanding of the animated image." In other words, rotoscoping's hybrid form creates ambiguity with regard to how to read the image: as (artificial) animation or as (real) film. The trace of the real in rotoscoping has been widely discussed, particularly in relation to both this (typically involuntary) phenomenological shift, its representational affordances, and the ethics implicit in re-embodying and/or appropriating captured movement.

While rotoscoping entangles an animation with an indexical (primarily film or video) image in order to capture a subject, motion capture takes the process of transferring embodiment even further.[6] Alberto Menache (2010, 1) defines motion capture as "the process of recording a live motion event and translating it into usable mathematical terms by tracking a number of key points in space over time and combining them to obtain a single three-dimension representation of the performance." Unlike rotoscoping, the image produced by motion capture is not a tracing of an indexical image but an instantiation of a captured performance (for Bouldin, it is significant that the technique is called motion "capture"). There are a number of different ways of capturing motion: cameras digitizing different views of the performance that are then analyzed to produce coordinates based on various markers, electromagnetic fields or ultrasound to track a group of sensors, mechanical systems using potentiometers to measure motion. As with rotoscoping, in some cases of non-fiction animation the motion capture data are in fact too specific, binding the motion to a no-longer-present corporeality that might not translate well onto a given animated character. While motion capture is more readily known for its presence in fiction filmmaking and digital games (most prominently the capture of "real" performances in sports and music games), its indexical affordances have also been engaged in Canadian documentary works such as Brigitte Berman's *The River of My Dreams: A Portrait of Gordon Pinsent* (2017). In this example, facial and body motion capture from Gordon Pinsent himself are used to animate sequences representing the actor's early life and career, creating an interesting tangle of actuality, embodiment, and displaced time. These hybrid captured images are explicitly contextualized through media releases and a documentation website demonstrating the process of capturing Pinsent (reinforcing a rhetoric of actuality) but not the extensive process of translating this data into compelling computationally animated images.[7]

These examples demonstrate that the networking surrounding other forms of hybrid images involves many of the same negotiations and intra-actions that can be seen in volumetric image contexts. Desires for presence, indexical effects, and embodiment intertwine with production practices, technological affordances, and interpretations bound to epistemic cultures, including documentary.

Network Fluidity

Volumetric images – like computational animated forms such as 3D modelling, computational rotoscope, and motion capture – can create images that are phenomenologically similar to filmic capture while being able to trade on some of the fluidity of animated imagery. For example, Holly Willis suggests another NFB production, *Way to Go* (2015), offers a potential future for VR by blurring the boundaries between human and animated character, live-action, and CGI, "by gently bending the ordinarily immutable limitations of live-action video," thus allowing it the mutability often missing from digital video (Willis 2016, 158). As Annabelle Honess Roe (2013, 25) notes, animation "offers freedom to explore possibilities for not only masking identities, but also interpreting the words of interviewees and illustrating and conveying a film's themes and issues." For example, artist Judith Doyle's 2014 *gestureLab* workshop, part of the Twentieth International Symposium on Electronic Art (ISEA) in Dubai, allowed UAE women to visualize themselves using custom depth camera technology. Doyle's work abstracts live hybrid video images into lines and point clouds. The resulting image preserves some aspects of volumetric video (motion gesture and an enhanced perception of spatiality), while downplaying photorealistic semblance in a controlled, expressive manner. In a video interview following this experience, the women note how such technology allows them to be seen and yet not be seen, giving them presence in representation but allowing them to maintain agency in upholding a standard of modesty with which they feel most comfortable. Abstract volumetric capture is discussed in, and through, the workshop as a way to "be seen, and not to be seen" – to preserve modesty, and anonymity, for its Muslim women participants.[8] As Honess Roe (2013, 87) notes, "There is a politics associated with visibility and, conversely, invisibility. To have a presence, you must be visible. To have a say, you must be both seen and heard." Such a conceit is also present in *Zero Days* (all versions), in which the volumetric image is originally presented as an obfuscation of an informant but is later revealed to be an actor representing an amalgam of informants.

Volumetric Images in Postmedia Documentary

While captured images have always involved complex relationships between machinic and social factors (Zylinska 2016), volumetric images present a powerful focal object for exploring late postmedia through the intra-action of human and computational agencies, the increasing blur between data and images, and desires and expectations surrounding digital capture. Canadian productions such as *Made This Way*, *The Choice VR*, and *Universe Within* demonstrate different ways in which volumetric images are networked within interactive documentary. *Universe Within* foregrounds the underlying digital process, using this as a cue for the digital hybridity of its subject. *Made This Way* and *The Choice* VR present an alternate networking, leveraging documentary ideals of indexicality and presence. However, these configurations are just two surrounding an emerging form, and, as the case of other hybrid capture entanglements such as those surrounding rotoscoping and motion capture have shown, there different ways not only of negotiating access to presence but also of generating the network – neither animation nor filmic capture, neither created nor captured, but potentially read as either or both. This is contingent on what we want these images to be and do, a process of negotiation that both draws upon past configurations and is open to the constant reconfiguration potential of postmedia.

Notes

1 Including unrealized prototypes attempting to capture the embodied performance of Inuit throat singers in association with performer Tanya Tagaq (Aylwin Lo NFB), personal discussion with author, July 2017.
2 Alexander Porter, personal correspondence with author, July 2017, emphasis in original.
3 *Made This Way* is based on an ongoing photo-documentary series by Harnak.
4 HotDocs Industry Conference 2018: *Creating Empathy* panel.
5 In addition to an ethically problematic re-corporealization that also manifests in motion capture (Allison 2015).
6 Performance capture is alternately used to describe the process of capturing motion using sensors and/or computer vision.
7 As Mihaela Mihailova (2016) notes, the motion data captured from actors provide a starting point upon which animators must build.
8 Video documentation is available at https://vimeo.com/118093318, but for the purposes of this chapter it was acquired directly from the artist, Judith Doyle, in July 2017.

References

Allison, Tanine. 2015. "Blackface, Happy Feet: The Politics of Race in Motion Capture and Animation." In *Special Effects: New Histories, Theories, Contexts*, ed. Dan North, Bob Rehak, and Michael S. Duffy, 114–26. London: Bloomsbury.
Barad, Karen. 2003. "Posthumanist Performativity: Toward an Understanding

of How Matter Comes to Matter." *Signs: Journal of Women in Culture and Society* 28 (3): 801–31. https://doi.org/10.1086/345321.
– 2007. *Meeting the Universe Halfway: Quantum Physics and the Entanglement of Matter and Meaning*. Durham, NC: Duke University Press.
Bazin, André. 1960. "The Ontology of the Photographic Image." Trans. Hugh Gray. *Film Quarterly* 13 (4): 4–9. https://doi.org/10.2307/1210183.
Belliger, Andréa, and David Krieger. 2014. *Interpreting Networks: Hermeneutics, Actor-Network Theory, and New Media*. Bielefeld: Transcript-Verlag.
Bouldin, Joanna. 2001. "Technologies of the Body and Politics of the Real: Race, Reality and the Rotoscope in Fleischer Animated Cartoons." Paper presented at Society for Animation Studies, Montreal, 23 October 2001.
Bryant, Antony, and Griselda Pollock, eds. 2010. *Digital and Other Virtualities: Renegotiating the Image*. London: IB Tauris.
Corner, John. 2002. "Documentary in a Post-Documentary Culture? A Note on Forms and Their Functions." http://lfbxmljy.blog.sohu.com/176601804.html.
de la Peña, Nonny, Peggy Weil, Joan Llobera, Elias Giannopoulos, Ausiàs Pomés, Bernhard Spanlang, Doron Friedman, Maria V Sanchez-Vives, and Mel Slater. 2010. "Immersive Journalism: Immersive Virtual Reality for the First-Person Experience of News." *Presence: Teleoperators and Virtual Environments* 19 (4): 291–301.
Dobbs, Jennifer Elizabeth. 2013. "A Changing Cinema: Re-Conceptualizing Indexicality and Digital Technologies." MA thesis, Carleton University.
Dolphijn, Rick, and Iris van der Tuin. 2012. *New Materialism: Interviews and Cartographies*. Ann Arbor: Open Humanities Press.
Fore, Steve. 2011. "Reenacting Ryan: The Fantasmatic and the Animated Documentary." *Animation* 6 (3): 277–92.
Fox, N.J., and P. Alldred. 2019. "New Materialism." In SAGE *Research Methods Foundations*, ed. P.A Atkinson, S. Delamont, A. Cernat, J.W. Sakshaug, and M. Williams, M. London: SAGE. https://methods.sagepub.com/foundations/new-materialism.
Gries, Laurie. 2015. *Still Life with Rhetoric: A New Materialist Approach for Visual Rhetorics*. Logan: Utah State University Press.
Grusin, Richard, ed. 2015. *The Nonhuman Turn*. Minneapolis: University of Minnesota Press.
Gunning, T. 2007. "Moving Away from the Index: Cinema and the Impression of Reality." *Differences* 18 (1): 29–52. https://doi.org/10.1215/10407391-2006-022.
Hébert, Pierre. 2006. "Les Trois Âges De La Rotoscopie." In *Quand Le Cinéma*

D'animation Rencontre Le Vivant, ed. Marcel Jean. Montreal, QC: Les 400 coups cinema.

Honess Roe, Annabelle. 2013. *Animated Documentary*. London: Palgrave Macmillan.

Kim, Jihoon. 2016. *Between Film, Video, and the Digital: Hybrid Moving Images in the Post-Media Age*. New York: Bloomsbury Academic.

– 2022. *Documentary's Expanded Fields: New Media and the Twenty-First-Century Documentary*. New York: Oxford University Press.

Latour, Bruno. 2005. *Reassembling the Social: An Introduction to Actor-Network Theory*. Oxford: Oxford University Press.

Manovich, Lev. 2001. "Post-Media Aesthetics." http://manovich.net/index.php/projects/post-media-aesthetics.

Menache, Alberto. 2010. *Understanding Motion Capture for Computer Animation*. 2nd ed. Burlington, MA: Morgan Kaufmann.

Mihailova, Mihaela. 2016. "Collaboration without Representation: Labor Issues in Motion and Performance Capture." *Animation* 11 (1): 40–58.

NFB. 2015. "Universe Within: Digital Lives in the Global Highrise - Process and Innovation." Video. https://youtu.be/MQcSSzSd5_4?si=IjzVIoEMbsG6bOBm.

Pasek, Anne. 2015. "The Problem of Nonhuman Phenomenology: Or, What Is It Like to Be a Kinect?" *InVisible Culture: An Electronic Journal for Visual Culture* no. 22 (April). https://ivc.lib.rochester.edu/the-problem-of-nonhuman-phenomenology-or-what-is-it-like-to-be-a-kinect.

Rosen, Philip. 2001. *Change Mummified: Cinema Historicity, Theory*. Minnesota: University of Minnesota Press.

Slater, Mel. 2003. "A Note on Presence Terminology." *Presence Connect* 3 (January): 3. https://www.researchgate.net/publication/242608507_A_Note_on_Presence_Terminology.

Steyerl, Hito. 2009. "In Defense of the Poor Image." *E-Flux Journal* 10. http://www.ocopy.net/wp-content/uploads/2016/04/steyerl-hito_in-defense-of-the-poor-image.pdf.

Uricchio, William. 2011. "The Algorithmic Turn: Photosynth, Augmented Reality and the Changing Implications of the Image." *Visual Studies* 26 (1): 25–35.

Ward, Paul. 2008. "Animated Realities: The Animated Film, Documentary, Realism." *Reconstruction: Studies in Contemporary Culture* 8 no. 2: n.p.

Weibel, Peter. 2006. "The Post-Media Condition." In AAVV, Postmedia Condition, cat., 96. Madrid: Centro Cultural Conde Duque. http://www.metamute.org/editorial/lab/post-media-condition.

Willis, Holly. 2016. *Fast Forward: The Future(s) of the Cinematic Arts*. London New York: Wallflower.

Wolf, Mark J.P. 2000. *Abstracting Reality: Art, Communication, and Cognition in the Digital Age*. Lanham, MD: University Press of America.

Wollen, Peter. 1969. *Signs and Meaning in the Cinema*. Bloomington: Indiana University Press.

Woodcock, Rose. 2003. "Instrumental Vision." In *Carnal Knowledge: Towards a New Materialism through the Arts*, ed. Barbara Bolt and Estelle Barrett, 171–84. London: IB Tauris.

XRMust. 2018. "Interview: 'Sharing a Relationship Through VR' Irem Harnak and Elli Raynai (Made This Way)." https://xrmust.com/interview-made-this-way. Link defunct.

Zylinska, Joanna. 2016. "Nonhuman Photography." MIT Press. https://mitpress.mit.edu/books/nonhuman-photography.3

16

INDIGENOUS FUTURISM AND THE IMMERSIVE WORLDING OF *INHERENT RIGHTS, VISION RIGHTS, 2167*, AND *BIIDAABAN: FIRST LIGHT*

Brenda Longfellow

This chapter may seem a very odd, even unsettling addition to a volume focused on Canadian interactive documentary. In the first instance, the works I propose to explore are a series of Indigenous artists' projects produced in virtual reality (VR), including Lawrence Paul Yuxweluptun's *Inherent Rights, Vision Rights* (1992) and his recent VR collaboration with Paisley Smith, *Unceded Territories* (2019); two VR projects commissioned by ImagineNATIVE under the rubric of *2167* – Scott Benesiinaabandan's *Blueberry Pie under the Martian Sky* (2017) and Danis Goulet's *The Hunt* (2017); and Lisa Jackson's *Biidaaban: First Light* (2018). Shaped and informed by the robust and long-standing tradition of Indigenous futurism, these projects feature provocative meditations on the future rendered through animation, CGI, and digital processing. They are speculative, fantastical, metaphorical, and mysterious. Each, in its own distinct way, is informed by and mediates Indigenous cosmologies, philosophies, and worldviews, embodying radical relationality, complex temporalities, and decolonial imaginaries of the future. They are, as should be evident by now, conceived and executed in a manner that is far removed from "the charge of the real" or the indexical properties and ontologies of documentary, as traditionally conceived. As I argue, this does not mean, however, that the works are devoid of political urgency. But it does mean that that the works' political implications are mediated less through rhetorics of persuasion or the articulation of claims around "reality" than through an immersive and affective embodiment of simulated worlds, visions, and prophecies.

Most important, these works unsettle any easy designation of the national or "Canada" as an unmarked frame. Ironically, while *2167* received financial support from the Canada and Ontario 150 Fund, intended to mark the celebration of Canada's sesquicentennial, and Jackson's project was produced by the National Film Board of Canada, all five projects implicitly contest the permanence and authority of the settler-colonial state as they assert the *survivance* (to evoke Gerald Vizenor's [1994] term) of Indigenous Peoples far into the future.[1] Indigenous sovereignty rather than national belonging is a fundament of the speculative imagination apparent in these projects.

Sitting more comfortably within the adjacent, yet distinct, field of Indigenous new media, these projects extend the long preoccupation of Indigenous new media artists with expanded forms of cinema, the internet, and innovative media technologies. As Candice Hopkins (2005, 135) writes in *Transference, Tradition, Technology*, a seminal anthology on Indigenous new media, "Cyberspace has been occupied, transformed, appropriated and reinvented by Native people in ways similar to how we've always approached real space." Far in advance of the contemporary scholarship, new critical language, and institutional support for interactive documentary, Indigenous new media has been at the forefront of artistic appropriations of new technologies into media-integrated performance, installation, and web-based art since the late 1990s. Some of the most resonant projects in this tradition have incorporated documentary elements and strategies such as Dana Claxton's *Sitting Bull and the Moose Jaw Sioux* (2004), a four-channel video installation that weaves contemporary documentary interviews with Elders, archival images, and panning shots of an empty prairie landscape to reflect on the history of the forced exodus of Sitting Bull and his people to Moosejaw, following the Battle of Little Bighorn. Stephen Foster,[2] Cheryl L'Hirondelle,[3] and David Garneau[4] also use modified documentary elements in their new media work, but, for the most part, Indigenous new media has been discursively and institutionally situated in the art world and disseminated through an international field of art festivals, galleries, universities, and community displays that have historically been quite separate from the extended exhibition circuits or broadcast medium of documentary.

Today, with the expansive and accessible affordances of Web 2.0, the proliferation of platforms, and new institutional priorities of support and programming of interactive and immersive digital media, these two worlds have come into closer proximity. That said, there are surprisingly few instances I could discover of interactive documentaries produced by

Indigenous directors in Canada. Stephen Foster's *The Prince George Métis Elders Documentary Project*, co-directed with sociologist Mike Evans in 2005, was not specifically designed for the web but was disseminated as an interactive DVD and multi-channel video installation. *God's Lake Narrows* (2011), an interactive photo-essay, was directed by Winnipeg artist Kevin Lee Burton and NFB producer Alicia Smith and features photos of the God's Lake Reserve community by Scott Benesiinaabandan. A clever use of GPS tracking allows *God's Lake Narrows* to challenge outsider perspectives of Indigenous reserves while exploring the faces and places of Burton's home reserve in northern Manitoba. *Ice Fishing* (2014), by Newfoundland Mi'kmaq artist Jordan Bennett, is an interactive sculptural, sound, and video installation that includes an actual ice fishing shack built by Bennett and his father, the process of which is documented in a short linear film.

While the NFB's Digital Mandate (2008–13) coincided with the agency's increased prioritization of support to Indigenous filmmakers (formalized in the NFB's 2017 three-year equity plan),[5] the actual convergence of these mandates has been intermittent and tenuous.[6] Both *God's Lake Narrows* and *Ice Fishing* involved co-productions and initiatives initiated outside the NFB. *God's Lake Narrows* grew out of Kevin Lee Burton and Caroline Monnet's installation piece RESERVE(d), which was shown in Winnipeg at the Shaman Urban Gallery in 2010 before being produced by the Winnipeg NFB as an interactive documentary. *Ice Fishing* was supported by the Vancouver Digital Studio through Canada's Digital Partnership with the ImagineNATIVE Film and Media Arts Festival. The NFB also collaborated with the Montreal Museum of Fine Arts on Kushapetshekan/Kosapitcikan – A Glimpse into the Other World (2017), an immersive installation by Atikamekw artists Eruoma Awashish and Meky Ottawa, and Innu artist Jani Bellefleur-Kaltush.

While documentary remains the core institutional project of the National Film Board, its Digital Studios have interpreted the NFB's digital mandate as an "experimental canvas for interactive storytelling" (NFB 2008–13) and have not confined themselves to strict definitions of documentary. The NFB Vancouver Digital Studio, in fact, was the producer on Lisa Jackson's *Biidaaban: First Light*, a project that the Canadian Screen Awards included in the category "immersive fiction."

While the five Indigenous VR projects I want to explore rely on new technologies of spatial storytelling, an investment they share with the broad spectrum of interactive documentary, there are some key and crucial differences. While accessed through new platforms and personalized modes of navigation, the interactive documentary frequently retains a core of traditional documentary elements, including witness testimony, interviews, and photorealistic depictions of place and subjects. All the VR projects I explore in this chapter embody complex mediations of the computational and the real that lean far more towards simulation and hyper-realism than actuality. Yuxweluptun's *Inherent Rights, Vision Rights* recreates a Coast Salish longhouse but in neon animated renderings in which space is populated by spirits and ghosts. Lisa Jackson's *Biidaaban: First Light* has an indexical relation to an actual location, the iconic Nathan Philips Square in downtown Toronto, whose image is then textured and remediated as a futurist post-apocalyptic landscape. Danis Goulet's 2167 project, *The Hunt*, mixes CGI with 360-degree lens-based video to create science fiction, and Scott Benesiinaabandan's *Blueberry Pie under the Martian Sky* reveals a dreamscape that is entirely computational. Either through the appropriation of the new technology of virtual reality or through the use of speculative fiction as a modality of Indigenous futurism, these projects operate outside of traditional ontologies of the real, and it is precisely for this reason that they are able to embody the distinctiveness of Indigenous cosmologies and worldviews in sublime, provocative, and powerful ways.

The central challenge of this chapter is how to engage with the rich philosophical provocations of these VR projects in a respectful mode that acknowledges their decolonizing impetus. As Mohawk and Anishinaabe scholar Vanessa Watts (2013) warns, translations of Indigenous cosmologies into Euro-Western scholarship often result in a reterritorializing of Indigenous thought into problematic abstractions or critical categories. Indigenous worldviews are embodied and embedded in specific places, she argues: they come into being and are sustained only through active and reciprocal tending of relations to those places and territories, a process that Glen Coulthard and Leanne Betasamosake Simpson (2016) term "grounded normativity." As a settler on occupied territories, I can never presume to fully know Indigenous epistemologies or cosmologies. There are, however, many brilliant Indigenous philosophers, scholars, and artists who I lean on and listen to in an effort to highlight how Indigenous worldviews are manifest in these VR projects. Each of these projects embodies a generous invitation to settler and Indigenous viewers alike to imagine alternative futures and to immerse themselves in other worlds. Of course, this invitation comes with the proviso that these virtual territories will be respected and not occupied or settled, and that the recognition (and even celebration) of Indigenous sovereignty is an a priori condition for all reformulations of settler and Indigenous relations.

Lawrence Paul Yuxweluptun's *Inherent Rights, Vision Rights* (1992)

Cree/Métis director and scholar Loretta Todd's (1996) seminal essay "Aboriginal Narratives in Cyberspace" and Mohawk multimedia installation/performance artist and cultural theorist Jackson 2bears's (2010) "A Conversation with Spirits Inside the Simulation of a Coast Salish Longhouse" provide rich frameworks for considering the evolution and specificity of what 2bears calls "an Indigenous theory of virtuality" (ibid.). For both, a touchstone project is Lawrence Paul Yuxweluptun's, *Inherent Rights, Vision Rights* (*IRVR*), the first ever Indigenous VR project developed during a residency at the Banff Centre in 1991 and the first VR project to be exhibited at the National Gallery of Canada. I turn to *IRVR* now in the hope of tracing its contemporary legacy and the critical discourse that it inspired.

By the early 1990s Yuxweluptun was well known for his large-scale, gorgeous, and politically explicit landscape paintings that highlighted Indigenous dispossession, environmental devastation, and the toxic fallout of colonialism, inflected, as one critic notes, as much by Coast Salish mythologies as by "acid rock" (Laurence 1995). *IRVR* borrows many of Yuxweluptun's signature ovoid shaped figures, psychedelic colours, and hybridizations of Northwest Coast mask traditions to immerse the participant in a sacred Coast Salish longhouse in which a spiritual ceremony is taking place. As Yuxweluptun (1996) writes, "the longhouse is a given space in time which I use to show a religious concept, to physically bring people into contact with a native worshiping aspect of life, praying Indians … What it is like being in a possessed state feeling rhythmic sounds in a longhouse, feeling sounds go through one's own self, feeling a spirit inside you." While *IRVR* might be seen as a departure from the exhortatory language of his paintings, the VR project is, nonetheless, deeply political in its assertion of the survival and integrity of Indigenous spirituality and millennial-old traditions that persist despite five hundred years of colonization, forced Christianization, and assimilation through the mechanisms of residential schools and state-sanctioned policies of cultural genocide. According to 2bears, *IRVR* is conditioned by Yuxweluptun's initiation as a dancer into the Sxwaixwe coast Salish secret society at the age of fourteen, but as a self-avowed "modernist" Yuxweluptun mediates the experience of the ceremony through the technology of VR and through his own syncretic and hybridized imagination.

From the standpoint of thirty years of technical refinement of virtual reality (for many a technology still in its infancy) *IRVR* seems crude. The project is only accessed through large headphones and a clunky Darth Vadar type helmet stuck into a plexiglass box containing two tiny monitors and a computer. A joystick provides the single participant with ability to navigate through this space. There are fragments of *IRVR* that exist online in the form of frame grabs on Yuxweluptun's website (http://lawrencepaulyuxweluptun.com/interdisciplinary.html) and in an extended excerpt included in *Man of Masks*, an NFB documentary on Yuxweluptun directed by Dana Claxton in 1998. Mostly for this writer, however, the experience of *IRVR* is mediated through the accounts of contemporary spectators such as 2bears and Todd, who viewed the project in its original incarnation, and through a more recent account by Sarah King who writes about *IRVR* in the context of the Yuxweluptun retrospective in 2016 at the Museum of Anthropology.

One thing that is clear from all these accounts is that, despite the clunky encumbrance of 1992 VR technology, the experience for all participants is intensely visceral and one of absolute immersion. Here is Jackson 2bears's (2010) account of his encounter with the project: "I begin to feel nauseous as this ecstatic feeling of disembodied-embodiment awakens feelings in me of a kind of psychoexistential transformation that has about it the quality of some ancient initiation ritual. Confused and discombobulated, my entire sense of 'self' has become distorted, dislocated and entirely uncertain … I feel submerged in a kind of digital underworld, caught in a technologically enabled illusion, set adrift in a liminal zone with the feeling of being simultaneously inside and outside my body." Loretta Todd (1996, 160) writes of how Yuxweluptun's virtual environment allowed for an uncanny experience of time, "the time of walking from the outside to the inside. The time of listening to a dog. The time of hearing the roar of the fire as the wood burns." Sarah King (2017, 190) also comments on *IRVR*'s immersive nature where "fire pits are active and ovoid beings are dancing, drumming and vocalizing.". When an ovoid figure looms up and seemingly passes through her, King finds the experience "overwhelming" (191).

Writing "Aboriginal Narratives in Cyberspace" in 1996 at the height of uncritical and pervasive techno-utopianism, Todd (1996, 154) is justifiably wary about the promise of these new technologies and asks whether cyberspace is not really "a clever guise for neo-colonialism," responsible for perpetuating the founding axioms of Western thought: "A fear of the body, aversion to nature, a desire for salvation and transcendence of the earthly plane" (155). While refusing to absolve the general ontology and practice of cyberspace from its colonial entanglements, Todd reads *IRVR* as a notable and critical exception to the rule. "Yuxweluptun does not want you to forget your body" (160), she insists, he "invites you into the mystery of the everyday. You must define yourself in relationship to the story around you" (161). Building on Todd's insight, 2bears (2010) points to the paradigm shifting nature of *IRVR* with its possibility, as he argues, "of recontextualizing the Western 'ontology of the virtual,' a transformation in which the focus becomes a return to the flesh as both an embodied and simulated experience under the sign of an *Indigenous Theory of Virtuality*" (emphasis in original).

While 2bears's argument is highly complex and built through a wide-ranging exegesis of texts from Carl Jung to Heidegger, what I believe is core to his argument is that Indigenous Virtuality as theory and as instantiated in *IRVR* moves beyond the logic of either/or to propose a simultaneous and even paradoxical conjoining of opposites: flesh and the virtual, spirit world and the world of matter. The conjoining of opposites, moreover, is mediated through the particular nature of virtual reality technology, which invites participatory immersion in a highly kinesthetic sensory experience whereby a user is able to move through a spatial surround that has volume, depth, and acoustic and visual presence. In other words, volumetric immersion may be virtual but the individual participant's experience is felt through the body, in waves of nausea, awe, fear, trembling, and surrender. As 2bears (2010) writes, "the people who experience the work [*IRVR*] are not mere spectators but participants In the phenomenological hallucination of a sacred ritual – they are users with agency who exercise free will while navigating a simulation of a Coast Salish longhouse." As with the traditional practices of ceremony, prayer, fasting, ritual, or ingestion of mind-altering substances, the VR experience facilitates the transposition of the subject into a state of altered consciousness. Yuxweluptun (1996), in fact, refers to the VR helmet as "the whiteman's mask," a device, which, like the traditional masks of Coast Salish peoples, operates to transport users into other-worldly encounters with ghosts, animated spirits, and sacred hauntings. For 2bears (2010), IRVR foregrounds the specific potential of VR technology as animistic "alive and filled with spirit" as it models a new participatory and embodied relation in which an active participant is "interconnected with the virtual, caught in a feedback loop in which … spirit-simulations move through the digital code and interface with the flesh."

In addition to the way in which VR facilitates a complex relay between the virtual and the body, 2bears and Todd argue that VR represents a technological mediation particularly consonant with Aboriginal modes of storytelling given its primary orientation towards space, an orientation embedded in the core precept of all Indigenous worldviews: namely, the sacredness of land. As Vine Deloria Jr (2003) points out in his canonical *God Is Red/A Native View of Religion*, while Western philosophy is preoccupied with time, Indigenous spirituality is based on a philosophy of space and understands land as an animate entity that possesses or inhabits the people. As is obvious, one can't stress enough how distinct this view is from Western ideologies for whom the land exists almost exclusively as an external, inanimate object whose value is dependent on its instrumental use as a resource for exploitation, extraction, and commodification. Even mainstream Western environmental discourses tend to portray the ravaged and polluted landscapes of the Anthropocene as an inert other. By contrast, Deloria and multiple Indigenous philosophers have meticulously delineated how, by virtue of their radical relationality, Indigenous ontologies stand in marked contrast to the founding subject/object dualism of Western thought. As Aboriginal scholar and activist Karen Martin so beautifully puts it: "We are part of the world as much as it is part of us, existing within a network of relations amongst Entities that are reciprocal" (Martin and Mirraboopa 2003, 209).

"Inherent Rights," the declarative title of Yuxweluptun's VR project, references the sacred trust invested in Indigenous Peoples to care and steward the land understood as a vast assemblage of interconnected life and human and non-human beings. While *IRVR* offers a generous invitation to Indigenous and non-Indigenous visitors to spiritual immersion in a Coast Salish longhouse, his recent VR project, *Unceded Territories* (2019), produced in collaboration with VR artist Paisley Smith, takes a more confrontational stance (although tempered by Yuxweluptun's characteristic wry and ironic sense of humour), implicating the visitor as a colonizer and perpetrator of environmental devastation. Like IRVR, *Unceded Territories* appropriates the iconic figures of Yuxweluptun's Coast Salish surrealist aesthetic into an intense six minutes of hallucinogenic play. *Unceded*, however, adds elements of explicit game-like interactivity as the user is provided with hand controllers that turn into stylized bear claws inside the world of VR. As my "claw" touches a mosaic of rounded rectangles, the play begins and I'm encouraged to fling a ball into the world of the beautiful forest, each fling splattering neon colour into the environment. The gaming aspect is fun, driven by the pounding, intoxicating rhythms of *A Tribe Called Red*, but soon the tone changes. The forest is invaded by Super-Predators and Colonial Snake whose toxic presence begins to change the natural environment: forests catch on fire, fish are poisoned, and when one looks down, oil pools on the forest floor, growing with each insouciant fling of the ball. As the "game" reaches a crescendo, the landscape shifts into a swirling blur of neon mosaics, which finally resolve into a grey and ruined world as the voice of Yuxweluptun offers a final admonition: "You must not touch what is not yours!"

Unceded Territories is playful and deeply mischievous, but there is an obvious method to Yuxweluptun's madness. The "Unceded Territories" of the project's title might very well embrace the whole of Turtle Island or, indeed, the territories of the world that have been subject to colonial dispossession since Contact. But in British Columbia, the title makes an immediate reference to the large tracts of land in the province (the last to be colonized in Canada) where Aboriginal Title has neither been surrendered nor acquired by the Crown, much of which is in protracted legal dispute. For Yuxweluptun and for the late Arthur Manuel, Secwepemc activist, Indigenous leader, environmentalist, and writer, Indigenous struggles over rights and title represent the frontline of resistance and main legal challenge to the exploitation of lands and fossil fuel expansion. By referencing the ongoing struggle over Aboriginal Title, Yuxweluptun reminds users of who the inherent and rightful stewards of the land actually are while positioning Indigenous resistance as the embodied manifestation of the sacred responsibility to tend and care for Mother Earth. As Manuel writes: "In defending the land at this time of the international global warming crisis, we are defending something much larger than Indigenous rights. Our fight today is to preserve the planet in a livable form" (Manuel and Derrickson 2017, 242).

2167 and Indigenous Futurism

As part of the Toronto International Film Festival's sesquicentennial initiative, Canada on Screen, four Indigenous filmmakers and artists – Danis Goulet, Kent Monkman, Scott Benesiinaabandan, and the interdisciplinary arts collective Postcommodity – were commissioned to create VR projects envisioning Indigenous life 150 years in the future. A collaboration between ImagineNATIVE, TIFF, the Inuit media collective Pinnguaq, and Concordia University's Initiative for Indigenous Futures, the commission was intended as a crucial and decolonial counterpoint to the 150 years of Canadian Confederation celebrations that took place throughout 2017. Shepherded and produced by the artistic and managing director of ImagineNATIVE Film and Media Arts Festival, Jason Ryle, the commission clearly took up the insight first developed by Loretta Todd and Jackson 2bears that highlighted the particular compatibility of VR with Indigenous worldviews. As the program notes for a panel discussion on 2167 put it, "The art of story creation in virtual reality offers a point of view and presence of place, space and environment that may be the closest comparison yet to Indigenous oral storytelling practice" (Ryle 2017).

While Indigenous futurism has an extraordinarily robust presence in Canada, the movement is international and embraces a range of practices complexly entangled, as Karyn Recollet (2019) notes, with Afrofuturism as a discourse of speculative resistance. The term was first coined by Grace Dillon (2012) in *Walking the Clouds: An Anthology of Indigenous Science Fiction*, which includes contributions by Native Americans, First Nations, Aboriginal Australians, and New Zealand Maori authors. Rigorously framed by Dillon, the anthology provides a deconstructive critique of conventional science fiction with its traditional colonialist emphasis on conquering "alien" territories while highlighting the speculative and time-travelling traditions that have always informed Indigenous legends and oral storytelling. Indigenous futurism has expanded kinetically within the last decade as an integral part of Indigenous resurgence and, in its contemporary iterations, includes a diverse range of media and theory making, gaming, machinima, hip-hop, computer animation and zines, mixed tapes, science fiction films, and internet-based practices.

One of the best known and cutting-edge innovators in the field is AbTeC (Aboriginal Territories in Cyberspace), a research network of artists and academics who investigate and create Indigenous virtual environments at Concordia University directed by Jason Lewis (Cherokee/Hawaiian/Samoan) and Skawennati Fragitini Kawennati (a Mohawk multi-media artist). AbTeC hosts a range of symposia, "skins" workshops on Aboriginal storytelling and Videogame design for Indigenous youth, and ongoing research creation initiatives and scholarly interventions. Inspired by CyberPowWow, the pioneering online art gallery and chat space conceived in 1996, AbTeC has been developing an expansive conceptual framework around Indigenous futurism for the past fifteen years. Of particular note are the extraordinary and highly influential machinimas directed by Skawennati: *Time Traveller* (2008–13), which follows a young Indigenous hunter who travels through time to immerse himself in key chapters in Indigenous resistance, and *She Falls for Ages* (2016), a gorgeous sci-fi retelling of the Haudenosaunee (Iroquois) creation story that reimagines Sky World as a futuristic, utopic space and Sky Woman as a brave astronaut and world-builder. AbTeC was a collaborating partner with *2167*, through the Initiative for Indigenous Futures, and the lab hosted a residency for Scott Benesiinaabandan as he worked on *Blueberry Pie under a Martian Sky*.

As many of its practitioners have observed, Indigenous futurism evolves as a retort to the colonial imagination that views Indigeneity and Indigenous Peoples as artefacts of the past, frozen in time, and on the cusp of vanishing or being assimilated. Indigenous futurism insists that contemporary Indigenous Peoples are not outside the world of technological development and modernity but are recouping and appropriating new technologies as Indigenous Peoples have always done. As Grace Dillon points out, Indigenous futurism is markedly different from conventional science fiction and even, one might extrapolate, from contemporary post-apocalyptic imaginaries sparked by the increasing awareness of global environmental devastation and climate change. Indigenous scholars, artists, and allies such as Jolene Rickard (2016), Jessica L. Horton (2017), Thomas J. Demos (2017), Zoe Todd (2015), and Nicholas Mirzoeff (2014) are developing a crucial critique of the mainstream discourses of the Anthropocene that, while drawing attention to current and impending ecological disaster, serve to reinforce the colonial and Enlightenment centring of "man" at the apex of planetary transformations and history.

In their groundbreaking essay "On the Importance of a Date, or Decolonizing the Anthropocene" Métis artist and scholar Zoe Todd and settler scholar Heather Davis argue that such problematic philosophical alliances are reproduced in the universalizing rhetoric of the Anthropocene with its undifferentiated use of a culpable "humanity" and its obliviousness to the striations of power, privilege, and responsibility that have distributed massively unequal benefits and harms (Davis and Todd 2017). For these authors, the Anthropocene is not a new event but a continuation of the processes of dispossession and genocide that have been at work since Contact. Decolonizing the Anthropocene, as such, requires a massive revision of its conceptual apparatus to incorporate Indigenous philosophies and worldviews, beginning with the historicization of the new epoch at the commencement of colonization. Such a move, as much strategic as it is symbolic, foregrounds the violence at the core of colonization as a world-changing seismic event and pluralizes the disasters of the Anthropocene beyond anthropogenic climate disruption, including the transatlantic passage and Black chattel slavery. As Davis and Todd conclude, Indigenous Peoples have already faced the end of their worlds, apocalyptic annihilation in the form of mass dispossession, genocide, and ecological upheaval, and this experience conditions all Indigenous approaches to the future with the generational knowledge that, despite overwhelming odds, Indigenous people have survived and possess the resilience, wisdom, and skill to survive future apocalyptic iterations.

These insights certainly inform and shape the embodiment of Indigenous futurism in the *2167* VR projects. For reasons of space and thematic consistency, I'm only going to touch on two of these, Scott Benesiinaabandan's *Blueberry Pie under a Martian Sky* and Danis Goulet's *The Hunt*, which, perhaps more explicitly than the other VR projects, appropriate tropes of science fiction to re-imagine the future as a necessary efflorescence of Indigenous survivance.

Blueberry Pie under a Martian Sky

Of all the *2167* projects, *Blueberry Pie under a Martian Sky* feels most like a dreamscape or hallucination. As with *IRVR*, it provides a heightened kinesthetic experience, immersing the user in a space that is entirely abstract and mediated through computational rendering. We enter the story through a black void where a tall, stylized scaffold of bent branches forms around us, tethered with bark or sinew. Suddenly a flock of birds flies through the structure, escaping from the top as the structure rotates in space. Caught in a whorl of time, we are without horizon or gravity and surrender to the sensation of floating and turning, staring into deep space. We are in the wormhole.

The wormhole, of course, is a staple in science fiction, a speculative trope that is loosely predicted by the theory of general relativity and that inspires ideas of time travel, of moving through disparate points in spacetime. In *Blueberry Pie*, Benesiinaabandan Indigenizes the concept, linking it to two traditional Anishinaabe origin stories: one a prophetic Anishinaabe legend about a young boy who travels back in time to his people's place of origin and the other a story about Spider Woman who weaves a web from the stars along which the Anishinaabe people travelled to Earth. Benesiinaabandan adds a contemporary twist to these origin stories, inserting the wormhole as the metaphoric time-travel medium, a space of complex temporalities where the future is folded into the deep past.

We hear the artist's voice introducing the story world, telling us that one hundred years from now, in the spring of 2167, a research collaboration between Anishinaabe and Omega announced the discovery of a localized, fuzzy wormhole, confirming years of speculative theory. Spider Woman, he tells us, has also been seen in dreams and walking visions across the territory, and a little boy was selected for the first trip home. We are reminded that the wormhole is the conduit through which descendants return and that it represents an arduous journey during which "gravity will reshape us and we will get used to it, it will also reshape our minds."

Inside the black void of the wormhole, recursive geometric shapes spin and turn. A white and grey kaleidoscope of concentric pointed stars spins and dislocates, each band whirling off into the void. There are a few recognizable forms caught in the whorl – a teapot, an artefact of a bygone civilization, floats by – but the wormhole is mostly occupied by abstract and constantly mutating shapes. The narration is taken over by a female Anishinaabemowin speaker whom we hear in the right side of the headphone speaking Anishinaabemowin and on the left side speaking the English translation, the two languages woven together in a rich vocal invocation.

In a public panel at TIFF following the launch of *2167*, Benesiinaabandan spoke of how the project was inspired by his recognition that the Anishinaabemowin term for "blueberry pie" did not exist until relatively recently (blueberries having been around since time immemorial, but not pie). Indigenous languages, he felt, are immensely innovative, constantly in flux and capable of adapting to new technologies, situations, and new relations to kin and land, and he wanted to explore how the language might evolve seven generations into the future. Working with linguist Alan Corbiere, director of the Anishinaabemowin Revival Program Coordinator at Lakeview School, M'Chigeeng First Nation, they commissioned an Elder language group on Manitoulin Island to develop terms for the future such as "black hole" or "event horizon." Anishinaabemowin, like all Indigenous languages, is action oriented and implicitly embeds relations to human and non-human others in poetic and multi-syllabic words that function like short poems. These beautiful and melodic aural fragments are what Benesiinaabandan used to compose the narration, as a testament to the creativity and power of the language to survive into the deep future.

The Hunt

In his contribution to *Coded Territories*, new media artist and activist Archer Pechawis (2014, 38) writes: "I am looking for a future in which Indigenism is the protocol, an all-encompassing embrace of creation: the realms of earth, sky, water, plant animal, human, spirit and, most importantly, a profound humility with regards to our position as humans within that constellation." It seems to me that all the *2167* projects answer Pechawis's call for future imaginaries that centre Indigeneity as the dominant worldview, and Danis Goulet's *The Hunt* is no exception. Deploying a fictional mise-en-scène and 360-degree photo realist video to construct its story world, *The Hunt* is perhaps the most explicitly political of the VR projects I'm considering. While the other VR projects project a future where settler colonialism is extinct and Indigenous worlding takes precedence, *The Hunt* imagines the perpetuation of colonialism as a post-apocalyptic police state where automated orbs patrol the skies to survey and control the remaining pockets of Indigenous community. As with her 2014 short linear film, *Wakening*, in which a lone Cree woman warrior hunts the Weetigo through a dystopian urban landscape, Goulet's (2017) focus is on Indigenous resilience, celebrating, as she puts it, "the ingenious ways we resist colonization."

The Hunt opens with a drone shot that takes us over parched landscapes and ruined technoscapes (wind turbines, cracked and lying on the ground) void of traces of population to the edge of a field where a small group of Mohawk people are hunting. We realize we have been following the point of view of the surveying orb as it drops to ground level and the point of view switches to the hunters. As the orb hovers over his head, a man protests in

Mohawk (Kanien'keha) that they are on sovereign Mohawk territory and have the right to hunt, pulling out his state-issued hunting permit. His assertion of sovereignty mediated through the colonial state is suddenly eclipsed by the more forceful retort of a young woman hunter who takes aim wit' a laser crossbow and shoots the orb out of the sky. Joking about the men's feeble hunting prowess, the members of the group make their way back to their shelter, a ramshackle group of huts patched together with corrugated tin and tarps. We see an abandoned bulldozer and car around the settlement, the debris and detritus from another time, but the small community is vibrant and alive, multi-generational and ingenious in its tactical modes of survival. The camera follows the young woman hunter as she enters a storage space and pulls apart a black curtain to reveal a large mound of these glowing orbs. As the man exclaims "almost a full fleet," the woman hunter commands the orbs to Rise! Reprogrammed from state surveillance to resistance, the orbs obey her in a powerful move of Indigenous *détournement*, massing their energies towards a future confrontation with colonial power.

As with the other examples of Indigenous futurity I have discussed, *The Hunt* presupposes that Indigenous flourishing in the future is dependent on a deep and intimate knowledge of the land and a resurgence of language as the carrier of spiritual being and culture. These values are core to the future imagined in Lisa Jackson's *Biidaaban: First Light*, the final VR project I now consider in a more extended exegesis.

Biidaaban: First Light

Winner of the Canadian Screen Award for Best Immersive Feature in 2019 (among a host of other awards) and featured at dozens of international film and media festivals, Jackson's *Biidaaban: First Light* provides one of the more sublime experiences of virtual reality as it immerses viewers in a post-apocalyptic Indigenous future set in a landscape – Toronto's Nathan Philips Square. Crucially, the project was launched in the actual foyer of Toronto's city hall in Nathan Philip's Square, inscribing an uncanny link between the virtual and the real that was enhanced by the lush plants and vegetation that artfully surrounded the viewing booths.[7]

As soon as the project starts, I am viscerally catapulted into a dark abyss. Tiny beams of light that could be stars, atoms, or infinite galaxies float through the dark resolving into the project's title then dissolving into a new title: "Tkaronto," the Mohawk word for "where there are trees standing in the water" – the antecedent of the colonial place name of "Toronto."

The scene cuts to black and I am suddenly on the edge of the dilapidated and deserted underground subway station. I look down and see the water that fills the tunnel and instantly pull back. I'm dizzy and unmoored. I can feel the dankness, can almost smell the odour of decay and abandonment. I hear the steady drip of water. I turn my head to look behind me and see debris on the other side, and a fading and indecipherable Toronto subway map on one of the posts. The silence is eerie and foreboding. A red canoe is docked in the tunnel, another is overturned on the platform. As I'm wondering if these represent a sign of inhabitation, a woman's voice asks, "Änen shayo'tron' Shonywäa'tihchia'ih sentiohkwa'?" as a title reveals the translation: "Where did the Creator put your people?"

The next scene transitions from underground to the ground level of Nathan Philips Square, Toronto's iconic city hall with its modernist curved buildings designed in 1965 by Finnish architect Viljo Revell. Vegetation has taken over the buildings. Trees grow on roofs, ivy and vines coil down the crumbling sides of buildings. The Sheraton Centre and the CN Tower survive in the background as pathetic and decrepit reminders of commercial boosterism, now a sad reflection of mortal hubris. The scene is uncanny, familiar yet *unhemlich*, a vision of Toronto blasted into a post-apocalyptic future that is as stunning as it is remorseless.

Biidaaban's meticulously detailed vision of the future evolved through an impressive collaboration between Jackson, the Vancouver Digital Studio of the NFB, Jam3 – a design studio out of London, England – and Mathew Borrett, a Toronto-based digital artist whose original large-scale photo project, *Hypnagogic City*, reworked actual 3D models of Nathan Philips Square, fusing the real and the computational into a stunning series of two-dimensional views. Jam3 extended and adapted these views into immersive 3D spatial renderings.

One of the crucial distinctions, however, between Borret's original photo renderings and *Biidaaban* is that the future evoked in *Hypnagogic City* is devoid of human presence, an apocalyptic scenario increasingly prevalent in settler culture, in discourses of the Anthropocene, and in recent non-fiction accounts of climate change disaster such as David Wallace-Wells's recently released *The Uninhabitable Earth* (2019). Gerry Canavan (2014, 1), in fact, has coined a new term, "necrofuturism," to describe a contemporary pervasive imaginary that "posits a future that is doomed to continue modern capitalism's unsustainable and immoral practices even as those practices become more and more destructive and self-defeating."

Although I've used the term "post-apocalyptic" to signal some of the generic affinities of *Biidaaban* with contemporary instances of futurism, I should point out that, in an interview in *Filmmaker Magazine*, Jackson strongly eschews the idea of describing *Biidaaban* with that descriptor. Her intent, she insists, was to foreground the resurgence of nature as a verdant animate force and to evoke a cosmic sense of a futurity linked to Indigenous continuity. Indeed, while the future evoked in *Biidaaban* shares the iconography of ruin with much post-apocalyptic scenarios, nestled among the ruins are multiple signs of human survival. I can see a fire pit by an old patio table and chairs with animal remains and antlers scattered by the side. The sound of a bird cawing directs me to a crow perched on a ledge. I turn my head and see a ghostly apparition: an Indigenous woman in a white dress digging in the soil who looks up as the crow flies overhead. As subsequent scenes land us on the rooftop of a skyscraper looking down at the seemingly abandoned and deteriorating city, these visual signifiers of Indigeneity increase: strips of meat hung to dry on a traditional wooden rack, a wigwam built out of treated hides and branches. Most important, however, Indigenous presence is signified through voices speaking the traditional languages of the area – Wendat, Anishinaabemowin, and Kanyen'keha (Mohawk) – as the text translations float through space. The text is mainly composed of excerpts from the Haudenosaunee Thanksgiving Address, an invocation that expresses gratitude for all that sustains life while reminding listeners of a solemn promise to tend and care for the world with its abundant gifts. Jackson asked and received approval from members of Six Nations to use the prayer given its sacred and powerful status in the culture. The Address offers an expansive and "shimmering" vision of a world of interconnected relations of humans, non-humans, and all of creation, exhorting listeners that the proper stance before the bounty of creation is humility and ethical responsibility: "We give thanks and acknowledge her, our mother the Earth that supports our feet. All our minds are one."

Like *Blueberry Pie*, *Biidaaban* conjures a complex non-linear temporality in which the future is only imagined in communion with the deep past. The Anishinaabemowin title: Bi (the future coming at us), daa (the past), a Ban (after they go into the spirit world) poetically embodies this non-linear view of time. Settler industrial civilization may have collapsed but time loops into traces of pre-Contact habitation sustained by deep Indigenous knowledge of how to survive on the land.

There are many uncanny resonances between Heather Davis and Zoe Todd's essay "Decolonizing the Anthropocene" and *Biidaaban*. Indeed, it is as if *Biidaaban* answers the call that Davis and Todd (2017, 775) issue to "those studying and storying the Anthropocene" to "tend to the ruptures and cleavages between land and flesh, story and law, human and more than human." Could we read the apparition of the Indigenous woman digging in a patch of soil as an embodied instantiation of these relations and ruptures? Her digging does not appear to be a gesture connected to the instrumental ends of agriculture; rather, the gesture feels performative and mysterious, an acting out of what Davis and Todd, following Indigenous scholar Vanessa Watts, term "Place-Thought." Evoking Anishinaabe and Haudenosaunee history and philosophy, Watts (2013, 21) describes Place-Thought as "based upon the premise that land is alive and thinking and that humans and non-humans derive agency through the extensions of these thoughts." For Watts "we [i.e., Indigenous subjects] are made from the land, *our flesh is literally an extension of soil*" (27, emphasis added). Viewed from this perspective, the digging woman embodies multiple gendered and philosophical implications as the site and body of female generative energy, fashioning and generating new peoples of the land, through the "relatedness of land and flesh" (Davis and Todd 2017, 769). For Watts (2013, 27): "The feminine and land [are] fundamental to our extensions as people" and ensure the continued ability to act and think according to traditional cosmologies.

In one of the last scenes of this breathtaking experience, I am inside the domed wigwam looking up at the skins stretched taut over the bent poles as they glow with reflected light from the moon. Suddenly the skins dissolve and I'm immersed in an intoxicating surround of stars and night sky. There is no horizon, no form of any orientation that would ground me to the earth, so I surrender, my body floats as if lost in an immense void of time and space. A male and female voice continue to speak the Thanksgiving Address in the original languages of the territory, as if their voices emanated from the night stars themselves, wrapping me in an acoustic envelope of sacred incantation. The experience feels transcendent, deeply moving, and for a brief and ephemeral moment I can feel I'm inside a cosmic experience.

The acoustic envelope of incantatory vocalizations is obviously crucial to the experience of *Biidaaban*. *Biidaaban* and its sister installation project,

Transmissions, grew out of Jackson's interest in how Indigenous worldviews are intimately and profoundly embedded in Indigenous languages and convey distinct sets of relationships, as Jackson (2018) puts it, "to land, to each other and to time itself." While Wendat, Anishinaabemowin, and Kanyen'keha, the traditional languages heard in *Biidaaban*, have emerged over millennia of habitation and are shaped by the specificity of their territories, they also bear common orientations with all place-based Indigenous languages and ontologies. A core idea in Vanessa Watt's Place-Thought, shared with multiple Indigenous intellectual traditions, including Leroy Little Bear's Blackfoot Metaphysics, is that the singularity of Indigenous languages and, by implication, Indigenous worldviews has to do with their emphasis on radical relationality and the sacred connection between all beings, human and non-human. "Everything in creation is animate and imbued with spirit," Little Bear writes, a sentiment at the heart of the Haudenosaunee Thanksgiving Address, which offers gratitude to "the wind," to "our elder brother the sun," to "Grandmother moon and the stars in the sky," to "running water," "game animals," "food plants," and "birds." While Western thought is oriented around the foundational dualism of subject and object (with profound implications for how we are able to instrumentalize others and the land itself), radical relationality provides a powerful alternative of living in embedded dwelling on the Earth, in relations of kin and caring with all entities. This is the lesson that *Biidaaban* meticulously embodies, a lesson we all must learn if the Earth and all its inhabitants are to be lovingly sustained.

Conclusion

This chapter begins with an exploration of Jackson 2bears's Indigenous theory of virtuality to demonstrate why Indigenous new media artists have gravitated to VR, particularly artists invested in the tactical technological appropriations and interventions of Indigenous futurism. For 2bears, VR facilitates a particular form of embodiment and participatory engagement that is radically distinct from the transcendental spectator of conventional cinema. As he argues, wearing the "whiteman's mask," as Yuxwelputun names it, places us inside a "phenomenological hallucination" immersed in a highly kinesthetic sensory experience that can simulate alternate modes of knowing and being traditionally arrived at only through ritual practices.

In her essay "The World Navigated: Interactive Documentaries in Canada," Jessica Mulvogue (2019) calls on Heidegger and his theorization of "world picture" to distinguish the user experience of interactive documentary as one that potentially breaches the subject/object divide of Western ontologies. Conventional cinema, she argues, mirrors and reproduces Western modernity's othering of the world as an image: "The world stands before and apart from us ... as an object that we can define, conquer and control" (416). I would argue that, even more than interactive documentary, the affordances of VR provide for the possibility of such a breach. VR may embody interactive elements, but its key distinguishing feature is its ability to immerse us in a spatial and auditory surround in which the frame, with all of its complex ideological, ontological, and perceptual effects, is eclipsed through immersive worlding. There is no doubt that VR can also be used to deleterious ends as in commercial pornography or gaming, in which the story world invites the user to occupy the position of colonizer or conqueror of alien territories. However, in the hands of Indigenous artists, as I hope I have demonstrated, VR has been skilfully deployed to mediate complex Indigenous worldviews.

All of the works discussed here provide a speculative vision of the future, in which Indigeneity is centred as a necessary relational ontology that eclipses colonial modes of vision, knowing, and being in the world. This vision, as multiple Indigenous artists and scholars have argued, is embedded in the future-oriented nature of Indigenous worldviews, which, as Wade Churchill (2003, 253) writes, "stand[] in diametrical opposition to the totality of what might be termed 'Eurocentric business as usual' as they offer an antidote, a vision of how things might be that is based in how things have been since time immemorial, and how things must be once again if the human species, and perhaps the planet itself, is to survive much longer."

Notes

1 Anishinaabe cultural theorist and writer Gerald Vizenor coined the term *survivance*, an amalgam of "survival" and "resistance," in his book *Manifest Manners: Narratives on Postindian Survivance* (Vizenor 1994) to insist on the active presence, ingenuity, and continually evolving nature of Indigenous cultural and social realities throughout colonization.

2 *The Prince George Métis Elders Documentary Project* (2005), directed by Stephen Foster (Haida/European) and Mike Evans, is perhaps the most explicitly documentary in form, using interviews with Elders in the installation and CD Rom.

3 While not documentary interviews per se, *Why the Caged Bird Sings: Here I Am* (2014), directed by Cheryl L'Hirondelle, uses documentary performances of incarcerated women filmed in correctional institutions. L'Hirondelle is of Métis/Cree, French, German, and Polish descent.

4 Métis artist David Garneau's video installation *Black Pepper* (2000) uses an autobiographical story narrated by Garneau and a fixed video image of an Indigenous male actor to recount an episode in Garneau's experience as a camp counsellor when he was instructed to discipline a young Indigenous child with black pepper. The performative elements of the piece highlight the complex ways in which documentary elements have been employed in Indigenous new media work.

5 NFB equity plan: https://blog.nfb.ca/blog/2017/06/20/nfb-commits-indigenous-equity/.

6 Gauthier (2016) identifies a clear paradigm shift at the National Film Board as evidenced in public policy directives and statements, whereby support to Aboriginal media diminishes in the wake of the Board's digital priorities.

7 *Biidaaban*'s subtle insistence on the urgency of ecological materiality was apparently reinforced at the Tribeca Film Festival, where viewers exiting the project were confronted with a large turtle in a glass aquarium – for many, a shocking juxtaposition.

References

2bears, Jackson. 2010. "A Conversation with Spirits Inside the Simulation of a Coast Salish Longhouse." In *Code Drift: Essays in Critical Digital Studies*, ed. Arthur and Marilouise Kroker. https://journals.uvic.ca/index.php/ctheory/article/view/14679/5549.

Canavan, Gerry. 2014. "'If the Engine Ever Stops, We'd All Die': *Snowpiercer* and Necrofuturism." *Paradoxa*, no. 26: 1–26.

Churchill, Ward. 2003. "I Am Indigenist: Notes on the Ideology of the Fourth World." In *Acts of Rebellion: The Ward Churchill Reader*, 251–74. New York: Routledge.

Coulthard, Glen, and Leanne Betasamosake Simpson. 2016. "Grounded Normativity/Place-Based Solidarity." *American Quarterly* 68 (2): 249–55.

Davis, Heather, and Zoe Todd. 2017. "On the Importance of a Date, or, Decolonizing the Anthropocene." *ACME: An International Journal for Critical Geographies* 16 (4): 761–80. https://www.acme-journal.org/index.php/acme/article/view/1539.

Deloria, Vine, Jr. 2003. *God Is Red/A Native View of Religion*. Golden, CO: Fulcrum.

Demos, Thomas J. 2017. *Against the Anthropocene: Visual Culture and Environment Today*. Berlin: Sternberg Press.

Dillon, Grace. 2012. *Walking the Clouds: An Anthology of Indigenous Science Fiction*. Tucson: University of Arizona Press.

Gautier, Jennifer L. 2016. "Digital Not Diversity? Changing Aboriginal Media Policy at the National Film Board of Canada." *International Journal of Cultural Policy* 22 (3): 331–52.

Goulet, Danis. 2017. *Indigenous Storytelling in VR*. ImagineNative Industry Panel. https://www.youtube.com/watch?v=g7dTlB2ZjbY.

Hopkins, Candice. 2005. "Interventions in Digital Territories: Narrative in Native New Media." In *Transference, Tradition, Technology: Native New Media/Exploring Visual and Digital Culture*, ed. Melanie Townsend, Dana Claxton, and Stephen Loft. Banff, AB: Walter Phillips Gallery Editions.

Horton, Jessica L. 2017. "Indigenous Artists against the Anthropocene." *Art Journal* 76 (2): 48–69.

Jackson, Lisa. 2018. "'Our Culture Is in Our Language': Lisa Jackson on Her VR Film *Biidaaban: First Light* and Indigenous Futurism." *Filmmaker Magazine*. https://filmmakermagazine.com/105184-our-culture-is-in-our-language-lisa-jackson-on-her-vr-film-biidaaban-first-light-and-indigenous-futurism/#.XS9XoJNKjys.

King, Sarah. 2017. "In/consequential Relationships: Refusing Colonial Ethics of Engagement in Yuxweluptun's *Inherent Rights, Vision Rights*." *BC Studies*, no. 193 (Spring). https://doi.org/10.14288/bcs.v0i193.189202.

Laurence, Robin. 1995. "Man of Masks: Lawrence Paul Yuxweluptun's Iconoclastic Paintings Blend Tribal Motifs with Acid Rock Psychedelia." *Canadian Art* 12 (1): 50–5.

Manuel, Arthur, and Grand Chief Ronald Derrickson. 2017. *The Reconciliation Manifesto: Recovering the Land, Rebuilding the Economy*. Toronto: James Lorimer.

Martin, Karen, and Booran Mirraboopa. 2003. "Ways of Knowing, Being and Doing: A Theoretical Framework and Methods for Indigenous and Indigenist Research." *Journal of Australian Studies* 27 (76): 203–14.

Mirzoeff, Nicholas. 2014. "Visualizing the Anthropocene." *Public Culture* 26 (2): 213–32.

Mulvogue, Jessica. 2019. "The World Navigated: Interactive Documentaries in Canada." In *The Oxford Handbook of Canadian Cinema*, ed. Janine

Marchessault and Will Straw, 409–22. Oxford: Oxford University Press.

Pechawis, Arthur. 2014. “Indigenism: Aboriginal World View as Global Protocol.” In *Coded Territories: Tracing Indigenous Pathways in New Media Art*, ed. Kerry Swanson, 36–47. Calgary: University of Calgary Press.

Recollet, Karen. 2019. “Land-ing: City Land-based Knowledges for Those on the Move.” HASTAC plenary, University of British Columbia.

Rickard, Jolene. 2016. *Future Imaginary Symposium.* Winnipeg. https://www.youtube.com/watch?v=OkF6mwofaoY.

Ryle, Jason. 2017. “2167: Indigenous Storytelling in VR.” Moderated by Jason Ryle, artistic director of imagineNATIVE’s Festival, featuring Scott Benesiinaabandan, Raven Chacon and Denis Goulet.

Todd, Loretta. 2005. “Aboriginal Narratives in Cyberspace.” In *Transference, Tradition, Technology*, ed. Melanie Townsend, Dana Claxton and Stephen Loft, 152–63. Banff, AB: Walter Philips Gallery Editions. Originally published in 1996 in *Immersed in Technology, Art and Virtual Environments*, ed. Mary Anne Moser, 179–94 (Cambridge, MA: MIT Press).

Todd, Zoe. 2015. “Indigenizing the Anthropocene.” In *Art in the Anthropocene: Encounters Among Aesthetics, Politics, Environments and Epistemologies*, ed. Heather Davis and Etienne Turpin, 241–54. London: Open Humanities Press.

Vizenor, Gerald. 1994. *Manifest Manners: Narratives on Postindian Survivance.* Hanover: University Press of New England.

Watts, Vanessa. 2013. “Indigenous Place-Thought and Agency amongst Humans and Non-Humans (First Woman and Sky Woman Go on a European World Tour!).” *Decolonization: Indigeneity, Education and Society* 2 (1): 20–34. https://jps.library.utoronto.ca/index.php/des/article/view/19145.

Yuxweluptun, Lawrence Paul. 1996. “Inherent Rights, Vision Rights.” In *Immersed in Technology, Art and Virtual Environments*, ed. Mary Anne Moser, 315–18. Cambridge, MA: MIT Press.

AFTERWORD

ON THE OUTSIDE LOOKING IN

PERSPECTIVE ON THE NEW MEDIA DOCUMENTARY IN CANADA

Dale Hudson and Patricia R. Zimmermann

As scholars and programmers trained in the United States and working there, as well as in Singapore and the United Arab Emirates, our thinking has been reorganized and opened up by many of the documentaries discussed in *The Interactive Documentary in Canada*. We have experienced, programmed, taught, and written about interactive documentaries for almost twenty years now, understanding them as part of a massive shift in which emerging technologies have been used to engage localized conjunctions of people, place, and power in relation to broader ecological and social issues in what can only be described as a total reset for the entire Western documentary project. Much of the work discussed in the book has been supported by the National Film Board/l'Office national du film (NFB/ONF, hereafter NFB), extending its commitment to developing socially engaged ways to use new technologies – and even developing the technologies themselves.

Our view is shaped by admiration for Canada – who hasn't fantasized about fleeing the United States for Canada? – which is why we were energized by reading so many of the volume's contributors who reject a technology-driven approach to making, which often dominates US understandings of how media and technology meet. The NFB is a model of state support unimaginable in the United States. State funding for the arts through the National Endowment for the Arts and National Endowment for the Humanities supports makers with grants but lacks the larger institutional support of a space like the NFB and therefore increasingly relies upon public-private partnerships. The term "public-private partnerships" arouses suspicion in the United States given the history of such partnerships with the Hollywood industry, which produced propaganda to support hydropower's environmental devastation and wartime racism. These structures continued in the soft power of documentaries exported to so-called developing countries.

Although the NFB has produced its share of capitalist, settler-colonial, and wartime propaganda, it also has critiqued some of these ugly periods and supported alternative perspectives. In the United States, documentary makers are frequently dependent on corporate support for production funds, distribution, and exhibition, driven largely by marketing formulas rather than public interests or environmental and social justice. Even the Public Broadcasting System (PBS), sometimes called "public television," is managed by the Corporation for Public Broadcasting (CPB), a private non-profit. CPB replaced the National Educational Television (NET) funded by the Ford Foundation, better known globally for its support of "population control" (i.e., involuntary sterilization schemes) than for the arts. While Canadian arts funding is far from perfect, it is certainly idealized by many makers, programmers, and scholars in the United States. It is hardly surprising that anyone in the United States with an interest in documentary looks to Canada for direction.

Until we read this book, with its polyphony of interdisciplinary theories and spread of exemplary innovative interactive documentaries, we had not realized that we – and likely many other makers and scholars around the world – had not really understood these works as part of a Canadian set of debates, discourses, funding schemes, institutions, practices, and social relations. Interactive documentary operates over distributed networks of the internet and mobile networks. Typically, it does not compete in international festivals that impose national identities or reduce collaborative work to auteurs. Consequently, interactive documentary often circulates within a fanaticized miasma of border-lessness and author-lessness.

This book situates work within Canadian histories of media infrastructures and innovation. It shows how the NFB, in particular, provides spaces for the emergence of interactive documentaries, supplying funding, space, teams, and a commitment to showing the complexities of Canadian politics. This context implicitly explains why interactive documentary has developed in Canada in ways not evident elsewhere. Technological innovations threaded into community-located media have a long history at the NFB. It is not new to the digital turn in documentary. The NFB supported the development of cinéma direct in the 1950s through lightweight cameras and sound technology; animation, including early computer animation;

community-produced film through Challenge for Change/Société nouvelle (CFC/SN) in the 1960s and 1970s; and even IMAX – all of which flow into interactive documentary. The book's insistence that political complexity as a means to unsettle assumptions always be at the core of interactive documentary extends beyond the state borders of Canada.

Taken as a whole, the chapters show the lineage of this interdisciplinary theorization of interactive documentary, expanding on arguments from Western scholarship on documentary by Bill Nichols (2001) and Brian Winston (2013), among others, as well as scholarship on interactive documentary in edited collections by Craig Hight (2008) and by Judith Aston, Sandra Gaudenzi, and Mandy Rose (2017); and books by Patricia R. Zimmermann and Helen DeMichiel (2018) and Kate Nash (2021). *The Interactive Documentary in Canada* shows constant intellectual movement between inside (Canadian sets of social relations and contexts) and outside (interactive documentary practice around the planet and a community of documentary scholars). It asks us to consider Canada not as a homogenous nation-state but, instead, as a heterogenous set of regionally focused and multilingual debates often addressing environmental, epistemological, and physical violence by its settler-colonial founders. These debates and works suggest the urgent need for decolonial work towards land reparations as well as environmental and social justice. The book also moves beyond the techno-utopianism of early work on interactive documentaries (our own work included) that invests digital technologies with the potential to challenge some calcified assumptions in analogue-based scholarship. The book's chapters historicize the emergence of insights that develop through sustained discussion and debates between makers and scholars working collaboratively.

Polyvocality drives many of the elaborate interactive documentaries discussed in this book. Many chapters invoke it almost as a given in these new forms of documentary. *The Interactive Documentary in Canada* proposes that it is not so simple as to jettison the singular linear story and then draft some undeveloped amorphous notion of the non-linear. Instead, in many cases, it takes current political thinking in Canada about settler colonialism and Indigeneity both to restore complexity to ideas and to unsettle on every level the idea that the non-linear is what corrects the fallibilities and failings of the linear. In this volume, the unsettling is deliberate, incisive, and figured as something endlessly unfolding rather than resolved.

State Support for Documentary

The Interactive Documentary in Canada pulls into focus documentary practices that have been partly overshadowed by the commodification of feature-length documentary. Interactive work rejects the Hollywoodization of documentary through an oligarchy of the US Academy and its Oscars, HBO, Netflix, Sundance, SXSW, and Tribeca that functions as a cultural oligopoly. Taken as a whole, these organizations reconfigure documentary from a form premised on education into one focused on entertainment. Further, these corporations are indirectly supported by the US military and taxpayer monies. The United States famously argued against the "cultural exception" for film and audiovisual media at the Uruguay Round (1986–93) of the General Agreement on Tariffs and Trade (GATT). While corporate control is devastating for narrative media, it can be lethal for documentary. It reduces a limitless number of perspectives to entertaining formulas featuring the notorious character-driven narrative arc with resolution and catharsis that invites audiences to fantasize that all is well – and nothing really needs to change.

In this international media context, the book's contributors constitute part of Canada's long-standing efforts to focus on types of filmmaking that the classical-era Hollywood studios largely ignored – such as animation, documentary, experimental. With Canada's exhibition markets overrun by Hollywood, the NFB imagined other kinds of media practices that contributed to the arts and society.

Founded in 1939 with John Grierson as its first commissioner, the NFB became a leading centre for work in the not-narrative-film categories. Grierson believed documentaries should avoid the rational approach to journalism and instead aim for the emotional appeal of Hollywood films as a call to action. The NFB, however, moved from wartime propaganda in the *Canada Carries On* and *The World in Action* series to promoting a polyphony of voices. From 1967 to 1980, CFC/SN expanded the range of perspectives by equipping filmmakers with new technologies such as portable cameras and sound recorders to catalogue society and preserve local culture.

The contributors to this collection extend documentary's social engagement, an idea popularized by Grierson. This idea necessarily intervenes in documentary practice and scholarship that is too often distracted by technology, seeing it as a solution not only to debates within documentary studies but also to social problems. The early area of techo-utopianism with regard to the internet constitutes an earlier moment in this fetishization of technology, historically a tactic modern developmental schemes deploy and that has wrought ecological and social catastrophe around the world. *The Interactive Documentary in Canada*'s premise is that interactive documentaries need to be "observed, historicized and critiqued."

The NFB support for interactive documentary offered a modicum of autonomy from the market-driven business of many distributors, exhibitors, and festivals. However, public funding decreased as the culminative effects of neoliberal economic policy began to be felt not only in parts of the world that were exploited but also in parts of the world that exploited, including the United States. The political economies of interactive documentary remain underexamined in scholarship. In this regard, contributors to this volume bring important insights. Michael Brendan Baker's chapter offers an examination of the NFB's reorganization as a way to create a funding envelope focused specifically on new media production, the Digital Studio, while Frédéric Dubois historicizes the constraints of public funding with the ripple effects of the 2008 global recession triggered by financial corruption in the United States. More recent collaborations have been with private companies like Toronto-based Helios Design Labs, which places collaborative research over profit.

Learning from Makers

Several key chapters are written by (or feature interviews with) makers involved with the work discussed. They offer first-hand accounts of decision making, usually in conversations with others. These chapters show an awareness that digital technologies that generate the illusion of interactivity and immersivity need to be used critically. These insights from makers are invaluable, something we learned when interviewing various makers in our research for "Taking Things Apart" (2008), which became the basis of our book *Thinking about Digital Media* (2015).[1] In discussions with Ismail Farouk, Adriana Knouf, and Stephanie Rothenberg, we learned that makers work within the limits of technologies yet also push back against these restrictions. We argue that makers lead the way for the rest of us to understand how digital media differs from analogue media.

The terms "interactivity" and "immersivity" are often over-emphasized at the expense of issues of privacy and safety. Every movement online can be tracked: artificial intelligence (AI) is well trained to model our future behaviour. While privileged internet users in places like Canada and the United States may feel confident that their governments ensure them basic rights, they should not feel overconfident, as evidenced in the frequent US prosecution of whistleblowers. We use the term "locative media" for work that moves between physical and virtual spaces through GPS. Locative technologies for AR (augmented reality) seem innocuous since Pokémon GO (2016), yet they track users in time and space.

In our work, we draw upon insights from makers, who taught us to think *through* digital media rather than simply to *make* media-that-could-be-analogue with digital technologies, such as digital images that look like celluloid. Contributors to *The Interactive Documentary in Canada* define key differences in their own experiences with analogue (or old) and digital (or new) hardware. Analogue is associated with human perceptions and sensations, whereas digital is associated with machine perceptions and sensations. Cindy Poremba and Amy Siegel examine volumetric video that merges ideas of human lens-based and machine graphically rendered vision composed by algorithms rather than by human splicing of media. Algorithms or coding provides instructions for how an interactive documentary or any form of digital media operates through human-machine interface. The illusion of seamlessness hides these more complex operations. It also obscures the limits of what it allows. Users can contribute new data, but the underlying structure of the database remains even when its functionality is not the primary structure of the documentary.

Early new media theory pointed to the illusion of interactivity, much like the illusion of moving images in analogue media. Interactivity is limited to machine reactions to user input. In their chapter on their *Viewfinders* (2017) project, Gerda Cammaer and Max Schleser discuss AR as "responsive content" and interaction as "reciprocal action." Their work is motivated by the limited choices on offer that make the unexpected and unanticipated impossible. In general, users of interactive documentaries cannot change the machine programming or software operations unless they are sufficiently digitally literate to hack. The next evolution in interactivity will likely be the use of AI to allow interactive projects to alter fixed choices and predetermined paths of pre-set machine reactions. This situation underscores the need for centres where communities can train in coding and not simply in how to operate software and hardware.

The Interactive Documentary in Canada offers insights into how makers work with and against technologies. Rather than naming properties and qualities of interactive documentary according to the limited vocabulary of this emerging field, contributors move quickly beyond formalist and functionalist taxonomies to foreground the complexity of the issues that they engage through digital technologies. Interactive documentary is not fetishized as a goal unto itself in the way that corporations fetishize internet technologies (IT) with their lifestyle-branded consumer-grade hardware and software.

Ingenuity, then, emerges from working within both the limits and opportunities of digital technology. Technologies shape forms that, in turn, shape content, but none overdetermines potential meanings. The NFB was thinking about social impact before social media platforms Facebook and Twitter helped potential audiences locate and discuss digital media. Within the confines of increasingly privatized funding, Baker describes how its Digital Studio allowed makers the latitude to create work in different iterations, such as Jeremy Mendes and Leanne Allison's *Bear 71* (2012), which was web-based, installed in a gallery, performed with live musical accompaniment, and subsequently redesigned for VR. His participants also discuss the important question of how and whether to archive these digital works within the context of the NFB's partnership with Rhizome in the United States.

Interactivity and Immersivity Are Not a Goal

Learning from their experience sharing *The Shore Line* with teachers and students, Rachel Webb Jekanowski and Elizabeth Miller discovered that their interactive documentary worked best as preparation for student work outside the classroom and off the screen. Importantly, Jekanowski and Miller develop a pedagogy alongside Indigenous thinking. These insights move away from what, in an article (Hudson and Zimmermann 2009a) that became the basis for the final chapter in our book (Hudson and Zimmermann 2015), we call the uncritical technophilia in digital media that extended an uncritical cinephilia over "great auteurs." Documentary itself is associated with epistophilia, marking an uneasy fit for documentary with the dominant technophilia of IT corporations, which proffer technology as solutions, and the cinephilia of film festivals, which promote the filmmaker as auteur.

In her chapter, Laura Ann Fox outlines how her web documentary *Sackville Schools 2020* (2017) also enters the physical world in the sense of convening discussions between people inside and outside conventional education decision-makers. Again, the media object becomes "an activist's tool for network[ed] thinking" (175). She moves away from simplistic assumptions that media can evoke empowerment and empathy to consider the difficult work that actually needs to take place. "There is a risk in assuming that *interactivity* automatically means there will be *interaction*" (176), she acknowledges. In fact, many of the contributors acknowledge pandemic-amplified screen fatigue. Creators conceive, design, and make works that use digital technologies as a new way to engage with the physical world. Interactivity and immersivity are thus not conceived exclusively in terms of what takes place through *human-machine* interfaces but through *human-world* interfaces. They redirect attention away from technologies towards what the technologies can allow us to notice.

The book also re-examines missteps in past moments of techno-utopianism. Daniel Keyes and Mike Robbins argue that the NFB's efforts to archive *Fort McMoney* (2013) were well intended yet poorly conceived. Commenting on the poor representation of environmental and social justice within the work, they reflect upon the limitations of both interactive documentaries and strategy videogames with their promotion of depoliticized nostalgia. Jessica Mulvogue, meanwhile, examines Brenda Longfellow's *Offshore* (2013) and Dufresne's *Fort McMoney*, both of which analyze extreme oil extraction, where extremity is measured in the "devastating scale of their effects on the surrounding environment" (217). In these cases, the interactive documentaries activate strategies from game design to arrive at uncertainty, melancholy, or even despair rather than the fantasies of solutions and comforts of non-complicity and closure. Although makers and scholars (ourselves included) have praised them, we too often generalize our interactions and the meanings derived. Keyes and Robbins define *Fort McMoney*'s civics lessons as virtual tourism even as "*schadenfreude* tourism" – since users were "not implicated every time a furnace ignited or a car was filled up with gas" (78). We could add running the interactive documentary to this list of routine actions since much electricity is derived from fossil fuels.

The Interactive Documentary in Canada is also attentive to the lingering effects of the pandemic, foregrounding "fast technological change along with digital fatigue (and the overuse of the descriptor 'interactivity')" (3) as subjects that need to be unpacked. Important work in critical software studies by Wendy Chun, Alexander Galloway, and Craig Hight pushes back against fetishism for interactivity and immersivity. It cannot be ignored that both are entangled within neoliberal surveillance. Online exhibition for web-based documentaries appears to bypass the hindrances of censorship certificates for media and passport controls for makers and users, but it is only liberating for people with access who feel comfortable seeing the work on their own laptops and smartphones. As platforms for exhibition, the internet and mobile networks activate invisible layers of control through nodes across networks, much like global capital is controlled through corporations across nation-states, free zones, and other geopolitical entities. Questions of trust are important. Participation on social media is now a well-known form of data mining. Corporations monetize our digital footprints and also train AI (artificial intelligence) to anticipate our future thoughts and actions, modelling digital identities that we will likely inhabit in the future. Brett Gaylor's NFB interactive documentary *Do Not Track/Traque interdite* (2015) visualized ways the websites speak to these issues long before Jeff Orlowski-Yang's widely seen Netflix documentary, *The Social Dilemma* (2020).

Augmented Reality and Virtual Reality Are a Responsibility, Not Just Tools

One of the biggest takeaways from *The Interactive Documentary in Canada* emanates from its emphasis on how interactive documentary makers and scholars have not liberated documentary from the theatre or television screen only to constrain it to the laptop or mobile screen. Much of the work discussed emphasizes that AR and VR technologies put users back in touch with the physical world by visualizing what may no longer exist or what might not be possible to notice through limited human sensory perceptions. AR and VR are conceived not just as tools but as responsibilities. Inventors and uses also shape these technologies, but these two groups do not necessarily the share the same politics. Contributors are attentive to how AR and VR can be used to simulate how someone from another historical moment or ethno-racial group or even another species might perceive a shared physical world. We understand AR not only as more than portable screens but also as onsite projections onto screens mounted in public spaces.

AR and VR can be oriented towards the future as well as towards the past. Brenda Longfellow argues that Indigenous futurism is "conceived and executed in a manner that is far removed from 'the charge of the real' or the indexical properties and ontologies of documentary, as traditionally conceived" (303), a critical point with which to conclude this volume. Work by Lawrence Paul Yuxweluptun, Paisley Smith, Scott Benesiinaabandan, Danis Goulet, and Lisa Jackson, and work commission by ImagineNATIVE engage precisely with what settler colonies like Canada are reluctant to consider: land reparations. Although the work strives to contest settler-colonial authority and imagine a future of secured Indigenous sovereignty, it remains documentary and not activist media. It is more akin to Michael Kanentakeron Mitchell's *You Are on Indian Land* (1969) for the NFB than to the radical work of the Zapatista Army of National Liberation in Chiapas against the Mexican state's complicity with global capitalism. This larger international context makes us somewhat more ambivalent about the NFB. At the same time, after five centuries of unrelenting colonialism and racism, futurism has invaluable symbolic value. Longfellow situates the work within the context of Zoe Todd and Heather Davis's arguments that the Anthropocene, a geological epoch defined by human activity as the primary driver of change, is not new but, instead, a "continuation of the processes of dispossession and genocide" (314). They have the knowledge to survive. As Longfellow makes clear, the work asserts Indigenous sovereignty and rejects national belonging. This rejection of the idea of the nation-state, particularly as it has been romanticized as multicultural, gives us hope. VR technologies hold the potential to evoke Indigenous ways of knowing the planet. Non-human perspectives such as that of the earth and its numerous biosystems require translation by Indigenous and scientific communities. Rendered across a number of different piles-as-screens onsite, Nettie Wild's *Uninterrupted* (2017) – addressed herein by Chelsea Birks – disables humans from adopting a position of mastery by *seeing everything*, as in conventional time-based documentary, or by *controlling everything*, as in conventional interactive documentary. These chapters offer an impressive range of insights into what makers have learned by thinking through digital technologies.

Practice-and-Research-Entwined Polyvocalities

Our enthusiasm for this book is a response to the plethora of work across forms and technologies that unsettle the very definitions of documentary. Although we use the phrase "makers and scholars" throughout this afterword, this book makes clear that the term "maker" is insufficient and increasingly antiquated. Much of the work unfurls by makers who are also researchers (or researchers who actively engage with makers). Debates on how arts practice and scholarly research entwine have been productive for more than accreditation purposes: they mark an epistemological shift in higher education that recognizes that digital technologies have altered the possibilities for research. Digital humanities imagined ways that machines can perform labour on a scale impossible for humans, offering new insights into questions long thought settled. Although no one needs digital technologies to make the argument that arts practice is a form of research, they have made some of the technical aspects of arts practice easier, allowing artists to choose between in-depth focus on craft or interdisciplinary approaches. Among them are conceptions of practice-based or practice-led research and research-based or research-led practice. These entwine into integrated practice and research, sometimes called "research-creation" or "practice as research."[2] This work is theoretically driven to recognize different kinds of knowledge production. It often develops within communities and teams who work together to formulate inquiries too large for any one person alone to attempt.

For us, three differences in this kind of work, which are exemplified by many contributors to this book, stand out. First, there is funding in Canada for this kind of work, which embraces complexity, and this funding is not limited to state institutions like the NFB but is also available in many universities. Second, this work shares a common set of ideas about horizontal rather than vertical structures and about collaborative rather than individualistic practices. Third, this work is only possible in institutional structures that value exploration rather than in industries that value formulas and prioritize intellectual property and revenue extraction. Exploration takes on many forms and modes of engagement. It emanates from, operates within, and engages communities with a multitude of perspectives, unlike self, story, and industrial models. This kind of work through exploration can only happen when points of view are allowed to be polyphonic.

The contrast between what *The Interactive Documentary in Canada* unpacks and explores, and standard institutional and curricular contexts for film/media departments in the United States, could not be more extreme. The contributors show a variety of ways to move forward to develop new directions for documentary. Established film/media schools in the United States and elsewhere value individual makers, standardized forms, industry-defined production values, and uncomplicated issues. For both documentary and narrative, they champion almost identical preoccupations with individualistic self-expression that is imagined somehow also "universal," digital technologies used as though they are analogue, and character-driven linear narratives that rely on conflict and offer resolution or even "catharsis." Crews are hierarchical, with the director in control. Once they graduate, emerging directors learn that producers and funders are often the ones who are really in control. Goals are simple: film festivals, industry awards, commercial distribution.

The work in this book values community over self. It evaluates the ethics demanded for each subject and the questions required to interrogate the politics embedded in technology. It asks how to recalibrate funding, production, distribution, and exhibition that are based on principles of community media that are focused on use-value rather than on individual career advancement in highly competitive commercial sectors dominated by corporate entities, with their high barriers to entry typically requiring substantive unearned privileges (i.e., family and social connections more than ability or ingenuity).

Across all the chapters, there occurs an intervention into the idea that documentary is about representation, with this analogue concept being replaced by a digital concept of entanglements that reveals existing relations and that produces new configurations through digital architecture that structures encounters. Non-linear and resolutely unresolved, the interactive documentaries analyzed (as well as the theoretical journeys of the individual chapters) propose terms like "conversations," "ethical encounters," "a politics of care," "collaboration," "interconnectedness," "the relationship between making, researching, and thinking in interdependent ways." This conception of interactive media takes the term "interactive" and moves it beyond technology into the realms of how people engage with complex ideas and each other. At the core of this emphasis on the relational as an endlessly developing assemblage resides the practices of connections, dialogues, and polyvocality, whereby many voices, people, histories, and ideas combine to form new relational assemblages.

With its insistence on the plural, the complex, and the heterogeneous, ideas with which the linear conflicts and cannot hold, the book provides a way to think through new structures. These ideas elaborate ways to imagine complexity, complex stories, and issues as though they occur in a continual state of overlapping in which boundaries are dissolved. This collection puts forward concepts that depend on thinking in a heterogeneous and plural way, with terms such as "story worlds," "story living," "story environments," and "immersive worlding," which provide pathways towards how to construct documentaries in which space, time, people, and place are layered.

The Interactive Documentary in Canada proposes that polyphony occupies the centre of interactive documentary, a refutation of what some might see as a US-centric, de facto capitalist individualism fuelled by dreams of career success and recognition. The range of projects cross Canada from Montreal and Toronto, where documentary festivals flourish, to rural Alberta and an ever-gentrifying Vancouver, where histories are often undocumented. They reject the idea of a unified nation-state and instead express Canada as overlapping and sometimes competing pluralities. The critical framework and research methods in the chapters resonate with the polyphonic, irrefutably showing that a multi-disciplinary approach is necessary to address complexity in layered webs rather than conflicts unfolding along a straight line.

The contributors propose new ways of thinking beyond technology-driven solutions or spectacles. They situate interactive documentary within histories of work on archives, ethnography, oral history, and multiple epistemologies from Western philosophy to Indigenous knowledge. Polyphonies reside at the core of this book, encouraging thinking beyond the individual to the collective, the multiple, the heterogeneous, the complex. *The Interactive Documentary in Canada* variously argues that interactive documentaries embrace both physical and virtual dimensions of experience simultaneously. It shows that humans and non-humans are in constant contact, that they are not separate.

Notes

1 See Hudson and Zimmermann (2009b). On the potential distractions of technology, see also Hudson (2021).

2 Examples include Chapman and Sawchuk (2012) and Nelson (2013).

References

Aston, Judith, Sandra Gaudenzi, Mandy Rose, eds. 2017. *iDocs: The Evolving Practices of Interactive Documentary.* London: Wallflower.

Chapman, Owen, and Kim Sawchuk. 2012. "Research-Creation: Intervention, Analysis and 'Family Resemblances.'" *Canadian Journal of Communication* 37: 5–26.

Hight, Craig, ed. 2008. *Studies in Documentary Film* 2 (1) (special issue on digital documentary).

Hudson, Dale. 2021."Mapping Palestine/Israel through Interactive Documentary." *Journal of Palestine Studies* 50 (1): 51– 76.

Hudson, Dale, and Patricia R. Zimmermann. 2009a. "Cinephilia, Technophilia, and Collaborative Remix Zones." *Screen* 50, no. 1, "Screen Theorizing Today: A Celebration of Screen's Fiftieth Anniversary," ed. Annette Kuhn (Spring): 135–46.

– 2009b. "Taking Things Apart: Migratory Archives, Locative Media, and Micropublics." *Afterimage* 36 (4): 15–19.

– 2015. *Thinking through Digital Media: Transnational Environments and Locative Places.* New York: Palgrave Macmillan.

Nash, Kate. 2021. *Interactive Documentary: Theory and Debate.* New York: Routledge.

Nelson, Robin. 2013. "From Practitioner to Practitioner-Researcher." In *Practice as Research in the Arts: Principles, Protocols, Pedagogies, Resistances*, ed. Robin Nelson, 23–47. New York: Palgrave Macmillan.

Nichols, Bill. 2001. *Introduction to Documentary.* Indianapolis: University of Indiana Press.

Winston, Brian. 2013. *The Documentary Film Book.* London: British Film Institute.

Zimmermann, Patricia R., and Helen DeMichiel. 2018. *Open Space New Media Documentary: A Toolkit for Theory and Practice.* New York: Routledge.

CONTRIBUTORS

MICHAEL BRENDAN BAKER is professor of film studies at Sheridan College in the Faculty of Humanities and Social Sciences and the Honours Bachelor of Film and Television Program. He is co-editor, with Tom Waugh and Ezra Winton, of *Challenge for Change: Activist Documentary at the National Film Board of Canada* (McGill-Queen's University Press, 2010).

CHELSEA BIRKS is the director of Learning and Outreach at the Cinematheque, Vancouver. She won the 2017 SCMS Student Writing Award and has been published in *Cinema Journal* (now *JCMS*), *Film-Philosophy*, *New Review of Film and Television Studies*, and *Journal of Gender Studies*. Her first book, *Limit Cinema: Transgression and the Nonhuman in Contemporary Global Film* (Bloomsbury), was published in 2021.

GERDA CAMMAER, PhD, is a filmmaker, scholar, and curator. Her main research interests are experimental and documentary film, smartphone filmmaking and microcinema, overlooked film histories, the history of film technology, and new media technologies. Her own creative work entails found-footage films, collage works, video art, and poetic documentaries. Her films have been shown in galleries and at film festivals in Canada and abroad. She is the co-founder and organizer of the Moving_Image_Arts International Short Film Festival in the School of Image Arts at the Toronto Metropolitan University, and she is actively involved in the International Organization of Cinema, Audiovisual and Media Schools and the Mobile Innovation Network and Association. Among other publications, she is the co-editor of *Cinephemera: Archives, Ephemeral Cinema, and New Screen Histories in Canada* (McGill-Queen's University Press, 2014) and *Critical Distance in Documentary Media* (Palgrave Macmillan, 2018).

ZOË DRUICK is a professor in the School of Communication at Simon Fraser University. Her research considers histories, theories, and trajectories of documentary and reality-based media with an emphasis on their intersection with biopolitical projects. Her work on these topics has been published in numerous anthologies and journals, including the *Blackwell Companion to Documentary History*. She is author or editor of five books, including *Projecting Canada: Government Policy and Documentary Film at the National Film Board* and *The Grierson Effect: Documentary's International Movement*. She is currently PI on a major, multi-year SSHRC grant investigating the history of cybernetics and educational TV in Canada.

FRÉDÉRIC DUBOIS is professor of media theory in the MA Digital Narratives at Internationale Filmschule Köln, Germany. He is the founding and managing editor of *Internet Policy Review*, an open-access journal on internet regulation published by the Alexander von Humboldt Institute for Internet and Society. Dubois completed a research-creation PhD in film production at the Film University Babelsberg with a thesis entitled "Interactive Documentary Production and Societal Impact: The Case of Field Trip." Previously, he practised journalism and researched community media (*Autonomous Media*, Cumulus Press, 2005), mining (*Extraction! A Comix Reportage*, Cumulus Press, 2007), internet-based communications, and media impact. Frédéric is a maker of award-winning digital media, including those produced with the National Film Board of Canada.

LAURA ANN FOX is a writer, producer, and learning experience designer based in Toronto. She has an MA in Communication and Culture from York University, where she specialized in interactive documentary, as well as a BA in International Relations from Mount Allison University. With her combined background in international relations, educational media, and communications, Laura now creates learning and training solutions for a variety of different audiences. She has always held a particular interest in storytelling for non-profit organizations. In all of her work, Laura truly believes in the power of a good story to educate and inspire.

DALE HUDSON is an associate professor at New York University Abu Dhabi. His research and teaching focus on environmentalism and on film and visual media in Southwest Asia, North Africa, and South Asia. He is co-author of *Thinking through Digital Media: Transnational Environments and Locative Places* (2015), author of *Vampires, Race, and Transnational Hollywoods* (2017), and co-editor of a double issue of *Middle East Journal of Culture and Communication* on "Film and Visual Media in the Gulf" (2021) and "Reorienting the Middle East: Film and Digital Media Where the Persian Gulf, Arabian Sea, and Indian Ocean Meet" (2023). He programs exhibitions for the Finger Lakes Environmental Film Festival and coordinates Films from the Gulf for the Middle East Studies Association Film Festival.

RANDOLPH JORDAN teaches in the Department of Humanities at Champlain College in Montreal. His research, pedagogy, and creative practice reside at the intersections of film studies, sound studies, and critical geography. He is co-editor of *Sound, Media, Ecology* with Milena Droumeva (Palgrave 2019), and his monograph, *Acoustic Profiles: A Sound Ecology of the Cinema*, is forthcoming from Oxford University Press. His multi-media project *Bell Tower of False Creek* has been presented at film festivals and conferences internationally, and he collaborated on the sound design for the *Impostor Cities* exhibition, Canada's official entry for the Venice Architecture Biennale in 2021 and now opening at Toronto's Museum of Contemporary Art for summer 2023.

DANIEL KEYES serves as an associate professor of English and cultural studies in the Faculty of Creative and Critical Studies at the University of British Columbia Okanagan; he teaches cultural studies with a focus on media studies. He is a settler in the unceded Okanagan territories having been raised on farmland on the perimeter of the Canadian military base Camp Borden on Treaty 18 land (1818). He served as the secretary for Film and Media Studies Association of Canada from 2020 to 2022. His most recent publication, co-edited with Luis Aguiar at UBC Press, is the anthology *White Space: Race, Privilege and the Cultural Economics of the Okanagan* (2021). He currently researches born-digital ephemerality with a focus on Anglo-Canadian audio-visual heritage.

MONIKA KIN GAGNON is a professor of communication studies at Concordia University. She has published widely on cultural politics and the visual and experimental media arts since the 1980s. She is author of *Other Conundrums: Race, Culture and Canadian Art* (2000), and *13 Conversations about Art and Cultural Race Politics* (2002) with Richard Fung. She is co-editor of *Reimagining Cinema: Film at Expo 67* (2014) with Janine Marchessault and *In Search of Expo 67* (2020) with Lesley Johnstone. Her most recent publication is with Alanis Obomsawin, "Before I Made Films, I Was Singing," in *Alanis Obomsawin: Lifework* (Berlin: HKW/Prestel, 2022). She is currently writing *Posthumous Cinema: Unfinished Films in the Archives.*

CAROLINE KLIMEK is a PhD candidate in the Department of Cinema and Media Arts at York University. Her SSHRC-funded dissertation focuses on how Canadian cultural institutions are incorporating XR media by examining how film festivals, artist-run centres, and legacy institutions are including virtual and augmented reality in their mandates and how that affects their exhibition practices. She is currently a sessional instructor at Wilfrid Laurier University, the University of Toronto Information School, and at York University. She is published in the *Canadian Journal of Film Studies* and *Shameless Magazine*.

BRENDA LONGFELLOW is a professor in the Department of Cinema and Media Arts at York University, Toronto. She is an award-winning filmmaker whose documentaries have been screened and broadcast internationally. Her work includes the interactive documentary *Offshore*. She is currently co-director of the Circle Project, an evolving collaboration of artists and formerly incarcerated women in Vancouver who have produced several new media works, including *The Circle*, *What Fools These Mortals Be*, and *The Dreaming*. In addition to her film and media practice, she has also published articles on documentary, feminist film theory, and Canadian cinema in *Public*, *Camera Obscura*, *CineTracts*, *Screen*, and the *Journal of Canadian Film Studies*. She is also the co-editor (with Scott MacKenzie and Tom Waugh) of the anthology *The Perils of Pedagogy: the Works of John Greyson* (2013) and *Gendering the Nation: Canadian Women Filmmakers* (1992).

ELIZABETH (LIZ) MILLER is a documentary filmmaker and a full professor in communication studies at Concordia University in Tiohti:áke/Montreal. Her collaborative documentary projects on timely issues such as climate change, environmental justice, and refugee rights have won awards and influenced decision makers. She is the co-author of *Going Public: The Art of Participatory Practice* (2017) and has also written on collaborative documentary, environmental media, and place-based pedagogies. Her project, *The Shore Line* (2017), is used in classrooms around the world and features profiles of individuals who are responding to the threats of massive development and rising sea levels in coastal communities. Her recent project, *Wastescapes* (2023) engages critically with concepts and materials of waste.

JESSICA MULVOGUE is a lecturer in film studies at the University of St Andrews (Scotland). Her two main areas of research are the history and theory of immersive, expanded cinemas and the exigencies of environmental cinema in the period of climate change catastrophe. Jessica obtained her PhD in cinema and media studies at York University (Toronto, Canada). Her publications include essays in *The Routledge Companion to Contemporary Art, Visual Culture and Climate Change* (ed. T.J. Demos, Subhankar Banerjee, Emily Eliza Scott), *The Oxford Handbook of Canadian Cinema* (ed. Janine Marchessault and Will Straw), and in journals such as *Studies in World Cinema* and *Transformations.*

CINDY POREMBA is associate professor in digital futures at OCAD University (Tkaranto/Toronto) and co-director of OCAD's game:play Lab. They have maintained a scholarly, experimental gamemaking, and curatorial practice for almost two decades with a particular interest in captured media practices and emerging technologies. Cindy has published and presented extensively on topics relating to game art, postmedia, and interactive documentary. Their award-winning game, curation, and "New Arcade" work (independently and as a member ofkokoromi collective) have been featured in both game and digital art exhibitions.

MIKE ROBBINS is a director, producer, and creative technologist. As creative technologist and partner at his company Helios Design Labs in Toronto he led pioneering interactive documentary projects such as *Highrise* (2012, with director Kat Cizek), winning Emmy, Peabody, World Press Photo, and Canada Screen awards. Other projects include the Quipu Project, *Digital Me*, *After The Storm*, and *Offshore.*

MAX SCHLESER is associate professor in film and television and a researcher in the Centre for Transformative Media Technologies (CTMT) at Swinburne University of Technology (Melbourne, Australia), Adobe education leader, founder of the Mobile Innovation Network and Association, and screening director of the International Mobile Innovation Screening and Festival. He is an award-winning filmmaker with expertise in immersive media, documentary film, and creative arts 4.0, with a focus on cinematic VR and interactive filmmaking. His research explores screen production, emerging media, and smartphone filmmaking for community engagement, creative transformation, and transmedia storytelling. Schleser co-edited the books *Mobile Media Making in an Age of Smartphones, Mobile Story Making in an Age of Smartphones*, and *Mobile Storytelling in an Age of Smartphones*, and he has edited journals for *Studies in Documentary Film*, *Ubiquity*, the *Journal of Pervasive Media*, and the *Journal of Creative Technologies*. His monograph *Smartphone Filmmaking: Theory and Practice* was published by Bloomsbury in 2021.

AMY SIEGEL is a queer and feminist multimedia artist, scholar, educator, and organizer of artistic projects. Amy is currently pursuing a SSHRC-funded PhD in communication and culture at York University. Amy holds an MFA in documentary media from Toronto Metropolitan University and an MA in adult education and community development from the University of Toronto.

MATT SOAR is emeritus professor of communication studies at Concordia University in Tiohtià:ke/Montreal. From 2008 to 2016 he was co-developer of the Korsakow System, an opensource software application for digital non-linear storytelling, particularly web documentaries. He is co-editor, with Monika Kin Gagnon, of Database|Narrative|Archive: An anthology of seven interactive essays on digital non-linear storytelling (2013), and author of "Making (with) the Korsakow System: Database Documentaries as Articulation and Assemblage" in C. Summerhayes, C. Hight, and K. Nash, eds., *New Documentary Ecologies: Emerging Platforms, Practices and Discourses* (2014) . Soar's Korsakow films include the web doc *Les Enseignistes de Montréal* (2018), co-directed with Dr Dayna McLeod, the formal experiment Fibonacci Korsakow #1 (2013), and the "database diary" film *Ceci N'est Pas Embres* (2012).

PETER URQUHART is associate professor in communication studies at Wilfrid Laurier University.

RACHEL WEBB JEKANOWSKI is an interdisciplinary scholar working between film and media studies and the energy humanities. Her current book project, *Cinemas of Extraction: Land, Resources, Settler Imaginaries*, examines environmental and colonial entanglements of twentieth-century non-theatrical and documentary filmmaking in North America. She is a co-editor of *The Goose: A Journal of Arts, Environment, and Culture in*

Canada and reviews co-editor for the *Journal of Environmental Media*. Rachel works as an assistant professor at Memorial University's Grenfell Campus in Newfoundland.

FREYA WRIGHT-BROUGH has taught film, screen, and animation at QUT's School of Creative Practice since 2015 and is currently a lecturer in learning and teaching development, impact, and recognition within QUT's Academy of Learning and Teaching (QALT). She has also worked as a screenwriter for clients in the US, UK, and Australia, contributing to digital and factual content. Her research focuses on ethical encounter in arts-based collaboration as well as social justice in higher education.

PATRICIA R. ZIMMERMANN was the Charles A. Dana Professor of Screen Studies and director of the Finger Lakes Environmental Film Festival in the Roy H. Park School of Communications at Ithaca College in Ithaca, New York. The author or editor of ten books, her most recent include *Thinking through Digital Media: Transnational Environments and Locative Places* (with Dale Hudson, 2015), *Documentary across Platforms: Reverse Engineering Media, Place, and Politics* (2019), and *Flash Flaherty: Tales from a Film Seminar* (2021). She served as editor-at-large for the online magazine, *The Edge*, dedicated to countering mainstream media.

INDEX

THE INTERACTIVE DOCUMENTARY IN CANADA